NEW TRENDS IN
COMPUTER NETWORKS

Advances in Computer Science and Engineering: Reports

Published

Vol. 1 New Trends in Computer Networks
edited by T. Tuğcu, M. Çağlayan, F. Alagöz (Bogazici Univ., Turkey) and E. Gelenbe (Imperial College, UK)

NEW TRENDS IN COMPUTER NETWORKS

editors

Tuna Tuğcu
(Bogazici University, Turkey)

Erol Gelenbe
(Imperial College, UK)

M. Ufuk Çağlayan
(Bogazici University, Turkey)

Fatih Alagöz
(Bogazici University, Turkey)

ICP Imperial College Press

Published by

Imperial College Press
57 Shelton Street
Covent Garden
London WC2H 9HE

Distributed by

World Scientific Publishing Co. Pte. Ltd.
5 Toh Tuck Link, Singapore 596224
USA office: 27 Warren Street, Suite 401-402, Hackensack, NJ 07601
UK office: 57 Shelton Street, Covent Garden, London WC2H 9HE

British Library Cataloguing-in-Publication Data
A catalogue record for this book is available from the British Library.

NEW TRENDS IN COMPUTER NETWROKS
Advances in Computer Science and Engineering: Reports — Vol. 1

ISSN 1793-2416
ISBN 1-86094-611-9

Printed in Singapore by World Scientific Printers (S) Pte Ltd

PREFACE

Welcome to the 20th International Symposium on Computer and Information Sciences, (ISCIS'05). ISCIS has attained international recognition, disseminating research results from the best work of various research and academic communities. This is a result of a constant effort made every year to improve ISCIS, and to publicise it more effectively. Many colleagues in various countries from all over the world have been instrumental in helping us regularly in this goal.

This year over 490 papers from more than 30 countries in five continents were submitted to ISCIS'05. As a result of the evaluation process, less than one third of the papers were accepted as full papers. The accepted papers are published in LNCS Springer Verlag and IC Press Series. The papers published in this book are selected from the topics of:

- Computer networks
- Internet and multimedia
- Security and cryptography
- Wireless networks
- Parallel and distributed computing
- Performance evaluation.

We would especially like to mention our colleagues who served in the program and organizing committees, members of Boğaziçi University Computer Engineering Department, and our honorary chair, Prof. Erol Gelenbe. We also would like to thank to the authors for submitting the results of their research and helping to make ISCIS 2005 a success.

We hope that the participants benefited from the technical content and enjoyed the social program, the hospitality of Turkish hosts and Istanbul.

October 2005

Editors
Tuna Tuğcu
Erol Gelenbe
M. Ufuk Çağlayan
Fatih Alagöz

INVITED TALKS

Jacques Stern
Professor and Chair
Department of Computer Science
Ecole normale supérieure, France

Alternatives to RSA: An Overview

Since the invention of public key cryptography by Diffie and Hellman in 1976, very few public key schemes have been deployed in applications, besides the celebrated RSA algorithm designed by Rivest, Shamir, and Adleman. While millions of RSA keys are used in WEB browsers, most public key cryptosystems are only present in textbooks, with the noticeable exception of those based on elliptic curves, which seem to slowly make their way to the market.

There are however, several other challenging lines of research proposing public key schemes of a different flavour. Some use elliptic/hyperelliptic curves as mentioned, some are based on the computational hardness of various problems from coding theory or from the geometry of numbers. Some stem from considering the mathematical formula describing RSA as a univariate modular polynomial, and attempt to use multivariate polynomials instead. All hope to achieve a lower cost for encryption and/or decryption and/or communication.

While some of the original proposals have been shown insecure, many further schemes have been designed. In turn, these have been subject to active cryptanalytic work. The aim of the talk is to review some of the schemes, to explain some of the methods that have been used to attack them, and to assess their level of security. In other words, are these alternatives now ready for practical applications?

Yanghee Choi
Professor and Chair
School of Computer Science and Engineering
Seoul National University, Gwanak-gu, Seoul, Korea

Location and Address Issues in Ubiquitous Computing

There will be billions of new nodes in ubiquitous computing environment within not-so-far future. Telephone-based or IP-based addressing may not be adequate for identifying moving, transient or temporary network nodes. And location information will become very important in ubiquitous network applications. Issues and solutions for the two important problems will be discussed in this talk.

HONORARY CHAIRMAN

Erol Gelenbe

ORGANIZING COMMITTEE

Technical Program Chair
Fatih Alagöz

Local Organizing Committee Chair
Tunga Güngör

Best Paper Award Chair
Fikret Gürgen

Publicity Chair
Pınar Yolum

Finance Chair
Tuna Tuğcu

Sponsorship Chair
Can Özturan

LOCAL ORGANIZING COMMITTEE

İlker Demirkol

Hatice Köse (Bağcı)

Arzucan Özgür

Fatma Canan Pembe

Albert Ali Salah

Burak Turhan

TECHNICAL PROGRAM COMMITTEE

Bulent Abali
Mohammed Abdel-Hafez
Sibel Adali
Ozgur B. Akan
Lale Akarun
Levent Akin
Sahin Albayrak
Reda Alhajj
Ethem Alpaydin
Emin Anarim
I. Budak Arpinar
Cevdet Aykanat
Fevzi Belli
Ufuk Caglayan
Mariacarla Calzarossa
K. Selcuk Candan
Ugur Cetintemel
Gabriel Ciobanu
Vedat Coskun
Andrea D'Ambrogio
Tugrul Dayar
Oguz Dikenelli
Iain Duff
Eylem Ekici
Marc Emmelman
Cem Ersoy
Jean-Michel Fourneau

REFEREES

Ebru Celikel
Ugur Cetintemel
Heung Seok Chae
Nizamuddin Channa
Alexander G. Chefranov
Jessica Chen
Xiao Chen
Yan Chen
Haengrae Cho
Dae-Young Choi
Jin-Hee Choi
Lynn Choi
WoongChul Choi
Gabriel Ciobanu
Selim Ciraci
Vedat Coskun
Diogo Costa
Mate J. Csorba
Haydar Cukurtepe
Andrea D'Ambrogio
Tomas Danikauskas
Tugrul Dayar
Hakan Delic
Engin Demir
Engin Deveci
Oguz Dikenelli
B. Taner Dincer
Banu Diri
Erdogan Dogdu
Ugur Dogrusoz
Inshil Doh
M. Yunus Donmez
Iain Duff
Claudiu Duma
Gunhan Dundar
Nurcan Durak
Taner Dursun
Tobias Eggendorfer
Eylem Ekici
Atilla Elci
Nahit Emanet
Marc Emmelman
Kayhan Erciyes
Zeki Erdem
Nadia Erdogan
Riza Cenk Erdur
Murat Ergun
Cem Ersoy
Gurdal Ertek
Y. Murat Erten
Sarp Erturk
Mustafa Taner Eskil
Yu Fei
Dan Feng
Fernando Z. Flores
Jean-Michel Fourneau
Mario Marques Freire
Peng Fu
Laura Galluccio
Alexander Gelbukh
George Ghinea
Katja Gilly
Sertan Girgin
Berk Gokberk
Erek Gokturk
Janaki Gopalan
Robert Griffioen
Ugur Gudukbay
Cigdem Gunduz
Gurkan Gur
Burak Gurdag
Attila Gursoy
H. Altay Guvenir
Michael Hadjitheodosiou
JungHyun Han
Su-Young Han
Sof. Galicia Haro
Jed Hassell
Jane Hillston
Eui Kyeong Hong
David C. Hooge
Mark Hoogendoorn
Jia Hou
Zhang Hu
Adriana Iamnitchi
Giuseppe Iazeolla
Sinan Isik
Ali Iskurt
Jie Jiang
KyoHong Jin
Carlos Juiz
Hu Jun
Kyungkoo Jun
Eui-Hyun Jung
Jinhee Jung
Fatih Kahraman
Ozan Kahramanogullari
Utku Kalay
Oya Kalipsiz
JungMin Kang
NamO Kang
Seokhoon Kang
Aylin Kantarci
Ahmet Kara
Dervis Karaboga
Dilek Karabudak
Manolya Kavakli
Cem Keskin
Hurevren Kilic
Cheol Hong Kim
Dong Seong Kim
Jangha Kim
Seong-Woon Kim
Young-Pil Kim
Fatih Koksal
Ahmet Koltuksuz
Can Komar
Hyunjang Kong
Jung-Shik Kong
Ibrahim Korpeoglu
Rabun Kosar
Alexander Kostin
Sastri Kota
Ulas Kozat
Gurhan Kucuk
Ugur Kucuk
Ayse Kucukyilmaz
Tayfun Kucukyilmaz
Omer E. Kundakcioglu
Sukru Kuran
Marek Kurzynski
Mustafa Kuscu
Jong Wook Kwak
Bo-Hee Lee
Chang-Gun Lee
Chang-Hwan Lee
Junsoo Lee
Kangsun Lee

ShinHyoung Lee
SungYoung Lee
Yong-Jin Lee
Ricardo Lent
Albert Levi
Bin Li
Huaqing Li
Jinyan Li
Minglu Li
Weimin Li
Jinqian Liang
Hyotaek Lim
Hyung-Jin Lim
Ming-Hua Lin
Fuyu Liu
Jian-Wei Liu
Alok Madhukar
Margarida Mamede
Alessandro Marchetto
Robert LR Mattson
Carlos A. B. de Mello
Boanerges A. Meza
Alok Mishra
Sangman Moh
Higinio Mora Mora
Giacomo Morabito
Omer K. Morgul
Syed S. Murtaza
Lauro Nakayama
Kim Anh Pham Ngoc
Hu Ning
Kemal Oflazer
Kazuhiro Ogata
Hasan Ogul
Hayoung Oh
Sema Oktug
Onur Onder
Tolga Onel
Ertan Onur
Bulent Orencik
Mehmet Orgun
Zeynep Orhan
Cemil Oz
Selma Ayse Ozalp
Ender Ozcan
Mahmut Ozcan
Ibrahim Ozcelik
Ali Haydar Ozer
Atay Ozgovde
Bulent Ozguc
Fusun Ozguner
Eray Ozkural
Ahmet Ozmen
Gultekin Ozsoyoglu
Tamer Ozsu
Ercan Oztemel
Tansel Ozyer
Lale Ozyilmaz
Hasan Palaz
Jaesung Park
Jihun Park
Jun-Cheol Park
Jungkeun Park
SungHoon Park
Saeed Parsa
Ferhan Pekergin
Zhang Peng
Rui G. Pereira
Yusuf Pisan
Faruk Polat
Viara Popova
Ramon Puigjaner
Jae-Young Pyun
Franck Quessette
Behnam Rahnama
Omar Ramadan
Ren Ren
Ana Regina C. da Rocha
Joel J. P. C. Rodrigues
Minsoo Ryu
Ali Vahit Sahiner
Mohammad Salamah
Pinar Sanac
Kristian Sandahl
Hasan Sarper
Erkay Savas
Cem Say
Yucel Saygin
Martijn Schut
Onur Tolga Sehitoglu
Canan Senol
Jungtaek Seo
Gabriela Serban
Ahmet Sertbas
Erdogan Sevilgen
Nahid Shahmehri
Huagang Shao
Alexei Sharpanskykh
Dongyu Shi
Xuanhua Shi
Nikolay V. Shilov
SungHoon Shim
Dongwan Shin
Soong Hyun Shin
Taeshik Shon
Fikret Sivrikaya
Ibrahim Sogukpinar
A. Coskun Sonmez
Omer Ozan Sonmez
Nuanwan Soonthornphisaj
Onur Soysal
Boleslaw Szymansky
Martin Takac
A. Cagatay Talay
Abdullah Uz Tansel
Fatma Tansu
Samir Tartir
K.Tuncay Tekle
Umit Tezcan
Yuan Tian
Igor Timchenko
Petia Todorova
Yasemin Topaloglu
Vedat Topuz
Oguz Tosun
Fehime Tufekcioglu
Borahan Tumer
Betul Turgut
Cigdem Turhan
Ata Turk
Aysegul Tuysuz
Devrim Unal
Mustafa Unel
Alper Ungor
Tonguc Unluyurt
Suzan Uskudarli
Mutlu Uysal
Yasin Uzun

Binod Vaidya
Alessandro Vanelli-Coralli
Krzysztof Walkowiak
Michal Wozniak
Wu Xiaoling
Zhiwen Xu
Pan Yantao
Adnan Yazici
Husnu Yenigun
Yakup Yildirim
Turker Yilmaz
Jiadi Yu
Erkan Zergeroglu
Xinyu Zhao
Xuefeng Zhu
S. Valli
Rosa Vicari
Fang Wang
Robert Wrembel
Xin Xu
Soomi Yang
Hongxun Yao
Ali Yazici
Meltem Yildirim
Olcay Taner Yildiz
Meltem Turhan Yondem
Arda Yurdakul
Jia Zhai
Liao Zhigang
S.D. Zorzo
George Valvis
Branimir R. Vojcic
Kainam Tom Wong
Chi-Jen Wu
Zeshui Xu
Zhu Yanqin
Sirma Yavuz
Bulent Yener
Tulay Yildirim
Birkan Yilmaz
Chuck Yoo
Lingfang Zeng
YongZhong Zhang
Wang Zhiqi

CONTENTS

Preface v

Invited Talks vii

Organization ix

A Lightweight Passive Replication Protocol for Deterministic Servers 1
Jinho Ahn

A Simple Partial-Path Combination Approach for Constrained Path Selection 11
Murat Sensoy and Murat Zeren

TCP Start-up Behavior under the Proportional Fair Scheduling Policy 19
J.H. Choi, J.G. Choi and C. Yoo

The Hop-Limit Approach for Flow Assignment in Survivable Connection-Oriented Networks 30
K. Walkowiak

A Fair Bandwidth Allocation Scheme for Multimedia Handoff Calls in Cellular Networks 40
M. Salamah and I. Candan

Improving the Performance of Video Streaming Systems Using Video-Locality and Distributed Redundant Hierarchy Servers 50
Hasan Sarper, Mohammed Ahmed, Isik Aybay

Searching for Low Latency Routes in CPN with Reduced Packet Overhead 63
R. Lent and P. Liu

A Required Level for Optical Networks Business Model: Integrated Neutral Topology Optimizer (INTO) 73
Haydar Cukurtepe, Sefer Kurnaz and A. Behzat Sahin

Characterizing Voice and Video Traffic Behavior over the Internet 83
Prasad Calyam and Chang-Gun Lee

Dynamic Bandwidth Allocation Considering Utilization and QoS in Cellular Networks 93
Kyungkoo Jun, Seokhoon Kang and Byoungjo Choi

A Path Restoration Algorithm Sharing the Resource in GMPLS Network 103
Tae-Man Han, You-Hyeon Jeong, Jun-Hwa Lee, Sang-Ha Kim and Dong-Won Kim

Design of a Chirped Fiber Bragg Grating for Use in Wideband Dispersion Compensation 114
Isa Navruz and Ahmet Altuncu

Voronoi-Based Approach for Constructing Connected Cover Set in Wireless Sensor Networks 124
Jie Jiang, Zhen Song, Heying Zhang and Wenhua Dou

Messages Scheduling of CAN-Based Network for a Humanoid Robot 134
J.-S. Kong, Y.-K. Sung, J.-G. Kim and B.-H. Lee

More Efficient Java RMI for GPRS Devices 144
Jalal Kawash, Ghassan Samara and Ahmad El-Halabi

Implementation and Performance Analysis of iSCSI-Based Virtual Storage System with Wireless Networks 154
Hyotaek Lim, Saebom Choi and Daehun Nyang

A Robust Cluster-Based Multi-Hop Routing Algorithm in Wireless Sensor Networks 165
Xiao Chen, Mingwei Xu and Yong Cui

Cluster-Based Security Mechanism for Sensor Network Communication 175
Inshil Doh, Hayoung Oh and Kijoon Chae

HTTP-MPLEX: An Application Layer Multiplexing Protocol for the Hypertext Transfer Protocol (HTTP) 190
R.L.R. Mattson and S. Ghosh

A New Approach to Detect DDOS Attacks Using Support Vector Machine 202
Jungtaek Seo, Cheolho Lee, Taeshik Shon and Jongsub Moon

Performance Evaluation of End-to-End Security in Wireless Applications Using WTLS Handshake Protocol 211
Burak Bayoglu, Albert Levi and Erkay Savas

Integrating Semantic Context Model into Adaptive Middleware for Ubiquitous Computing 222
Qing Wu, Zhaohui Wu and Jie Sun

An Infrastructure for Context-Aware Authorization in Ubiquitous Computing Environments 232
Young-Chul Shim

Performance Considerations for Elliptic Curve Cryptography in Communications 242
Omer Ozgur Bozkurt

Minimum Power Multicasting with Delay Bound Constraints in Ad Hoc Wireless Networks 252
O.E. Kundakcioglu, K. Bulbul, T. Unluyurt, K. Kilic and O. Ercetin

Video Segmentation with Block Based Change Detection Using Numerous Preceding Image Frames 264
O. Urhan and S. Erturk

An Ethernet-Oriented Receiver-Initiated Reliable Multicast Protocol with an Early Message Loss Detection Scheme 274
Yilmaz Kemal Yuce, Alexander Kostin and Erhan Basri

A Dynamic Route Optimization to Support Network Mobility by Using HMNR Scheme 288
Moon-Sang Jeong, Jong-Tae Park and Yeong-Hun Cho

Prediction Accuracy Study of an Adaptive Algorithm in Cluster-Based Network Servers with Resource Allocation 298
Katja Gilly, Salvador Alcaraz, Carlos Juiz and Ramon Puigjaner

A Fuzzy-Based Vertical Handoff Scheme for Interworking Between WLAN and GSM 309
Fatma Tansu and Muhammed Salamah

Performance Analysis of Reliable Multicast Protocols 319
Coskun Celik and Cuneyt F. Bazlamacci

Emulating Ad Hoc Networks: Differences from Simulations and Emulation Specific Problems 329
Erek Gokturk

Energy Efficient and Reliable Routing with Cooperative Diversity in Wireless Ad-Hoc Networks 339
A. Aksu, O. Ercetin, T. Unluyurt, K. Bulbul and K. Kilic

Visual Device Identification for Security Services in Ad-Hoc Wireless Networks 349
Dongwan Shin and Seunghyun Im

A New Algorithm for Horizontal Handover Management in Wireless Mobile Networks 359
A. Tuysuz and M. Yildirim

An AAA Based Solution for the Secure Interoperability of 3G and 802.11 Networks 368
B. Turgut and M.U. Çaglayan

A LIGHTWEIGHT PASSIVE REPLICATION PROTOCOL FOR DETERMINISTIC SERVERS

JINHO AHN

Dept. of Computer Science, Kyonggi University,
San 94-6 Iui-dong, Yeongtong-gu,
Suwon-si Gyeonggi-do 443-760, Korea
E-mail: jhahn@kyonggi.ac.kr

This paper presents a lightweight passive replication protocol for deterministic servers in message-passing distributed systems. The protocol allows any server, not necessarily the primary, to take responsibility for processing its received client request and coordinating with the other replica servers after obtaining the delivery sequence number of the request from the primary. Thanks to this feature, the protocol with conventional load balancing techniques can avoid extreme load conditions on the primary. Therefore, the protocol promises better scalability of deterministic and replicated services compared with traditional protocols. Simulation results indicate that the proposed protocol can reduce 22.4% $\sim$ 52.3% of the average response time of a client request.

1. Introduction

When an application executes in parallel on multiple computers in a distributed system, the failure of a single computer may lead to the failure of the entire execution of the applications. In particular, as the distributed systems scale up, their failure probability may also be higher. Thus, the systems require efficient techniques for supporting fault-tolerance. Process replication is a well-known fault-tolerance technique to ensure high availability of a service in a distributed system by using a group of servers all executing the same service on physically independent computers. In other words, if all servers know what service requests are currently being handled, live servers can continue the work that was not completed by failed ones. In this technique, each replica server of a service should maintain a globally consistent state even in case of failures. In order to ensure the consistency, several specific replication protocols are generally used [6]. Software-based replication protocols are classified into two categories: Active and Passive. In the active replication approach [8], every non-faulty replica server receives each request from its client in the same order, processes it and sends a reply to the client. The approach requires the operations on the replica server to be deterministic: given the initial state of each replica server and the same sequence of client requests previously performed by the replica server, it will produce the same result. It provides failure transparency for clients because even if some replica servers fail, the other normal ones can handle the requests and send their replies to the clients. Additionally, it may provide low response time in some failure cases compared with the passive approach. However, the approach has two important drawbacks: high resource consumption during normal operations because all replica servers have to process client requests, and determinism constraint as mentioned above.

In the passive replication approach [4], only one of the replica servers, called *primary*, receives a request from a client, processes it and then forwards a message including its updated state to the other replica servers, called *backups*. When receiving the message, each backup updates its state using it and sends an acknowledgement message to the primary. After the primary receives the messages from all non-faulty backups, it sends a reply to the client. When the primary fails, it cannot mask the failure to the client and requires high reconfiguration cost. However, this approach has three desirable features as follows. First, the approach enables its consistency to be guaranteed even if replicated servers handle requests in a non-deterministic manner. Thus, it can be applied to replicate any service regardless of the execution behavior of the service. Second, it needs lower processing power during failure-free execution than the active replication one. Third, clients only has to use a unicast primitive, not a multicast one because they send service requests only to the primary server. Therefore, the approach can be applied to message-passing distributed systems as a general-purpose and low-cost fault-tolerant technique.

However, in this approach, clients send requests only to the primary, which executes each request and sends its updated state to the backups. When receiving all acknowledgements from the backups, the primary returns a response. This constraint results from satisfying the consistency condition for non-deterministic services. The behavior may cause the primary to be overloaded when the number of client requests is high. In this case, the entire system performance significantly becomes degraded. In particular, if replicated servers handle requests in deterministic manners only, the primary need not necessarily play the special role in order to ensure the system consistency. In this paper, we present a partially decentralized passive replication protocol designed for deterministic servers in the systems. When a backup receives a request directly from a client, this protocol allows the backup to play the role of the primary in the traditional passive replication approach except determining the processing order of the request. If it is integrated with traditional client based, DNS-based, dispatcher-based or server-based load balancing techniques [3], the protocol can diffuse extreme load conditions on the primary. Therefore, the protocol promises better scalability compared with conventional passive replication ones.

2. Traditional Passive Replication Approach

When a client sends a request message to the primary in the traditional passive replication approach, the following four steps are performed to ensure linearizability during the failure-free operation.

[Step 1]
The primary receives the message from the client.
[Step 2]
The primary processes the message. After the execution, (*resp*, *handledrsn*, *updated-state*) is generated, where *resp* is the response to the message, *handledrsn* identifies the handled request message and *updated-state* is the state of the primary updated by handling the request.
[Step 3]
The primary sends all backups the update message (*resp*, *handledrsn*, *updated-state*, *cid*, *reqid*) respectively, where *cid* identifies the client and *reqid* is the send sequence number of the client request message. When each backup receives the update message, it updates its state using *updated-state*, maintains $(resp, cid, reqid)$ in its buffer and then sends an acknowledgement message to the primary.
[Step 4]
After receiving an acknowledgement message from every live backup, the primary sends *resp* to the client.

However, to ensure linearizability even in case of the crash of the primary, the traditional approach includes several additional steps. Consider the critical cases in figure 1, which is an example for showing how to execute the above mentioned steps . Let $request_i{}^x$ be the x-th request message client i sends to a server process and $resp_i{}^x$ the response message of $request_i{}^x$. $update_i{}^x$ is the update message containing the state of the primary updated by handling $request_i{}^x$, and $ack_i{}^x$ the acknowledgement message of $update_i{}^x$.

(Case 1) The primary p crashes before executing the step 3.

In this case, a new primary q is elected among all backups and client i suspects that p fails because the client cannot receive any response of $request_i{}^x$ from p. After learning the identity of q, the client will resend $request_i{}^x$ to q. When receiving $request_i{}^x$, q has only to perform the step 1 through 4.

(Case 2) The primary p crashes after sending $update_i{}^x$ to all backups, but before sending $resp_i{}^x$ to client i.

Like in case 1, a new primary q is selected, and client i perceives that p fails and identifies q. To ensure linearizability in this case, either all the backups receive $update_i{}^x$, or none of them receive it. **View Synchronous Multicast**($VSCAST$) [6] is used to satisfy the atomicity condition of linearizability in case of an asynchronous system with an unreliable failure detector. If no backup receives $update_i{}^x$, this case is similar to case 1. Otherwise, $(resp, cid, reqid)$ in the step 3 is used to ensure the exactly-once semantics [9]. In other words, when client i sends $request_i{}^x$ to the new primary q again, it immediately sends the response $resp_i{}^x$ to the client without handling the request.

(Case 3) The primary p crashes after sending $resp_i{}^x$ to client i.

Like in case 1, a new primary q is selected, and client i suspects that p fails and identifies q.

As shown in figure 1, all requests from clients are sent to the primary p to satisfy the ordering condition of linearizability. Thus, the operations triggered by the requests are totally ordered based on their *handledrsn*. However, if a large number of clients send requests to the primary p concurrently, p handles the requests in order and coordinates with all backups in the traditional approach. This behavior may cause the extreme load condition to occur and the average client response time to be increased.

3. The Proposed Protocol

In the system model, replicated services are generally classified into deterministic and non-deterministic according to their execution behavior. However, to the best of our knowledge, previous works [1,4,5] uniformly applied the traditional passive replication approach to each replicated ser-

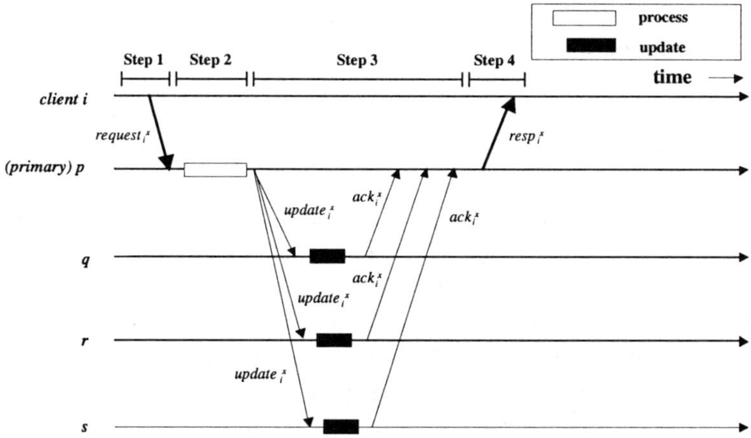

Figure 1. The Traditional Passive Replication Approach

vice regardless of whether it is deterministic or non-deterministic. However, this strategy is not appropriate to the system because the deterministic services require weaker constraints to ensure their consistency than non-deterministic ones. Thus, the traditional passive replication protocols should be applied to non-deterministic services, and more lightweight passive replication protocol, to deterministic services. Therefore, we attempt to propose the protocol $PDPR$ (Partially Decentralized Passive Replication) for deterministic servers to alleviate the problem of the traditional approach and support the increased loads on replicated and deterministic services while ensuring linearizability. This protocol is based on one observation: even if the primary and backups concurrently process the requests in the same order like in the active replication approach, the consistency is ensured in case of deterministic servers. Thus, after the primary has determined the processing order of every client request, it is not necessary that only the primary handles all client requests, and coordinates with the other replica servers like in the traditional approach.

With this observation in mind, the $PDPR$ protocol has the following features.

• Every client can send a service request to the primary or a backup.

• Only the primary determines the processing order of every client request.

• After a backup has received a client request and obtained the order of the request from the primary, the backup, not the primary, processes the request and coordinates with the other replica servers.

In order to satisfy the desirable requirements, the proposed protocol is designed as follows.

[Step 1]
Replica p receives a request message from a client.
[Step 2]
If replica server p is the primary, the step 2 through 4 of the traditional approach are performed. Otherwise, p asks the primary *handledrsn* of the request message. In this case, after the primary determines the *handledrsn* of the message, it notifies p of the *handledrsn*. Then, the primary processes the request message and saves (*resp*, *handledrsn*, *updated-state*, *cid*, *reqid*) of the message in its buffer. When receiving the *handledrsn*, replica server p handles the corresponding request and generates (*resp*, *handledrsn*, *updated-state*) of the request.
[Step 3]
Replica p sends the other replica servers the update message (*resp*, *handledrsn*, *updated-state*, *cid*, *reqid*) respectively. When each replica server except for the primary receives the update message, it updates its state using *updated-state*, maintains (*resp*, *cid*, *reqid*) in its buffer and then sends an acknowledgement message to replica server p. If the primary receives the update message from p, it just removes (*resp*, *handledrsn*, *updated-state*, *cid*, *reqid*) for the message from its buffer, saves (*resp*, *cid*, *reqid*) in the buffer and sends an acknowledgement message to p.
[Step 4]
Once replica server p receives an acknowledgement message from every other live replica server, it sends *resp* to the client.

Figure 2 illustrates how the *PDPR* protocol is performed in case that a backup receives a client request. In the first step, client i sends the x-th request message $request_i^x$ to a backup q. In the second step, q asks the primary p the processing order of the request. At this point, p determines the order and immediately informs q of it. Afterwards, p processes $request_i^x$ and saves its state and the order and response of the request in its buffer. Concurrently, when obtaining the order from p, q handles $request_i^x$. In the third step, it sends its state, $update_i^x$, and $request_i^x$'s order and response, $resp_i^x$, to the other replica servers p, r and s. In this case, r and s update their states using $update_i^x$, save $resp_i^x$ in their buffers, and send each an acknowledgement ack_i^x to q respectively. However, p just removes the corresponding element for $request_i^x$ from its buffer, saves $resp_i^x$ in the buffer and sends ack_i^x to q. After receiving all ack_i^xs from p, r and s, q sends $resp_i^x$ to client i in the last step.

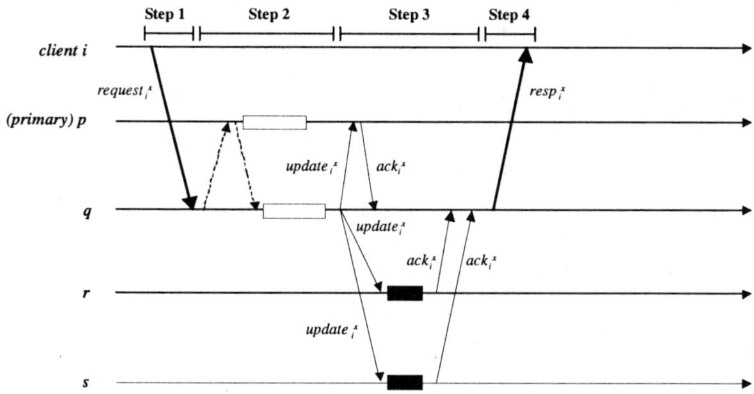

Figure 2. Our Passive Replication Protocol

As shown in the example, the $PDPR$ protocol can diffuse extreme load conditions on the primary and in the network by allowing each backup to be responsible for handling its received client request after obtaining its delivery order from the primary. Thus, the protocol with load balancing techniques may significantly reduce the average client response time and provide better scalability compared with the traditional approach.

When the primary crashes, our protocol performs the same steps for the failure of the traditional one as mentioned in the previous section. However, to satisfy the consistency criterion despite future failures of the other replica servers, the protocol considers the following critical cases. The step performed for each case in the protocol is informally described using figure 2.

(Case 1) Replica q crashes before executing the step 2.

In this case, the replica server q is just removed from its group. Afterwards, client i can detect q's failure because of no response of $request_i{}^x$ from q.

(Case 2) Replica q crashes after sending $request_i{}^x$ to the primary, but before performing the step 3.

(Case 2.1) The primary fails.

All the replica servers except for q and the primary select a new primary, for example r, among them. Also, client i perceives that q crashes.
(Case 2.2) The primary is alive.

When the primary detects q's failure, it retrieves every update information, which is form of (*resp*, *handledrsn*, *updated-state*, *cid*, *reqid*), from its buffer and sends it to all the live replica servers. In this case, $VSCAST$ is used to ensure linearizability. If client i perceives that q fails, it will resend $request_i{}^x$ to another replica server, for example r. Then, r immediately sends the response $resp_i{}^x$ in its buffer to the client without processing the request, which provides the exactly-once semantics.
(Case 3) Replica q crashes after sending $update_i{}^x$ to the other replica servers in the step 3, but before receiving $ack_i{}^x$s from all live replica servers.

As q sent $update_i{}^x$ to the other replica servers by using $VSCAST$, the entire consistency is ensured. Therefore, the group of q has only to eliminate q.
(Case 4) Replica q crashes after $resp_i{}^x$ has been sent to client i.

q is removed from its group and client i detects that q fails.

4. Performance Evaluation

In this section, extensive simulations are performed to compare our passive replication protocol (*PDPR*) with the traditional Centralized Passive Replication one (*CPR*) using PARSEC discrete-event simulation language [2]. A performance index is used for comparison; the mean response time of a client request. The network modelled is a multi-access LAN (100Mbps Ethernet). Nodes connected to the network are identical and uniformly distributed along the physical medium. Each node has at most one process executed on it. Every process communicates with each other using UDP/IP protocol. The message transmission delay between two processes consists of: 1) T_s, the time to execute a send operation on the sending node, 2) T_t, the time to transfer a message from the network interface of the sending node to that of the receiving node, 3) T_r, the time to execute a receive operation on the receiving node. If a process attempts to send or receive a message while its CPU is busy, the message will have to wait until the CPU becomes idle. The network resource is allocated locally based on a FIFO policy, and randomly between nodes. A similar communication model can be found in [7]. In the simulation, $T_s = 0.269$ milliseconds (ms), $T_t = 0.120\ ms$ and $T_r = 0.292\ ms$ for each message frame (1500 bytes). The time required to process a client request is $1ms$ and the time needed for updating the server state is $80\mu s$. For *PDPR*, the destination of each client request is a uniformly distributed random variable among server processes. Client request messages are sent to the network with a interval following an exponential distribution with a mean T_{ms}. Also, to consider more various network environments, the two protocols CPR and $PDPR$ are implemented and simulated depending on whether the network type is point-to-point communication(CPR-P and $PDPR$-P) or multicast communication, i.e., IP multicast(CPR-M and $PDPR$-M).

Figure 3 shows the average response time of *CPR-P*, *CPR-M*, *PDPR-P* and *PDPR-M* for the specified range of the number of replicated servers ($NORS$) in a network in case that no server failure occurs. In this figure, their mean request sending intervals(T_{ms}s) is 30 ms. In figure 3, as $NORS$s of the four protocols increase, their response times also increase. The reason is that as the degree of replication scales up, they require higher coordination overhead of the server group. However, the response time of *PDPR-P* is much lower than that of *CPR-P*. In particular, as $NORS$ is higher, the gap between their increasing rates is larger. In this case, $PDPR$-P reduces 24.5% $\sim$ 45.1% of the response time compared with CPR-P. Also, as expected, the response time of *CPR-M* and *PDPR-M* is considerably smaller than that of *CPR-P* and *PDPR-P* because a smaller number of messages were generated in the multicast case than the point-to-point one. Thus, we can see that as the mean sending interval T_{ms} increases, the gap between the increasing rates of *CPR* and *PDPR* becomes much larger and if the two protocols are implemented to use mulicast communication, their response time is more reduced.

5. Conclusion

The proposed passive replication protocol was designed for deterministic servers to be more lightweight than the traditional passive replication protocols because the deterministic services require weaker constraints to ensure the system consistency than non-deterministic services. The proposed protocol allows any server, not necessarily the primary, to process each client request and coordinate with the other replica servers after receiving the request and obtaining its delivery sequence number from the primary. Thus, integrating it with the conventional load balancing techniques, the protocol can promise lower response time in the increased load condition compared with the traditional ones. The simulation results showed that our protocol is more scalable than the centralized passive replication protocol

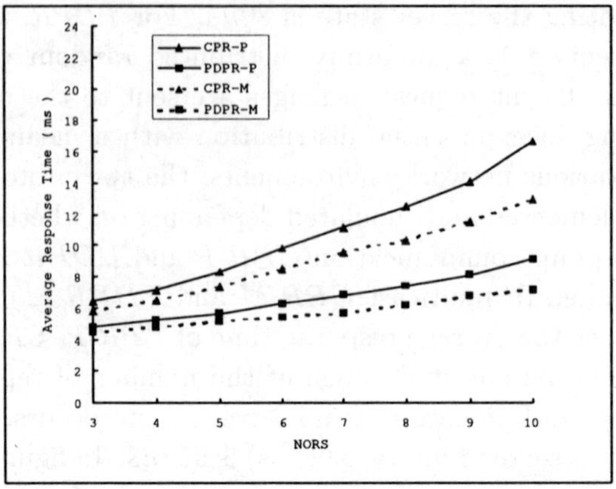

Figure 3. Average response time vs. $NORS$ ($T_{ms} = 30\ ms$)

with respect to the number of servers and client requests.

References

1. K. P. Birman and T. A. Joseph, T. Raeuchle and A. E. Abbadi. Implementing fault-tolerant distributed objects. *IEEE Transactions on Software Engineering*, Vol. 11, No. 6, pp. 502-508, (1985).
2. R. Bagrodia, R. Meyer, M. Takai, Y. Chen, X. Zeng, J. Martin and H. Y. Song. Parsec: A Parallel Simulation Environments for Complex Systems. *IEEE Computer*, pp. 77-85, (1998).
3. H. Bryhni, E. Klovning and O. Kure. A Comparison of Load Balancing Techniques for Scalable Web Servers. *IEEE Network*, 14:58-64, (2000).
4. N. Budhiraja, K. Marzullo, F. B. Schneider and S. Toueg. The primary-backup approach. *Distributed Systems(S. Mullender ed.*, ch. 8, 199-216, Addison-Wesley, second ed., (1993).
5. X. Defago and A. Schiper. Semi-passive Replication and Lazy Consensus. *Journal of Parallel and Distributed Computing Systems*, 64(12), pp. 1380-1398, (2004).
6. R. Guerraoui and A. Schiper. Software-Based Replication for Fault Tolerance. *IEEE Computer*, 30(4):68-74, (1997).
7. M. Malcom and W. Zhao Hard real time communication in multiple-access networks. *Real-Time Systems*, Vol.8, pp. 35-77, (1995).
8. F. B. Schneider. Implementing fault-tolerant services using the state machine approach: A tutorial. *ACM Computing Surveys*, 22(4):299-319, (1990).
9. A. Spector. Performing remote operations efficiently on local computer network. *Communications of the ACM*, 25(4):246-260, (1982).

A SIMPLE PARTIAL-PATH COMBINATION APPROACH FOR CONSTRAINED PATH SELECTION

MURAT ŞENSOY AND MURAT ZEREN

Bogazici University,
Department of Computer Engineering,
P.K. 2 TR-34342 Bebek, Istanbul, TURKEY
E-mail: murat.sensoy@boun.edu.tr

In this paper, PAS (partial-path combination approach for constrained path selection) is proposed to find delay-constrained paths with the same order of complexity as Dijkstra's algorithm. Performance of PAS as an underlying path selection heuristic in multicast routing is evaluated using randomly generated sessions on random networks. Simulations show that PAS produces delay-constrained paths very fast without significantly trading-off tree cost for speed.

1. Introduction

For real-time communications, such as teleconferencing, videoconferencing or real-time online multicast routing applications, connection establishment time can be crucial. Especially for online multicast sessions where new members join and some members leave the session, immediate establishment of new admissible paths may be as important as constructing low cost delay-constrained paths. The proposed heuristic PAS (partial-path combination approach for constrained path selection) can easily be employed in such time-critical path selection tasks. PAS is a heuristic proposed to find best effort least-cost delay-constrained paths between nodes or trees with the same order of complexity as Dijkstra's algorithm.

In order to formulate the problem of finding delay-constrained least-cost paths, the network is modeled as a directed, connected graph $G = (V, E)$, where V is the set of nodes and E is the set of directed links. Each link, e, is characterized by a cost, $C(e)$, and a delay, $D(e)$ and n is the number of nodes. Given a source node $s \in V$, a destination node $d \in V$, and a positive delay constraint Δ, delay-constrained least-cost path problem is summarized in Eq. 1, where $P_{set}^{\Delta}(s,d)$ is the set of paths from s to d for which the end-to-end delay is bounded by Δ.

$$\min_{P \in P^{\Delta}_{set}(s,d)} \sum_{e \in P} C(e) \tag{1}$$

Although the problem is NP-complete, there are polynomial time heuristics. A substantial portion of those heuristics depends on k-shortest path algorithms [1,2,3]. Performance of such heuristics highly depends on *k* parameter and performance of underlying k-shortest path algorithm. They can find near optimum paths for appropriately large *k* values with a drawback of high computation time.

2. Partial-Path Combination Approach For Constrained Path Selection

PAS is based on Dijkstra and Reverse-Dijkstra algorithms. In Dijkstra algorithm, objective is to find the shortest paths from a source node to other nodes. Each node keeps the least-cost path from source node to itself by keeping the predecessor node on that path. By back tracking this predecessor node, this path can be constructed. Similarly Reverse-Dijkstra algorithm can be used to find paths to a destination from other nodes. This time each node keeps a path from itself to destination by keeping the forward node information. In both algorithms, nodes also should keep total cost and total delay of the paths. For each node in the network, PAS finds one complete path from source node to destination node, which is the shortest path containing the corresponding node according to the calculation metric, by simply combining partial paths derived from Dijkstra and Reverse-Dijkstra algorithms. Combination of partial paths can be done by using predecessor node ID coming from Dijkstra algorithm and forward node ID coming from Reverse-Dijkstra algorithm, additionally delay and cost of the complete path can be calculated using delay and cost of the partial paths. A sample graph and calculated complete paths are demonstrated in Figure 1.

Table 1 and Table 2 tabulates the combined paths derived from the example in Figure 1. For each node, two paths are derived; one path for cost metric and one path for delay metric. Paths in Table 1 and Table 2 are not unique. Table 3 tabulates the combined unique paths derived from the example in Figure 1. Usefulness of a path can be determined by inspecting its total cost, total delay and other path information. So paths violating delay constrain can easily be disregarded. Path selection can be done by traversing paths and selecting the cheapest delay-constrained path. PAS

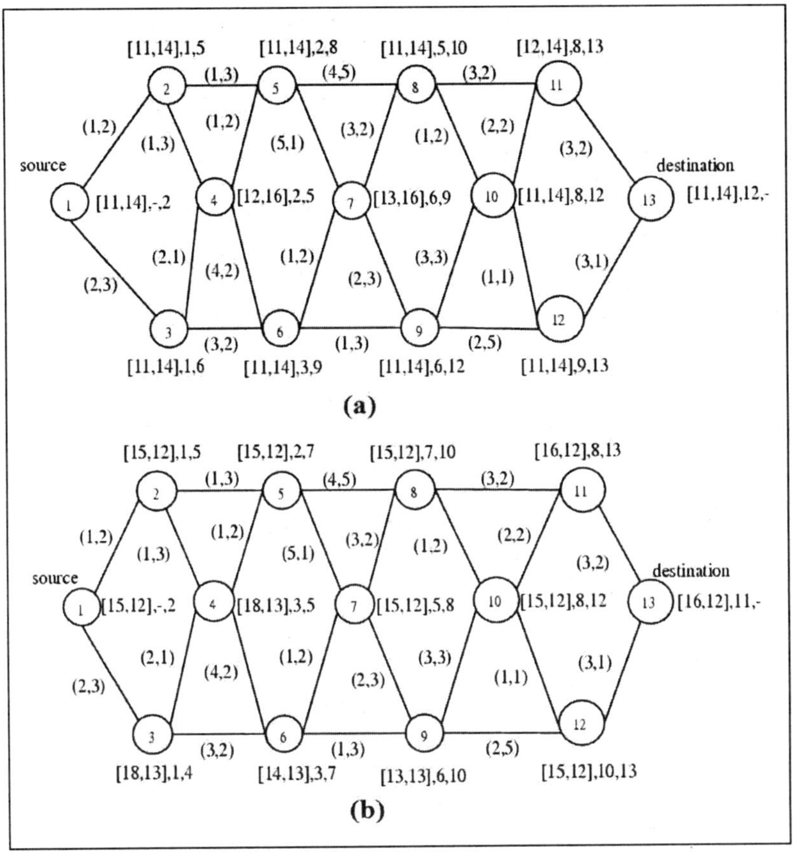

Figure 1. A sample graph and combined partial paths of Dijkstra and Reverse-Dijkstra algoritms. Nodes are labeled with *[path cost, path delay], PredecessorNodeID, ForwardNodeID* format. Edges are labeled according to *(cost,delay)* format. (a) Cost metric calculations, (b) Delay metric calculations.

can find a delay-constrained path, if one exists, because it employs both delay metric and cost metric calculations.

Making small modifications on Dijkstra and Reverse-Dijkstra algorithms, PAS can find paths between a source tree and a destination tree in a graph. In the modified Dijkstra algorithm, each source-tree-node should be regarded as the source node. However, during relaxation of a graph node using a source-tree-node, delay of the path on the source tree from the source node to the source-tree-node is used instead of using zero, be-

Table 1. Cost metric paths

Node	Cost	Delay	Path
1	11	14	1,2,5,8,10,12,13
2	11	14	1,2,5,8,10,12,13
3	11	14	1,3,6,9,12,13
4	12	16	1,2,4,5,8,10,12,13
5	11	14	1,2,5,8,10,12,13
6	11	14	1,3,6,9,12,13
7	13	16	1,3,6,7,9,12,13
8	11	14	1,2,5,8,10,12,13
9	11	14	1,3,6,9,12,13
10	11	14	1,2,5,8,10,12,13
11	12	14	1,2,5,8,11,13
12	11	14	1,2,5,8,10,12,13
13	11	14	1,2,5,8,10,12,13

Table 2. Delay metric paths

Node	Cost	Delay	Path
1	15	12	1,2,5,7,8,10,12,13
2	15	12	1,2,5,7,8,10,12,13
3	18	13	1,3,4,5,7,8,10,12,13
4	18	13	1,3,4,5,7,8,10,12,13
5	15	12	1,2,5,7,8,10,12,13
6	14	13	1,3,6,7,8,10,12,13
7	15	12	1,2,5,7,8,10,12,13
8	15	12	1,2,5,7,8,10,12,13
9	13	13	1,3,6,9,10,12,13
10	15	12	1,2,5,7,8,10,12,13
11	16	12	1,2,5,7,8,11,13
12	15	12	1,2,5,7,8,10,12,13
13	16	12	1,2,5,7,8,11,13

Table 3. Unique paths sorted by cost

Node	Cost	Delay	Path	Metric
1	11	14	1,2,5,8,10,12,13	COST
3	11	14	1,3,6,9,12,13	COST
11	12	14	1,2,5,8,11,13	COST
7	13	16	1,3,6,7,9,12,13	COST
9	13	13	1,3,6,9,10,12,13	DELAY
6	14	13	1,3,6,7,8,10,12,13	DELAY
1	15	12	1,2,5,7,8,10,12,13	DELAY
11	16	12	1,2,5,7,8,11,13	DELAY
4	18	13	1,3,4,5,7,8,10,12,13	DELAY

cause delay is a source centric metric. In the modified Reverse-Dijkstra algorithm, each node on the destination tree is regarded as the destination node.

3. FAST-BSMA

BSMA is an iterative heuristic proposed by Parsa et al [4] for the delay-constrained multicast routing problem. It starts by computing a least-delay tree using Dijkstra algorithm for a given source and multicast group members. Then BSMA iteratively replaces superedges in the tree with cheaper superedges, without violating the delay constraint. A superedge is a path in the tree between two branching nodes, or two multicast group members, or a branching node and a multicast group member. This iterative procedure stops, when the total cost of the tree cannot be reduced any further. BSMA uses a k-shortest path algorithm to find cheaper superedges. Fast-BSMA (FBSMA) is a version of BSMA heuristic in which PAS is used instead of a k-shortest path algorithm based delay-constrained path heuristic. BSMA is known to be one of the best polynomial-time heuristics in terms of the multicast tree cost in the literature and its high time complexity is its only bottleneck [5]. This bottleneck is relaxed by using PAS instead of a k-shortest path based algorithm without significantly compromising tree cost performance.

4. Performance Evaluation

Performance of PAS as an underlying path-selection heuristic in delay-constrained multicast routing is evaluated using simulations on randomly generated networks. An online multicast session is simulated for each network. Each multicast session has 100 join/leave requests. Random network generation and random request generation models are adopted from the Waxman's models [6,7]. Random request generation model is configured so that join and leave requests are equally likely. After each request a new delay-constrained multicast tree is computed for the new set of multicast members using BSMA and FBSMA. BSMA heuristic is run for different k values of its k-shortest path algorithm, which are 100 and 1000, for better comparison. Total 800 different networks are simulated, 400 for 50-node networks and 400 for 100-node networks. Simulations are performed for different multicast group sizes ranging from 10 percent of network size (sparse multicast groups) to 60 percent of network size (dense multicast groups).

For the comparison of FBSMA and BSMA, two metrics are used. Those are cost competitiveness and CPU time. Cost competitiveness metric is the average multicast tree cost of a heuristic throughout a multicast session as the percentage of that of BSMA. So cost competitiveness of BSMA is always 100. Table 4 and Table 5 show average cost competitiveness for FBSMA.

Difference between average cost competitiveness of FBSMA and BSMA heuristics is negligible for different multicast group sizes, network sizes and k values. This means that both BSMA and FBSMA produce almost the same quality delay-constrained multicast trees in terms of multicast tree cost.

Table 4. Average cost competitiveness for FBSMA (k = 100 for BSMA)

Multicast Group Size	50-node Networks	100-node Networks
10%	100.009	99.970
20%	100.014	100.037
40%	99.998	100.018
60%	99.996	100.001

Table 5. Average cost competitiveness for FBSMA (k = 1000 for BSMA)

Multicast Group Size	50-node Networks	100-node Networks
10%	100.014	99.990
20%	100.022	100.054
40%	100.038	100.035
60%	100.020	100.015

Table 6. Average CPU time (sec.) (k = 100 for BSMA)

Multicast Group Size	**50-node Networks**		**100-node Networks**	
	FBSMA	**BSMA**	**FBSMA**	**BSMA**
10%	0.091	0.588	0.637	8.451
20%	0.094	0.778	0.778	10.755
40%	0.107	1.064	1.087	19.205
60%	0.131	1.285	1.428	34.342

Table 7. Average CPU time (sec.) (k = 1000 for BSMA)

Multicast Group Size	**50-node Networks**		**100-node Networks**	
	FBSMA	**BSMA**	**FBSMA**	**BSMA**
10%	0.091	0.795	0.637	11.103
20%	0.094	0.861	0.778	15.211
40%	0.107	1.101	1.087	26.721
60%	0.131	1.757	1.428	50.055

CPU time metric is the average CPU time required to compute multicast trees throughout a multicast session. Table 6 and Table 7 show average

CPU time of BSMA and FBSMA heuristics for 50-node and 100-node networks for different k values. It is shown that CPU time of BSMA increases dramatically with increasing number of nodes in the network or multicast group. However, CPU time of FBSMA is minor with respect to that of BSMA. This means that FBSMA can compute multicast trees as good as that of BSMA much faster.

5. Conclusions

Fast and efficient delay-constrained multicast tree construction is becoming an essential part of multimedia communication applications. Our work is motivated by the need for fast and efficient constrained path selection heuristics to be used in delay-constrained multicast routing. Proposed heuristic, PAS, is convenient for the applications, which require fast computation of delay-constrained paths without significantly trading off performance for speed. So it can easily be used in delay-constrained online multicast routing. BSMA, which is one of the best polynomial-time heuristics for delay-constrained multicast routing problem, is used for the performance evaluation of PAS. A delay-constrained path selection heuristic basing on k-shortest path algorithm is used in BSMA. However k-shortest path algorithms have high time complexities. Therefore, the high time complexity of BSMA is its bottleneck. This bottleneck is relaxed by using PAS instead of a k-shortest path based heuristic without significantly compromising cost competitiveness. Our simulation results confirm that PAS is very convenient to be used in delay sensitive multicast routing applications as underlying path selection heuristic. FBSMA using PAS can produce the same quality multicast trees much faster than the original BSMA heuristic. So, PAS can be used as a stand-alone unicast routing heuristic or an underlying path selection heuristic in delay-constrained multicast routing.

References

1. Zhanfeng Jia and Pravin Varaiya, Heuristic Methods for Delay Constrained Least Cost Routing Using k-Shortest-Paths, *Proceedings of 20th Joint Conference IEEE Computer and Communications Societies, INFOCOM'01*, (2001).
2. Liang Guo and Ibrahim Matta, Search Space Reduction in QoS Routing, *Computer Networks*, **42**(2003), pp. 73–88.
3. M. F. Mokbel, W. A. El-Haweet and M. N. El-Derini, A Delay-Constrained Shortest Path Algorithm for Multicast Routing in Multimedia Applications,*Proceedings of IEEE Middle East Workshop on Networking*, (1999).
4. Mehrdad Parsa, Qing Zhu, and J. J. Garcia-Luna-Aceves, An Iterative Algo-

rithm for Delay-Constrained Minimum-Cost Multicasting, *IEEE/ACM Transactions on Networking*, **6**, 4 (1998).

5. Hussein F. Salama, Douglas S. Reeves, and Yannis Viniotis, Evaluation of Multicast Routing Algorithms for Real-Time Communications on High-Speed Networks, *IEEE Journal on Selected Areas in Communications*, **15**, 3 (1997) pp. 332–345.
6. Bernard M. Waxman, Routing Multipoint Connections, *IEEE Journal on Selected Areas in Communications*, **6**, 9 (1988).
7. M. Doar and I. Leslie, How bad is naive multicast routing, *Proceedings of IEEE INFOCOM'93*, (1993) pp. 82–89.

TCP START-UP BEHAVIOR UNDER THE PROPORTIONAL FAIR SCHEDULING POLICY*

J. H. CHOI [†], J. G. CHOI [‡], AND C. YOO [†]

[†] *Department of Computer Science and Engineering*
Korea University
Seoul, Korea
E-mail: {jhchoi, hxy}@os.korea.ac.kr

[‡] *KT Convergence Laboratory*
Seoul, Korea
E-mail: jinchoi@kt.co.kr

It is expected that the proportional fair (PF) scheduler will be used widely in cdma2000 1xEV-DO systems because it maximizes the sum of each user's utility, which is given by the logarithm of its average throughput. However, in terms of short-term average throughput, PF scheduler may lead to a large RTT variation. We analyze the impact of PF scheduler on TCP start-up behavior through NS-2 simulation. To show the impact of PF scheduling on TCP, we also analyze the packet transmission delay under the PF scheduling policy through mathematical model.

1. Introduction

Recent advances in communication technology make appearance of the packet-based cellular systems such as cdma2000 1xEV-DO [1] and UMTS-HSDPA [2]. Being mainly targeted on high-speed data applications that are tolerant of some packet delay, it is reasonable that their schedulers focus on maximizing the sum of each user's utility. A good way of achieving it is to serve the users with good channel condition first utilizing the time-varying feature of wireless channels. This approach increases the system throughput significantly. But, some users can be sacrificed since, in wireless environment, users have very different channel condition according to their location.

*This work is supported by grant no.r01-2004-000-10588-0 from the basic research program of the korea science and engineering foundation.

The proportional fair scheduler [3] is one of the most promising opportunistic schemes balancing system throughput and user fairness. It is very simple to implement, and also it is optimal in the sense of maximizing the sum of each user's utility that is given by the logarithm of average throughput for elastic traffic. However, it does not provide fair service in short-term scale even if it achieves the proportional fairness in long-term. In addition, owing to its reflection on channel state, the scheduler induces some variation on scheduling delay. So, PF scheduler can make a serious influence on the performance of TCP since it uses path delay or round trip time (RTT) to estimate network state.

Previous researches [6] [7] [8] have already addressed the issue of TCP performance in cellular networks. However, to our best knowledge, it is not investigated how the opportunistic scheduler like PF one affects the behavior of TCP. In this paper, we focus on the impact of PF scheduler on TCP excluding other reasons such as handoff, packet error, and so on.

This paper is organized as follows. The following section provides the description of our target system and background knowledge. In Section 3, we introduce the simulation environments and show how the TCP fairness and throughput is affected by PF scheduler. Section 4 presents our analysis for TCP start-up behavior under PF scheduler. Finally, in Section 5, we demonstrate our next plan and conclude the paper.

2. System Model and Background

2.1. *System model description*

We consider the downlink channel of cellular networks where a BS serves N mobile terminals. The downlink is a single broadband channel shared by all users in the time division multiplexing manner[a]. The BS exploits the pilot signal, which is pre-defined by the protocol, in the specified position of each time slot, and every mobile measures it to obtain the channel gain. The BS receives the fed back signal from all the users to collect the current channel status. Based on the channel information, the radio frequency scheduler selects a user among the active ones to be served in the next slot.

2.2. *PF scheduler*

Let us examine the operation of the PF scheduler. The average throughput of each user is tracked by an exponential moving average. At the beginning

[a]The downlink structure is very similar to that of the IS-856 system.

of each time slot, each user feeds back the channel state (or the feasible rate) to the BS. The BS calculates the ratio of the feasible rate to the average throughput for each user, which is defined as the preference metric and is the key selection criterion. The user with the maximum preference metric will be selected for transmission at the next coming slot.

This is described formally as follows. In time slot n, the feasible rate of user k is $R_k[n]$ and its moving average is denoted by $\tilde{R_k}[n]$. Then, user $k^* = argmax_k(\frac{R_k[n]}{\tilde{R_k}[n]})$ is served in time slot n, and the average throughput of each user is updated by

$$\tilde{R_k}[n+1] = \begin{cases} (1-\frac{1}{t_c})\tilde{R_k}[n] + \frac{1}{t_c}R_k[n], & k = k^* \\ (1-\frac{1}{t_c})\tilde{R_k}[n], & k \neq k^* \end{cases} \tag{1}$$

where t_c is the time constant for the moving average. It is clear that the PF scheduler affects relative preference to users with good channels as opposed to absolute preference.

3. Observation and Problems

We are easily able to guess that PF scheduler makes an influence on RTT variation of TCP, but the key problem is to investigate the degree of such impact. If the impact does not severely harm TCP, mere influence of RTT variation could be ignored. But if TCP misbehavior results from the variation can lead to a serious performance drop, we have to find the core condition to make the wrong action.

3.1. *Simulation environments*

The simulation study is performed by NS-2 2.27 version, and topology is a typical cellular network shown in Fig.1. There is a link that has 2Mbps bandwidth and 100ms latency between MH (Mobile Host) and BS (Base Station). Also, a wired link has 10Mbps bandwidth and 50ms latency, and it is placed between BS and CH (Corresponding Host). The queue between MH and BS uses PF scheduler, and the other uses FIFO (First-In-First-Out) policy.

3.2. *Observation: TCP startup behavior*

From the analysis of the simulation results, TCP's RTO mechanism generally keeps track of RTT variation well in most cases except timeouts.

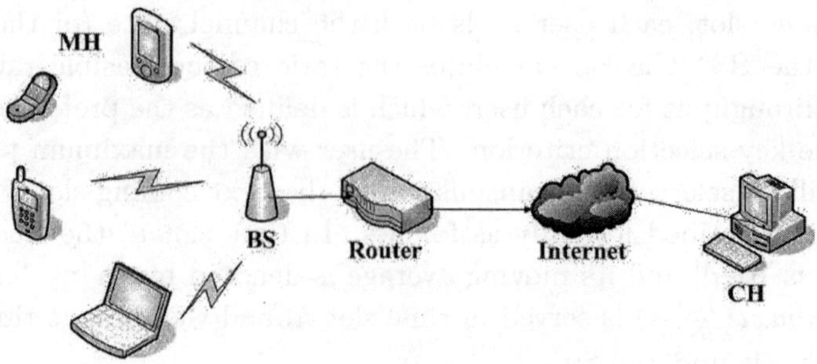

Figure 1. Simulation topology.

Specially, our observation says that timeout event often happens in slow start phase as shown in Fig.2.

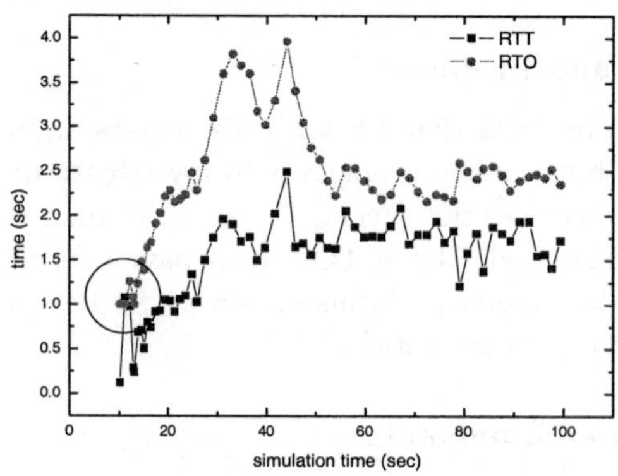

Figure 2. Initial timeout.

Due to the timeout in the slow start phase, TCP sessions cannot keep fairness in short-term average throughput, and this unfairness is in a serious degree (see Fig.3) even if we allow that PF scheduler does not consider short-term traffic. A good way to look into a problem of the initial timeout is to compare the timeout case with the non-timeout case under the same condition. Fig.3 shows well the effect of the initial timeout on TCP fairness and aggregate throughput. In Fig.3(a), we can see that the sessions with the initial timeout are not nearly able to use the network bandwidth (in 11 of 20 sessions, the timeout occurred), and the others aggressively use the remains so the fairness comes to harm severely. In Fig.3(b), it is observed that both the aggregate throughput and the fairness are improved by just preventing the unnecessary timeout from happening. That is, according to Jain's fairness index [4], the experiment in Fig.3(a) shows the fairness of 68.5%, and the study in Fig.3(b) shows the fairness of 86.2%. Also, in point of view of the aggregate throughput, Fig.3(b) obtains the throughput of 2296 Kbps while Fig.3(a) gets the throughput of 1998.4 Kbps. Fig.5

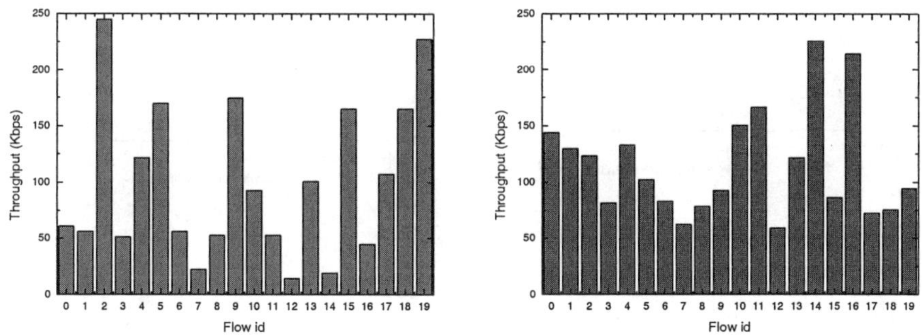

(a) Without holding timeout

(b) With holding timeout

Figure 3. Throughput of 20 flows under PF scheduler in short-term.

draws the results of the fairness and the aggregate throughput varying the number of sessions from 20 to 50. Comparing normal case with holding-timeout case, we can see that both the fairness and the throughput shows better performance in the holding-timeout case independent of the number of flows.

However, the case of Fig.3(b) also shows considerably lower fairness than that of Fig.4, in which FIFO is used in queuing policy (FIFO case got the 99.09% fairness). The performance gap of Fig.3(b) and Fig.4 could be understood as the result from the difference of the scheduling policies since we force to hold the initial timeout in Fig.3(b).

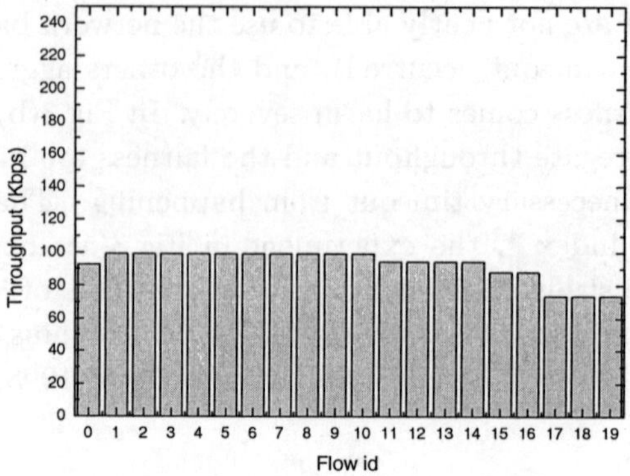

Figure 4. Throughput of 20 flows under FIFO scheduler in short-term.

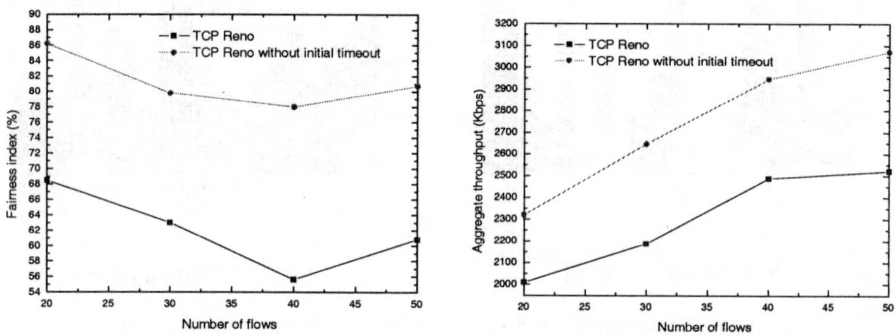

(a) Fairness index

(b) Aggregate throughput

Figure 5. Comparisons depending on the number of flows.

4. Analysis

4.1. *Condition of TCP timeout*

TCP retransmission timer expires when an ACK packet is not returned during RTO interval. So, we can describe the condition of the timeout occurrence as follows.

$$RTO < RTT = Q.D. + P.D., \tag{2}$$

where $Q.D.$ denotes queuing delay and $P.D.$ is propagation delay in all links. $Q.D.$ is the sum of queuing delays in wired and wireless link. We assume that the queuing delay in the wired link is steady, and PF scheduling delay is dominant factor in $Q.D.$.

TCP starts data transmission by setting the initial RTO to 6 seconds, and hereafter updates the RTO value, referencing the measured RTT. Because TCP begins the slow start phase sending a few segments (generally 2 segments), RTT is relatively small in the initial phase (when there is not much packets to be scheduled, usually the queuing and scheduling delay decrease). Based on this measurement, TCP usually sets RTO to MIN RTO that is 1 seconds according to RFC 2988 [5]4.

After this, RTT increases when the amount of data increases by TCP or other traffic. The problem is that the scheduling delay of PF scheduler leads to rapid RTT increase, which causes TCP's timer expired. Because the scheduling interval of PF scheduler is 1.667 ms, if a channel is not allocated to during n turns, $1.667 \times n$ ms is added to TCP session's RTT in the flow. Supposing that this additional time gets RTT over RTO, the sender will expire the retransmission timer. In our experiments, the timeout usually happens when RTT is over 1 second in the slow start phase. The reason of the boundary is that TCP rounds the calculation value below MIN RTO up to MIN RTO second.

4.2. *Analysis of the packet transmission delay in the cellular networks*

Above one second RTT is not rare in the wireless networks. The wireless networks sometimes have a quite long delay because a base station may have many tasks to reduce the impact of the errors such as Forward Error Correction (FEC), interleaving, retransmission, and so on. In this section, we show an analytic model for BS delay, which is simplified with only the scheduling delay and the retransmission delay.

First, we build the model with 1 user. The user has the packet size of T bytes and is able to transmit X bytes whenever the scheduling slot is allocated. For example, if T is 1500 and X is 100 in constant, the time for servicing the packet is 15 slots. But when X changes depending on the channel state, the analysis comes to be more difficult.

For convenience of the analysis, we assume that X has an exponential distribution with average m (actually this assumption is exactly correct when the transmission rate linearly increases in proportion as SNR (Signal-to-Noise Ratio) on the Rayleigh channel). When we denote the data size that is successfully transmitted in flow i as X_i, the number of slots that is required to service the packet is $N(T)$. $N(T)$ is minimum N that satisfies $\sum_{i=1}^{N} X_i \geq T$. Analyzing this problem as the Poisson counting process, we can see that $N(T) - 1$ has a Poisson distribution with both average and variance $\frac{T}{m}$.

We obtain the required number of slots to service a packet as above. However, owing to wireless channel error, the transmission does not always make a success even if BS successfully transmits the packet. In this model, we denote the error rate of each flow as p and assume that the error rate is independent of the transmission rate. At this time, to transmit the packet successfully in flow i, actually Y_i slots are taken. Because Y_i follows the discrete probability distribution with $Pr(Y_i = n) = p^{n-1}(1-p)$, we get $E(Y_i) = \frac{1}{1-p}$ and $Var(Y_i) = \frac{p}{(1-p)^2}$.

Actual number of slots to transmit a packet is given by $S = \sum_{i=1}^{N}(T)Y_i$, and we can obtain its average and variance as follows.

$$E(S) = E\{N(T)\}E(Y_i) = (\frac{T}{m} + 1)(1-p)^{-1}, \tag{3}$$

$$\begin{aligned} Var(S) &= E\{N(T)\}Var(Y_i) + E^2Y_iVar\{N(T)\} \\ &= (\tfrac{T}{m} + 1)p(1-p)^{-2} + (1-p)^{-2}(\tfrac{T}{m} + 1) \\ &= (\tfrac{T}{m} + 1)(1+p)(1-p)^{-2} \end{aligned} \tag{4}$$

Let's consider the case of K users. We assume that each user has a packet to transmit, and the packet size, T, and channel state are same in every user. Also assuming that the scheduler chooses a user and, only after transmitting the user's one packet, selects another user, we analyze the packet transmission time of the last-selected user. When the transmission time of $k-th$ selected user is denoted as D_k, our finding time is $D = D_1 + D_2 + ... + D_k = \sum_{k=1}^{K} D_k$. By applying Central limit theorem, we approximate D to a Gaussian distribution with the average $K \cdot E(D_k)$ and the variance $K \cdot Var(D_k)$.

$$\begin{aligned} E(D_k) &= E(S) = (\tfrac{T}{m} + 1)(1-p)^{-1}, \\ Var(D_k) &= Var(S) = (\tfrac{T}{m} + 1)(1+p)(1-p)^{-2}, \end{aligned} \tag{5}$$

Finally D follows the Gaussian distribution with the average $K(\frac{T}{m}+1)(1-p)^{-1}$ and the variance $K(\frac{T}{m}+1)(1+p)(1-p)^{-2}$.

For example, when we consider the case of T=1500, m=100, K=50, and p=0.1, the packet transmission time of the last selected user is as follows[b]. It is necessary to keep in mind that the inter-packet interval of a user comes from the scheduling delay.

- Constant rate with no channel error: 750 slots.
- Variable rate with no channel error: 800 slots with 50% and 847 slots with 5%.
- Variable rate with channel error, p: 889 slots with 50% and 943 slots with 5%.

In this model, the scheduler services a user's packet sequentially but real PF scheduler services several users' packet little by little, depending on the channel state. Thus, every user finishes the packet transmission at similar time due to their mixed service time while the average rate of the allocated slots is so high as to have a better possibility that reduces the entire transmission time. Consequently every user has a similar finish time with the "last" user.

4.3. *Condition of the initial timeout under PF scheduler*

In previous subsection, we showed the possibility that BS delay leads to TCP timeout, but above MIN RTO RTT does not always make the timeout. Although RTT comes to over 1 second, the timeout occurs only if RTO in previous turn should be 1 second which is MIN RTO. Such type of the timeout event does not happen often because several long RTTs make also RTO large (As we already mention it, TCP's RTO mechanism keeps track of the network state in most cases). That is, the condition of the initial timeout is not just long RTT but also long relative gap of consecutive RTTs.

From the result, the condition of the initial timeout can be summarized as follows.

- RTT in previous turn has to make RTO value small enough.
- RTT in next turn increases sharply, and consequently it should be over the RTO value.

[b]Note that one slot takes 1.667 ms.

4.4. *Tendency analysis*

Such initial timeout happened often as the number of session increases. Fig.6(a) draws the number of the initial timeouts varying the number of sessions. As shown in Fig.6(a), we can observe that the sacrificed sessions also increase as the number of sessions increase, and as a result RTT comes to over RTO in several sessions. Also, it is observed that increasing the number of flows leads to consecutive timeout in the slow start phase even if the event does not happen frequently.

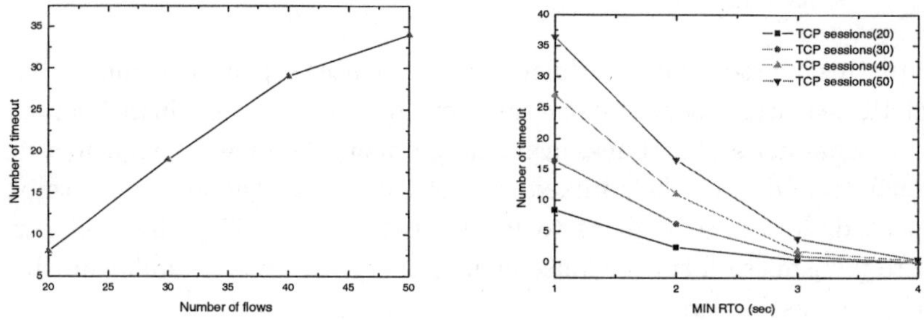

(a) Number of timeout depending on number of flows

(b) MIN RTO value and the number of flows

Figure 6. Tendency of the timeout number and MIN RTO value.

The timeout does not occur at all TCP sessions, and it is because the slot count for each TCP session can be extremely different in PF scheduler though other delaying factors are similar in each flow. Since PF scheduler preferentially allocates the slot to good channel depending on the channel state, the allocation may be converged on the specific session from the point of view on the short-term. Also, the scheduler may almost not assign the slot to some flows during considerable period.

TCP's initial timeout occurs more frequently, for minimum RTO is briefly set to 1 second. We could see that as MIN RTO increases, the number of the initial timeout in the slow start phase remarkably decreases (refer to Fig.6(b)). Both the throughput and the fairness achieve conspicuous improvement in the performance as the number of the initial timeout decreases, and we can see that in Fig.5. But we cannot say that increasing MIN RTO is not best choice since TCP reacts too slowly in handling the segment loss if the value is large. In addition, it is a difficult problem to propose any specific value as a recommended MIN RTO, as the suitable value for the various network environments is different according to circumstances. However, our a clear opinion is that current TCP's MIN RTO is set too short under the PF scheduling policy, and the value had better be larger.

5. Conclusion and Future work

In this paper, we analyzed the impact of PF scheduler on TCP start-up behavior. We introduced the initial timeout in the slow start phase from PF scheduling and demonstrated the cause and effect of the timeout through the simulation experiments. From the simulation results and their analysis, a conclusion is that TCP's MIN RTO is so short as to lead to non-necessary timeout under the PF scheduling policy. We do not recommend any specific MIN RTO value in this paper, and the reason is that a fitful MIN RTO is so different depending on the network environments that determining the value is a difficult problem. However, we plan to investigate the method to determine a proper MIN RTO for a variety of network environments.

References

1. Qi Bi, S. Vitebsky, *Performance analysis of 3G-1X EVDO high data rate system*, **Proc. of IEEE WCNC**, March(2002).
2. M. Assaad, B. Jouaber, and D. Zeohlache, *Effect of TCP on UMTS-HSDPA system performance and capacity*, bf Proc. of IEEE GLOBECOM, November(2004).
3. F. Kelly, *Charging and Rate Control for Elastic Traffic*, **European Transactions on Telecommunications**, volume 8 (1997) pages 33-37.
4. R. Jain, W. Hawe, D. Chiu, *A Quantitative measure of fairness and discrimination for resource allocation in Shared Computer Systems*, **DEC-TR-301**, September(1984).
5. V. Paxson, M. Allman, *Computing TCP's Retransmission Timer*, **RFC 2988**, November(2000).
6. Khafizov, F. and M. Yavuz, *Running TCP over IS-2000*, **Proc. of IEEE ICC**, April(2002).
7. Yavuz, M. and F. Khafizov, *TCP over Wireless Links with Variable Bandwidth*, **Proc. of IEEE VTC**, September(2002).
8. H. Inamura, G. Montenegro, R. Ludwig, A. Gurtov, F. Khafizov, *TCP over Second (2.5G) and Third (3G) Generation Wireless Networks*, **RFC 3481**, February(2003).

THE HOP-LIMIT APPROACH FOR FLOW ASSIGNMENT IN SURVIVABLE CONNECTION-ORIENTED NETWORKS

K WALKOWIAK

Chair of Systems and Computer Networks, Faculty of Electronics, Wroclaw University of Technology, Wybrzeze Wyspianskiego 27, 50-370 Wroclaw, Poland
E-mail: Krzysztof.Walkowiak@pwr.wroc.pl

This paper describes a novel method for flow assignment in survivable connection-oriented networks. The considered optimization problem is NP-complete and computationally difficult. In order to reduce size of the problem we propose to consider all networks eligible routes, which do not violate a predetermined hop-limit value. We focus on one of restoration methods - local rerouting – used in popular network technique MultiProtocol Label Switching (MPLS) to provide survivability. Seven various networks are analyzed to examine and evaluate the proposed approach.

1 Introduction

Problems of network survivability have gained much attention recently due to the tremendous development of computer networks, expansion of new services and growing expectations of users. The main objective of this paper is to study the hop-limit approach applied to the flow assignment (FA) problem in survivable connection-oriented (c-o) network. In c-o networks prior to transmitting the data, a virtual connection is established and the data is carried along this connection. Popular network technique using this approach is MultiProtocol Label Switching (MPLS). The standard method to enable survivability in c-o networks is as follows. Each label switched path has a primary route and a backup route. The primary route is used for transmitting of data in normal, failure-free state of the network. After a failure of the primary route, the failed circuit is switched to the backup route that uses spare capacity not used in non-failure state of the network. We concentrate on local restoration (called also local rerouting, local repair, link restoration). In this method the backup route is found only around the failed arc and the origin node of the failed arc is responsible for rerouting [3], [6-10].

We consider an existing facility network, i.e. we do not design capacity and topology. The objective function is lost flow – flow that cannot be restored after failure due to limited resources of spare capacity [6], [9-10]. Combined assignment of primary and backup routes must be carried out to find a global optimum of the lost flow due to a network failure for a projected traffic demand. Because the optimization is performed jointly over primary and backup routes, the complexity of the problem grows tremendously. Therefore, an interesting method is to partition the problem into two simpler problems: first optimize primary routes and next find backup routes for already established primary routes. Since there is mutual dependency between primary and backup routes assignment, the obtained solution cannot be claimed to be an optimum if these problems are treated separately. The key issue of this approach is to use for primary routes assignment an effective objective function that denotes preparation of the network to the rerouting process. In this work we examine the influence of the hop-limit approach on the flow assignment in c-o networks using two such objective functions.

2 Hop-Limit Approach

The flow assignment problem in c-o networks is very complex and NP-complete [5], [7]. Especially, for large networks the number of possible routes is extremely huge. The size (number of flow variables) of the optimization problems in the link-path formulations (with predefined sets of routes) depends on the total size of candidate route lists. Since the total number of network routes increases exponentially with the number of nodes, the total number of potential flow variables also grows exponentially [7]. To make the flow assignment problem computationally feasible we must reduce the number of routes. However, if we do not consider all possible routes, the obtained solution cannot be claimed to be optimal. The major issue is to select a small subset of routes keeping the objective function close to the minimum (or maximum) value. The hop-limit approach proposed in [4] for spare capacity assignment is an interesting method to solve FA problem. Under this approach the process of reducing the size of the FA problem is achieved by taking into account all networks eligible routes, which do not violate a predetermined hop-limit value. In particular, if for a given origin-destination node pair the length of the shortest route is *n* hops and the hop limit is *hl*, then we consider all routes which are not longer than (*n*+*hl*) hops. Authors of [11] discuss the hop-limit approach to provide ATM group communication.

Table 1. Effects of network connectivity and hop limit on number of routes.

Hop limit	0	1	2	3	4	5	6	7
avnd=2.88	2.3E+03	5.3E+03	1.2E+04	2.3E+04	4.4E+04	7.8E+04	1.3E+05	2.2E+05
avnd=3.17	2.4E+03	6.9E+03	1.7E+04	4.0E+04	8.8E+04	1.8E+05	3.5E+05	6.4E+05
avnd=3.56	3.6E+03	1.1E+04	3.5E+04	9.4E+04	2.4E+05	5.5E+05	1.2E+06	2.6E+06
avnd=4.00	3.9E+03	1.7E+04	6.6E+04	2.2E+05	6.5E+05	1.8E+06	4.7E+06	1.2E+07
avnd=4.50	4.4E+03	2.7E+04	1.2E+05	4.9E+05	1.7E+06	5.7E+06	1.7E+07	5.0E+07
avnd=5.00	3.7E+03	2.7E+04	1.4E+05	6.6E+05	2.7E+06	1.0E+07	3.5E+07	1.2E+08
avnd=5.56	3.8E+03	3.0E+04	1.8E+05	9.6E+05	4.5E+06	2.0E+07	7.9E+07	3.0E+08

To illustrate the problem we show a simple example. We calculate the number of routes generated according to the given hop limit for 7 similar networks having 36 nodes and having 104, 114, 128, 144, 162, 180 and 200 links respectively.

Connectivity of tested networks denoted by the average node degree parameter (*avnd*) is in the range from 2.88 to 5.56. Table. 1 depicts number of routes as a function of hop limit, using *avnd* as a parameter. Since in the link-path formulation number of variables and size of the flow assignment problem depends on the number of possible routes, even for low-connected networks considering hop limit greater than 5 is not reasonable for 36-nodes networks. Therefore, if we want to solve the optimization problem of flow assignment in c-o networks in computationally reasonable time, we must reduce size of the problem and consider only a subset of routes with small value of hop limit.

In this work we propose to use the hop-limit approach for flow assignment in c-o networks using the local restoration. We verify this approach for two objective functions presented in next section. It should be noted that also other techniques facilitating the computational size of FA problem in c-o networks have been proposed, e.g. the route generation technique discussed in [7].

3 Definition of Functions for Link Restoration

A network (G,c) is given, where $G=(V,A)$ is a directed graph with *n* vertices and *m* arcs, $c: A \rightarrow R^{+}$ is a function that defines capacities of the arcs. We denote by $o: A \rightarrow V$ and $d: A \rightarrow V$ functions defining the origin and destination node of each arc. For each $a \in A$ we call $\mathrm{in}(a)=\{k \in A \mid d(k)=d(a), k \neq a\}$ the set of incoming arcs of $d(a)$ except *a*, and $\mathrm{out}(a)=\{k \in A \mid o(k)=o(a), k \neq a\}$ the set of outgoing arcs of $o(a)$ except *a*. We introduce the following further notations

f_a	Represents the total flow on arc *a*.
c_a	Capacity of arc *a*.
$g_v^{\mathrm{out}} = \sum_{i:o(i)=v} f_i$	Aggregate flow of outgoing arcs of *v*.
$g_v^{\mathrm{in}} = \sum_{i:d(i)=v} f_i$	Aggregate flow of incoming arcs of *v*.
$e_v^{\mathrm{out}} = \sum_{i:o(i)=v} c_i$	Aggregate capacity of outgoing arcs of *v*.
$e_v^{\mathrm{in}} = \sum_{i:d(i)=v} c_i$	Aggregate capacity of incoming arcs of *v*.

Definition 1. *The global non-bifurcated m.c. flow denoted by* $\underline{f}=[f_1, f_2, \ldots, f_m]$ *is defined as a vector of flows in all arcs. We call a flow* $\underline{f}$ *feasible if for every arc* $a \in A$ *the inequality (1) holds. Inequality (1) ensures that in every arc flow is not greater then capacity. This inequality is called a capacity constraint.*

$$\forall a \in A: f_a \leq c_a \tag{1}$$

For the sake of simplicity we introduce the following function

$$\varepsilon(x) = \begin{cases} 0 & \text{for} \quad x \le 0 \\ x & \text{for} \quad x > 0 \end{cases} \tag{2}$$

Function L_k given by (3) is a linear combination of flow lost in arcs outgoing $o(k)$ and arcs incoming $d(k)$. This function considers only arcs adjacent to the failed arc a. Arcs remote to k, which can block some flow of the failed arc during the rerouting process, aren't taken into account. Therefore, L_k only estimates the lost flow and it is a lower bound of the flow of arc k lost due a failure of k.

$$L_k(\underline{f}) = (\varepsilon\left(g_{o(k)}^{\text{out}} - (e_{o(k)}^{\text{out}} - c_k)\right) + \varepsilon\left(g_{d(k)}^{\text{in}} - (e_{d(k)}^{\text{in}} - c_k)\right))/2 \tag{3}$$

Using $L_k(\underline{f})$ we can define a function $L(\underline{f})$ that shows preparation of the network to the local restoration after a failure of any single arc. We assume that probability of each arc failure is the same.

$$L(\underline{f}) = \sum_{k \in A} L_k(\underline{f}) \tag{4}$$

Functions (3) and (4) are convex for any feasible flow $\underline{f}$. For the sake of simplicity in the remainder of the paper we use the term LFL (Lost Flow in Link) to refer to the function (4). For more details refer to [9-10].

An alternative function that can be used for estimation of lost flow after the local restoration is based on k-shortest paths (KSP) algorithm, which works as follows. The failed arc k is removed from the network. Next, the KSP algorithm finds k-successively shortest disjoint paths between the origin and the destination node of the failed arc. These paths one by one are saturated with flow of the failed arc and are used for restoration of flow f_k. The fraction of the flow f_k not restored during running KSP algorithm is lost. Let $KSP(k)$ denote flow of the failed arc k restored by the KSP method. The lost flow of k using KSP rerouting is given by $\varepsilon(f_k - KSP(k))$. The lost flow after a failure of any single arc using KSP approach is calculated similarly to (4)

$$L_{KSP}(\underline{f}) = \sum_{k \in A} \varepsilon(f_k - KSP(k)) \tag{5}$$

4 Results of Numerical Experiments

Flows in c-o networks are modeled as non-bifurcated multicommodity flows. Therefore the optimization problem of FA is 0/1 problem, which can be solved optimally only using branch and bound techniques for relatively small networks and limited sets of candidate routes [7]. Thus, to obtain feasible solutions of considered problem and evaluate the hop-limit approach we apply a modification of heuristic Flow Deviation (FD) algorithm [2]. FD is one of the most effective heuristics for FA problems and it has been applied to many computer network optimization problems [1], [6-7] [9]. A comprehensive description of the applied algorithm is given in [9]. We implement the algorithm in C++. We test two objective functions: LFL (lost flow in link) and lost flow after KSP (k-shortest route) rerouting. Both functions can be used to evaluate survivability of network using the local restoration method. The function LFL can be applied for static [9] and dynamic [10] optimization of routes in survivable c-o networks. For more information on issues on survivable networks and optimization of computer networks refer to [3], [6-10].

We now describe our simulation setup and scenarios. In order to evaluate the effectiveness of hop-limit approach we run two kinds of experiment. First, we solve the FA problem considering only routes generated according to the given hop limit. Then, we examine the performance of obtained solutions as a function of hop limit. In the second experiment, we solve the problem without any hop limit, i.e. we take into account all possible route. After that, we analyze the distribution of routes' lengths in obtained solution comparing it to the hop limit.

Table 2. Paramters of tested networks.

Name of network	104	114	128	144	162	108ring	120mesh
Number of nodes	36	36	36	36	36	36	36
Number of links	104	114	128	144	162	108	120
Topology	irregular mesh					ring	regular mesh
Node degree (average)	2.88	3.17	3.56	4.00	4.50	3.00	3.33
Node degree (minimum)	2	2	3	3	3	3	2
Node degree (maximum)	5	5	6	6	6	3	4
Number of tests (identical bandwidth requirement)	29	20	18	18	17	19	19
Number of tests (random bandwidth requirement)	20	20	20	20	20	0	0

Results presented in this section are obtained from simulations on 7 sample networks. Three topologies are shown in Fig. 1. All networks have 36 nodes. Name of each network indicates the number of links in the network and type of topology. Table 2 summarizes the parameters of all tested networks. We assume that for all networks capacity of each link is 5000 BU (bandwidth unit). Since, according to theoretical analysis presented in [9], functions LFL and KSP depends on the node degree and network topology; we selected to numerical experiments networks with different values of the average node degree and different topologies. Networks 104, 114, 128, 144 and 162 have irregular mesh topology and the average node degree parameter in the range from 2.88 to 4.50. Network 120mesh have regular 6x6 mesh topology and network 108ring is based on the ring topology.

We assume that there is a requirement to set up a connection for each direction of every node pair. Thus, the total number of demands is 1260. To make more comprehensive tests several demand patterns are examined for each network. The flow requirement for all demands is the same. For instance, in network 114 we perform 20 simulations with flow requirement of each demand from 45 BU to 64 BU. Moreover, for networks 104, 114, 128, 144 and 162 we generate random demand patterns. For each of these networks 20 various random demand patterns are considered.

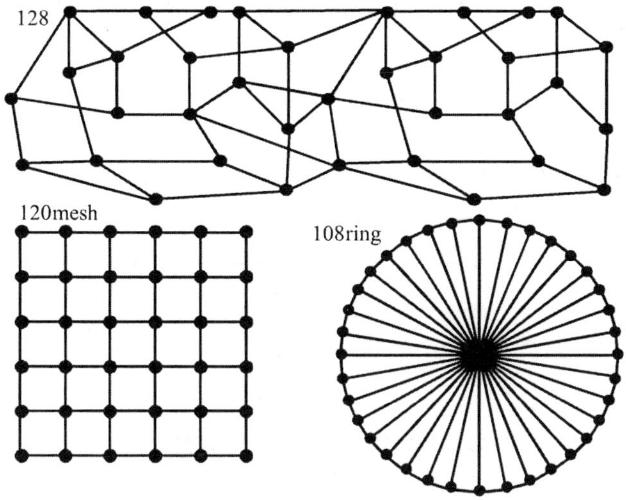

Figure 1. Topologies of tested networks 128, 120mesh and 108ring.

Fig. 2 shows aggregate value of function LFL summed over various traffic demands as a function of the hop limit. Fig. 3 depicts aggregate value of function KSP summed over various traffic demands as a function of the hop limit. In Fig. 3 we use randomly generated traffic demands for irregular mesh networks. In both figures we present results obtained for values of hop limit in the range 1-5 and result obtained without hop-limit restriction, (since we analyze 36-nodes networks in this case hop limit is 36). From Fig. 2 and Fig. 3 we can watch the general trade-off between considered objective functions and hop limit. The results evidently indicate that, for various types of networks, with the increase of the hop-limit value both functions rapidly converge to the solution obtained without hop-limit constraint. Therefore, a good-quality solution of the flow assignment problem using functions LFL and KSP can be found with relatively small value of hop limit. Furthermore, we observe different performance between curves, reflecting results obtained for various networks. The largest differences are observed for low-connected irregular topologies. For instance, in network 104 the value of LFL calculated for *hl*=1 is 14% bigger than for the case *hl*=36, in network 144 the corresponding gap is 5%. Finally, for regular 108ring topology the value of LFL obtained for *hl*=1 is the same as for *hl*=36. The same trend can be observed for function KSP. However, the difference in results obtained for various hop-limit values is smaller than for the LFL function. The average gap between results of LFL obtained for hop limit equal to 5 and results without hop limit is 0.37%. The related value for the KSP function is only 0.01%. Generally, trends observed in Fig. 2 and Fig. 3 can be explained by the fact that for regular network topologies there are relatively more routes having small values of hop limit. The second explanation comes from the specific features of functions LFL and KSP, which depend strongly on the network connectivity and topology.

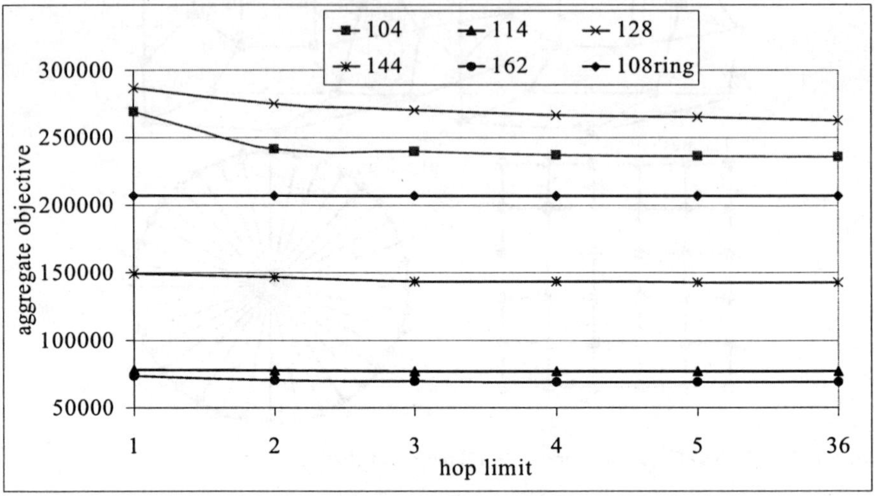

Figure 2. Trade-off between aggregate values of LFL function and hop limit.

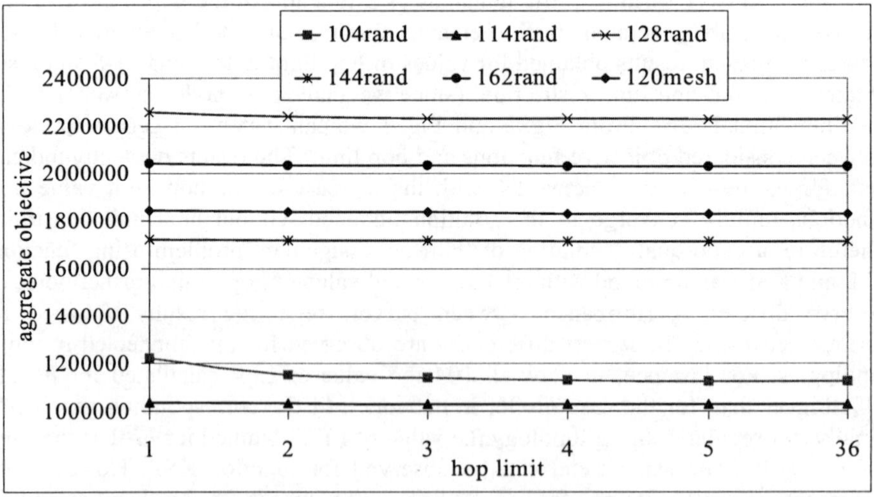

Figure 3. Trade-off between aggregate values of KSP function and hop limit.

It should be noted that in irregular mesh topologies for 106 of 202 tested traffic demands the FD algorithm was not able to find a feasible solution for *hl*=0. Thus, on Fig. 2 and Fig. 3 we show aggregate results for hop-limit values 1-5 and 36.

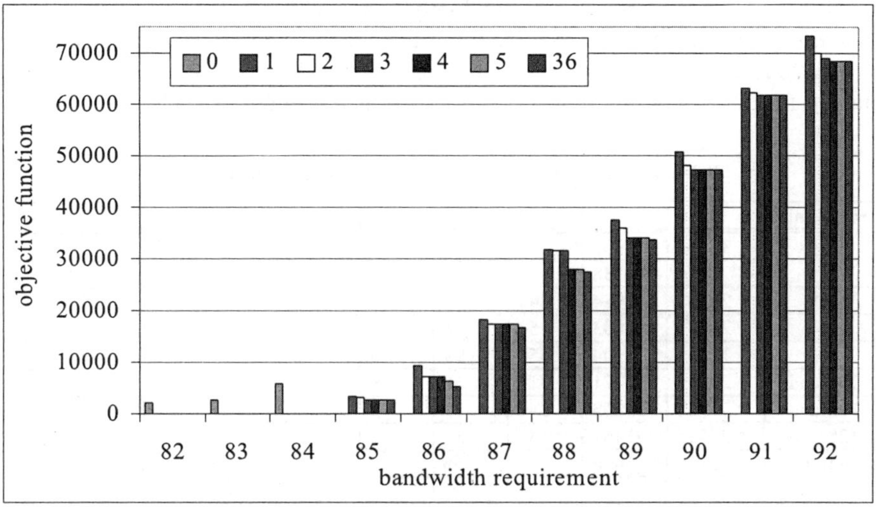

Figure 4. The LFL as a function of bandwidth requirement for various hop limit values obtained for network 128.

Fig. 4 plots the relative performance of LFL function for increasing traffic load in network 128. The x-axis represents bandwidth requirement of each demand. The y-axis shows value of LFL function. Under low load conditions, only for *hl*=0 value of LFL is greater than 0. Under high, near saturation, loads values of LFL function obtained for *hl*>2 are the same. Similar trend was observed for the function KSP and for other tested networks.

Table 3 shows results of the routes' length distribution obtained for function LFL. To find these results we solve the FA optimization problem for each considered network and traffic demand without hop limit restriction, i.e. we consider all possible routes. Next, we analyze the routes' length distribution with respect to the hop limit in the following way. For each demand we calculate the length of the shortest route between end nodes of the demand. Next, we compare this value with the length of the route in the obtained solution and calculate the hop limit. For instance, for network 104 - summarizing over 29 tests with various demands patterns - 33862 of routes have the same length as the shortest route for a particular demand (hop limit is 0), 1903 routes is one hop longer than the shortest route and etc.

Analysis of Table 3 shows that 99.3% routes have the hop limit 0. Only 0.28% routes have hop limit larger than 2. For network 120mesh 99.7% routes have the length the same as the shortest route. The data is reasonably well explained by the fact that for regular network topologies considered in this work there are relatively more routes with small values of hop limit. Moreover, if the network is irregular and the traffic demand is asymmetrical, the solution of the FA problem includes more relatively long routes. Therefore, the lowest ratio of routes having *hl*=0 is obtained for the network 114rand with randomly generated demand pattern. During simulations we also observed that the number of routes having *hl*>2 increases as the network load grows. It is worth remarking that the distribution of routes' length obtained for function KSP are analogous to results presented in Table 3.

Table 3. Distribution of the number of routes for function LFL.

Hop limit	0	1	2	3	4	5	6	7	8	9
104	33862	1903	707	44	24	0	0	0	0	0
114	22774	2158	239	29	0	0	0	0	0	0
128	21401	984	249	35	8	2	1	0	0	0
144	21971	603	54	28	5	19	0	0	0	0
162	18840	1904	558	99	19	0	0	0	0	0
104rand	22419	1771	914	66	29	1	0	0	0	0
114rand	21768	2863	548	19	2	0	0	0	0	0
128rand	23535	1461	185	17	2	0	0	0	0	0
144rand	23879	1006	199	65	20	26	3	2	0	0
162rand	21269	3072	584	208	45	13	1	6	0	0
108ring	23498	170	270	2	0	0	0	0	0	0
120mesh	23858	0	82	0	0	0	0	0	0	0

5 Concluding Remarks

The main contribution in this paper is a successful evaluation of the hop-limit approach for flow assignment in survivable connection-oriented networks. We have verified the hypothesis that the hop-limit approach can be effectively applied in solving FA problem in survivable networks by extensive simulations run on seven networks and using two kinds of experiments. In the former experiment method, we solved the considered problem with various values of hop limit and evaluated obtained results. In the latter approach, we analyzed the routes' length distribution for the solution calculated without hop limit. The first method shows that a valuable solution for functions LFL and KSP can be found with a relatively small hop-limit. The second kind of experiments indicates that solutions obtained without constraints on the hop limit include mostly routes with small hop limit, especially for regular network topologies. Therefore, in order to reduce size of the problem and make the problem computationally feasible, we can reduce the number of considered candidate routes and use the hop-limit approach for assignment of primary routes for local restoration. As an ongoing work we want to examine the hop-limit approach for objective functions used in flow assignment problems of survivable networks using other restoration methods.

6 Acknowledgements

This work was supported by a research project of the Polish State Committee for Scientific Research carried out in years 2005-2007.

References

1. Burns, J., Ott, T., Krzesinski, A., Muller, K., Route selection and bandwidth allocation in MPLS networks. Performance Evaluation, 52 (2003) pp. 133-152.
2. Fratta, L., Gerla, M., Kleinrock, L., The Flow Deviation Method: An Approach to Store-and-Forward Communication Network Design. Networks Vol. 3 (1973), pp. 97–133.
3. Grover, W., Mesh-based Survivable Networks: Options and Strategies for Optical, MPLS, SONET and ATM Networking. Prentice Hall PTR (2004).
4. Herzberg, M., Bye, S., Utano, A., The Hop-Limit Approach for Spare-Capacity Assignment in Survivable Networks. IEEE/ACM Transactions on Networking, 6 (1995), pp. 775-784.
5. Karp, R., On the Computational Complexity of Combinatorical Problems. Networks (1975), pp. 45-68.
6. Murakami, K., Kim, H., Virtual Route Routing for Survivable ATM Networks. IEEE/ACM Transactions on Networking, 2 (1996), pp. 22-39.
7. Pióro, M., Medhi, D., Routing, Flow, and Capacity Design in Communication and Computer Networks. Morgan Kaufman Publishers (2004).
8. Sharma, V., Hellstrand, F. (ed.), Framework for MPLS-based Recovery. RFC 3469 (2003).
9. Walkowiak, K., A New Method of Primary Routes Selection for Local Restoration. Lectures Notes in Computer Science, LNCS 3042 (2004), pp. 1024-1035.
10. Walkowiak, K., Survivable Online Routing for MPLS Traffic Engineering. Lectures Notes in Computer Science, LNCS 3266 (2004), pp. 288-297.
11. Yurcik, W., Tipper, D., Medhi, D., The Use of Hop-Limits to Provide Survivable ATM Group Communications. In Proc. NGC (2000), pp. 131-140.

A FAIR BANDWIDTH ALLOCATION SCHEME FOR MULTIMEDIA HANDOFF CALLS IN CELLULAR NETWORKS

M. SALAMAH AND I. CANDAN

Computer Engineering Department, Eastern Mediterranean University, Gazimagosa, K.K.T.C. –Mersin 10- TURKEY
E-mail: {muhammed.salamah, idil.candan@emu.edu.tr}

This paper focuses on how to allocate bandwidth fairly for new and handoff calls in multimedia cellular networks. Most (if not all) of the proposed schemes in the literature give priority to handoff calls at the expense of blocking new calls and degrading channel utilization. We present a new bandwidth allocation scheme based on guard policy. Accordingly, new calls are blocked if the amount of occupied bandwidth is greater than a predefined bandwidth threshold. The scheme is based on monitoring the elapsed real time of handoff calls and according to both, a time threshold parameter, and the call type, handoff calls are either prioritized or treated as new calls. Also in this paper, we introduce a crucial general performance metric Z that can be used to measure the performance of different bandwidth allocation schemes and compare them. Z, which is a performance/cost ratio, is a function of the new call blocking probability, handoff call dropping probability and system utilization all together. Simulation results show that, our scheme outperforms other traditional schemes in terms of performance/cost ratio, and maintains its superiority under different network circumstances.

1 Introduction

In recent years there is a rapid growth in the population of mobile users and in order to support the drastic increase in demand for resources, wireless systems need to incorporate multimedia services such as data, voice and video. Providing multimedia services with a quality of service (QoS) guarantee presents more challenges due to the limited bandwidth resources and user's mobility. One of the central issues in the performance characterization of cellular mobile and personal communication systems is the problem of handoff [1]. Handoff is the change of radio resources when a mobile user moves from one cell to another. Cell boundary crossing or a deteriorated quality of signal in the current cell causes the handoff initiation. One of the traditional well-known schemes proposed in [2] is the guard channel scheme (GCS). GCS scheme gives higher priority to handoff calls as compared to the new calls by reserving a number of guard channels for handoff calls. The remaining channels are shared by both new and handoff calls. GCS scheme achieves low handoff dropping probability (P_h) compared to the new call blocking probability (P_n) at the cost of degrading channel utilization. On the other hand, another well-known scheme, called fully shared scheme (FSS) treats new and handoff calls equally and therefore all channels are shared. The FSS scheme improves P_n and channel utilization at the expense of increasing P_h. In literature, most of the proposed schemes [3-8] give priority to handoff calls at the expense of blocking originating calls. Their claim is "dropping ongoing calls is more annoying than blocking new calls". We believe that this is true to some extent, as the annoyance is a fuzzy term which depends on the elapsed time of the ongoing call. For example, dropping an ongoing data call is very annoying if it is approaching to its end, whereas it is not that much annoying if it has just started. On the contrary, dropping an ongoing voice call is very annoying if it does not last for a moderate duration, whereas it is not that much annoying if it is approaching to its end. This is in addition to the fact that, priority is usually associated with pricing, and therefore, some uncritical conversations may tolerate reasonable handoff dropping at a lower price. Motivated with these arguments, we introduce a novel bandwidth allocation scheme for multimedia calls which outperforms both GCS and FSS schemes. The main idea of our scheme is based on monitoring the elapsed real time of handoff calls and according to both, a time threshold parameter, and the call type, handoff calls are either prioritized or treated as new calls.

The rest of the paper is organized as follows. We describe our proposed handoff scheme in section 2. In section 3, we present the simulation parameters, performance metrics, and introduce a new general performance metric Z that can be used to measure the performance of different bandwidth allocation schemes. Simulation results and discussions are given in section 4. Finally, concluding remarks are given in section 5.

2 The Time Threshold Based Scheme (TTS)

In our scheme, we focus on a single cell as a reference cell in a cellular wireless network. The arrival traffic at the BS of the reference cell is either voice or data type. We assume that the cell has a total capacity of B bandwidth units (BUs), and we used two threshold values B_v and B_d for the voice and data calls respectively. Each voice call requires one BU and each data call requires two BUs. Fig. 1 above shows the bandwidth allocation of our TTS scheme for new and handoff calls. A new data or a non-prioritized handoff data call is served if it finds less than B_d bandwidth units. A new voice or a non-prioritized handoff voice call is served if it finds less than B_v bandwidth units. A prioritized handoff call is served if it finds less than B bandwidth units. A successful handoff without interruption is very important to real-time services, but not so critical for non-real time services [9]. Therefore, higher priority is given to voice calls.

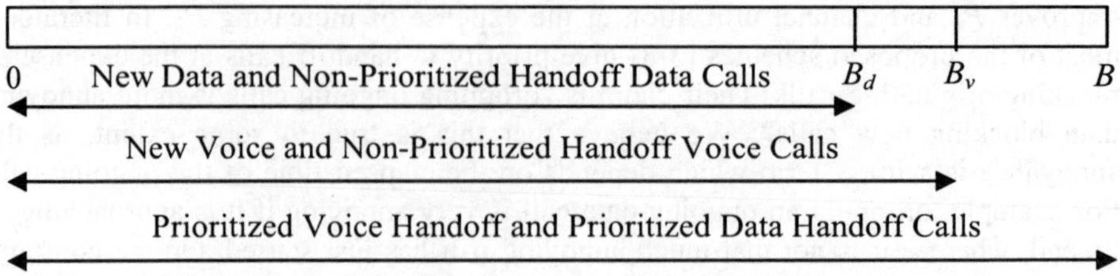

Figure 1. Bandwidth Allocation of the TTS Scheme

The proposed TTS scheme handles handoff and new calls belonging to voice traffic and data traffic together. Fig.2 below shows the flowchart of processing a voice call in the TTS scheme. Accordingly, voice handoff calls that have elapsed real time smaller than time threshold t_{ev}, are prioritized. That is to say, such handoff calls are accepted as long as the occupied amount of bandwidth in the cell is smaller than the total capacity, *B*. On the other hand, handoff calls that have elapsed real time greater than or equal to time threshold t_{ev}, and new voice calls are treated according to the guard policy. That is, such calls are accepted as long as the occupied amount of bandwidth in the cell is less than a bandwidth threshold B_v, where B_v is a value less than *B*.

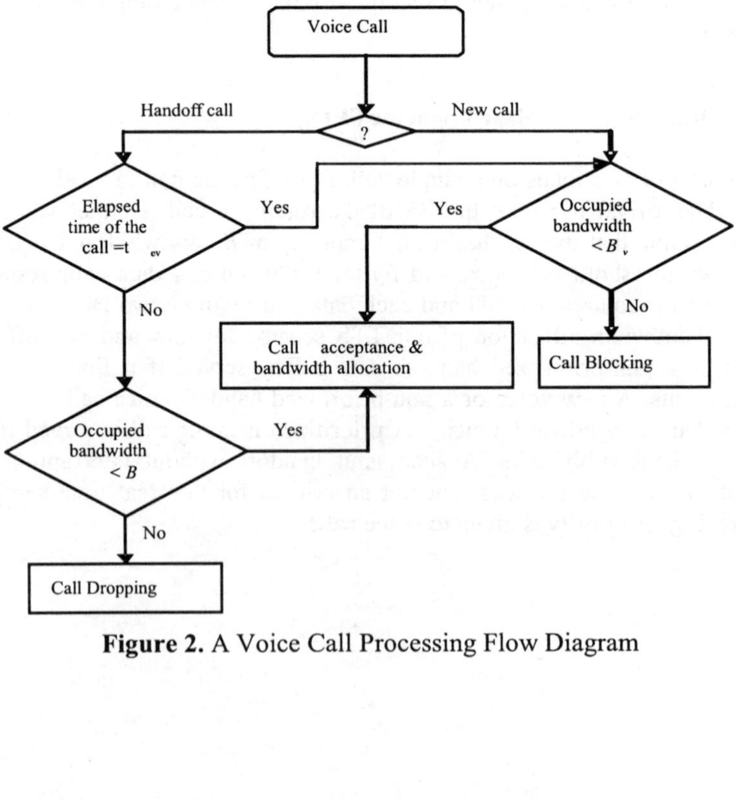

Figure 2. A Voice Call Processing Flow Diagram

As mentioned before, dropping an ongoing data call is very annoying if it is approaching to its end, whereas it is not that much annoying if it has just started. Therefore, the reverse strategy is applied to data calls as seen in Fig.3. Accordingly, data handoff calls that have elapsed time greater than time threshold t_{ed}, are prioritized. That is to say, such handoff calls are accepted as long as the occupied amount of bandwidth in the cell is smaller than the total capacity B-1 (recall that a data call requires 2 BUs). On the other hand, handoff calls that have elapsed real time smaller than or equal to time threshold t_{ed} and new data calls are treated according to the guard policy. That is, such calls are accepted as long as the occupied amount of bandwidth in the cell is less than a bandwidth threshold B_d, where B_d is a value less than B-1. It is worth to mention that B_v is taken to be greater than $B_d^{'}$, as seen in Fig. 1, so that higher priority is given to voice handoff calls.

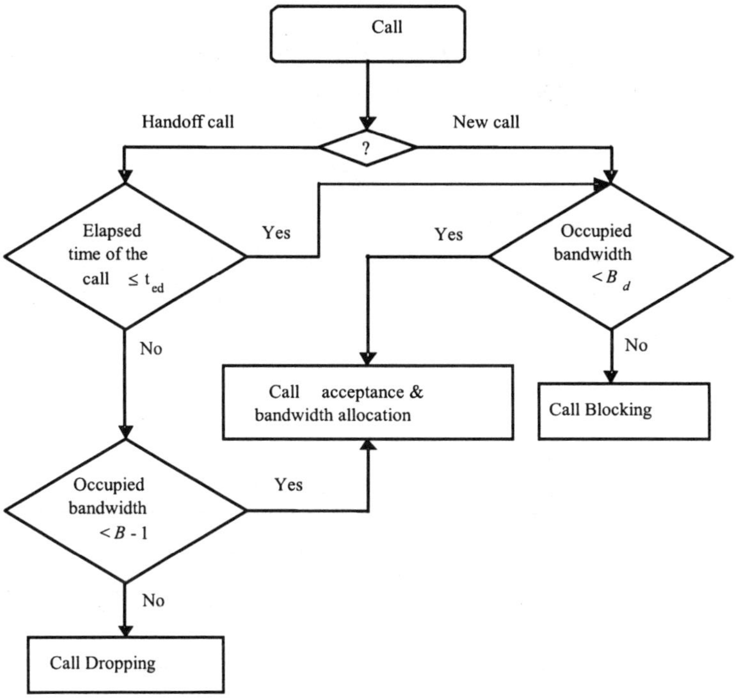

Figure 3. A Data Call Processing Flow Diagram

3 Simulation Parameters and Performance Metrics

The simulation has been performed using the Ptolemy simulation tool, developed by the University of California at Berkley. During simulation, more than 30 runs are taken for each point in order to reach 95% confidence level. As we mentioned before, we concentrate on a single reference cell. The interarrival times of new voice, handoff voice, new data and handoff data calls are assumed to follow Poisson processes with means $1/\lambda_{nv}$, $1/\lambda_{hv}$, $1/\lambda_{nd}$ and $1/\lambda_{hd}$ respectively. The call holding times also follow exponential distribution with means $1/\mu_n$ for new calls, and $1/\mu_h$ for handoff calls.

The mean service time is defined as

$$\frac{1}{\mu}=\frac{\lambda_{nv}+\lambda_{nd}}{\lambda_{nv}+\lambda_{nd}+\lambda_{hv}+\lambda_{hd}}\cdot\frac{1}{\mu_n}+\frac{\lambda_{hv}+\lambda_{hd}}{\lambda_{nv}+\lambda_{nd}+\lambda_{hv}+\lambda_{hd}}\cdot\frac{1}{\mu_h} \tag{1}$$

The normalized offered load of the system (in Erlang) is defined as

$$\rho=\frac{\lambda_n+\lambda_h}{B\mu} \tag{2}$$

where $\lambda_n=\lambda_{nv}+\lambda_{nd}$ and $\lambda_h=\lambda_{hv}+\lambda_{hd}$.

The mobility (γ) of calls is a measure of terminal mobility and is defined as the ratio of handoff call arrival rate to new call arrival rate, and can be written as

$$\gamma=\frac{\lambda_h}{\lambda_n} \tag{3}$$

The simulation input parameters used are given in Table 1 below.

Table 1. Simulation Parameters

Mobility(γ)	0.5, 1, 1.5
Load (ρ)	2 Erlangs
Time threshold values (t_{ev}, t_{ed})	15, 30, 60, 90, 120, 150, and 165 sec.
Total bandwidth (B)	100 units
Bandwidth threshold for voice calls (B_v)	90 units
Bandwidth threshold for data calls (B_d)	85 units
New call average service time ($1/\mu_n$)	180 sec. (Exp. Dist.)
Handoff call average service time ($1/\mu_h$)	180 sec. (Exp. Dist.)
Average elapsed time of a handoff call	90 sec. (Unif. Dist.)

The design goals of handoff schemes should also include minimizing the Grade of Service (GoS) cost function. Although sophisticated cost functions have been proposed [10], in practice, a simple weighted average is useful for most design purposes. The weighted sum of the new voice call blocking probability (P_{nv}), prioritized voice handoff call dropping probability (P_{h1v}) , non-prioritized voice handoff call dropping probability (P_{h2v}), new data call blocking probability (P_{nd}), prioritized data handoff call dropping probability (P_{h1d}) and non-prioritized data handoff call dropping probability (P_{h2d}) is introduced as a measure of grade of service (GoS) and can be defined as

$$GoS = P_{nv} + k_1 \cdot P_{h1v} + P_{h2v} + P_{nd} + k_2 \cdot P_{h1d} + P_{h2d} \tag{4}$$

where k_1 and k_2 are the penalty factors used to reflect the effect of the handoff dropping over the new call blocking probability. A penalty of 5 to 20 times is commonly recommended [11]. In accordance with our proposed scheme, we used the penalty for the prioritized handoff calls, whereas the non-prioritized handoff calls have the same weight as the new calls. Of course, from the mobile user's point of view, the objective is to minimize the GoS cost function in order to improve the performance of the system. Therefore, the performance of a system can be defined as

$$Performance = \frac{1}{GoS} \tag{5}$$

Another objective, from the service provider's perspective is to decrease the cost by increasing utilization of the system. Therefore, the cost of a system can be defined as

$$Cost = \frac{1}{Utilization} \tag{6}$$

In order to make a fair balance between both user satisfaction and service provider satisfaction, a crucial performance metric Z is introduced to measure the performance of different bandwidth allocation schemes and compare them. It is clear that, Z is a function of new call blocking probability, handoff dropping probability and system utilization all together and it can be defined as

$$Z = \frac{Performance}{Cost} \tag{7}$$

Of course, the design goals of a handoff scheme are increasing the performance and decreasing the cost, which means maximizing Z.

4 Simulation Results

The proposed scheme is evaluated for different values of system parameters. The performance measures obtained through the simulation are the blocking probability of new voice calls (P_{nv}), the total dropping probability of handoff voice calls (P_{hv})

which includes both prioritized and non-prioritized handoff voice call dropping probabilities, blocking probability of new data calls (P_{nd}), the total dropping probability of handoff data calls (P_{hd}) which includes both prioritized and non-prioritized handoff data call dropping probabilities , grade of service (GoS) and Z. Simulation parameters are set as follows: ρ =2Erlangs, B_v=90 BU, B_d=85 BU, k_1=k_2=20, λ_n =0.33-0.47 call/sec and λ_h =0.23-0.5 call/sec.

Fig. 4 below shows the dropping and blocking probabilities versus elapsed time threshold for a mobility of 1. As the time threshold increases, both P_{nv} and P_{hv} decrease. This is because, when t_{ev} increases, the number of prioritized handoff voice calls increases, therefore P_{hv} decreases. The decrease in P_{nv} is natural, since higher priority is given to voice calls over data calls. In addition to this, as t_{ed} increases, P_{nd} decreases smoothly at the expense of increasing P_{hd}. This is because, as t_{ed} increases, the number of prioritized handoff data calls decreases, therefore the number of handoff data calls that are treated as new calls increases. We can recommend service providers to set the value of t_{ev} between 120 – 165 sec. (approximately 4/6 – 11/12 of the average call duration). It is also reasonable to set the value of t_{ed} less than 30 sec (approximately 1/6 and 2/6 of the average call duration). The service providers may make use of the history of average call durations for a specific time period and can adjust t_{ev} and t_{ed} accordingly.

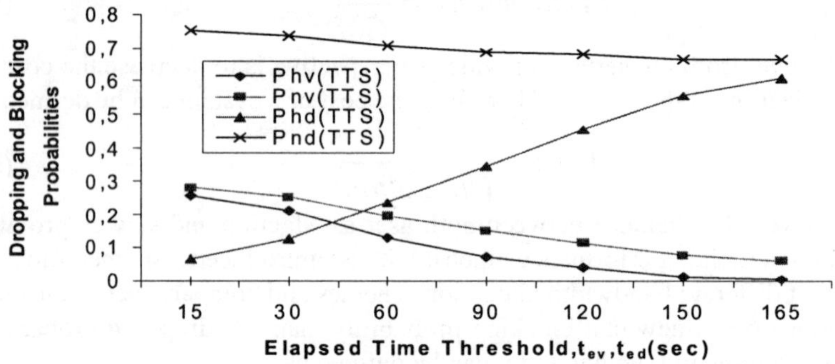

Figure 4. Dropping and blocking probabilities versus time threshold $t_{ev,}$ t_{ed} for γ =1

Fig. 5 below shows the grade of service (GoS) versus mobility for FSS, GCS, and TTS scheme with t_{ev}=120 sec, and t_{ed}=60 sec. As mentioned above, minimizing the GoS cost function improves the user satisfaction. As seen from the figure, our TTS scheme achieves the minimum GoS compared to GCS and FSS schemes. More than that, TTS scheme does not show a serious deterioration in the GoS as mobility increases.

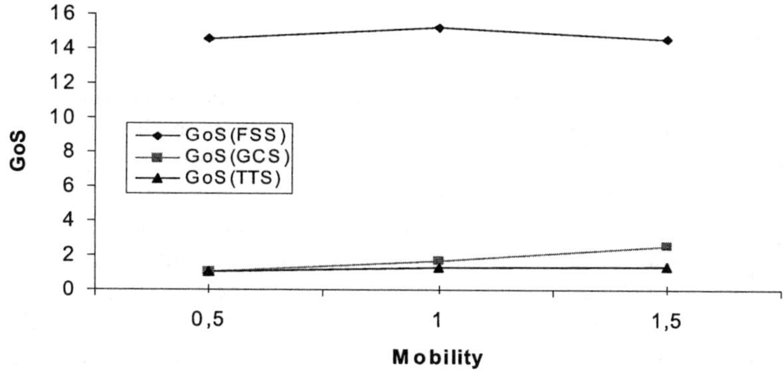

Figure 5. GoS versus mobility for the three different schemes

The last figure, Fig. 6 shows the general performance metric Z versus mobility for FSS, GCS, and TTS scheme with t_{ev}=120 sec, and t_{ed}=60 sec. It is clear that our TTS scheme outperforms the other schemes, since it has the highest Z for almost all mobility values. As expected the Z value of the FSS is constant with respect to mobility, because all channels are shared between new and handoff calls. The Z value of the GCS decreases sharply with mobility, because of the increase in its GoS, and its low utilization. The slight decrease of the Z value of the TTS at high mobility is due to the increase in the percentage of the non-prioritized handoff calls which may cause a marginal deterioration in the GoS. Although at low mobility, TTS scheme has approximately the same performance as the GCS scheme, the superiority of the TTS scheme becomes clearer as mobility increases, and the TTS improvements over GCS and FSS schemes reaches 50% and 70% respectively at γ=1.5.

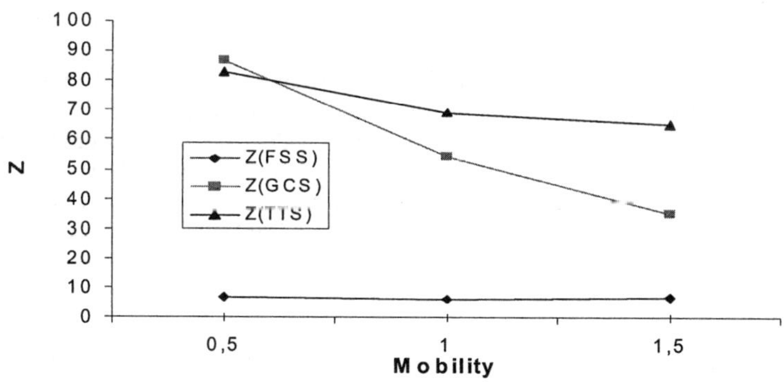

Figure 6. *Z* versus mobility for the three different schemes

5 Conclusion

In this paper, we propose a novel bandwidth allocation scheme based on monitoring the elapsed real time of handoff calls and according to both a time threshold parameter and the call type, the handoff calls are either prioritized or treated as new calls. The proposed TTS scheme relies on fairness among new calls and handoff calls that may tolerate uncritical dropping. It is well known that the GCS aims to increase user satisfaction by decreasing the dropping probability; and the FSS aims to increase service provider satisfaction by decreasing the blocking probability and increasing bandwidth utilization. To have a tradeoff between user and service provider satisfactions, we introduced a general performance metric Z as a performance/cost ratio that can be used to compare different bandwidth allocation schemes. The simulation results show the superiority of our scheme over GCS and FSS schemes. It is worthy to mention that TTS can be implemented easily since it uses the elapsed real time of a call which is already recorded in all systems for billing and other purposes. As a future work, we are planning to develop an analytical model for the proposed scheme.

References

1. S. Tekinay and B. Jabbari: Handover and Channel Assignment in Mobile Cellular Networks. IEEE Communications Magazine, **29**(11) (1991) 42-46
2. I. Katzela and M. Naghshineh: Channel Assignment Schemes for Cellular Mobile Telecommunications Systems: A Comprehensive Survey. IEEE Personal Communications Magazine, **3**(3) (1996) 10-31
3. J. Y. Lee, J. G. Choi, K. Park and S. Bahk: Realistic Cell-Oriented Adaptive Admission Control for QoS Support in Wireless Multimedia Networks. IEEE Transactions on Vehicular Technology, **52**(3) (2003) 512-525
4. Y. Kim, D. Lee and B. Lee: Dynamic Channel Reservation based on Mobility in Wireless ATM networks. IEEE Communications Magazine, **37**(11) (1999) 47-51
5. J. Hou and Y. Fang: Mobility-Based Call Admission Control Schemes for Wireless Mobile Networks. Wireless Communications and Mobile Computing, **1**(3) (2001) 269-282
6. S. Choi and K. G. Shin: Predictive and Adaptive Bandwidth Reservation for Handoffs in QoS-Sensitive Cellular Networks. Proc. ACM SOGCOMM'98, (1998) 155-166
7. J. Wang, Q. Zeng and D. P. Agrawala: Performance Analysis of a Preemptive and Priority Reservation Handoff Scheme for Integrated Service-Based Wireless Mobile Networks. IEEE Transactions on Mobile Computing, **2**(1) (2003) 65-75
8. L. Huang, S. Kumar and C. C. Kuo: Adaptive Resource Allocation for Multimedia QoS Management in Wireless Networks. IEEE Transactions on Vehicular Technology, **53**(2) (2004) 547-558
9. Q. Zeng and D. P. Agrawal: Modeling and Efficient Handling of Handoffs in Integrated Wireless Mobile Networks. IEEE Transactions on Vehicular Technology, **51**(6) (2002) 1469-1478

10. ETSI Standard ETR 310,, Radio Equipment and Systems; Digital Enhanced Cordless Telecommunications; Traffic Capacity and Spectrum Requirements, (1996)
11. F. Barcelo: Performance Analysis of Handoff Resource Allocation Strategies through the State-Dependent Rejection Scheme. IEEE Transactions on Wireless Communications, **3**(3) (2004) 900-909

IMPROVING THE PERFORMANCE OF VIDEO STREAMING SYSTEMS USİNG VIDEO-LOCALITY AND DISTRIBUTED REDUNDANT HIERARCHY SERVERS

HASAN SARPER, MOHAMMED AHMED SHAH, IŞIK AYBAY

Computer Enginnering Department, Eastern Mediterranean University, Magosa, North Cyprus

E-mail:{hasan.sarper, ahmed.shah, isik.aybay}@emu.edu.tr

This study proposes two new systems for the client and server sides of video streaming systems. The client side performance is improved by employing inactive clients as local servers for their peers, while the server side performance is increased by a redundant hierarchy of servers.

1 Introduction

Recent progresses in desktop processing, audio and video compression, high bandwidth storage systems and Internet opened the way for new multimedia applications. These applications include video-on demand, live broadcasts, distance learning, video games, interactive television, and video conferencing. A common property of these applications is that media files are delivered on-demand to clients.

A typical Video-on-Demand (VOD) system consists of a client in a local area network (LAN) requesting a video clip and a video server on the Internet. Usually each client creates a single connection with the video server and the server supplies video streams over this connection. Unfortunately, a single connection to the video server cannot use the available bandwidth efficiently.

A popular VOD server is likely to store hundreds of media files, and provide real-time media access to several hundreds (or thousands) of clients. The stored media files are very large. To ensure playback without pauses or delays, the requested media has to be retrieved from storage subsystems and transmitted at a fixed rate over the Internet. Since a large number of streams might be in progress at a given point in time, server resources such as disk bandwidth and network bandwidth must be carefully managed.

A number of techniques have been proposed to increase the performance of VOD systems. In techniques based on multicasting, a client request waits at the server side for more requests for the same video data from other clients to come. After a timeout, all requests waiting for the same video object are serviced by the server with multicasting packets [5]. These implementations require reliable multicasting over the Internet, which is still a challenging task [17].

In [3], a multithreaded video streaming system is described and it is shown that multithreading can be an important factor for improving the performance of a video streaming system.

Caching ‘frequently used data’ at proxies close to clients can reduce client access latencies and server/network loads [16]. Actually, a dedicated proxy server can be used with an intelligent cache [6], but since the proxy server acts as a coordinator of the LAN for video streaming, it becomes a single point of failure.

Since video objects have a large size, it is costly to store them as a whole in proxy servers or client caches. Instead, it is reasonable to divide these objects into smaller parts, or segments, and store only segments of an object. Different segmentation techniques are proposed for proxy caching [7].

Taking into consideration video streams are processed at client nodes, storing and using those segments can further improve the performance of video streaming [1], [2].

In the Global Video Environment (GloVE) system [2], client buffers form a cooperative video cache. A centralized cooperative video cache manager controls the execution of the system. Consequently, a single point of failure and client overloading may be problems in this technique.

In [1], it is shown that a peer-to peer architecture improves the performance of a VOD system considerably. ‘groups’ with similar interests should be formed, and clients should store video clips as a whole.

In this paper, a novel architecture for VOD is proposed and a performance study is conducted. The client architecture is based on multithreading (concurrency), and it uses video clip segments from LAN in cooperation with the back-end module of a video player application. (Fig. 1)

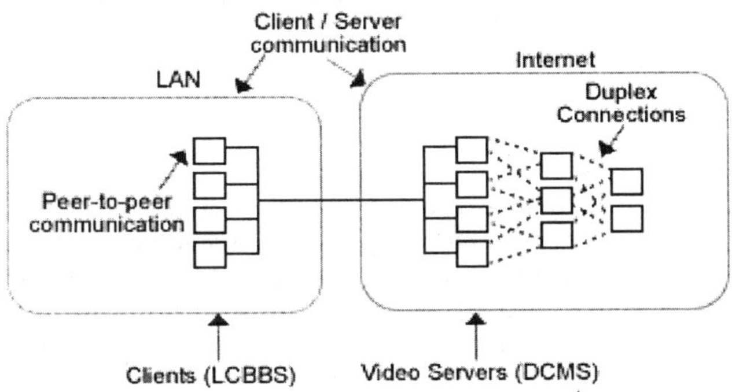

Figure 1 The general structure of the proposed VOD system

In the proposed system, multicasting is used only locally. Furthermore, a centralized coordinator is not needed for cooperation among the clients. Video objects are divided into fixed sized segments. The system module can be installed at the clients, or can be integrated into a video player application.

Employing only one large Centralized Continuous Media Server (CCMS) to support all distributed clients results in inefficient resource allocations and requires extremely high bandwidth connections. The overall bandwidth requirement to implement an interactive VOD system with such a design is estimated to be as high as 1.54 Pb/s (Peta-bits/second) for the US [8].

Therefore, the proposed VOD system considers a different distributed server architecture on the Internet, called the Redundant Hierarchy Distributed Server Architecture (RHDSA) (Figure 1). We propose employing a number of media servers for streaming. Distributed continuous media server (DCMS) architectures designed based on a similar approach [9], [10], are shown to be able to provide the minimum communication storage [11], [12].

The rest of the paper is structured in the following way. Section 2 describes the proposed client architecture. In Section 3, the proposed server architecture is described. The Petri-net model developed for simulation is discussed briefly in Section 4. Simulation details and results can be found in Section 5. Finally, Section 6 concludes the paper and outlines some future work.

2 The Client System Architecture

In a typical VOD system, a video player application running on the client downloads video clips from a remote server and displays them. Video clip data are temporarily stored in the client's buffers before displaying, and are discarded afterwards.

User interests in the same LAN tend to be similar, and different clients may display the same video clips over and over in a short period of time. We call this the *video-locality* principle. To make use of video-locality, and to search for the availability of some requested video clip firstly on the LAN, a novel scheme called the LAN Concurrent Back-End Buffering System (LCBBS) is implemented (Fig 2). Basically, if video clip data is not discarded after display on a client, a newly requested video clip may be located on the same LAN.

A special LCBBS module is installed on each client on the LAN so that the client can operate both in the client mode and in the LAN server mode. In this scheme, to receive requested video clips faster, clients can first try buffers of other clients in the same LAN. In this case, the LAN communication becomes peer-to-peer. The communication between the client and the remote server is similar to the typical VOD case, with multithreading to receive multiple parts of the video clip simultaneously (Fig 1).

Storing entire video clips at the clients need a large space in client buffers. Instead, clips are thought to consist of a number of segments of a fixed size. The client keeps in its buffer only some segments of recently displayed video clips.

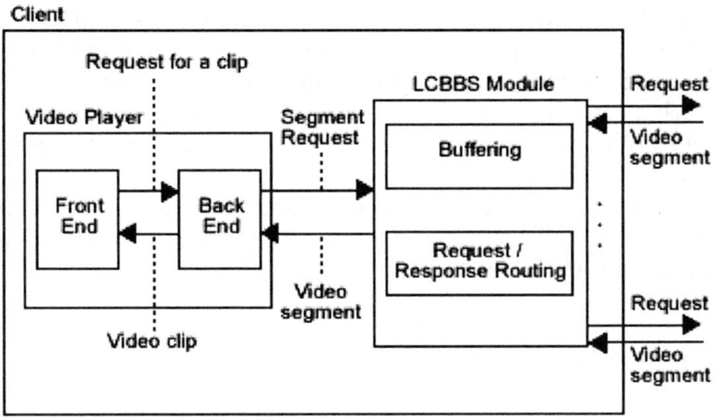

Figure 2 VOD Client with an LCBBS module

2.1 Client Mode

When a video clip request is received from the video player (Fig 1), a Segment Availability Table (SAT) is created to store the status of segments for this clip. The LCBBS module sends a multicast inquiry message to other LAN clients to find out whether segments of the requested video clip are available within the LAN. After receiving replies from other clients, the requesting client marks all segments that are available in the LAN as "LAN". The rest of the segments are labeled as "Internet" to indicate that those segments should be downloaded from a remote server.

Then, multiple threads are created to start downloading segments of the desired clip from other clients in the LAN and/or from the remote video server in the Internet. After downloading is completed, segments are transferred to the back-end module of the video player, which feeds the segments in the correct order to the front-end module for actual video display.

The time elapsed from the moment the video clip request is generated, to the moment the last segment arrives represents the '*response time*' for the requesting client. It includes downloading delays, transmission times of segments in the LAN and the Internet, and queuing delays. Response time is considered as the main performance measure for LCBBS simulations.

2.2 LAN Server Mode

Clients working in the LAN server mode act like a LAN video data provider. In this role, a client needs to carry out the following operations on requests coming from other clients in the LAN:

1. Preparing and sending a reply message that contains information about segments of the requested video clip available in its buffer,

2. Uploading segments of the requested video clip available in its buffer.

When a client receives a new request for segments of a video clip, it might be heavily loaded by displaying some other video clip, or uploading video data to some other client. In such a case, the client ignores the received request, leaving this request to be served by other, less loaded clients in the LAN, or in the worst case, by a remote video server on the Internet.

Each client sets its status to 'active' when it starts receiving a video clip, and sets its status to 'inactive' when it finishes displaying a video clip. Only inactive clients can switch to the LAN server mode.

3 The Server System Architecture

In a typical DCMS system, when a client requests some streaming service, the request is forwarded to the entry-level server of the distributed streaming system through the Internet. Using some set of policies defined by the system administrators and developers, the entry-level server decides which exact server is to be used to provide the media content to the client. After selecting the server responsible for streaming, actual streaming is done through the entry-level server, over the Internet, to the requesting client.

Therefore, distributed media server architecture has two main issues to handle:

1. Choosing an appropriate server which has a copy of the requested media object (object location).
2. Streaming the located media object over the Internet to the client (streaming).

3.1 The Proposed Object Location Scheme

The object location scheme proposed in this study runs as an application layer middleware on a DCMS network. A topology called Redundant Hierarchy [13] or, briefly, RedHi (see Fig. 3) mechanism is used to connect the media servers involved.

RedHi relaxes the degree-1 parent connectivity restriction of the pure hierarchy to be degree-2 or more. Main advantages of this approach are faster object location and redundancy (hence, no single point of failure). RedHi does not impose higher bandwidth requirements, it only requires higher connectivity. In the proposed scheme, we use degree-2 connectivity from a server node in the system to its parents.

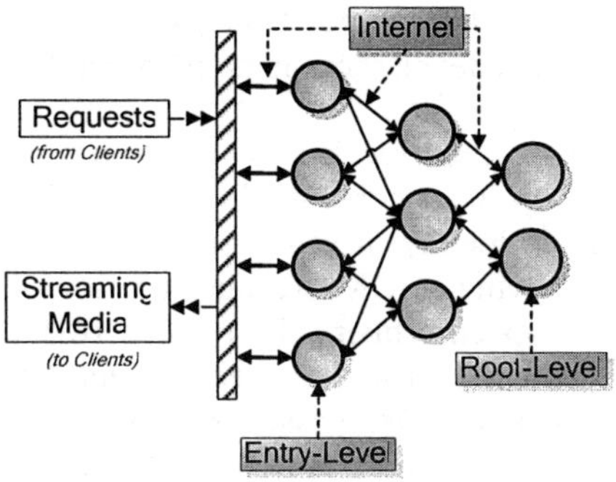

Figure 3 Redundant Hierarchy Distributed Server Architecture (RHDSA).

Other properties of the RHDSA are as follows:

1. Nodes of the architecture are multimedia servers (possibly heterogeneous), each with limited streaming bandwidth and storage space.
2. Links of the architecture are provided by some underlying telecommunication infrastructure that guarantees the availability of a fixed limited bandwidth.
3. There are two root nodes at the top of the redundant hierarchy.
4. A child node has exactly two parents.

The proposed object location method involves an algorithm, and a message passing mechanism. The algorithm runs in each node of the system, and it has two modules. One module is dedicated to receive queries from the child nodes. Entry-level servers receive queries from the client through the Internet. The second module is devoted to processing queries in the node and sending queries to parents and/or children nodes. If media required is not available locally, the query is passed to both parent nodes.

For object location, we use a message passing mechanism which involves three message types:

1. *Query Message*: When an entry-level node receives a request from the Internet for a specific media file, it checks its contents in order to find out whether the required media file is available in this node or not. If yes, then no query message is sent to parents and the media file is streamed to the client. In case the entry-level node finds out that it does not have any knowledge of the required media file, it forwards the client request to its parents as a query message.
2. *Negative Acknowledgement Message* (NAM): A negative acknowledgement message is sent from a node to a child when upon receiving a Query message; a parent node finds that the requested media file is not available locally. In addition, the parent node sends the same query message it received from its child to its own parents. This process is repeated by all the nodes until either the root nodes are reached, or the media file is found in some node. In case both roots send NAM messages, the child node prepares a NAM message for its own child, and in this manner, the whole hierarchy is traversed. In case the entry-

level node receives NAM messages from all servers in the hierarchy, it indicates that from this entry-level, there is no path that leads to the required media file.

3. *OK Message :* When a node receives a Query message from its child node it looks the media file up in its contents. In case a node finds that the requested media file is available locally, it sends an OK message to the corresponding child node. Upon receiving an OK message, a child node checks whether this is the first reply to the specific query. If it is the first OK reply, then it is forwarded down the hierarchy. If it is the second reply then the new OK message is discarded. In this manner, OK messages are filtered and passed down the hierarchy from parent to child nodes until one OK message reaches the client.

3.2 Request Life Cycle

When an entry-level server receives a request from a client for a media object, it generates a query packet and propagates/floods it to the network. Instances of the flooded query packet traverse different paths and incrementally evaluate the cost of the paths as they are forwarded from node to node. Some query packets reach the nodes that have a copy of the requested media file locally. Those nodes send OK messages back along the same path traversed by the corresponding query packets to report the availability of the requested media file, as well as the cost of the path. The nodes along the path compare the responses and select the best path. They also filter out the rest of the responses, so that finally the head-end receives the response that indicates the best path. When the path is determined, the selected server starts streaming the media file.

4 Petri-net Model Developed for the Server Architecture

A Petri-net model [14] of the RHDSA object location system was developed for simulation purposes. Three levels of hierarchy are considered between the servers. The requests made by clients are accepted through Level 1 servers, called entry-level servers. The general input/output model of the servers is shown in Figure 4.

Figure 4 General input/output mechanisms for a server in the RHDSA system.

4.1 *Assumptions for the Petri-net Model*

The Petri-net model for RHDSA is composed of three basic parts: the Petri-net model for clients, the Petri-net model for non-root level servers, and the Petri-net model for root-level servers. Due to limited space, only the Petri-net graph for non-root level servers is given in Figure 5. The Petri-net graph representing the root level servers are similar, but simpler, since no query will be forwarded to parents.

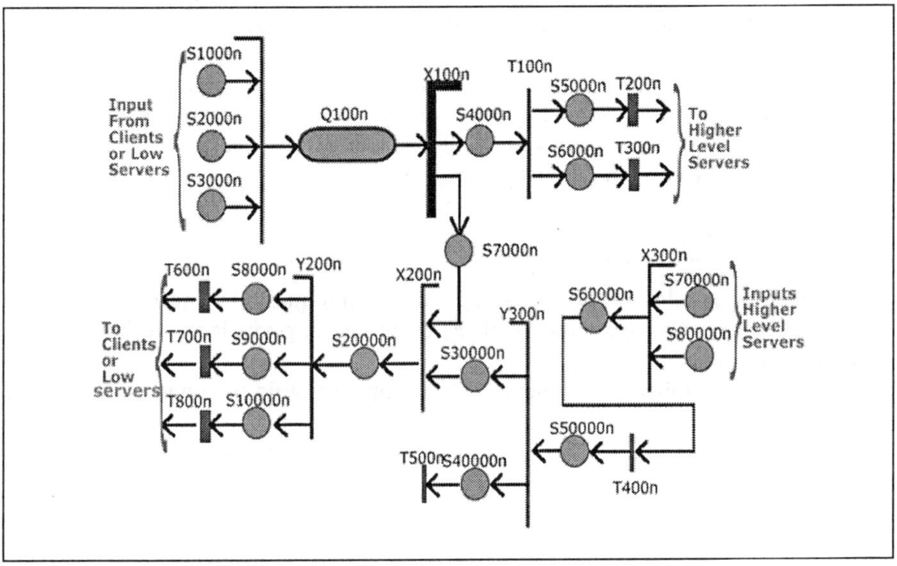

Figure 5 Petri-net graph for non-root level servers of RHDSA.

In the Petri-net model, it is assumed that all servers are connected to each other through the Internet, and they may be geographically dispersed. It is also assumed that nodes do not fail and there is no timeout mechanism.

Other assumptions are:

1. Each client, with equal probability, sends a request to an entry-level server and waits for the response. Only after one request is fully processed, a client may generate a new request.
2. Requests from clients arrive to entry-level servers through the Internet.
3. Transmission in the Internet is modeled as a random delay, distributed exponentially with some specific mean time 'TN'.

5 Simulation and Results

5.1 *Simulation Model*

The simulation model for the proposed client architecture is developed using the Petri-net-based simulation system Winsim [14]. The Petri-net model for the client side has three separate interconnected modules; the client module, the remote video server module and the LAN module. For simulation purposes, it is assumed that there are five clients and three remote servers in the LCBBS video streaming system.

The remote video server is organized considering a multithreaded scheme. The delays associated with message transmission on the Internet are reflected in the server module. Simulation studies show that these delays considerably affect the performance of the video streaming system.

5.2 *Simulation Parameters*

Let N be the total number of segments in a video clip requested by some client,
$N_{LOC} \leq N$ be the number of segments of the requested clip available in the buffer of the same client,
$N_{LAN} \leq N$ be the number of segments of the clip available at other clients in the LAN.

Then, the requesting client will need to download $(N - (N_{LOC} + N_{LAN}))$ segments from some remote video server in the Internet.
Defining p_{LOC} as the ratio of segments that will be accessed locally,
p_{LAN} as the ratio of the segments that will be accessed in the LAN,
p_{INT} as the ratio of the segments that will be accessed on the Internet:

$$p_{LOC} + p_{LAN} + p_{INT} = 1. \quad \textbf{(1)}$$

$$p_{LOC} = N_{LOC} / N, \ p_{LAN} = N_{LAN} / N, \ and \quad p_{INT} = (N - (N_{LOC} + N_{LAN})) / N. \quad \textbf{(2)}$$

For sufficiently large N, ratios p_{LOC}, p_{LAN} and p_{INT} can be considered as approximations of probabilities. Clearly, with an increase in probability p_{INT} , the time to get the requested video clip from the Internet will also increase. This is indicated in our simulation experiments, where probability p_{INT} is used as a varying parameter.

We consider the ratio of local segments to be approximated by probability $p_{LOC} = 0.05$ in all simulation experiments, with the exception where all segments are on the Internet ($p_{INT} = 1.00$). When $p_{LOC} = 0.05$, for each value of p_{INT}, the value of p_{LAN} can be calculated using formula (1).

Earlier, 'response time' was defined as the time elapsed from the moment the video clip request is generated, to the moment the last segment arrives. The average response time is calculated over all requests of all clients during a simulation run. The average response time is used as a performance measure of the simulated system. To see the effect of multithreading, simulation runs are repeated for different numbers of threads in remote video servers and clients.

In all simulation experiments, the main variable parameter was the ratio (probability) p_{INT}. For different values of p_{INT}, the following parameters were fixed: the number of threads in clients and a remote server, the mean Internet packet transfer time, and the packet transfer time in LAN.

The main goal of the simulation experiments was to observe the behavior of the average response time for a client when it makes a sufficiently large number of requests for video clips according to the proposed LCBBS scheme.

5.3 Discussion of Results

Figure 6 shows the simulation results with the mean Internet packet transfer time equal to 250 ms. This experiment is repeated for three different transmission speeds in the underlying LAN (10 Mbps, 100 Mbps, 1 Gbps). The number of threads is varied between 1, 2, 4 and 8. A packet is assumed to be 1500 bytes and the video size is assumed to be uniformly distributed between 1 MB to 25 MB.

A typical VOD system with a remote video server can be simulated by setting p_{INT}=1 and the number of threads to one. This is the topmost and rightmost point in the figures.

250 ms Internet packet transfer time is corresponds to a 56Kbps connection. The average response time is high (4000 seconds) when a single thread is used because of this slow connection and other delays (queuing, segment reading, packet preparation, and LAN delays).

When the number of threads is doubled, the average response time is reduced nearly to its half. Up to 8 threads, the average response time is reduced linearly. When p_{INT} becomes 0.2, with 8 threads, the average response time is reduced by almost 1.6 times.

When p_{INT} is decreased by 0.2, in other words when the number of segments located on the Internet is reduced by 20%, the average response time is reduced nearly 1.5 times (p_{INT}=1 to 0.8, p_{INT}=0.8 to 0.6, p_{INT}=0.6 to 0.4).

The average response time is reduced by almost 50% when p_{INT} is reduced from 0.4 to 0.2. When p_{INT} is reduced from 0.2 to 0 (i.e., all segments are available in the LAN), the average response time is reduced nearly 12, 6, 3 and 1.5 times with one, two, four and eight threads, respectively. The experiments show that that the LAN packet transfer time has no significant and direct effect on the average response time.

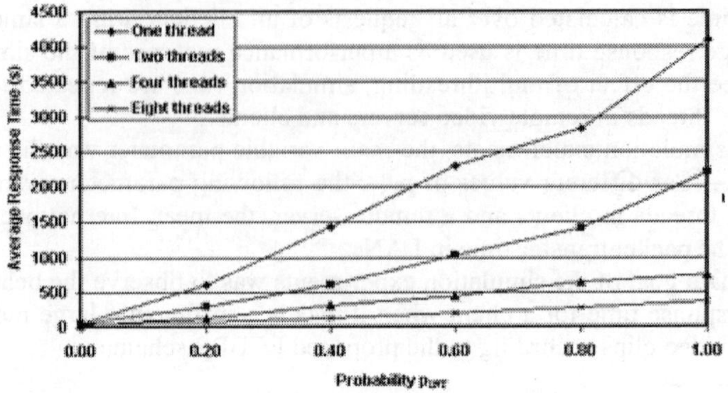

Figure 6 Average response time for a video client vs. probability p_{int} for different numbers of threads with mean Internet packet transfer time of 250 ms and LAN packet transfer time of (0.5 - 2.5) ms (approximately 10 Mbps) .

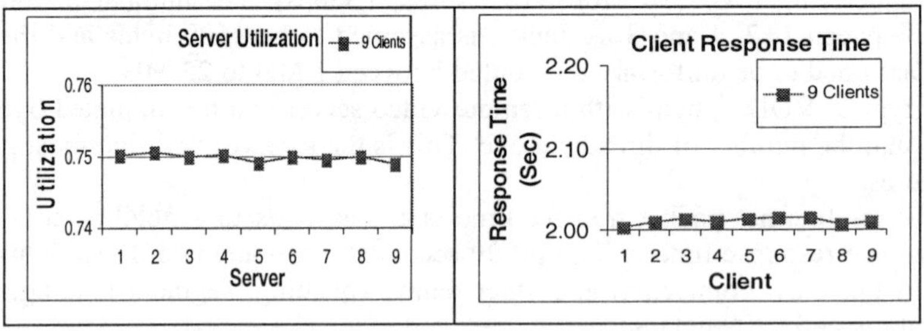

Figure 7 a) Server utilization (9 Clients), b) Response time (9 clients).

For the server side, the simulation results for the object location scheme were obtained using a mean of 50000 request messages from a client, and a 0.3 probability of finding a requested media in a server, After receiving a reply the clients waits a mean of 20 minutes before making a new request to the system in case the earlier requested media was found. This delay is the viewing time of the media whereas if the earlier request received a negative message then the client can immediately initiate a new request. The system consisted of 9 servers and three sets of simulations were conducted; one with 3 clients, another with 6 clients and the third one with 9 clients in the system, the average server utilization of the system with 9 clients is shown in figure 7a, and the average response times for each client in the system with 9 clients is shown in figure 7b. At the end of the simulation, the overall percentage of having the requested media located in the RHDSA was 98%. The average response time was found to be in the vicinity of 2.004 to 2.024 sec. This diminutive range, although the system was simulated with 150000 to 450000 request messages, promises scalability. Another important simulation parameter checked was server utilization, and from the simulation results we see that server utilization ranges from 0.748 to 0.75. These results show that our object location scheme is highly scalable, for example even for a system with 9 clients and a total of 450000 requests, our object location scheme shows that the average response time for the clients is 2.01 sec and the average server utilization is 0.745.

6 Conclusion

Current video server systems suffer from two major problems. These are firstly the difficulty of handling a huge amount of client requests coming from different local area networks for the same video file, and secondly the overhead in locating a server which contains a video file requested by a client among a farm of servers. In addition, Internet connection speed restrictions also reduce the quality of service.

This study proposes two techniques to overcome the performance constraining issues cited above. To improve the performance of the server side, the servers are organized as a redundant hierarchy. This increases the communication paths between servers, while reducing the overhead in locating a server which has the requested video contents using a multi-search strategy over multiple paths.

The client side problems are reduced by making use of client peers to load portions of requested video files. The main idea used is that due to video-locality, clients on the same LAN will have similar interests, which means a video requested by a client is likely already requested, viewed, and stored in another peer on the same LAN. Simulation studies show that both proposals are valid and improve video-streaming performance.

Currently, the client side system (LCBBS) is completed. The object location part of the server side is also finished and we are working on the streaming issues from servers to clients over the Internet.

Some other studies published recently [1], [7] indicate that this is a relevant research topic. This study differs from [1] in that we do not employ a special architecture like Peer-to-Peer Grid, our LCBBS system works on any LAN structure. We use segmentation as proposed in [7], however, we do not fix our attention only on proxy caching, and we extend the concept to LAN's on the client side. We also propose improved server architecture, the redundant hierarchy.

References

1. X. He, X. Tang, J. You, G. Xue, Network-Aware Multicasting for Video-on-Demand Services, IEEE Transactions on Consumer Electronics, Vol.50, No. 3 (2004), pp. 864-869.
2. Leonardo B. Pinho, Claudio L. Amorim, Edison Ishikawa, GloVE: A Distributed Environment for Low Cost Scalable VoD Systems, IEEE Symposium on

Computer Architecture and High Performance Computing (SBAC-PAD) (2002), pp. 117-124.

3. Gwang Jung, Kyung Kang, Qutaiah Malluhi, "Multithreaded Distributed MPEG1 Video Delivery in the Internet Environment", ACM Symposium on Applied Computing (SAC) (2000), pp. 592-597.
4. Aidong Zhang, Yuqing Song, Markus Mielke, "Netmedia: Streaming Multimedia Presentations in Distributed Environments", IEEE Multimedia (2002), pp.56-73.
5. Y. Cai and K. A. Hua, "An efficient bandwidth-sharing technique for true video on demand systems", ACM Multimedia (1999), pp. 211-214.
6. Chung-Ming Huang, Tz-Heng Hsu, and Chi-Kuang Chang, "A Proxy Based Adaptive Flow Control Scheme for Media Streaming", ACM SAC (Symposium on Applied Computing) (2002), pp.750-754.
7. K. Wu, P. S. Yu, J. L. Wolf, "Segmentation of Multimedia Streams for Proxy Caching", IEEE Transactions on Multimedia, vol 6 no:5 (2004), pp. 770-780.
8. J. Nussbaumer, B. Patel, F. Schaffa, and J. Sterbenz, "Network Requirements for Interactive Video-on-Demand," IEEE J. Selected Areas in Comm., vol. 13, no. 5 (1995), pp. 779-787.
9. A.D. Gelman, H. Kobrinski, L.S. Smoot, S.B. Weinstein, M. Fortier, and D. Lemay, "A Store-and-Forward Architecture for Video-on-Demand Service," Proc. IEEE Int'l Conf. Comm. (ICC '91), vol. 2 (1991), pp. 842-846.
10. L. De Giovanni, A.M. Langellotti, L.M. Patitucci, and L. Petrini, "Dimensioning of Hierarchical Storage for Video-on-Demand Services," Proc. IEEE Int'l Conf. Comm. (ICC '94), vol. 3 (1994), pp. 1739-1743.
11. F. Schaffa and J.P. Nussbaumer, "On Bandwidth and Storage Tradeoffs in Multimedia Distribution Networks," INFOCOM '95 Proc. 14th Ann. Joint Conf. IEEE Computer and Comm Soc., vol. 3 (1995), pp. 1020-1026.
12. S.A. Barnett and G.J. Anido, "A Cost Comparison of Distributed and Centralized Approaches to Video-on-Demand," IEEE J. Selected Areas in Comm., vol. 14, no. 6 (1996), pp. 1173-1183.
13. C. Shahabi, M. Alshayeji, and S. Wang, "A Redundant Hierarchical Structure for a Distributed Continuous Media Server," Proc. Fourth European Workshop Interactive Distributed Multimedia Systems and Telecomm. Services (IDMS '97) (1997)
14. Alexander Kostin, Ljudmila Ilushechkina, "Winsim: A Tool for Performance Evaluation of Parallel and Distributed Systems", Advances in Information Systems (ADVIS), Izmir, Turkey (2004), pp.312-321.
15. J. Liu and J. Xu, "A Survey of Streaming Media Caching", Technical Report, Hong Kong Baptist University (2003).
16. J. W. Atwood, "A Classification of Reliable Multicast Protocols", IEEE Network, May/June (2004), pp. 24-34.

SEARCHING FOR LOW LATENCY ROUTES IN CPN WITH REDUCED PACKET OVERHEAD *

R. LENT AND P. LIU
Imperial College London,
London SW7 2AZ, UK
E-mail: {r.lent, p.liu}@imperial.ac.uk

Most applications consider network latency as an important metric for their operation. Latency plays a particular role in time-sensitive applications, such as, data transfers or interactive sessions. Smart packets in cognitive packet networks, can learn to find low-latency paths by explicitly expressing delay in their routing goal functions. However, to maintain the quality of paths, packets need to continuously monitor the round-trip delay that paths produce, to allow the algorithm learn any change. The acquisition of network status requires space in packets and lengthens their transmission time. This paper proposes an alternative composite goal consisting of path length and buffer occupancy of nodes that requires less storage space in packets, while offering a similar performance to a delay based goal. Measurements in a network testbed and simulation studies illustrate the problem and solution addressed in this study.

1. Introduction

Quality-of-Service (QoS) routing has become an important solution for Internet service providers and corporate networks to intelligently deal with the growing amounts of traffic and concurrent diversity of applications. While different applications expect different characteristics from the network, most applications demand at least low latency. Low latency is of particular importance in time-sensitive applications, such as mission critical services or interactive sessions.

The latency of an end-to-end communication is the product of a number of factors. These factors include the processing speed of nodes in the path, as well as the propagation delay, which becomes significant in networks of long links. However, in the majority of cases, the dominant factors in

*This work was supported by the Engineering and Physical Sciences Research Council, U.K. under Grant GR/S52360/01.

network latency are the waiting time of packets in nodes' buffers and the store-and-forward transmission delays.

An effective way to achieve low latency in a communication is by dynamically identifying and using the paths in the network that produce the lowest latency as an alternative to using pre-defined paths as intra-AS Internet protocols do [1,2]. Routing algorithms based on the link state or distance vector algorithms are in general not suitable to find delay sensitive paths because of the relative slow process of information exchange among neighbors.

Most algorithms determine path selection in the path length, which uses hop-count (number of nodes in a path) as metric. Shortest paths are usually desirable because they tend to minimize the use of resources, such as the number of transmissions or buffer occupancies. However, shortest paths may produce an undesirable distribution of traffic that may lead to higher buffer occupancies and therefore to higher delays.

It is worthy of note that in some cases QoS routing algorithms are required to satisfy more than one constraint. The problem of path selection with multiple constraints is a problem extensively studied as a general unicast routing problem in the literature. A few examples follow. Wang and Crowcroft proposed a bandwidth-delay constrained solution based on Dijkstra's shortest path algorithm [3]. The bandwidth and delay constrained path selection under imprecise knowledge of network states was undertaken by Guerin and Orda [4], who suggested the use of probability distribution functions to statistically determine the capacity for new connections. Awebuch et al. proposed an algorithm to try to maximize the long-term average throughput of the network by associating an exponential cost of the bandwidth utilization [5]. Salama et al. proposed a distributed heuristic algorithm for a delay constrained and cost constrained problem [6]. Chen and Ansari [7] showed that linear cost functions of additive metric can produce low computation complexity in their algorithm that is based on an extended Bellman-Ford. The effectiveness of these algorithms largely depends on the accuracy of the network state information that is available to them, which usually involves moving large amounts of information traffic and therefore limiting their application.

The advantage of cognitive packet networks (CPN) over other routing algorithms is in that network state collection is focused on active paths and that the algorithm is able to make decisions with limited information [8]. As the algorithm learns more information, decisions are refined and routes become better in their QoS sense. CPN uses smart packets as control packets that are sent out by source nodes to discover routes on demand. Discovered routes are exploited by streams of dumb packets, which transport user data and use source routing to reach their destinations. Packet flows create a collaborative feedback system via acknowledgement packets. These acknowledgments disseminate network status to the nodes on the routes the packets use. For this, packets include a storage area (cognitive map) in addition to a header and payload area, to collect and disseminate network knowledge. Knowledge is accumulated via reinforcement learning in random neural networks located in the nodes of the network and is utilized by future smart packets to make better routing decisions.

CPN can identify low-latency paths by explicitly expressing delay as a goal for smart packets in the reinforcement-learning algorithm. However, the use of delay implies a collection of timestamps along packets' paths, which add overhead to the packets that may become significant in long routes.

This paper proposes an alternative mechanism for CPN to achieve traffic balancing and to identify low-delay paths in a network. The proposal introduces a routing metric for smart packets, which combines path length and buffer occupancy information to replace the explicit expression of delay in the routing goal of smart packets. As a result, a significant amount of overhead can be removed from packets while achieving similar results.

2. QoS Goal Functions

We refer the reader to the literature for further details on the CPN algorithm [8]. This section focuses on defining new goal functions (the inverse of the reward function) for smart packets in the reinforcement learning of CPN.

Assuming that packets of a given flow move along path $P = (n_1, n_2, \ldots, n_h, \ldots, n_d)$, where n_h represents the h-th node on the path and (n_h, n_{h+1}) represents the link between nodes n_h and n_{h+1}. The goal computed at node n_h is:

$$G(n_h, n_d) = \sum_{j=h+1}^{d} \eta C(n_j) \tag{1}$$

where $C(n_j)$ represents the measured cost of a metric of interest when the packet visits node n_j and may be a metric of the node itself or of the link used to reach the node. η is a constant that can be used to balance the resulting function. For example, delay can be minimized by simply making the goal equal to this metric:

$$G(n_h, n_d) = \sum_{j=h}^{d-1} \eta D(n_j, n_{j+1}) \tag{2}$$

where $D(n_j, n_{j+1})$ is the latency in moving a packet from node n_j to n_{j+1}. CPN uses round-trip delay as a metric (instead of forward delay) to avoid synchronize nodes' clocks. Round-trip delay is calculated from the arrival time difference of packets and their corresponding acknowledgments.

Shortest paths in hop count terms can be achieved by defining:

$$G(n_h, n_d) = \sum_{j=h+1}^{d} \eta \times 1 = \eta(d-h) \tag{3}$$

This paper proposes a way to achieve traffic load balancing by composing hop count and buffer occupancy:

$$G(n_h, n_d) = \sum_{j=h+1}^{d} \eta_1 + \eta_2 Q(n_j) \tag{4}$$

where $Q(n_j)$ is the buffer occupancy of node n_j. Through load balancing, we attempt to indirectly make smart packets discover low delay paths. The benefit is in the significant savings that can be achieved in packet overhead after replacing equation (2) with (4).

3. Testbed Measurements

A performance comparison of smart packets either using delay or path length as goals was conducted in a network testbed of 26 nodes. Testbed nodes are PC computers equipped with 4 Ethernet network ports and configured to transmit at a nominal rate of 10 Mbps. The topology consisted of 6 rings of 4 nodes connected in a grid fashion with two additional nodes connected to the ends of the resulting cylinder, which acted as source and destination for the experiments. An implementation of CPN runs in a Linux 2.4.x kernel space as a network layer protocol.

The experiments consisted in observing the round-trip delay and path length of packets in a single traffic stream. A constant bit rate traffic (UDP) was established between these two nodes with packets of size 1024 bytes, which were sent either at a rate of 200 pps or 500 pps. After an initial route was established, one smart packet was sent every 4 dumb packets on average, of which 5% employed random search instead of RNN/RL driven search.

Fig. 3 depicts the path length as measured by consecutive dumb packets within the first 2 minutes of the experiments with a sending rate of 200 pps and 500 pps respectively. The curves compare the ensemble average of at least 20 samples along with the 95% interval of routing cases when path length (hop count) or delay was the routing goal of smart packets. Both curves approximately tend to the value of 8.3.

The ideal shortest path length between source and destination was 8. The observed variation from the ideal value is because of the 5% smart packets that randomly decided their next hop. Randomness is a mechanism in CPN that avoids trapping the algorithm in local minima. For reference purposes, the average path length when using pure random decisions was measured as 14 hops, which gives: $8 * 0.95 + 14 * 0.05 = 8.3$ hops–the value learnt by smart packets in the experiments.

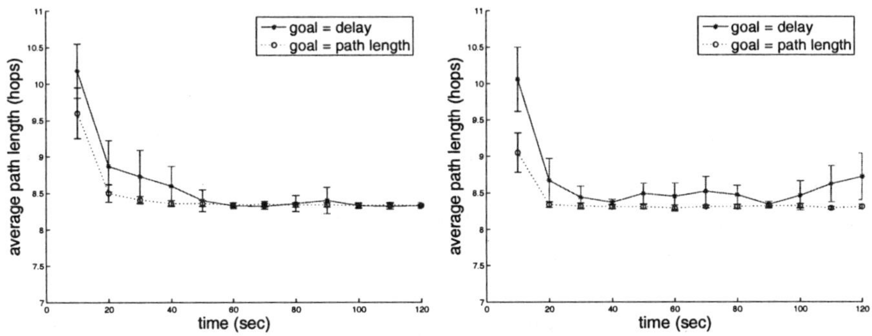

Figure 1. Average path length over time of dumb packets either when delay or path length (hop count) was the minimization goal for 200 pps and 500 pps respectively

Routing based on delay offers the advantage of load balancing while maintaining the path length close to the shortest path. The case is visible under heavier traffic load as shown in Fig. 3. However, routing based on delay requires significant higher overhead than routing based on path length as packets carry extra fields to collect timestamp information at each hop, which implies longer transmission times. In fact, when no other flows are present in the network, routing based on delay performs worse than routing based on hop count because of this extra overhead as reported in Fig. 3, which shows the corresponding average round-trip delay of the packets for the experiments.

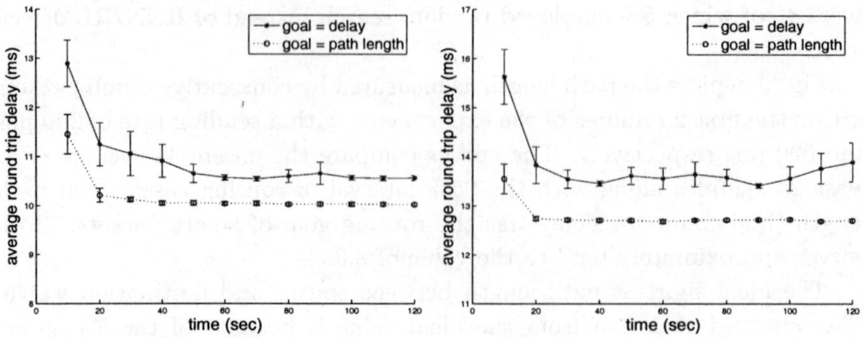

Figure 2. Average round-trip delay over time of dumb packets either when delay or path length (hop count) was the minimization goal for 200 pps and 500 pps respectively

These results confirm the ability of the algorithm to minimize a target cost function and shows the problem that this paper is addressing. In the next section, a simulation based study reports on the solution that we propose.

4. Wireless Ad Hoc Simulations

A simulation study was conducted in *Network Simulator 2* (NS-2) to test the algorithm in a wireless setting.

The algorithm differs in a few details to the one used in the experimental testbed study. Simulations were based on AHCPN [9] and not CPN, so a proportion of smart packets (5%) employed broadcast (flooding) to move in the network. The topology consisted of 7×7 equally-spaced stationary nodes producing a grid setting where only horizontal or vertical communications were possible. The smart to dumb packet ratio was fixed to 0.20 for all experiments and nodes' buffers prioritized smart packets and their acknowledgments.

Ad hoc CPN (AHCPN) is a mobile ad hoc network protocol [10]. As opposed to other protocols in the area [11,12,13,14], the AHCPN protocol restricts the use of flooding (broadcast) and replaces most of the routing decisions with decisions driven by the RNN/RL algorithm. The rate of broadcasts is controlled by a fixed parameter, which was defined as indicated before.

Four CBR traffic streams of 500 byte-length packets were established from each corner of the grid and destined to the opposite diagonal corner. Experiments were repeated to consider three different types of goals: round-trip delay, hop count or a composition of hop count and buffer occupancy. The capacity of each node's buffer was defined as 50 packets.

The average results for the four flows in round trip delay of both smart packet and dumb packets are reported in Fig. 3. The average delay experienced by smart packets and their acknowledgments is much smaller than the corresponding delay of dumb packets because of the priority queuing for these packets (i.e. a high priority packet moves to the head of the queue regardless of the number of packets waiting). The delay observed in packets, either smart or dumb, is better when delay was an explicit metric in the goal of smart packets than when using hop count.

The exposed terminal problem present in the network, may starve nodes located in the vicinity of congested areas. These nodes will report empty buffers even if their channels are congested because of others' transmissions. However, smart packets were able to make the right decisions and the observed performance of the combined metric of hop count and buffer occupancy was almost indistinguishable from that of explicit round-trip delay. An explanation for this effect is in the feedback flow that acknowledgements create. If a smart packet selects a path containing starved nodes, future dumb packets will start congesting the buffers of the path. The information about congested areas will eventually become available to future smart packets, which will have the necessary information to avoid these areas.

Fig. 5 shows the packet loss ratio for smart and dumb packets. Fig. 6 shows the loss ratio for their respective acknowledgments for the experiment. The loss experienced by smart packets and their acknowledgments is approximately constant because of their higher priority in the nodes' queues. Hop count as the unique metric performed the worst of the three cases. The other two cases offered a very similar packet loss ratio.

5. Conclusions

This paper has proposed the use of alternative metrics for CPN routing, expressed as a combined goal formula for smart packets that effectively produce a balancing of network traffic and low-delay paths for end-to-end streams of dumb packets. A routing goal that combines path length and buffer occupancy in nodes offers the advantage of producing approximately the same performance as that of using delay but with a smaller packet overhead. In some cases, as demonstrated by measurements done in a network testbed, delay based routing may produce higher latency than path length-

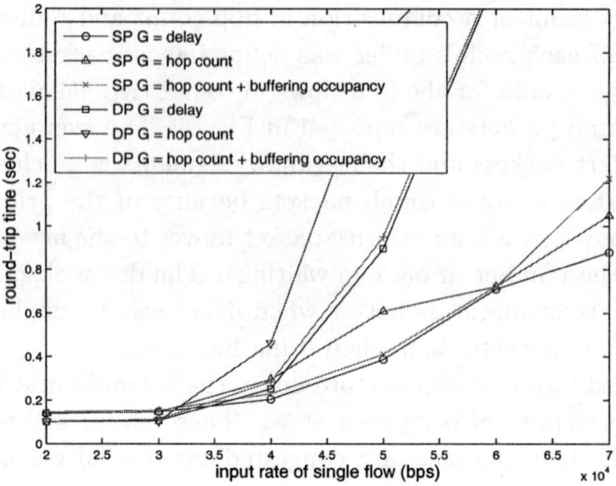

Figure 3. Round-trip latency of smart and dumb packets

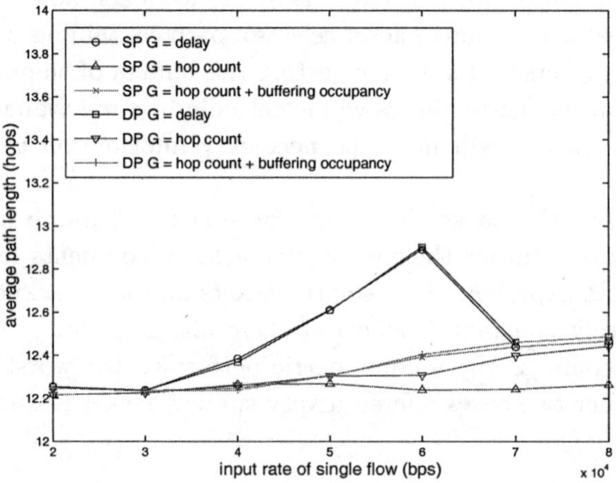

Figure 4. Average path length of smart and dumb packets. Note that after 60 Kbps, congestion becomes network-wide and delay based goal routing starts preferring again the shortest path.

based route as the extra overhead in packets impose a longer transmission time. Simulations have shown that smart packets that consider individual nodes' congestion can discover paths with similar performance dynamics to considering delay, but with a significant saving in packet length and transmission time.

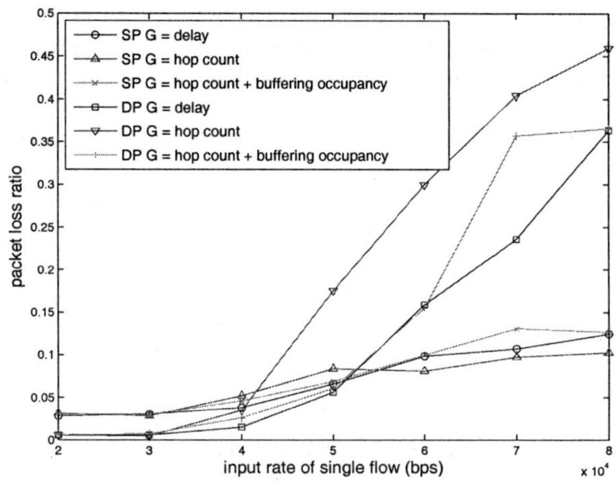

Figure 5. Smart and dumb packets loss ratio

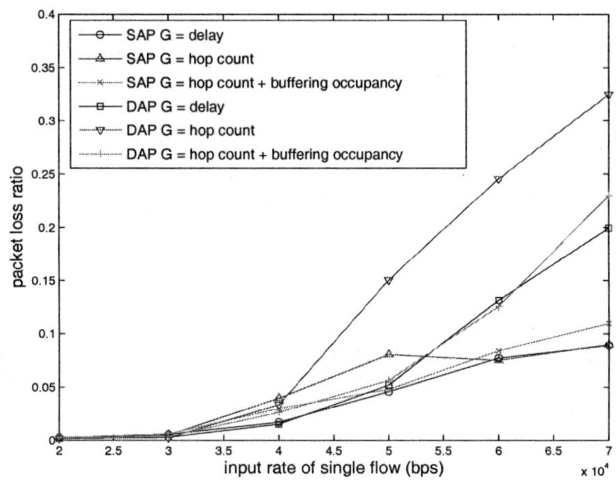

Figure 6. Acknowledgement packets loss ratio

Acknowledgments

The authors wish to express their gratitude to Prof. E. Gelenbe for his support in the completion of this research work.

References

1. G. Malkin, Routing information protocol version 2, *Internet RFC 2453* (1998).

2. J. Moy, Open shortest path first version 2, *Internet RFC 2328* (1998).
3. Z. Wang and J. Crowcroft, Qos routing for supporting resource reservation, *IEEE Journal of Selected Areas in Communications*, **14**, 7 (1996) pp. 1228–1234.
4. R. Guering and A. Orda, QoS-based routing in networks with inaccurate information, in *Proceedings of Infocom* (Japan 1997).
5. B. Awerbuch, Y. Azar, and S. Plotkin, Throughput-competitive online routing, in *Proceeding of the 34th Symposium Foundations of Computer Science* (1993) pp. 32–40.
6. H. F. Salama, D. S. Reeves, and Y. Viniotis, A distributed algorithm for delay-constrained unicast routing, in *Proceedings of Infocom* (Japan 1997).
7. G. Chen and N. Ansari, Multiple additively constrained path selection, *IEE Proceedings* **149** 5 (2002) pp. 237–241.
8. Erol Gelenbe, Ricardo Lent, and Zhiguang Xu, Design and performance of cognitive packet networks, *Performance Evaluation* **46** (2001) pp. 155–176.
9. Erol Gelenbe and Ricardo Lent, Power-aware ad hoc cognitive packet networks, Ad Hoc Networks Journal **3** 2 (2004) pp. 205–216.
10. Elizabeth Royer and C-K. Toh, A review of current routing protocols for ad-hoc mobile wireless networks, *IEEE Personal Communications* (1999) pp. 46–55.
11. David B. Johnson, Davis A. Maltz, Yih-Chun Hu, and Jorjeta G. Jetcheva, The dynamic source routing protocol for mobile ad hoc networks *IETF DRAFT* (2001).
12. Charles E. Perkins and Elizabeth M. Royer, Ad hoc on demand distance vector routing, in *Proceedings of the 2nd IEEE Workshop on Mobile Computing Systems and Applications* (1999) pp. 90–100.
13. Chai-Keong Toh, A novel distributed routing protocol to support ad-hoc mobile computing, in *Proceedings of the IEEE fifteenth annual international conference on computers and communications* (Phoenix 1996) pp. 480–486.
14. S. Corson, S. Papademetriou, P. Papadopoulos, and V. Park, An internet manet encapsulation protocol (IMEP) specification, *IETF DRAFT* (1998).

A REQUIRED LEVEL FOR OPTICAL NETWORKS BUSINESS MODEL: INTEGRATED NEUTRAL TOPOLOGY OPTIMIZER (INTO)

Haydar CUKURTEPE[1], Sefer KURNAZ[1]
[1]Aeronautics and Space Technologies Institute (ASTIN) Computer Science Dept. 34149 Yesilyurt/Istanbul TURKEY

A.Behzat SAHIN[2]
[2]Electrical-Electronic Eng. Dept. Middle East Technical University 06531 Ankara TURKEY

Abstract. Today's business model, although boundaries are not clear, comprises of several layers: End users, Internet Service Providers (ISP), exchange points, and carriers. Arbitrary technological upgrades and absence of interaction in this layered business model, have led to critical system shortcomings. Foremost issues caused by this model are: 1.) unoptimized topology, 2.) low-liquidity, 3.) waste of resources, 4.) reduced interoperability.

We introduce a new and novel concept for coping with the issues and shortcomings of today's business model. Integrated Neutral Topology Optimizer (INTO) is an over all arbiter layer with commercial functionality. This layer operates with ISPs and carriers during leasing process and continually monitors the traffic to optimize the bandwidth usage. Inter-and-intra carrier connections are made and maintained according to the decisions of this layer.

1. Introduction

The proliferation of Internet usage has led telecommunication corporations to invest more resources in communication networks in order to provide widespread and enhanced quality of services with more capacity via newly developed techniques. All optical networks employing Wavelength Division Multiplexing (WDM), which is an advanced technology that enables the transmission of multiple wavelengths over a single fiber, are believed [1][2] to be the next generation networks that can meet the increasing demand for bandwidth of the end users.

Today's business model, although boundaries are not clear, comprises of several layers: End users, Internet Service Providers (ISP), Exchange Points, and Carriers. The proliferation of both demand and supply caused diversity in all layers of telecommunication market. Arbitrary technological upgrades and absence of interaction in this layered business model, have led to critical system shortcomings. Foremost issues caused by this model are: 1.) unoptimized topology, 2.) low-liquidity, 3.) waste of resources, 4.) reduced interoperability.

We introduce a new and novel concept for coping with the issues and shortcomings of today's business model. Integrated Neutral Topology Optimizer (INTO) is an over all arbiter layer with commercial functionality. This layer operates with ISPs and carriers during leasing process and continually monitors the traffic to optimize the bandwidth

usage. Inter-and-intra carrier connections are made and maintained according to the decisions of this layer.
Network utilization, protection, investment consultations, growing revenues are some of the benefits we may expect from employing INTO.
We simulated a sample topology with three carriers, each of them reluctant to use others' topologies. After 1000000 random attempts with 0.9 weights of fitting simulated sample physical model, we obtained that the carriers' average bandwidth consumption is ± %70 more than optimal solution.
The paper is organized as follows. In section 2 we give an overview of current state of bandwidth market. Section 3 mentions about bandwidth as a commodity. Section 4 describes the shortcomings of the business model in use. Section 5 provides a sample scenario and simulation results. In section 6, we present our novel model. In section 7, we summarize our discussions and point out the future steps in our research.

2. Business model

The "business model" we mentioned is a wholesale model that distinguishes itself from its retail telecommunications counterpart in the aspect that participants (hereafter referred to as Carriers) in this model does not provide services to "end users". Rather they provide capacity and other services to Internet service providers (ISP), or other large institutional users of bandwidth.
This model, consists of: i.) Carriers (Carriers' Carrier, Interexchange Carriers, Network Providers, Communication Suppliers, and Local Exchange Carriers), ii.) Internet Service Providers, and iii.) Exchange Points (Carrier Hotels, Pooling Points, Exchange Hotels) [2] [3] [4].
Several different types of telecom carriers offer wholesale services in the marketplace, including carriers, local exchange carriers, resellers and even ISPs and other service providers [5] [6] [7] [8] [9].
ISPs provide Internet access to end users (whether at a scale of a person or an institution) by leasing wavelength or sub-wavelength granularity channels from carriers, and flexibly managing their backbone to resell the bandwidth with added values (Quality of Service (QoS), security, applications for end users, etc.) [3].
Newly constructed structure of the backbone network conduced to the emergence of several bandwidth Exchange Points, e.g., Band-X, Arbinet, Telco Exchange, and Bandwidth Market [10] [11] [12] [13] which include a marketplace for suppliers and buyers of bandwidth. These companies act as bandwidth market intermediaries where several functionalities can be provided to both buyers and sellers. A bandwidth intermediary can function as an exchange, broker or hybrid of the two.[14] Physically an exchange point may be a fiber interconnection and switching site in a particular geographical location.
It is assumed that a bandwidth exchange trades well-defined bandwidth contracts [15]. Each contract refers to a bandwidth segment between two exchange points where a bandwidth segment is an abstraction of one or more high capacity networks

providing connectivity between the two exchange points on definite duration at a specified QoS.

3. Bandwidth as a Commodity

Seeing that bandwidth became an article of trade which can be sold, purchased, or leased on a global scale, network markets declared it as their primary commodity. They are expected to mature quickly into markets similar to today's electricity markets where even ten-minute blocks are priced, traded, and settled [3]. In this perspective bandwidth markets will allow service providers to drastically reduce their capital and operational expenditure, by employing online bandwidth provisioning.

Commodities need to fulfill three criteria to be tradable on an exchange. Firstly, the market of the commodity must be liquid enough in demand and supply. This means that a market participant can be sure of finding counterparty willing to buy or sell the good at any time. Secondly, commodities are characterized as being interchangeable regardless of its source. Lastly, price volatility is a prerequisite for functional derivatives markets. [16].

Nonstorability is one of the most important properties of bandwidth which means that the unused capacity is an immediate loss of revenue for carriers [17].

The network structure and the market's optimal point-to-point routing selection introduce a new arbitrage condition called geographical or network arbitrage [18]

4. Disadvantages of Today's Business Model

In today's business model every ISP has to ensure its own topology's cost efficiency. On the other hand carriers are reluctant to share information about their routing tables, paths and the traffic load in the meantime, because of commercial concerns. ISPs cannot monitor the traffic on the path, over which their packets flow. Consequently they cannot optimize their virtual topology.

Today's technology allows ISPs to purchase or lease bandwidth in a matter of seconds or less whereas the business model does not allow this allocation in such a short time. Bandwidth allocation is realized by a contract, including the capacity, source and destination nodes, QoS, and the time period. Trading by contract impedes the business, and this causes illiquidity. In today's network, bandwidth provisioning can take weeks, or even months [2]. Whereas observations on real networks show that the traffic rates between node pairs fluctuate distinguishably during the day. The figure-1 depicted below shows a sample daily traffic fluctiotion [21].

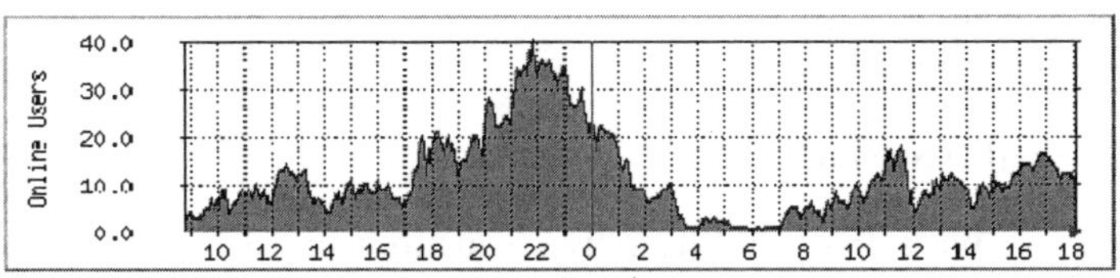

Fig. 1 Daily Traffic Fluctuation

ISPs have to provide confident Internet access to their customers. One popular way of overcoming the difficulty in providing assured services is to provide more capacity than the average demand. ISPs mostly have no opportunity to buy or lease bandwidth as needed. However traded bandwidth is monthly priced, the contracts are usually but not obligatory made for at least twelve months [10] [11] [12] [13].
Waste of sources caused by coarsely made business model is compensated with higher prices which causes demand mitigation in long term.
With respect to the nonstorability of bandwidth, contract making durations cause revenue loss for carriers. Even if there exists some bandwidth on which both buyers and sellers would agree, this loss occurs. When we consider the mean contract making time of 15 days, regarding the real prices, carriers' revenue loss caused by this contract making process can be estimated as shown in the Figure-2. Contract making time does not differ with respect to the contract duration, that is, the time required for 12 month contracts is the same as that for 24 months.
While working with more than one carrier, interoperability and management gets harder and becomes almost impossible to deal with, due to developing technologies and increasing demand. Carriers have different costs, capacities, technologies and different types of management in providing their services.

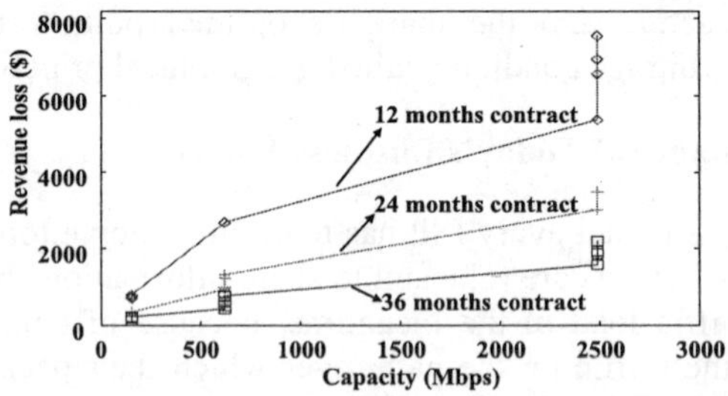

Fig. 2- Revenue loss caused by Contract Making Process The actual cost values used in the figure belongs to Los Angeles-New York pair taken from [13] on April 2005.

An ISP that leases more than one bandwidth from different carriers (e.g. carriers' carriers, resellers) to recover its data packets may unintentionally fail to attain its aim. Different carriers may use the same physical connection to transmit that ISP's packets. Since the carriers keep their geographical topology secret, an ISP can never be %100 certain about their packet's protection.
Today's business model suffers in the sense that a true network arbitrage condition is not maintained due to the lack of cooperation among carriers and overly complicated interrelations in the business layers [22].

5. An illustrative Scenario

Model description: We employ an illustrative scenario, using a 7-node sample model in Figure 3, to demonstrate how shortcomings of present model occur.

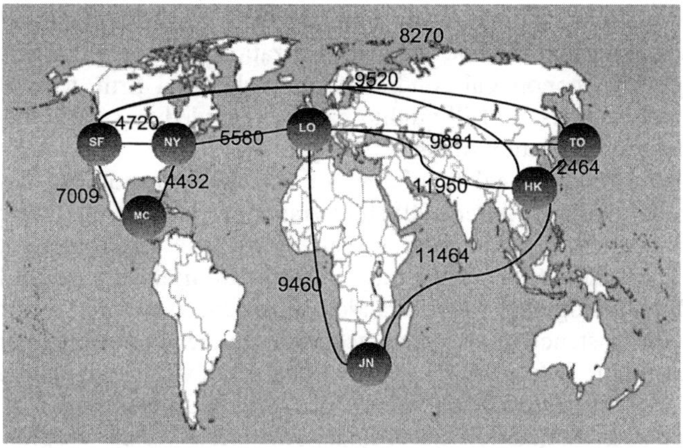

Fig. 3 Sample topology

These seven nodes represent seven major cities of the global Internet network. Physical links, depicted by lines, and node to node distances are assigned from the actual data, where in some cases intermediate junctions are not considered.

Assumptions: We assume an undirected virtual topology comprising of bidirectional lightpaths in this example. Physical distance is assumed to be the dominating factor in cost calculation. The capacity of the links and their respective traffic loads are considered to be not significantly different.

We considered three carriers, and each carrier can access throughout the whole network by using only its own physical topology. We evaluated random generated physical topologies for these carriers in order to estimate the advantage of the optimal access case. Carriers are reluctant to share any information about their topologies due to commercial concerns. Moreover carriers would like to employ only their own infrastructure while routing the packets, neglecting any surplus topology capacity. An exemplary case in which carriers utilize their own topologies for providing lightpaths from Mexico City (MC) to Johannesburg (JN), neglecting other carriers' infrastructures is given in Table 1.

Table 1 A sample case demonstrating the source waste during lightpath assignment

1	Optimum	MC,NY,LO,JN	19472	-	-
	Carriers	Intermediary Nodes	Total Distance (km)	Difference from optimum path (km)	(%)
2	A	MC,SF,HK,JN	27993	8521	44
3	B	MC,NY,LO,HK,JN	33426	13954	72
4	C	MC,SF,TO,HK,JN	29007	9535	49

The optimum path is given at the first row, which can only be provided by an over carriers approach. The differences given at the fourth and fifth columns account for the unused topology capacity, in other words waste of resources. This waste, which is caused by carriers' inclination on utilizing their own topology, is one of the most important factors that impede the standardization of bandwidth pricing, incidentally the firm policy, economical conditions of market and firm, temporary congestions, different technologies, and illiquidity can be regarded as some other factors that are stalling the standardization of bandwidth pricing.

We simulated the physical topologies of carriers with possible connections on the given sample topology. After 100*10000 random trials with 0.9 weights, the carriers' average bandwidth consumption is calculated as ± %70 more than the optimal solution. The distribution graph obtained from 100 trials is given in Figure 4 (a). The edges of the topology are formed randomly and the associated weight determines the possibility of existence of any edge, according to the given sample physical topology. As seen in Figure 4 (a), the range of surplus bandwidth usage varies from ±%55 to ±%78 for weight of 0.9. When the weight is varied between 0.1 and 1, the average surplus topology utilization accordingly changes.Average surplus utilization with respect to weight is shown in Figure 4 (b) When the weight is less than 0.6, carriers cannot access the whole topology on solely their own infrastructures. Surplus bandwidth usage decreases as the weight increases.

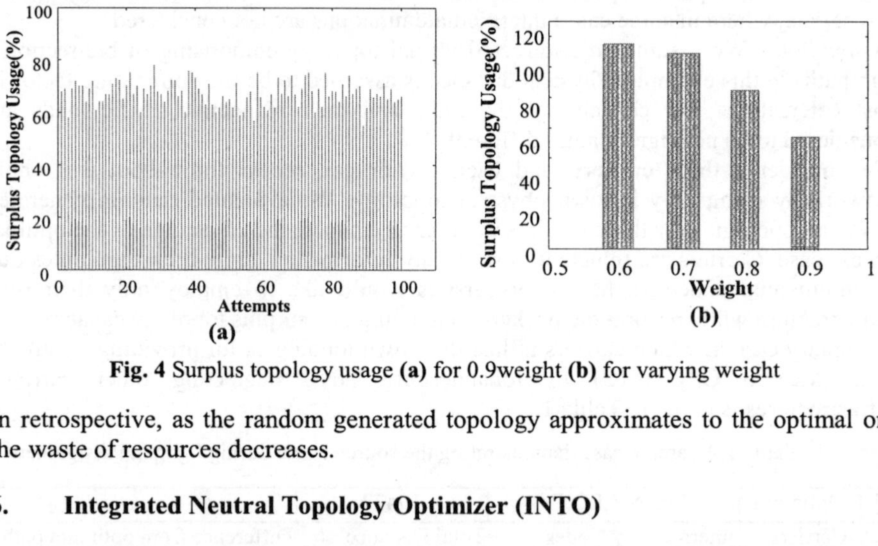

Fig. 4 Surplus topology usage **(a)** for 0.9weight **(b)** for varying weight

In retrospective, as the random generated topology approximates to the optimal one the waste of resources decreases.

6. Integrated Neutral Topology Optimizer (INTO)

A new model conducing liquidity, low-cost, protection, flexibility and rapid provisioning is what is required after the outgrowth of the present defective business model. Integrated Neutral Topology Optimizer (INTO) (Figure 5) is an arbiter layer over ISPs and carriers, which realizes the ISPs' demands via the most suitable carriers' resources. This layer operates through protocols, set up with both the ISPs and carriers, which gives INTO the responsibility for: i.) ISPs' assurance for establishing the optimum virtual topology, ii.)Not disclosing any commercial secret, iii.)Consulting for investment, iv.) Being neutral against any institution bound within the protocols.

Although integrated network management is unavoidable, the business model in use is far from facilitating efficient interoperability and manageability. ISPs have to ensure its own topology's optimality while working with many carriers. Every path on the virtual topology of ISPs is established by a contract, which includes so much difficulty. New techniques are not adopted simultaneously and many techniques are in use. It gets harder and becomes almost impossible to deal with, due to developing technologies and increasing demand. Since today's business model suffers in the sense that a true network arbitrage condition is not maintained due to the lack of cooperation among carriers and overly complicated interrelations in the business layers, employing an "integrated layer" entitled to access the whole network's infrastructure and traffic information is necessary.
Another factor makes manageability harder is the diversity in capacity that is sold. In bandwidth market, companies sell different types of capacity (e.g. point-to-point fiber or coaxial lines, satellite frequency band) with various parameters: assured rate, burst rate, contract term. As a result a layer that is expected to bring solution must be integrated and have the ability to operate over different types of capacity in order to interoperate through carriers.

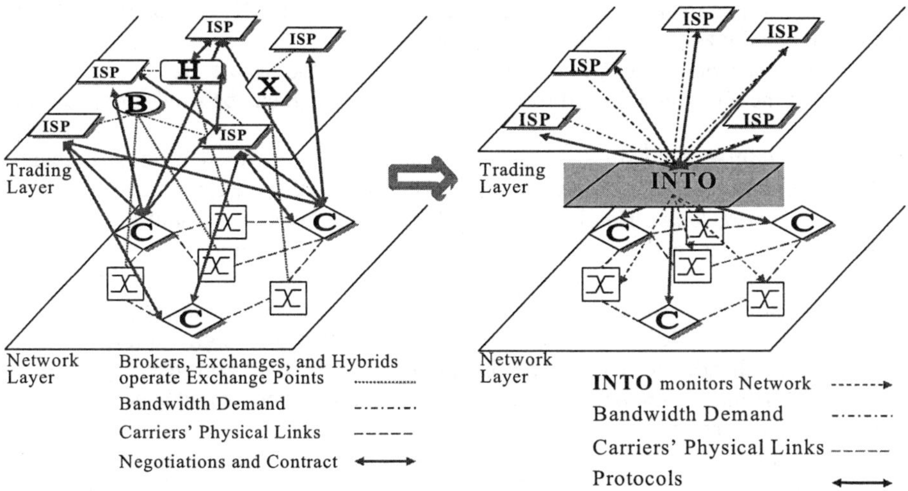

Fig. 5 (a) Today's Business Model (b) Proposed Business Model

As the bandwidth is a commodity good, both buyers and sellers of the market must be satisfied. This satisfaction can occur only by a neutral approach. It is estimated that about $25 billion worth of telecommunication capacity is bought and sold worldwide annually [23]. However, in the view of the fact that the participants in the bandwidth market operate regarding only their own commercial concerns, the market would not reach the expected liquidity and stability. Employing a commercially "neutral layer" operating through maximized mutual gains principle will provide the market with improved liquidity, stability, maturity, and robustness. Continuously traded liquid markets allow the participants to continuously adjust their position.

Optimization of virtual topology has two aspects. One of them is minimizing the total cost of the flowing traffic over the whole physical topology and the other is maximizing the throughput. INTO continually monitors the traffic to optimize the bandwidth usage with the authority of both carriers and ISPs. Inter-and-intra carrier connections are made and maintained according to its decisions.

7. Expected Benefits of INTO

Development of a global arbitrage system which is not monopolistic will lead to utilization of fair-share, fair- access principle in the bandwidth market. By employing INTO we may expect improvements in the issues mentioned below.

Protection: On the grounds that INTO monitors the traffic and makes decisions about routing, with the authority of both carriers and ISPs, protection can be guaranteed whenever any ISP asks for.

Topology optimization: Cost optimization can be achieved by sustaining the network arbitrage condition, which states that the market price for any point-to-point capacity must be minimized over all possible routings. Employing an INTO provides not only cost efficiency but also maximum throughput.

Consulting Investment: INTO, due to its monitoring the whole traffic over many carriers, has the most reliable and recent information which can be used for consulting investment.

Price Estimation: Price estimation is one of the main issues for market participants. All factors can be controlled or watched closely, and possibly be estimated by INTO.

Reduction of work loads: Employing an INTO reduces operational and trading work loads thus let carriers and ISPs concentrate on their service quality.

Growing Revenue: Revenue growth provided by INTO have more than one aspect. Carriers are protected from revenue loss that caused by contract making process. The virtual topologies of ISPs are optimized. An optimized and high liquidity market eliminates the handicaps caused by institutional and other end users' access to Internet. Consequently the perfect market stimulates the numbers and access demands of end users to increase.

Developed algorithms on topology reconfiguration and adaptation rely on the assumption that the ISPs or enterprises are running their own WDM networks [24] [25] [26] [27]. On the contrary, this perfect situation scarcely occurs in real world. Employing an INTO gives researchers the opportunity to develop such algorithms with ideal market assumptions.

Online Bandwidth Provisioning: Likewise the variety of suppliers, ISPs' demands diversify in time and capacity. They usually do not demand standard capacity for specific period of time. Problems caused by diversity of demands are expected to be overcome by online bandwidth provisioning, that is hour-by-hour real-time online market trading with little delay and without any of the current business model's encumbrances.

8. Conclusion

We introduce a new and novel concept for coping with the issues and shortcomings of today's business model. Integrated Neutral Topology Optimizer (INTO) is an over all arbiter layer with commercial functionality. This layer operates with ISPs and carriers during leasing process and continually monitors the traffic to optimize the bandwidth usage. Inter-and-intra carrier connections are made and maintained according to the decisions of this layer. When working with more than one carrier, interoperability and management gets harder and becomes almost impossible to deal with. Although today's business model operates without an institution such as INTO, due to the developing technologies, proliferation of usage, and diversification of access demands, it will be essential to employ INTO in order to cope with such a complicated market.

Network utilization, protection, investment consultations, and growing revenues are some of the benefits we may expect from employing INTO. Once a functional market emerges, telecommunications companies may mitigate the investment related risks.

References

[1] Gencata A., Singhal N. and Mukherjee B, Overview of Optical Communication Networks: Current and Future Trends, (2002).

[2] Mukherjee B., R&D Priorities and Challenges for Optical Networking: Migrating Theory to Practice, preprint (2002).

[3] Gencata A. and Mukherjee B., Virtual Topology Adaptation for WDM Mesh Networks Under Dynamic Traffic, IEEE/ACM Transactions on networking, (2003) Vol. 11, No,2.

[4] Bhatia R., et al. Algorithmic Aspects of Bandwidth Trading, Bell Labs. (2003).

[5] Level 3 Communications, Inc. www.level3.com

[6] Nortel Communications, http://www.nortel.com

[7] AT&T Communications, http://www.att.com

[8] Sprint Communications, http://www.sprint.com

[9] Lucent Communications, http://www.lucent.com

[10] Band-x, www.band-x.com

[11] Arbinet, www.arbinet.com

[12] Telco Exchange, www.telcoexchange.com

[13] Bandwidth Market, http://www.bandwidthmarket.com

[14] Aboulfadl M., Gupta A., Pradhan R., Kalyanaraman S., A Spot Pricing Framework To Enable Pricing And Risk Management of Inter-Domain Assured Bandwidth Services, Proceedings of the 2002 Winter Simulation Conference (2002).

[15] Cheliotis G., Bandwidth Trading in the Real World: Findings and Implications for Commodities Brokerage, IBM Res. Zurich Research Laboratory (2000).

[16] Arte K., Bandwidth Derivatives under Network Arbitrage, MS., Helsinki Univ. of Technology, (2002).

[17] Kenyon C., Cheliotis G, Stochastic Models for Telecom Commodity Prices, Computer Networks 36, 533-555, (2001).

[18] Chiu, Samuel, S. and Crametz, Jean-Pascal, Taking Advantage of The Emerging Bandwidth Exchange Market, RateXchange Ltd. (1999).

[19] Chiu, Samuel, S. and Crametz, Jean-Pascal, Arbitrage: surprising pricing relationship. Risk Magazine, Bandwidth Special Report, (2000).
[20] Phone+ Magazine http://www.phoneplusmag.com/articles/1c1trade3.html.
[21] Middle East Technical University, http://modems.metu.edu.tr/annexpri1.html.
[22] Broker N., Hrishikesh S., Man. Challenges in the Opt. Telecom. Industry, (2002).
[23] Keppo J., Price of point-to-point bandwidth contracts, University of Michigan, (2003).
[24] Gencata A., Topology and bandwidth adaptation in optical WDM backbone networks with dynamic traffic, Ph.D. Thesis, Istanbul Technical University, Turkey, (2003).
[25] Hu X.D., Jia X., Zhang Mu-H., and Shuai T.P. Multicast Routing and Wavelength Assignment in WDM Networks with Limited Drop-offs, IEEE INFOCOM (2004).
[26] Ramaswami R. and Sivarajan K. N., Routing and wavelength assignment in all-optical networks , IEEE/ACM Trans. Networking, (1995) vol. 3, pp. 489–500.
[27] Mokhtar A. and Azizoglu M., Adaptive wavelength routing in all-optical networks, IEEE/ACM Trans. Networking, vol. 6, pp. (1998) 197–206.

CHARACTERIZING VOICE AND VIDEO TRAFFIC BEHAVIOR OVER THE INTERNET*

PRASAD CALYAM, CHANG-GUN LEE

Department of Electrical and Computer Engineering,
The Ohio State University, Columbus, OH 43210
E-mail: pcalyam@oar.net, cglee@ece.osu.edu

In this paper, we present our research on characterizing voice and video traffic behavior in large-scale Internet Videoconferencing systems. We built a voice and video traffic quality measurement testbed to collect Videoconferencing traffic traces from several sites all over the world that were connected to our testbed via disparate network paths on the Internet. Our testbed also featured the H.323 Beacon, an H.323 session performance assessment tool we have developed, and various other open-source and commercial tools. Our findings obtained by analyzing the collected traffic traces demonstrate the impact of: 1) end-point technologies that use popular audio and video codecs and 2) network health status that is characterized by the variations of delay, jitter, lost and re-ordered packets in the network, on the end-user perception of audiovisual quality. The perceptual data used in our analysis includes both objective and subjective quality measures. These measures were collected from our testbed experiments for a few sample tasks involving various levels of human interaction in Internet Videoconferences.

1. Introduction

Technologies that support Voice and Video conferencing applications over IP networks (VVoIP) [1] [2] have already gained wide acceptance in todays end-user communities. It is becoming increasingly necessary to develop VVoIP friendly network protocols and devices such as firewalls, Network Address Translators (NATs), packet shapers and call-admission control systems that augment existing VVoIP system functionalities, without however affecting end-user experience of audiovisual quality. Developing VVoIP friendly network protocols and system devices requires a sound understanding of the VVoIP traffic characteristics. Simulation studies fail to provide a realistic environment in which vital VVoIP traffic characteristics can be

*This work has been supported in part by The Ohio Board of Regents

understood at a fundamental level. Hence, we have developed a novel measurement methodology for collecting real-world Videoconferencing traces. We have also developed techniques that could be used to effectively analyze the trace data in order to better understand the impact of factors such as end-point technologies and network health status on the end-user perception of audiovisual quality.

Many of the earlier attempts to characterize VVoIP traffic [4] [5] focused on voice traffic studies alone, and among these only few addressed issues of traffic characterization in the purview of end-user perception of audio quality. Studies such as [6] [7] discussed QoS issues relating to video traffic, in only a LAN environment, with a minimal setup of test cases and end-points. Their main focus was on studying frame rates issues, again without emphasis on end-user perception of the video quality for the various test scenarios. Other studies such as [8] chose a wider group of participants for obtaining perceptual quality evaluations of video. However, the results of their study were limited in scope since they covered only jitter and packet loss issues for streams originating from a single video codec (MPEG-1).

To the best of our knowledge, our study is the first to comprehensively characterize both audio and video traffic streams with the following considerations:

- The use of various network health scenarios and multiple end-point technologies (Ex., codecs, vendors, pc-based vs. appliance-based equipment) and diverse end-user demographics to obtain subjective and objective audiovisual quality assessments
- A study of the above audiovisual quality assessments for various Videoconferencing tasks that feature various levels of end-user interactions routinely seen in Internet Videoconferences

The remainder of the paper is organized as follows: Section 2 describes the methodology for collecting the traffic traces. Section 3 discusses our analysis of the collected traffic traces. Section 4 concludes the paper.

2. Measurement Methodology

2.1. *World-wide Testbed Setup*

Our world-wide testbed (shown in Fig. 1) was used to collect over 300 VVoIP traffic traces from 26 sites in 14 countries (shown in Fig. 2) that participated in one-on-one testing to rate audiovisual quality for various Videoconferencing tasks. Prior to our testing with each site, we gathered various types of information such as the participant profile, experience of the participant with VVoIP, site-network connectivity, and end-point technology routinely used for audio and video conferences . The participants included various demographics of end-users: Videoconferencing Co-ordinators, Network Engineers, Instructors, Graduate Students and IT Managers. Internet connectivity at the sites included LAN, research, commercial and last-mile DSL, Cable Modem and Satellite network links. Participating sites used various commercial and open-source VVoIP end-point technologies. The various audio codecs observed to be used at the endpoints included GSM, G.711 and G.722 and the various video codecs included H.261, H.262 and H.263.

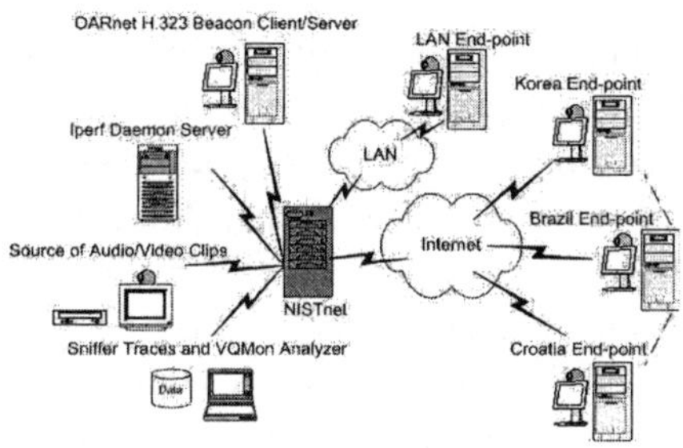

Figure 1. Overall World-wide Test Setup

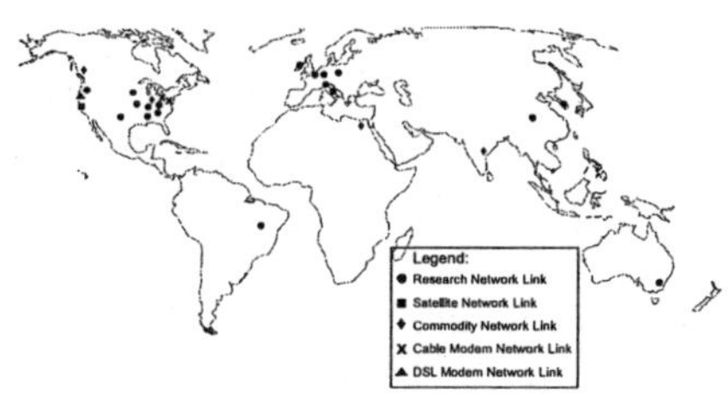

Figure 2. World-wide sites participating in the testing

Many tools were used to obtain the VVoIP traffic traces necessary for analysis. Table 1 shows the various tools used and their purpose in the testing. Measurement data was collected for both LAN and Internet tests. The basic difference between the LAN and Internet tests in terms of the NISTnet settings for generating different network health scenarios was that- in the LAN environment, the delay, jitter and loss values configured on the NISTnet were the overall values in the end-to-end path. In the Internet tests, the network paths had inherent values of delay, jitter and loss. Hence to configure any necessary end-to-end delay, jitter and loss values for the Internet tests, a network path characteristics pre-determination step was required for each site. To accurately obtain the inherent network path characteristics, we used a heuristic approach using the data obtained from the OARnet H.323 Beacon and NLANR Iperf. The end-to-end delay, jitter and loss values configured on the NISTnet were obtained by deducting inherent path characteristics values from the LAN settings.

Table 1. Tools Used in the Testing

Tool Name	Tool Description	Purpose of Tool in Testing
OARnet H.323 Beacon	H.323 session performance measurement tool	For network path characterization and subjective quality ratings
Ethereal	Network traffic sniffer and trace analysis tool	To capture traffic traces for analysis
Telchemy VQMon	Network traffic trace analyzer for VoIP Systems	For objective quality ratings
NISTnet	Network-emulation tool	To introduce delay, jitter and loss in network paths
NLANR Iperf	TCP/UDP throughput measurement tool	For network path characterization

In our study, we employed both the subjective and objective quality assessment methods to determine end-user perception of audiovisual quality for various network health scenarios. To obtain subjective quality assessment scores from the test participants, we extended the Quality Assessment Slider methodology presented in [3] and developed our own slider that was integrated into our H.323 Beacon Client GUI. Participants ranked the audiovisual quality for the various Videoconferencing tasks on a scale of 1 to 5, which is the Mean Opinion Score (MOS) ranking technique. To obtain objective quality assessment scores, we utilized the Telchemy VQMon tool [11] that implements the E-Model and uses traffic traces obtained for the various Videoconferencing tasks as an input for the analysis. The E-Model is a well established computational model that uses transmission parameters to predict the subjective quality.

2.2. *Quantizing Network Health Scenarios*

Table 2. Nine Network health scenarios for NISTnet Settings

	S1	S2	S3	S4	S5	S6	S7	S8	S9
Delay	G	A	P	G	G	P	G	G	A
Jitter	G	A	P	G	P	G	G	A	G
Loss	G	A	P	P	G	G	A	G	G

Legend: G: Good, A: Acceptable, P: Poor, S1-S9: Scenario (1-9)

Our definition of network health refers to the effect of the combined interaction of delay, jitter and loss. The three network parameters co-exist for every path in the Internet at any given point of time. In our design of experiments, we employed a full factorial design for the three parameters i.e. we emulated 3^3=27 scenarios that covered every possible network health status; each status comprising of different levels of delay, jitter and loss. The levels chosen for the scenarios were derived from our earlier work [9] where the performance bounds of the network parameters were mapped to Good, Acceptable and Poor grades of quality as experienced by an end-user. The Good grade corresponds to delay values of (0-150) ms, jitter values of (0-20) ms and loss values of (0-0.5) %. The Acceptable grade corresponds to delay values of (150-300) ms, jitter values of (20-50) ms and loss values of (0.5-1.5) %. The Poor grade corresponds to delay values $>$ 300ms, jitter values $>$ 50ms, loss values $>$ 1.5%.

We performed extensive LAN tests that covered all of the 27 scenarios and selected 9 scenarios shown in Table 2 for Internet measurements whose results in essence reflected the results of the 27 scenarios. To understand this selection process, we can consider an example that uses a three-letter notation which will be used in the remainder of this paper to indicate network health status. A (GGG) notation implies values of (delay, jitter, loss) in the good performance bounds and in that order. Letters A and P are used to indicate values in the acceptable and poor performance bounds respectively. Hence, a GGG condition refers to the best provisioned network path and a PPP condition refers to the worst provisioned network path, that can be seen in real-networks today.

2.3. *Videoconferencing Tasks*

For each of the 9 scenarios described in Section 2.2, a Videoconferencing task was assigned. A Videoconferencing task can basically be any activity that takes place in a routine Videoconference. We associated every Videoconferencing task with an activity level based on the interaction intensity. The activity levels were: low, moderate, or high. There is significant literature recommending strategies for tasks that could be part of assessments of audiovisual quality [3]. All of them recommend that in the participants must be presented with realistic scenarios. Key guidelines proposed in the above literature were followed in the tasks creation, tasks ordering, participants training to score the audiovisual quality and overall environment setup for the assessment.

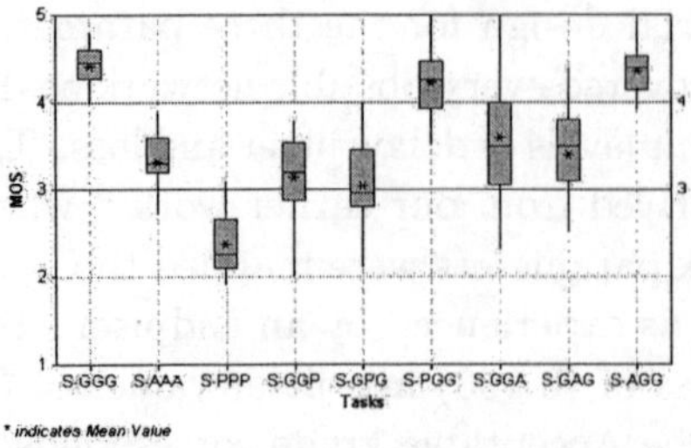

Figure 3. Subjective Quality Rankings for the 9 Network Health Scenarios

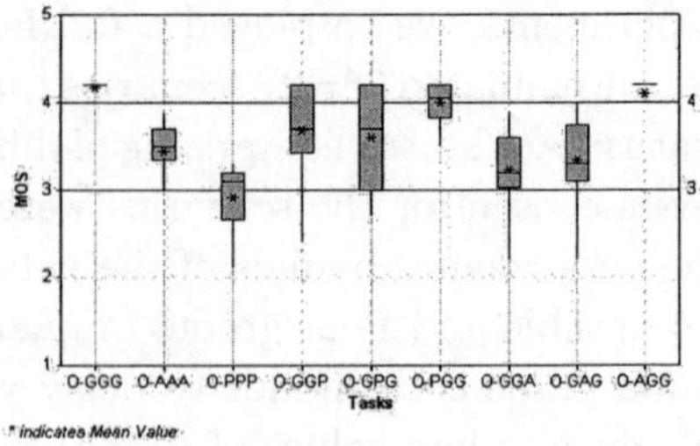

Figure 4. Objective Quality Rankings for the 9 Network Health Scenarios

3. Analysis Of Traffic Traces

3.1. *Subjective versus Objective Quality Rankings*

Figs. 3 and 4 show the box-plots for the various subjective and objective quality rankings determined from the experiments, respectively. We can analyze the results in relation to the horizontal lines marked at MOS values of 3 and 4 which are the boundaries for acceptable and poor grades of perceived audiovisual quality respectively. It can be noticed that both in the case of subjective and objective assessments, the MOS was least affected by the values of delay being in the acceptable or poor performance bounds. A more detailed discussion relating to this observation can be found in Section 3.3. From Figs. 3 and 4, the degradation of the perception of audiovisual quality can be seen to be more sensitive in the case of values of jitter in the acceptable or poor performance bounds compared to that of loss values. This observation illustrates that jitter is the most dominating factor amongst delay, jitter and loss that affects end-user perception of audiovisual quality. The Pearson-Correlation values for delay, jitter and loss for the subjective and objective quality rankings when compared on an individual basis were 82.7%, 73.7% and 71.2%, respectively.

3.2. *Packet-size Distributions versus Activity Levels*

A better understanding of how the network handles various packet size distributions could help in determining important trade-offs at the application level. We explored the packet size distributions for Videoconferencing tasks involving high, moderate and low activity levels. Fig. 5 shows the video packet-sizes distribution data aggregated for all the sites traces for the high-activity level in the GGG network health setting. The video packet-size distributions for moderate and low activity levels were nearly similar to the high-activity level characteristics.

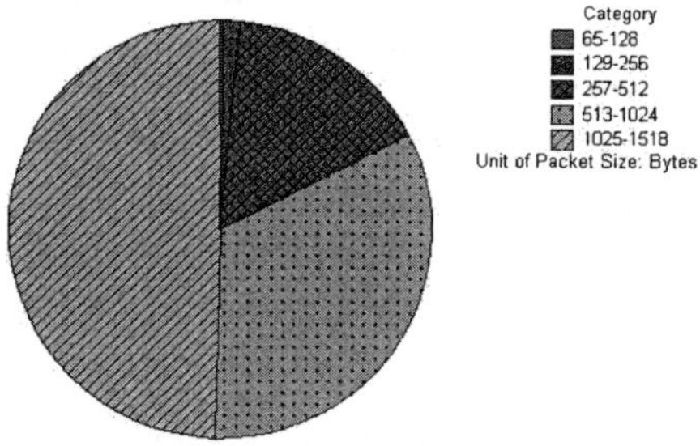

Figure 5. Video Packet-sizes Distribution for High-activity level and GGG Network Health Scenario

Our observations are in accord with the fact that packet sizes generated at the sources are mainly affected by the details and movements encoded in the transmitted images. Since routine Videoconferencing tasks do not generally contain video with high temporal aspects (e.g. Soccer or Hockey sports telecast videos), similarity in the aggregation of packet size distributions for the various network health scenarios and high, moderate and low activity levels in our experiments can be expected.

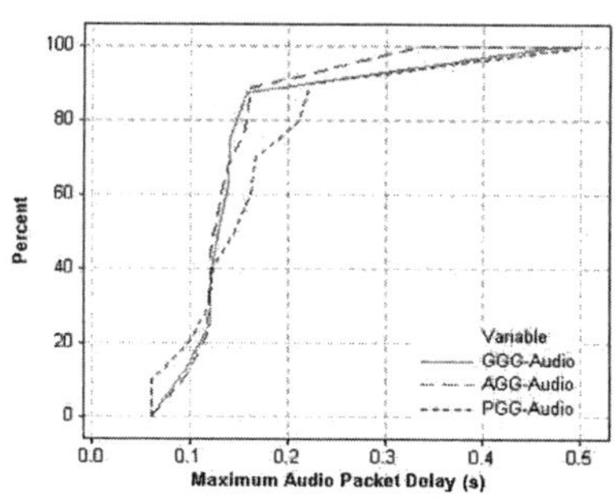

Figure 6. Cumulative Distribution Function of Maximum Inter-packet Audio Delay

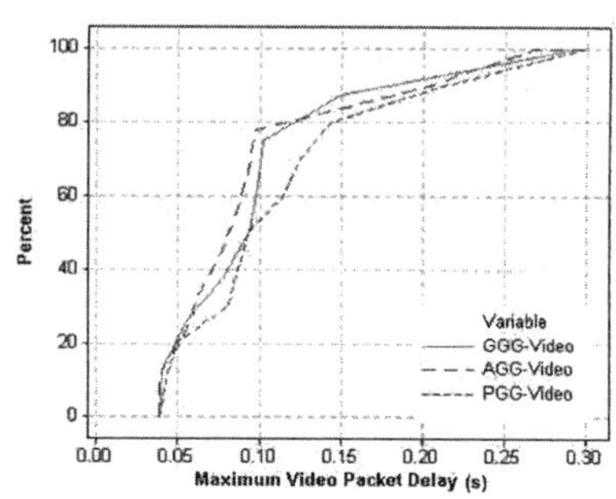

Figure 7. Cumulative Distribution Function of Maximum Inter-packet Video Delay

3.3. *Audio and Video Inter-packet Delays*

Figs. 6 and 7 illustrate the impact of good, acceptable and poor grade network delay values in the network on the maximum inter-packet delays aggregated from all the sites for the audio and video streams at the application level, respectively.

It can be observed from Figs. 6 and 7 that the cdf curves are almost close to one-another, i.e. the maximum packet delays of audio and video packets at the application level are not affected by the delay magnitudes (GGG, AGG, PGG) in the end-to-end network path. This observation concurs with the conclusion presented in Section 3.1 that large values of end-to-end delay do not affect the end-user perception of audiovisual quality. Irrespective of the delay conditions in the network, the packets get relatively offset as they traverse the network. However, it should be noted that large end-to-end delay values hamper the interactivity of human conversations in a Videoconference though not the end-user perception of audiovisual quality.

3.4. *Inter-packet Jitter versus Network Health and Packet Sizes*

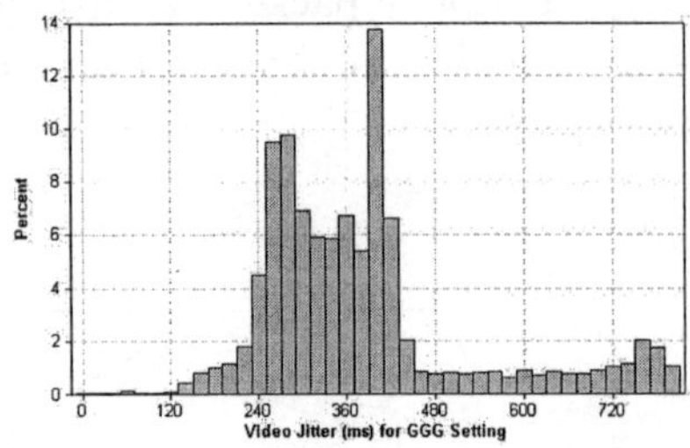

Figure 8. Probability Mass Function of Inter-packet Video Jitter for the GGG Network Health Scenario

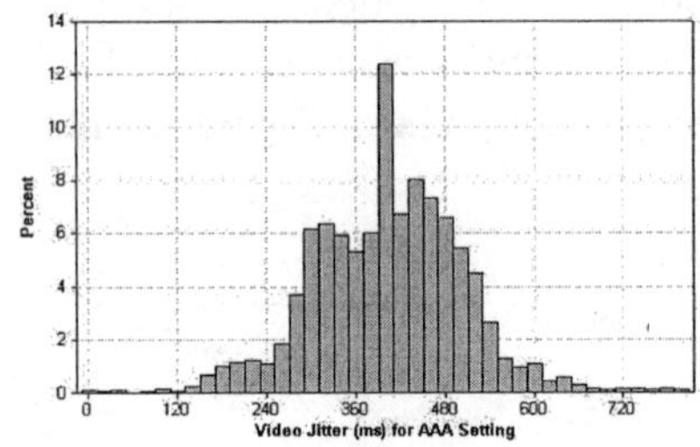

Figure 9. Probability Mass Function of Inter-packet Video Jitter for the AAA Network Health Scenario

Figs. 8 and 9 show the probability mass function or the occurrence frequency of the inter-packet jitter data aggregated from all the sites for the GGG, AAA and PPP network health scenarios. It can be observed from Figs. 8 and 9 that the mass of the inter-packet jitter in the graphs shifts in the direction of the larger jitter values as the network health deteriorates. For the GGG setting, the inter-packet jitter values are all clustered around 400ms, while for the AAA setting, though the highest frequency of inter-packet jitter values are around the 400ms range, there is a relatively higher spread of values greater than 400ms. Depending on the video jitter buffer settings at the end-points, the packets with large inter-packet jitter values get dropped at the application level.

Fig. 10 shows the impact of increasing packet sizes on inter-packet video jitter values for the GGG, AAA and PPP network health scenarios for all the sites. We can note that the inter-packet video jitter tends to decrease when higher packet-sizes are used. Hence, the optimization of the performance of VVoIP traffic streams may be achieved by using relatively larger packet-sizes. If we refer back to Fig. 5, we can notice that general Videoconferencing traffic utilize a higher percentage of large packet-sizes.

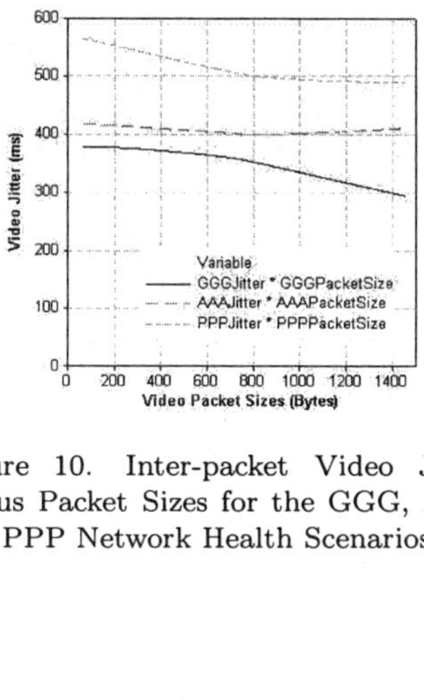

Figure 10. Inter-packet Video Jitter versus Packet Sizes for the GGG, AAA and PPP Network Health Scenarios

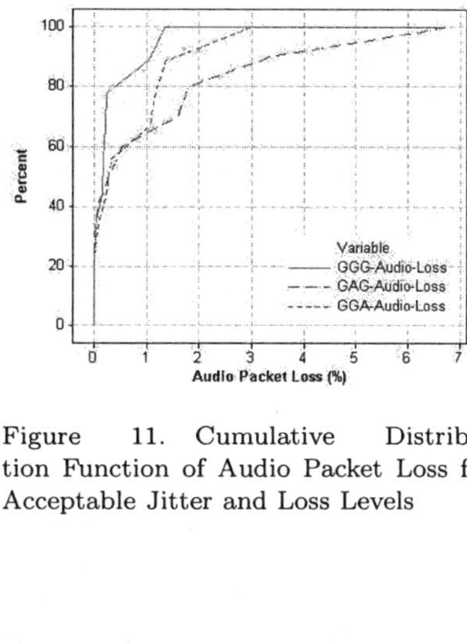

Figure 11. Cumulative Distribution Function of Audio Packet Loss for Acceptable Jitter and Loss Levels

3.5. *Application-level Packet Loss versus Network Health*

Fig. 11 shows the impact of jitter and loss (GAG and GGA) on audio packet loss data aggregated from all the sites at the application level. It is evident that network jitter has a higher impact on the audio packet loss compared to the impact of network delay or loss. Although end-point jitter buffers can be made to dynamically adapt to any significant presence of network jitter for minimizing the jitter buffer discards for packets that do not meet the play-out deadline, they do not significantly ameliorate the stream performance because of the high variability of the network characteristics in the timescale of a typical Videoconferencing session.

4. Conclusion

In this paper, we presented our carefully designed and executed experiments for obtaining VVoIP traffic traces from a testbed involving 26 sites world-wide. The results of our experiments demonstrated the impact of the various end-point technologies and network parameters on the end-user experience of audiovisual quality while using VVoIP applications. We also presented a comparative analysis of the objective and subjective quality assessments for various network health diagnostics. Further, we analyzed the end-to-end performance variations of VVoIP applications by characterizing packet size distributions, packet delay, jitter and loss, for both audio and video streams.

References

1. ITU-T Recommendation H.323, "Infrastructure of audiovisual services- Systems and terminal equipment for audiovisual services", 1999.
2. M. Handley, H. Schulzrinne, E. Schooler, and J. Rosenberg, "SIP: Session Initiation Protocol," IETF RFC 2543, 1999.
3. J. Mullin, L. Smallwood, et.al, "New techniques for assessing audio and video quality in real-time interactive communications", IHM-HCI Tutorial 2001.
4. I. Marsh, F. Li, "Wide-Area measurements of Voice over IP quality", QoFIS 2003.
5. A. Markopoulou, F. Tobagi, M. Karam, "Assessment of VoIP quality over Internet backbones", IEEE INFOCOM 2002.
6. V. Chandrashekar, "A framework for Quality of Service analysis of IP-based video networks", Masters Thesis, North Carolina State University, 2003.
7. R. Finger, A. Davis, "Measuring video quality in Videoconferencing systems", Wainhouse Research Whitepaper, 1998.
8. M. Claypool, J. Tanner, "The effects of jitter on the perceptual quality of video", ACM Multimedia, 1999.
9. P. Calyam, M. Sridharan, W. Mandrawa, P. Schopis, "Performance measurement and analysis of H.323 traffic", PAM 2004.
10. P. Calyam, W. Mandrawa, M. Sridharan, A. Khan, P. Schopis, "H.323 Beacon: An H.323 application related end-to-end performance troubleshooting tool", ACM SIGCOMM NetTs 2004.
11. A. Clark, "Modeling the effects of burst packet loss and recency on subjective voice quality", http://www.telchemy.com
12. ITU-T Recommendation G.107, "The E-Model: A computational model for use in transmission planning", 1998.

DYNAMIC BANDWIDTH ALLOCATION CONSIDERING UTILIZATION AND QOS IN CELLULAR NETWORKS

KYUNGKOO JUN, SEOKHOON KANG AND BYOUNGJO CHOI

Department of Multimedia System Engineering,
University of Incheon
177 Dohwa-dong, Nam-gu, Incheon, Korea
Email: {kjun, hana, bjc97r}@incheon.ac.kr

We propose a dynamic bandwidth allocation scheme for the downlink real–time video streaming in cellular networks. Our scheme is able to maximize the bandwidth utilization, while satisfying QoS constraints, e.g., the packet loss probability. Our scheme dynamically determines the amount of bandwidth to be allocated at each unit time interval by measuring the queue length and the accumulated packet loss probability. The simulation results show that our scheme is able to achieve the same level of performance as what can be accomplished with the pre-calculated effective bandwidth in terms of the bandwidth utilization and the packet loss probability.

1. Introduction

It is non-trivial task to determine the proper amount of bandwidth to be assigned for the video streaming service in terms of the utilization and the QoS satisfaction, considering the VBR-originated burst nature of the video streaming. For example, assigning bandwidth equal to the mean throughput of the stream may not satisfy the associated QoS constraints such as the packet loss probability. On the other hand, allocating the bandwidth corresponding to the peak rate is undesirable in terms of bandwidth utilization.

Effective bandwidth is a statistical concept devised to cope with the above problem of optimal bandwidth allocation [1]. The effective bandwidth lying between the peak rate and the mean rate is known to be the value satisfying the requirements in terms of both the utilization and the QoS satisfaction. The exact effective bandwidth for streams can be calculated only by processing the actual traces of the data streaming rate. However it is very difficult to obtain the exact traffic traces in a real cellular network environment.

To supplement these shortcomings concerning the effective bandwidth calculation, several schemes to estimate the effective bandwidth without using the trace files have been proposed, mostly exploiting on–line measurement and prediction [2 3 4 5 6].

Our proposed scheme is also based on the on-line measurement, predicting the required bandwidth during next time interval from current measurement results. In our scheme, the bandwidth to be allocated is determined in real-time aiming to maximize the bandwidth utilization as well as satisfy the required QoS constraints. The contribution of this paper is that, without using the traffic trace files, it is still feasible to achieve the same level of performance as what can be accomplished with the trace-based effective bandwidth in terms of the bandwidth utilization and the QoS satisfaction.

This paper is organized as follows. Section 2 presents the dynamic bandwidth allocation scheme in detail. Section 3 compares the utilization and the QoS satisfaction of our scheme with those of the pre-calculated effective bandwidth case and the peak-rate bandwidth allocation. Section 4 concludes this paper.

2. Dynamic Bandwidth Allocation Model and Algorithm

We propose a dynamic bandwidth allocation scheme by which the utilization of the allocated bandwidth is maximized while at the same time, the QoS constraints are met, for the downlink video streaming. The fundamental idea of our scheme is to predict the amount of bandwidth allocation for next unit time interval based on the measured bandwidth utilization and the QoS satisfaction level during current interval.

A prominent advantage of our suggested scheme is that the effective bandwidth can be calculated in real–time without a priori knowledge about the target traffic. Thus, our scheme can be employed for the case of real-time video conference about which the effective bandwidth is rarely known in advance.

2.1. *Algorithm*

In this section, we discuss in detail the algorithm by which the base station determines the amount of the bandwidth to be allocated. Figure 1 shows the flow diagram of our proposed algorithm.

The amount of bandwidth allocated for each flow during next unit time is determined by measuring the queue length at the end of every unit time interval. In our proposed scheme, we use the queue length as the metric

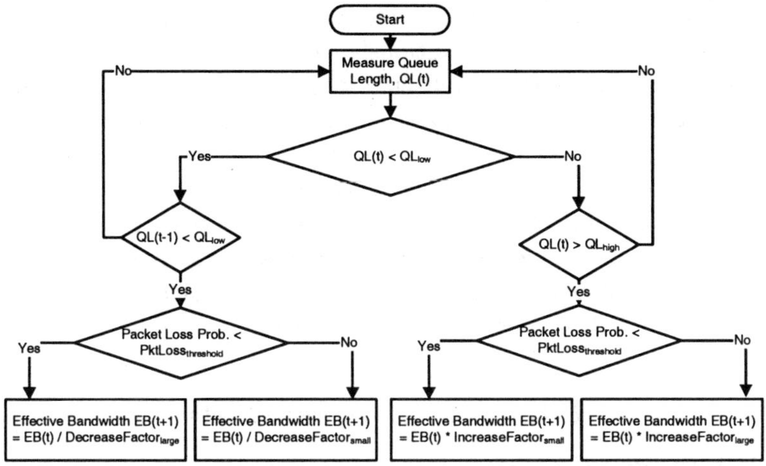

Figure 1. The flow chart of our proposed algorithm

to represent the utilization of the allocated bandwidth. It should be noted that we assume that each user service flow is assigned with a queue to store the downstreaming data once the service is admitted by the base station.

The queue length shorter than threshold is understood as the sign of the waste of the allocated bandwidth, while the longer queue length than the threshold indicates the state of insufficient bandwidth. According to the queue length comparison, either the increase or the decrease of the amount of bandwidth for next unit interval is determined compared with that of current interval.

To determine to decrease the allocated bandwidth, over two consecutive unit time periods, the measured queue length should be shorter than the threshold, QL_{low}. In the case of the increase, only one unit time period during which the queue length is longer than the threshold, QL_{high}, is required.

The difference in the required number of unit time periods when deciding the increase or the decrease stems from the fact that our proposed scheme puts emphasis on conservative QoS provision. For example, unless the increase of the bandwidth allocation is carried out promptly when it is needed, it directly leads to the packet loss, which then affects the experienced QoS level negatively. Thus, our scheme is designed to decide the bandwidth increase only over one unit time period measurement. On the contrary, in the case of the bandwidth decrease, considering the sporadic burst occurrences observed in the video streaming, it is desirable to determine the bandwidth decrease cautiously even when some of the bandwidth is wasted. This carefulness is reflected in our scheme as the two unit time period measurement before actually decreasing the bandwidth.

Once the increase or the decrease of the bandwidth is determined, the next step is to determine the change ratio by considering the accumulated packet loss probability. Depending on the measured packet loss probability, the magnitude of the increase or the decrease factor is determined, and then the allocated bandwidth for next interval is calculated by changing the current amount of allocated bandwidth as follows.

$$EB_{next} = EB_{cur}/DecreaseFactor \tag{1}$$

by which the decreased bandwidth EB_{next} is calculated by dividing the current bandwidth EB_{cur} by $DecreaseFactor$.

$$EBnext = EB_{cur} * IncreaseFactor \tag{2}$$

by which the increased bandwidth EB_{next} is calculated by multiplying the current bandwidth EB_{cur} by $IncreaseFactor$.

In the case of the increase, if the measured packet loss probability is bigger than a threshold, $PktLoss_{threshold}$, a relatively large $IncreaseFactor_{large}$ is employed in order to prevent further packet loss by raising the allocated bandwidth rapidly. On the other hand, if the packet loss is smaller than $PktLoss_{threshold}$, comparably small factor, $IncreaseFactor_{small}$, is adopted to increase the bandwidth slowly since it does not reach the packet loss threshold.

In the case of the decrease, we also compare the packet loss probability to determine the magnitude of the decrease factor. However, the determination logic is contrary to that of the increase case. For example, if the packet loss probability is bigger than $PktLoss_{threshold}$, relatively small factor, $DecreaseFactor_{small}$, is used to prevent packet loss. It contributes to the conservative bandwidth decrease.

With the aforementioned algorithm, we intuitively predict that our proposed scheme has the characteristic of the fast increase and slow decrease in the bandwidth allocation. We prove this asymmetric aspect of our scheme by the simulation results as shown in Figure 2. In the experiment, we observe how our proposed scheme dynamically allocates the bandwidth for the simulated video streaming traffic with an intentional surge; between time interval 2000 and 3000, we temporarily doubles the amount of generated traffic. The details concerning the video traffic generation and the simulation are discussed in next section.

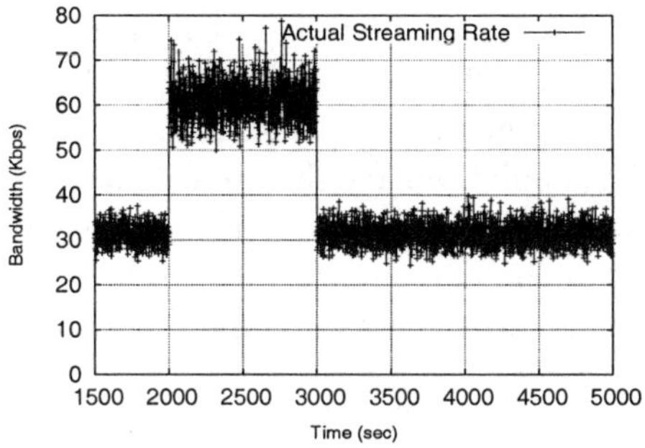

(a) Actual streaming

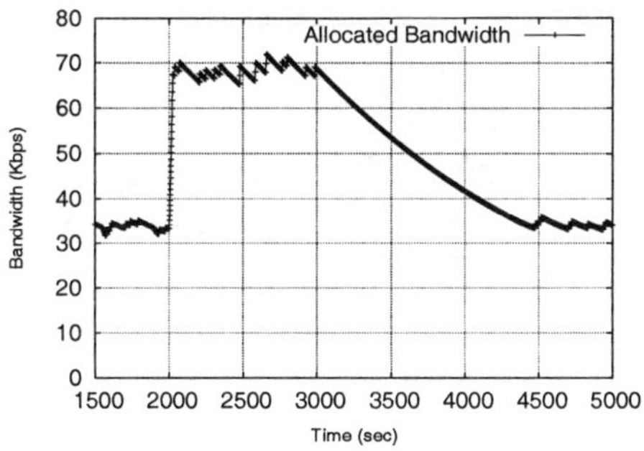

(b) Allocated bandwidth

Figure 2. The packet rate of video streaming with an intentional surge (a) and the allocated bandwidth by our proposed algorithm (b)

The allocated bandwidth by our algorithm grows very rapidly once the traffic volume increases fast at time 2000. However, from time 3000 at which the traffic amount returns to previous level, it is observed that the decrease of the allocated bandwidth starts to move down very slowly contrary to the increase case. Its slow decrease is to prevent further packet loss,

In conclusion, our proposed algorithm is designed to put emphasis on the provision of required QoS level by sacrificing the bandwidth utilization. However, with the modifications to the algorithm parameters presented in Table 1, our scheme can be made to behave in the opposite way, i.e., the slow increase and fast decrease.

3. Performance Evaluation

In this section, we evaluate our proposed scheme in terms of the bandwidth utilization and the required packet loss probability by the use of the simulation. The simulation results are compared with those of the peak rate allocation scheme and the pre-calculated effective bandwidth scheme. In the peak rate scheme, the fixed bandwidth 41.93 Kbps, corresponding to the maximum packet rate of the simulated video streaming, is allocated throughout the simulation. By the pre-calculated effective bandwidth scheme, the fixed bandwidth 33.76 Kbps is allocated throughout the simulation. 33.76 Kbps is the effective bandwidth that satisfies the required packet loss probability, 0.001. It was obtained by processing and analyzing the simulated video traffic.

Table 1. Algorithm Parameters

Parameter	Value
QL_{low}	50 bytes
QL_{high}	500 bytes
$PktLoss_{threshold}$	0.00098
Allowable Packet Loss Probability	0.001
$DecreaseFactor_{large}$	1.008
$DecreaseFactor_{small}$	1.001
$IncreaseFactor_{large}$	1.03
$IncreaseFactor_{small}$	1.01
Initial Bandwidth	41.93 Kbps

To generate the simulated video streaming traffic, we employ the parameters listed in Table 2. It produces average 32 Kbps video streaming [7]. The parameters of our algorithm are listed in Table 2. Of them, *IncreaseFactors* are set relatively larger than *DecreaseFactors*. It contributes to the characteristic of our algorithm, i.e., the fast increase and the slow decrease. Of other parameters, the allowable packet loss probability is set to 0.001, the initial bandwidth is set to 41.93 Kbps, the peak rate of the simulated video streaming. The thresholds for the queue length and the packet loss probability are also listed.

3.1. *Comparison with other schemes*

Figure 3(a) shows the utilization comparison of our scheme with two other schemes. The utilization of the peak rate allocation, 0.74, is the lowest of the three schemes. It is because its highly conservative approach leads to

Table 2. Parameters of simulated video streaming

Category	Distribution	Distribution Parameters
Inter–arrival time between the beginning of each frame	Deterministic (based on 10 fps)	100 ms
Number of packets (slices) in a frame	Deterministic	8
Packet Size	Truncated Pareto (Mean = 50 bytes, Max = 125 bytes)	K = 20 bytes, α=1.2
Inter-arrival time between packets in a frame	Truncated Pareto (Mean = 6 ms, Max = 12.5ms)	K = 2.5 ms, α=1.2

the waste of most of its allocated bandwidth. Secondly, the pre-calculated scheme achieves the utilization as high as 0.92. Our scheme, the dynamic bandwidth allocation, achieves the utilization of 0.92 which is similar to that of the pre-calculated effective bandwidth scheme.

Figure 3(b) shows the results of the packet loss probability comparison. The peak rate scheme has 0% loss rate because it literally allocates the "maximum" peak rate of the simulated video stream. Both our scheme and the pre–calculated effective bandwidth scheme show similar packet loss probabilities, around 0.099%, slightly less than the maximum allowable loss probability 0.1%.

In summary, our scheme succeeded to achieve the utilization level similar to that of the pre-calculated effective bandwidth, while at the same time satisfying the required packet loss probability. However, our scheme is superior to the pre-calculated effective bandwidth scheme in the sense that our method does not involve the pre-processing overhead for the effective bandwidth calculation.

3.2. *Effect of the bandwidth update interval*

In another experiment, we tried to understand how the bandwidth update interval affects the utilization and the packet loss probability. The bandwidth update interval in our proposed algorithm means the time period between [t-1, t], two consecutive bandwidth adjustment moments. During this period, the performance data needed to determine the bandwidth for next period are collected.

According to the results of this experiment shown in Figure 4(a) and 4(b), the longer the bandwidth update interval, the higher the utilization

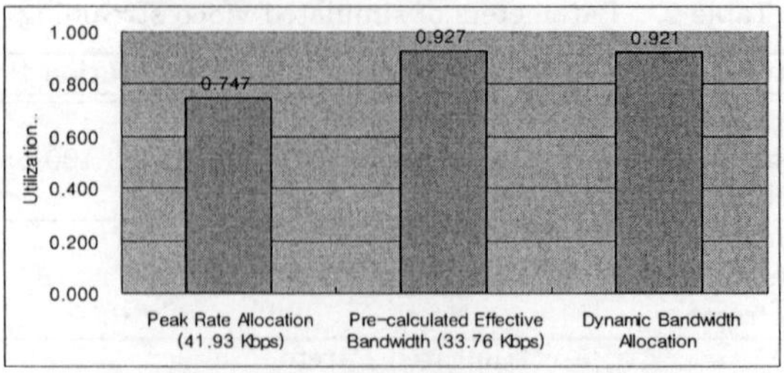

(a) Utilization

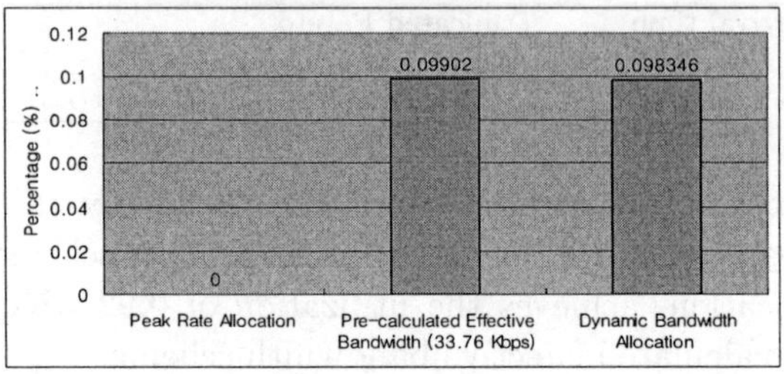

(b) Packet loss rate

Figure 3. Comparison of our scheme with the peak rate allocation and the pre-calculated effective bandwidth by (a) utilization and (b) packet loss rate

as well as the packet loss probability is. Figure 4(a) and 4(b) show the utilization and the packet loss rate, respectively. We measured the results as we changed the bandwidth update interval from 1 sec. to 20 sec. In the figure, only the packet loss probabilities at the update interval, 1, 2, 3, 4, 5, 10, and 20 sec., are plotted.

The utilization increases linearly as the update interval increases as shown in Figure 4(a). However all the corresponding packet loss rates are larger than the required level, except the case of the 1 sec. update interval.

From these experiment results, we can draw a conclusion that, if the update interval is longer than the average time between the packet rate changes, it is difficult to meet the required packet loss probability. With the video streaming model in Table 2, the update interval, 1 sec., seems to be short enough to reflect the packet rate changes, accompanying with decent level of utilization.

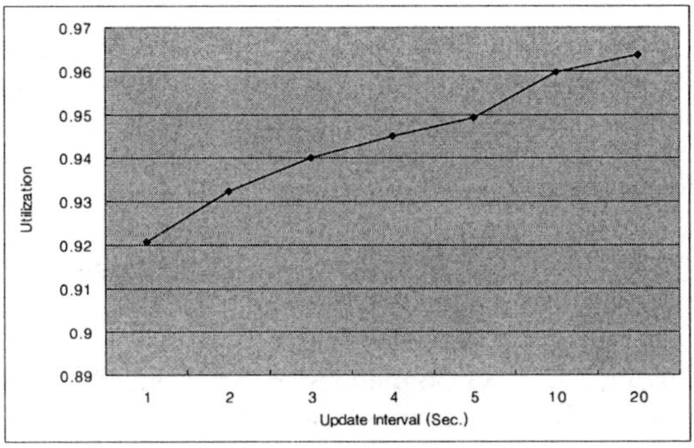

(a) Utilization

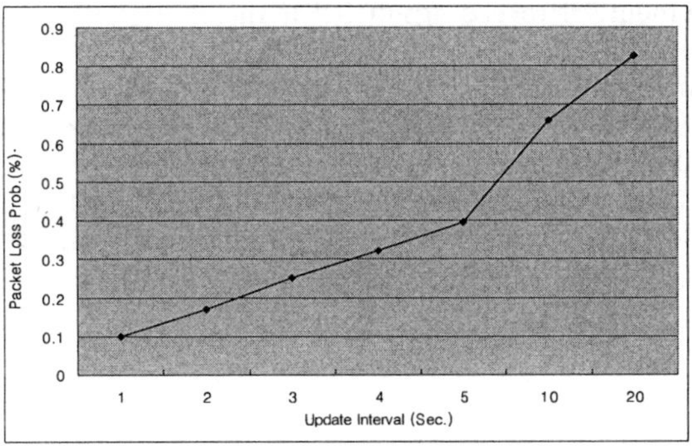

(b) Packet loss rate

Figure 4. The changes of the utilization and the packet loss rate depending on the bandwidth update interval (a) utilization and (b) packet loss rate

4. Conclusions

In this paper, we proposed a dynamic bandwidth allocation scheme for the downlink real-time video streaming in the cellular networks. Our scheme is able to maximize the utilization of the allocated bandwidth, while satisfying the required packet loss probability by dynamically changing the amount of bandwidth by measuring the queue length and the packet loss probability. Our proposed algorithm has the property of the fast increase, slow decrease in allocating the bandwidth. By the use of the simulation, it has been shown that our scheme produces similar results to those of the pre-calculated effective bandwidth case.

References

1. F. Kelly, "Notes on Effective Bandwidths", Stochastic Networks : Theory and Applications, Oxford University Press, 1996.
2. F. Ramos, P. Luan, and L. Lee, "An Effective Bandwidth Allocation Approach for Self-Similar Traffic in a Single ATM Connection," Proceedings of the GlobeCom 1999
3. J. Evans and D. Everitt, "Effective Bandwidth–based Admission Control for Multiservice CDMA Cellular Networks," IEEE Transaction on Vehicular Technology, vol. 48, no. 1, January, 1999.
4. N. Duffield, J. Lewis, N. O'Connell, R. Russell, and F. Tomey, "Entropy of ATM Streams : a Tool for Estimating QoS Parameters," IEEE Journal on Selected Areas in Communications, vol. 13, no.6, Auguest, 1995.
5. S. Valaee and J. Gregoire, "Resource Allocation for Video Streaming in Wireless Environment," Proceedings of IEEE International Symposium on Wireless Personal Multimedia Communications.
6. H. Li, Changcheng Huang, M. Devetsikiotis, and G. Damm, "Extending the Concept of Effective Bandwidths to Diffserv Networks", Proceedings of CCECE 2004.
7. F. Khan, "Traffic Models for IEEE 802.20 MBWA System Simulations (Ver 02)", IEEE 802.20 Working Group on Mobile Broadband Wireless Access.

A PATH RESTORATION ALGORITHM SHARING THE RESOURCE IN GMPLS NETWORK

TAE-MAN HAN AND YOU-HYEON JEONG

BcN Lab., Electronics and Telecommunications Research Institute (ETRI)
161 Gajeong-dong, Yuseong-gu, Daejeon, 305-350, KOREA
E-mail:{tmhan, yhjong}@etri.re.kr

JUN-HWA LEE AND SANG-HA KIM

Department of Computer Science, Chungnam National University
220 Gung-dong, Yuseong-gu, Daejeon, 305-764, KOREA
E-mail: {jhlee,shkim }@cclab.cnu.ac.kr

DONG-WON KIM

Department of Information and Communication, Chungbuk Provincial University
40 Gumgu-ri, Okchon-gun, Chungbuk, 373-807, KOREA

The restoration methods for the MPLS (Multi-Protocol Label Switching) network are 1+1, 1:1, 1:N, and M:N. However, these methods have a problem that it wastes network resources and cannot afford a perfect restoration when the physical connectivity is cut down. There is no guarantee that this problem is not present when the restoration methods are applied to the GMPLS (Generalized MPLS) network. This paper proposes the restoration mechanism that decreases the chances of getting the same problem where the Kini mechanism is applied over the GMPLS network. This mechanism computes a backup path at the time of a working path computation, and the resource allocation can maximize the resource utilization if the resource allocation is executed after the network fault. When the network fault is occured, this method extends the PATH or RESV message in RSVP-TE to allocate the resource as soon as it can.

1 Introduction

As the number of Internet user increases, there is a strong tendency in having the high speed Internet and the guaranteed quality of service. There could be two simple solutions to solve this problem. One is to offer various services which use the IP protocol in the network layer. The other is to introduce an optical technology for supplying high speed and broad bandwidth in the transmission layer. Therefore, the Internet needs to admit these two layers in providing an efficient solution, and this is the rationale where the GMPLS (Generalized MPLS) network begins.

The GMPLS network is an extension of the MPLS (Multi-Protocol Label Switching) technique, such that it is based on the routing technique in combination with the switching technique. For example, the data and transmission network is composed of not only routers and switches, but also DWDM (Dense Wavelength

Division Multiplexing) systems, ADMs, PXCs, OXCs, and etc. The GMPLS technology could include a switching technology as well as a forwarding technology. Therefore, it layers the network implemented various techniques, not only packet switching but also time-division like SONET, lambda-division, fiver switching etc in the current MPLS network.

When the Internet is used in public network, it should offer continuous services to users, and it should have a management scheme that can handle a network failure and a throughput adjustment. The use of DWDM system by implement of the optical internet to the high speed of Internet network makes to go past unnumbered lengths in a fiber. The bandwidth per a wavelength increases from 2.5 Gbps to 10 Gbps, and the number of traffic flow increases as much in a wavelength. As we can see, it could be happened that over a thousand traffic flow can be abruptly terminated even though one fiber is cut. Therefore, the next generation Internet should cover the guarantee of survivability.

To provide a reliable network service, we need to setup a backup path for the working path. When a backup path is established in network, it has to establish allocated bandwidth which can guarantee the allocated bandwidth in the working path to satisfy the required service condition. However, the efficiency factor of all networks also must guarantee. In this paper, the efficiency factor of all networks may increase by sharing a backup path which is not directly related to the network fault.

In the near future, the importance about guarantee of survivability in the Internet will be increased. The importance of the aspect of the network efficiency also will be increased. The algorithm suggested in this paper provides an efficient solution such that it can share a backup path for the paths that are not directly related to each other in terms of the network fault.

This paper is organized as follows. The section 2 will introduce about the protection schemes to share the resource, and the section 3 will present how it applies to the GMPLS network. The section 4 will explain some necessary extension parts for apply in the proposed algorithm the RSVP-TE protocol which is used when the label is allocated in the GMPLS network. The section 5 will present the result of the performance evaluation. Finally, the section 6 will conclude.

An old question in ecology is *how many species are there in a given place with a given level of fluctuations?* [14,15,17]. In fact, richness prediction is a fundamental problem both, in theoretical and applied ecology. Much of the variance in species richness of terrestrial organisms has been related to levels of available energy [10]; however, local patterns may be considered as depending on disturbance regimes.

Several models to describe the richness variation along a disturbance gradient have been proposed [11,13,15]; however, these models are either phenomenological [15] or very general [12], and they fail to predict, with the same mathematical and biological framework, a variety of data sets [1]. Models like those proposed by

Dayton and Hessler [8], Connell [6], Huston [12] and Barradas [2] predict highest species richness under intermediate perturbations, but, in some cases [6,13], their predictions are qualitative; in the case of [2] the model only consider competitive interactions. There are no testable mathematical models considering simultaneously competition and stress. Moreover, the classical succession theory [5] states the existence of immature communities in fluctuating environments and mature or climacic communities in stable environments; on the light of this theory, the possibility of a low richness at intermediate disturbance regimes becomes plausible.

In this paper, we present and analyze a general model linking environmental fluctuations and the number of species (richness). The model includes two biological mechanisms: competition and physiological stress. We analyze the model's behavior under different values of the involved parameters and contrast the model's predictions against field data sets. Finally we describe and analyze some modifications of the initial model, including a discrete version.

2 The restoration scheme sharing the resources

2.1 The problem of Kini algorithm

When the current MPLS network establishes a backup path for a working path, it uses the schemes such as 1+1, 1:1, 1:N, and M:N. However, some schemes, such as 1+1 and 1:N, establish the backup path for each working path which may cause waste of bandwidth for setting the backup path. A few years ago, Kini proposed an algorithm that can use resources effectively than the one establishes a backup path for each working path, because the Kini algorithm shares the bandwidth when it establishes a backup path. Figure 1 represents an example about the backup path that shares the bandwidth for three working paths.

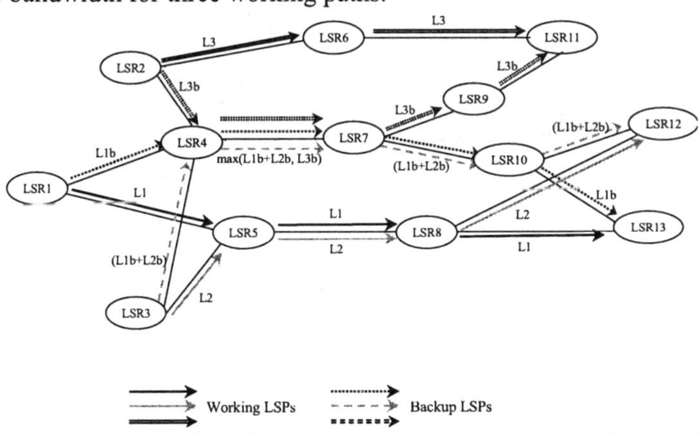

Figure 1. An example of the scheme to establish a backup path sharing the bandwidth

However, the algorithm that Kini proposes doesn't use the configuration information of the exact path to decrease the overhead which keeps and manages the configuration information of the path for all of the working path and the backup path which have already established, because it assigns the resources for the backup path in center of the largest bandwidth among the required bandwidths in the working path so that it wastes the resources of backup path as before.

2.2 *The proposed algorithm*

The proposed algorithm in this paper computes the backup path for a working path such that it does not actually allocate the resources until the network failure occurs. It is possible to share the backup path with other working paths that passes same links.

Figure 2 represents proposed algorithm. The backup path of LSP1b and LSP2b shares link F3. If they assign the resources at the same time, when GMPS network establishes the backup path, some problems will be occurred when the backup path is able to share the resources because the working paths including the LSP1b and LSP2b are not related about fault each other. If the label (lambda 1) is assigned before the LSP1b establishes the path, the LSP2b cannot use the label (lambda 1). In this reason, the backup path is computed in advance, as the resource allocation will holds off the label after the network failure.

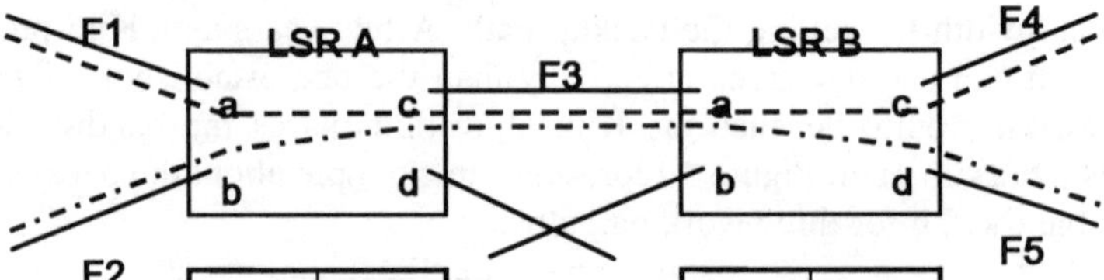

IN	OUT
$a_\lambda 1$	$c_\lambda 1$
$b_\lambda 1$	$c_\lambda 1$

IN	OUT
$a_\lambda 1$	?

Figure 2. The forwarding table of LSRs

However, the following conditions have to satisfy that this algorithm is able to exact restoration about fault. Given the fault to happen in the network is occurred in a place, the sharing of the backup paths which are in the proposed algorithm in this paper are possible to share each other on the each group that pass the afferent working paths. The reason is that the fault is occurred by fiber unit, when it is occurred in the network, but each lambda which is included in fiber has to be restored.

3 Applying scheme of GMPLS network

When it allocates the labels in the Internet, two protocols, RSVP-TE and CR-LDP, have been used, and these two protocols are extended to be used in the GMPLS network. However, the preference of using the RSVP-TE in the current venders has been increasing.

This section divides into two aspects. Firstly, we focus on the proposed algorithm in setting up the working path and the backup path in the GMPLS network. Secondly, we will discuss that the backup path replaces active path as the working path after the network failure.

3.1 Working Path

① GMPLS network computes the shortest path between the source and destination node. This is the working path. To establish the working path, it makes that the PATH message of RSVP-TE. This PATH message includes the Explicit Route Object, WP_LABEL_SET Object, and PATH_TYPE Object.
-Explicit Route Object: to decide the explicit route between source and destination node.
-WP_LABEL_SET Object: a label set that can be allocated to a working path after referencing a path information table.
-PATH_TYPE Object: to inform it the working path, establishing path now.

② GMPLS network remove their IP address in explicit route after receiving PATH message, and then transmit to next node. It sends to make the WP_LABEL_SET Object in the intersection between labels to be able to allocate the working path and the WP_LABEL_SET Object, at this time, it is good to refer the path information table to have.

③ The egress node selects one among label IDs in WP_LABEL_SET Object for PATH message. And it makes the RESV message to include the label selected former. It sends the RESV message to upstream, and the RESV message includes LABEL_SET Object and PATH_TYPE Object.
-LABEL_SET Object: the set of LSP ID to use same link to this working path.
-PATH_TYPE Object: to inform it working path.

3.2 Backup Path

① The backup path is to compute disjointed shortest path and the working path. The PATH message has PATH_TYPE Object, BP_LABEL_SET Object, and Explicit Route Object.
-Explicit Route Object: explicit route information from source to destination node.

-BP_LABEL_SET Object: a label set that can be allocated to the backup path after referencing path information table.

-PATH_TYPE Object: to inform it is the backup path establishing path now.

② After receiving the PATH message, GMPLS network remove their IP address from explicit route and send next node. it can reference the path information table to have and make the BP_LABEL_SET Object by the union between labels to be able to allocate the backup path and the BP_LABEL_SET Object in PATH message, and then send. The Hop Count value in the BP_LABEL_SET Object increases by 1.

③ The egress node selects one among label IDs in the BP_LABEL_SET Object which is included in the PATH message, and makes the RESV message to have the label. It sends the RESV message, which has the PATH_TYPE Object, to the upstream. In this stage, the RESV message sets the path information table in each LSR, but doesn't set the switching table and reserve necessary resources when it sends.

-PATH_TYPE Object: to inform it is the backup path.

3.3 The activity of the backup path when a fault occurs

① The network senses occurring fault. It uses the LOL (Loss of Light).

② The network decides the exact spot where the fail occurs, and this step is call to the localization. It uses the LMP (Link Management Protocol) protocol at this time.

③ The information which is sent to the ingress node is ChannelFial message of LMP at the spot where the fail occurs.

④ The ingress node must switch the flowing data to the backup path through the working path, and then it sends the PATH message after inserting the PATH_TYPE Object. The PATH_TYPE Object informs the activity of the backup path at this time.

⑤ The egress node receives the PATH message. When it sends the RESV message to the upstream node, it sets the actual switching table and reserves the necessary resource at the time of transmission of the data. At this time, it can find the used label from the path information table.

⑥ It switches to the backup path and makes to flow the flowing data, from to the ingress node to the working path by the backup path.

The control channel must do the O-E-O translation in hop-by-hop, but the data channel has to do the O-E-O translation in the ingress node. Other nodes only do the by-pass. All of the messages in the section 3 are carried and sent. Although the messages in ③ and ④ are a thing which is related with control, they are carried in the data channel and then sent. This is to decrease total restoration time because the middle hop nodes do not do for the message.

4 Requirements

To apply the proposed algorithm in this paper, it must have the path information table like Fig. 3 each port in a node.

LSP ID	LABEL	Type of Path

Figure 3. Path information table format

LSP ID column has the identity of each LSP, and LABEL column has the label value to be allocated in the channel. The type of Path column distinguishes between the working path and the backup path. LSP ID is composed of the combination of Tunnel ID like Fig. 4 in the IPv4 network. Tunnel ID makes a proper random value for low 15 bits of 16 bits in egress node. In the highest 1 bit, it is 0 if it is the working path, and it is 1 if it is the backup path. LSP has 48 bits identity in IPv4 network. However, in IPv6 network, LSP_TUNNEL_IPv6 Session Object is used, and the way to make LSP ID is same. Because IP address is 128 bits, LSP has 144 bits identity.

<table>
<tr><td colspan="2">IPv4 tunnel end point address</td></tr>
<tr><td>MUST be zero</td><td>Tunnel ID</td></tr>
<tr><td colspan="2">Extended Tunnel ID</td></tr>
</table>

Figure 4. LSP_TUNNEL_IPv4 Session Object

4.1 The extension RSVP-TE and the message format

To apply proposed algorithm in this paper, PATH_TYPE Object, PATH_TYPE Object, WP_LABEL_SET Object, BP_LABEL_SET Object, and LSP_SET Object has to be added.

4.1.1 PATH_TYPE Object

This Object must include all of the PATH message and RESV message. It doesn't need specific field for this object, and only the C-Type in common header can be used. C-Type values are summarized in Table 1.

Table 1. C-Type values of Common header

C-Type value	Path Type
1	Working Path
2	Backup Path
3	Activity of backup path

4.1.2 WP_LABEL_SET Object

This Object is included in the PATH message when it establishes the working path, and collects in order to be able to allocate labels. In GMPLS network, Label size can change variably by the encoding, and it can see the following Fig. 5 that shows the object architecture.

Channel ID 1
.
. Channel ID N
…

Figure 5. WP_LABEL_SET Object

4.1.3 BP_LABEL_SET Object

Channel ID 1	
…	
Channel ID 1 LSR count	…
…	Channel ID N
	…
Channel ID N	Channel ID N LSR count
…	

Figure 6. BP_LABEL_SET Object

4.1.4 LSP_SET Object

This object is included in the RESV message when it establishes the working path, and it collects LSP identities that pass the same path with establishing LSP. LSP ID length is decided in accordance with the length of LSP ID is 48 bits or 144 bits. Therefore, the object which is used in IPv4 network is called to LSP_SET_IPv4 object and the object which is used in IPv6 network is called to LSP_SET_IPv6 Object. Following Fig. 7 represent LSP_SET_IPv4 Object.

LSP ID 1	
LSP ID 1	LSP ID 2
LSP ID 2	
…	

Figure 7. LSP_SET_IPv4 Object

5 Performance Evaluation

In this section, we will provide a simple analysis and simulation of the proposed mechanism, and compare it with the Kini's algorithm. We used the ns-2 (network simulator-2) simulator and the simulation model is in Fig. 8. This network topology has 15 nodes and 26 link, and is designed for the optical communication network of the Middle Korea. Calls arriving at each node have a Poisson distribution. We assume that the number of wavelength is 15. Also, all simulations are the 100 simulated seconds.

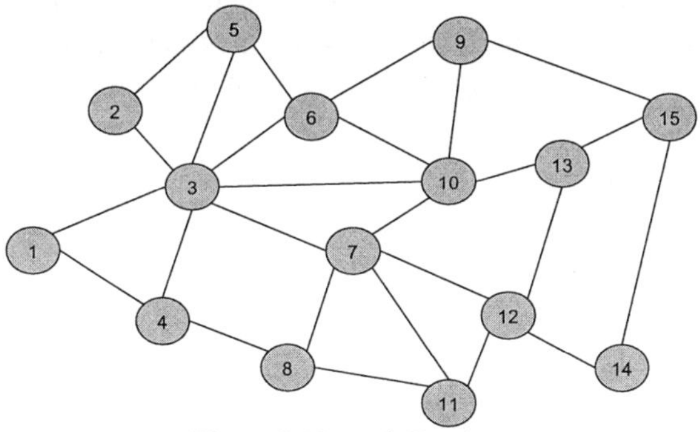

Figure 8. Network Topology

Fig. 9 shows the blocking rate of the proposed algorithm compared to the Kini's algorithm. This simulation result shows that the proposed algorithm has less blocking rate than the Kini's algorithm even with a high traffic load. As the proposed algorithm can allocate a minimum resource in a backup path, it can accept more requested calls. On the other hand, the Kini's algorithm allocates more resource than the proposed algorithm in a backup, because the proposed algorithm exactly computes amount of resource needed in a backup path.

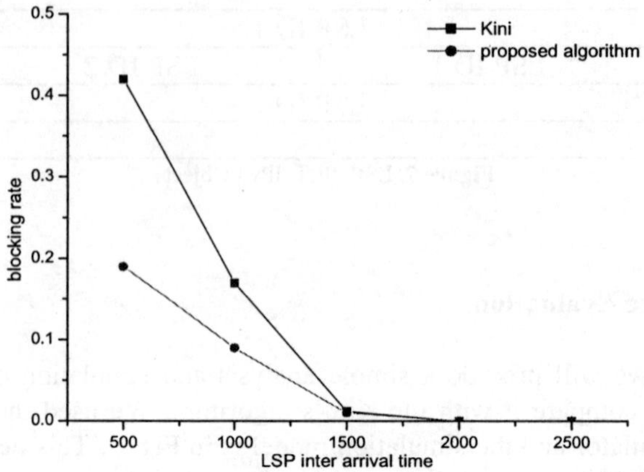

Figure 9. Blocking rate

Fig. 10 plots the normalized utilization for the proposed algorithm and the Kini's algorithm. The normalized utilization is defined as the number of entire wavelength divided by the number of the used wavelength. This figure shows that the utilization with the proposed algorithm is higher than that with the Kini's algorithm.

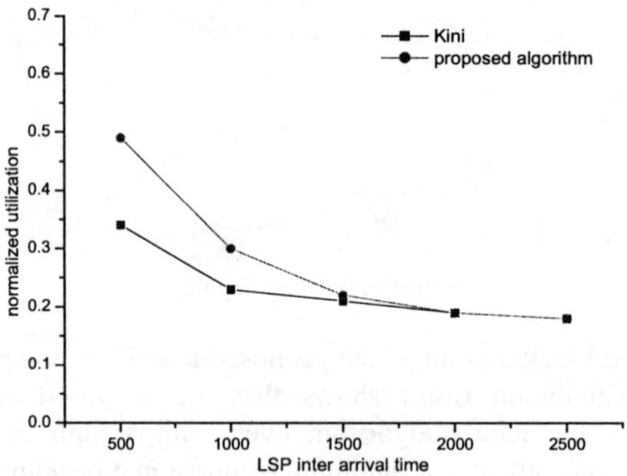

Figure 10. Normalized ultilization

6 Performance Evaluation

The survivability issues of the GMPLS network are of importance when it is first introduced as an Internet backbone networks. The network algorithms that have been used to resolve the problems in the aspects of the protection and resource, and these problems are occurred in GMPLS network. Therefore, this paper proposes the restoration algorithm which can be applied to the GMPLS network. This algorithm would achive high network utilization by using exact information about the paths when it establishes the backup path for the working path. Because of using exact information for the paths, it can guarantee the perfect protection. When it establishes the backup path at first, it set only the path information table, and allocates resources in real network after the fault. This is possible to extend the RSVP-TE protocol.

This paper only discusses the unidirectional path establishment. But GMPLS network can establish bidirectional path and allocate label in the ingress node. The future work need to extend proposed algorithm to apply in two environments.

References

1. O. Gerstel et al., "Optical Layer Survivability-An Implementation Perspective," IEEE J.S.A.C., vol. 18. no. 10, October 2000, pp. 1885-1889.
2. P. Ashwood-Smith et al., "Generalized Multi-Protocol Switching (GMPLS) Architecture," Internet Draft, draft-many-gmpls-architecture-00.txt, February 2001.
3. A. Banerjee et al., "Generalized Multiprotocol Label Switching: An Overview of Routing and Management Enhancements," IEEE Communication Magazine, vol. 39, no. 1, July 2001, pp. 144-150.
4. P. Ashwood-Smith et al., "Generalized MPLS-Signaling Functional Description," Internet Draft, draft-ietf-mpls-generalized-signaling-04.txt, May 2001.
5. A. Banerjee et al, "Generalized Multiprotocol Label Switching: An Overview of Signaling Enhancements and Recovery Techniques," IEEE Communication Magazine, vol. 39, no. 7, July 2001, pp. 144-151.
6. R. Doverspike and J. Yates, "Challenges for MPLS in Optical Network Restoration," IEEE Communication Magazine, vol. 39, no. 2, February 2001, pp. 89-96.
7. D. O. Awduche et al., "RSVP-TE: Extensions to RSVP for LSP Tunnels," Internet Draft, draft-ietf-mpls-rsvp-lsp-tunnel-08.txt, February 2001.
8. P. Ashwood-Smith et al., "Generalized MPLS Signaling – RSVP-TE Extensions," Internet Draft, draft-ietf-mpls-generalized-rsvp-te-03.txt, May 2001.
9. S. Kini et al., "Shared Backup Label Switched Path Restoration," Internet Draft, draft-kini-restoration-shared-backup-01.txt, May 2001.
10. M. Kodialam et al., "Dynamic Routing of Bandwidth Guaranteed Tunnels with Restoration," IEEE INFOCOM 2000, 2000, pp. 902-911.

DESIGN OF A CHIRPED FIBER BRAGG GRATING FOR USE IN WIDEBAND DISPERSION COMPENSATION

ISA NAVRUZ

Ankara University, Faculty of Engineering, Dept. of Electronics Engineering. Ankara

E-mail: inavruz@eng.ankara.edu.tr

AHMET ALTUNCU

Dumlupinar University, Faculty of Engineering, Dept. of Electrical and Electronics Engineering Kutahya

E-mail: altuncu@dumlupinar.edu.tr

A wideband chirped fiber Bragg grating (FBG) dispersion compensator operating in C band is designed theoretically by numerically solving the coupled mode equations. The power reflectivity spectrum and dispersion characteristics of the chirped fiber Bragg gratings are analysed. In order to achieve wideband dispersion compensation with a low insertion loss, grating length, average refractive index change, apodization profile and chirp parameter of the grating should be precisely optimized. The chirped FBG designs achieved in this study have resulted in a negative dispersion of 4.95 ps/nm for a grating length of L = 10 mm and a negative dispersion of 9.76 ps/nm for a grating length of L = 20 mm with 16 nm bandwidth at around 1550 nm.

1 Introduction

The use of erbium doped fiber amplifiers (EDFA) in optical communication systems has made chromatic dispersion the most significant limitation for the transmission performance since EDFAs compensate for the transmission losses. The chromatic dispersion in optical fiber is a phenomenon caused by the wavelength dependence of its group refractive index. In optical fiber, the wavelength dependence of the fiber group refractive index causes a temporal broadening of the pulses as they are propagating. After a certain propagation distance, the broadening of the pulses causes a significant number of errors at the receiving end thus the information is lost. Amongst its alternatives, dispersion compensating fibers (DCF) and bulk type dispersion compensators have been widely used to compensate for the chromatic dispersion [1-2]. This scheme requires to periodically insert a few km of DCF with a negative dispersion coefficient in an optical link to counteract the positive dispersion effects of the conventional fiber. But the insertion of DCF increases the total loss, nonlinear effects and cost of the optical transmission system [3]. In addition, the amount of compensation is wavelength dependent and can only be perfectly achieved in a relatively narrow band. Chirped fiber Bragg grating (FBG) has also been proposed recently for chromatic dispersion compensation and is recognized as a perfect alternative to DCF.

The most significant advantages of chirped FBGs are low insertion loss, nonlinear effects and cost. The idea of dispersion compensation using chirped fiber gratings was firstly proposed by Qulette [4] and later demonstrated experimentally by Williams et.al. [5]. A fiber Bragg grating is a reflective device composed of an optical fiber that contains a modulation of its core refractive index over a certain length. The grating reflects light propagating through the fiber when its wavelength corresponds to the modulation periodicity. In a chirped FBG, the periodicity of the induced index modulation varies along the grating's length. As the grating period varies along the axis, the different wavelengths are reflected by different portions of the grating and accordingly are delayed by different amounts of time. The net effect is a compression of the input pulse that can be tailored to compensate for the chromatic dispersion accumulated along the fiber link. Due to its superior advantages, the variety of fiber Bragg gratings are now widely used in optical communication systems [6] and fiber optical sensor applications [7].

2 Theoretical Model

The operation of fiber Bragg grating is based on the reflection of light from grating fringes and coupling of the modes. In a single mode fiber Bragg grating, the coupling occurs between the forward and backward propagating fields of the same mode. The maximum reflectivity is obtained at the wavelength providing the Bragg condition [8]:

$$\lambda_B = 2n_{eff}\Lambda \tag{1}$$

Where, n_{eff} , Λ and λ_B , represent the effective core refractive index, grating period and Bragg wavelength, respectively. In a uniform Bragg grating having a constant grating period, the forward and backward propagating fields are given by "coupled mode equations" as [9]:

$$\begin{aligned} \frac{dU}{dz} &= i\hat{\sigma}U(z) + i\kappa V(z) \\ \frac{dV}{dz} &= -i\hat{\sigma}V(z) - i\kappa^{*}U(z) \end{aligned} \tag{2}$$

Where, U and V are the transmitted and reflected fields respectively. In equation (2), κ *is* AC coupling coefficient and $\hat{\sigma}$ is DC self-coupling coefficient and are given for single mode Bragg reflection gratings as:

$$\kappa(z)=\kappa^{*}(z)=\frac{\pi}{\lambda}\nu\overline{\delta_{neff}}(z) \tag{3}$$

$$\hat{\sigma}(z)=\delta+\sigma-\frac{1}{2}\frac{d\phi}{dz} \tag{4}$$

$$\sigma=\frac{2\pi}{\lambda}\overline{\delta n_{eff}} \tag{5}$$

$$\delta=2\pi n_{eff}\left(\frac{1}{\lambda}-\frac{1}{\lambda_D}\right) \tag{6}$$

Here, δ is called as detuning parameter and is the frequency deviation ratio from the design wavelength which is taken as a reference. The design wavelength λ_D is the wavelength at which the Bragg condition is satisfied when $\overline{\delta n_{eff}}$ approximates to zero and thus a maximum reflectivity occurs. The grating fringes are obtained by sinusoidal modulation of the refractive index of the fiber core with a small intensity and is described as :

$$\delta n_{eff}(z)=\overline{\delta n_{eff}}(z)\left\{1+\nu\cos\left[\frac{2\pi}{\Lambda}z+\phi(z)\right]\right\} \tag{7}$$

Here, $\overline{\delta n_{eff}}$ is the average refractive index difference along the grating, ν is the fringe visibility of index change, Λ is the grating period and $\phi(z)$ is the grating chirp. For a linear chirped fiber Bragg grating, the group delay and dispersion can be calculated from the phase information of power reflectivity spectrum as :

$$\tau_\rho=\frac{d\theta}{d\omega}=-\frac{\lambda^2}{2\pi c}\frac{d\theta}{d\lambda} \tag{8}$$

$$D_\rho=\frac{d\tau}{d\lambda}=\frac{2\tau_\rho}{\lambda}-\frac{\lambda^2}{2\pi c}\frac{d^2\theta}{d\lambda^2} \tag{9}$$

Here, τ_p and D_ρ represent group delay and dispersion parameters, respectively and θ is the phase of power reflectivity spectrum.

3 Numerical Results

The optical characteristics of a FBG are mainly the reflectivity spectrum, which shows the wavelength range of operation, and the group delay spectrum which provides the dispersion characteristics. The slope of the group delay spectrum is the dispersion of the device. The reflectivity spectrum of the grating can be obtained by numerically solving the coupled equation system given in (2) using matrix transfer method [10]. In Figure 1, the power reflectivity spectrum of uniform fiber reflection gratings with a 10 mm length is shown for different index difference ($\overline{\delta n}_{eff}$) values.

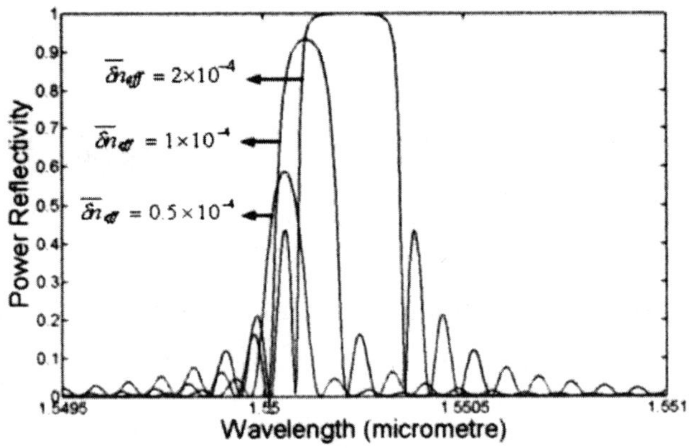

Figure 1. Power reflectivity and group delay spectrum of a linear chirped fiber Bragg grating. $\lambda_D = 1550nm$, L=10mm, $\overline{\delta n}_{eff} = 5\cdot10^{-4}$, $n_{eff} = 1.46$, $\frac{d\lambda_D}{dz} = -2.5$ nm/cm, grating period range : 530.82 nm -529.12 nm

As seen in this figure, the maximum reflection wavelength is shifted towards longer wavelength range when the index difference increases. The maximum wavelength deviation can be determined using,

$$\lambda_{\max} = \left(1 + \frac{\overline{\delta n}_{eff}}{n_{eff}}\right)\lambda_D \tag{10}$$

Since $\overline{\delta n}_{eff} << n_{eff}$, the deviation from design wavelength is usually considerably small. But this deviation must be taken into account in the design of fiber grating lasers and WDM fiber reflection gratings. Standard single mode fibers operating at 1.55 μm window usually have positive dispersion parameters. For a pulse propagating along an optical fiber with a positive dispersion, the short wavelength (high frequency) components of the pulse spectrum go faster than the long wavelength (low frequency) components and therefore, the pulse broadens with the increasing fiber length causing chromatic dispersion induced intersymbol interference (ISI) problem. It is possible to compensate chromatic dispersion using fiber Bragg gratings. In this scheme, a chirped FBG operates as a wavelength dependent dispersion compensator and light reflector. In Figure 2, the power reflectivity and group delay spectrum of a linear chirped fiber reflection grating operating at around 1550nm is shown.

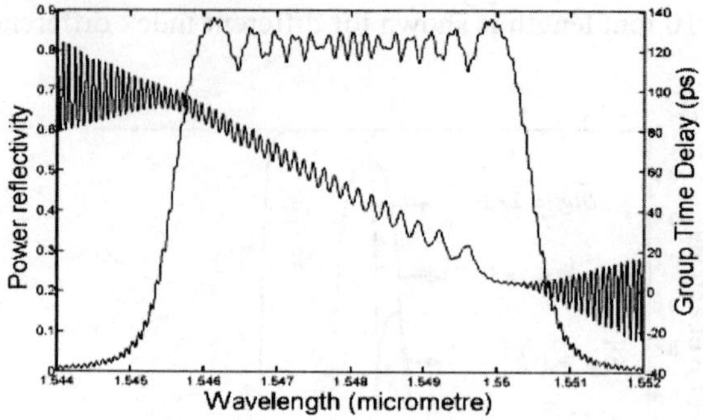

Figure 2. Power reflectivity and group delay spectrum of a linear chirped fiber Bragg grating. $\lambda_D = 1550nm$, L=10*mm*, $\overline{\delta n_{eff}} = 5 \cdot 10^{-4}$, $n_{eff} = 1.46$, $\frac{d\lambda_D}{dz} = -2.5$ nm/cm, grating period range : 530.82 nm -529.12 nm.

The power reflectivity and the group delay characteristics can be made more stable by applying apodization to fiber grating. Gaussian, Sinc and Tanh types of the apodization profile are seen in Figure 3 and the corresponding power reflectivity spectrums are shown in Figure 4.

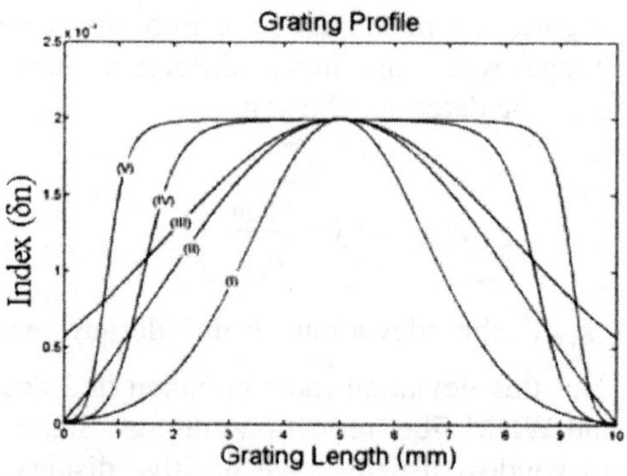

Figure 3. Different grating apodization profiles (I) Gaussian (a=20), (II) Sinc, (III) Gaussian (a=5), (IV) Tanh (α=2, β=3), (V) Tanh (α=4, β=3).

The grating apodization profiles used are described as a function of spatial distance as [11],[12],[13] :

Gaussian Profile: $$f(z) = \exp\left[-a\left(\frac{z - L/2}{L}\right)^2\right]$$

Sinc Profile: $$f(z) = \sin c\left(\frac{z - L/2}{FWHM}\right)$$

Tanh Profile: $$f(z) = \frac{1}{2}\left[1 + \tanh\left(\beta(1 - 2\left|\frac{2z}{L}\right|^{\alpha}\right)\right]$$

Where, a is the Gauss width parameter, FWHM is the full width at half maximum profile width, α and β are the tanh width parameters and L is the grating length.

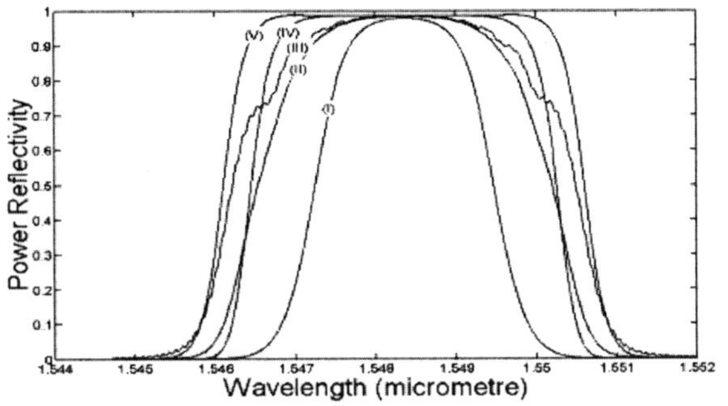

Figure 4. Power reflectivity spectrum for different grating apodization profiles. $\lambda_D = 1550nm$, L=10mm, $\overline{\delta n_{eff}} = 8 \cdot 10^{-4}$, $n_{eff} = 1.46$, $\frac{d\lambda_D}{dz} = -2.5$ nm/cm, v=100

Figure 4 shows the power reflectivity spectrum of a chirped FBG for different grating profiles. It can be seen that when the fiber grating is apodized with tanh (α=4, β=3) profile (V), the reflection band is more stable and wider in contrast to the other profiles. The power reflectivity (dB) and group delay spectrum of a FBG apodized with this profile is shown in Figure 5.

The reflection band of a chirped FBG can be more broadened by increasing chirp parameter which is given by the $\frac{d\lambda_D}{dz}$. The grating reflection spectra for two different chirp parameters are shown in Figure 6. For a chirp parameter of -6 nm/cm, the grating period decreases from 535.59 nm to 531.48 nm linearly whereas for a chirp parameter of -10 nm/cm, this variation occurs between 535.59 nm and 528.77 nm. The reflection bandwidth increases with increasing chirp parameter but in this case the reflection power decreases.

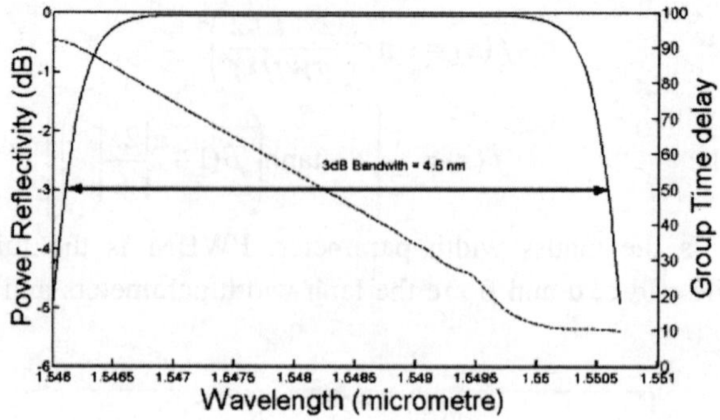

Figure 5. Power reflectivity (solid line) and group delay (dashed line) spectra of a chirped FBG apodized with Tanh (α=4, β=3) grating profile.

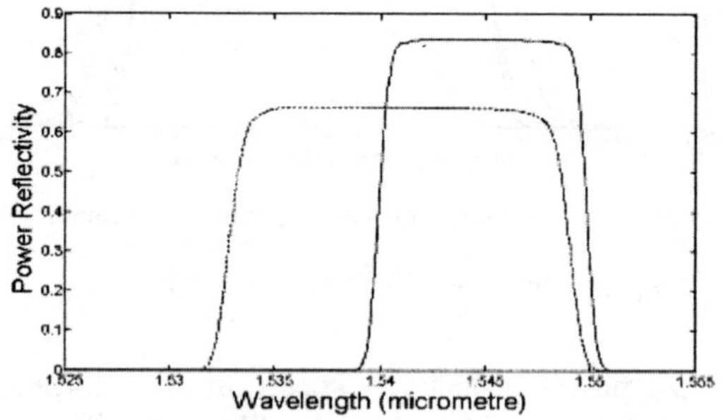

Figure 6. Power reflectivity spectrum of grating for two different chirp parameters: -6 nm/cm (solid line), -10 nm/cm (dashed line). L=10mm, $\overline{\delta n_{eff}} = 8 \cdot 10^{-4}$, $\lambda_D = 1550nm$, $n_{eff} = 1.447$, v=100, tanh apodization (α=4, β=3).

In order to compensate for this extra power loss, the grating length should be increased for the reduced chirp parameters. The power reflectivity spectra of two different gratings with the chirp parameters of -10 nm/cm and -5 nm/cm are shown in Figure 7. As seen in this figure, if the grating length is increased to twice and the chirp parameter is reduced to half of its previous values, the reflection spectrum stays nearly same but the power reflectivity increases. The power reflectivity and group delay spectra of two different grating designs are shown in Figure 8.

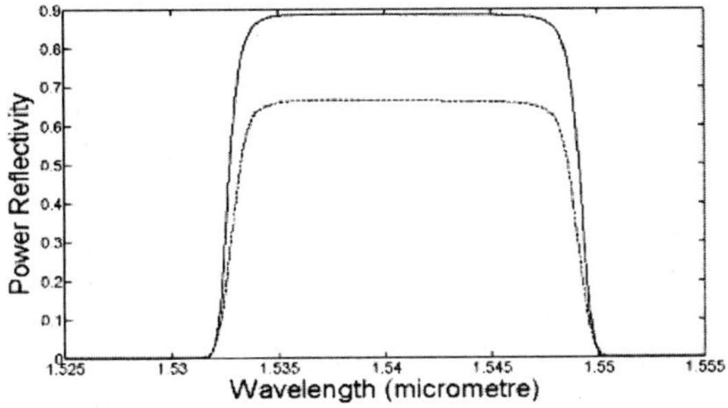

Figure 7. Power reflectivity spectra of two different grating designs, a) Chirp parameter = -5 nm/cm and L = 20 mm (solid line), b) Chirp parameter = -10 nm/cm and L = 10mm (dashed line).

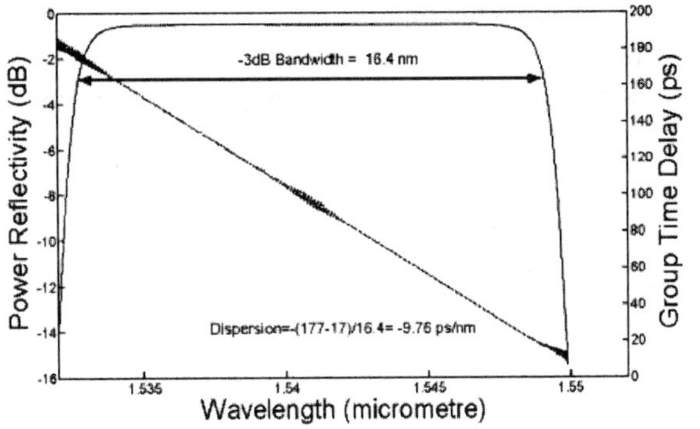

(a)

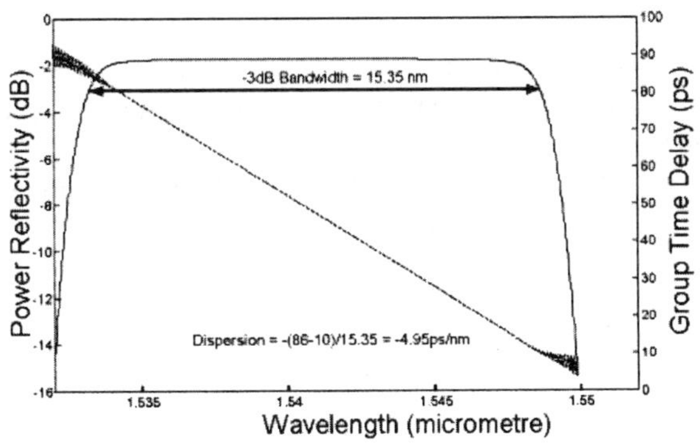

(b)

Figure 8. Power reflectivity (solid line) and group delay (dashes line) spectra of two different grating designs: a) Chirp parameter = -5 nm/cm and L = 20 mm (solid line), b) Chirp parameter = -10 nm/cm and L = 10 mm (dashed line).

4 Results and Discussion

A wideband chirped fiber Bragg grating dispersion compensator operating in C band was designed theoretically by numerically solving the coupled mode equations. The effects of grating length and chirp parameter of the FBG on power reflectivity and group delay spectra are investigated in detail. The results obtained have shown that increasing the chirp parameter broadens the reflection spectrum but decreases the reflectivity power for a certain grating length. On the other hand, if the grating length increases, group delay of the reflection band and therefore dispersion compensated bandwidth increases. The chirped FBG designs achieved in this study have resulted in a negative dispersion of 4.95 ps/nm for a grating length of L = 10 mm and a negative dispersion of 9.76 ps/nm for a grating length of L = 20 mm with a bandwidth of about 16 nm at around 1550 nm. According to these results, a higher group delay and a wider bandwidth covering all of the C or L bands in optical fiber can be achieved by precisely optimizing the grating length, the average refractive index deviation, the apodization profile and the grating chirp parameter.

References

1. A. M. Vengsarkar and W. A. Reed, “Dispersion-compensating single-mode fibers: efficient designs for first and second-order compensation,” Opt. Lett. 18, 924-926, (1993).
2. L. G. Nielsen, S. N. Knudsen, “Dispersion Compensating Fibers”, Optical Fiber Technology 6, 164-180, (2000).
3. G.P. Agrawal, Optical Fiber Communications Systems, John Wiley, 1997.
4. F. Qullette, "Dispersion cancellation using linearly chirped Bragg grating filters in optical waveguides" Opt. Lett. 12, 847-849, (1987).
5. J. A. R. Williams, I. Bennion, K. Sugden, and N. J. Doran, “Fiber dispersion compensation using a chirped in fiber Bragg grating,” Electron. Lett. 30, 985-987, (1994).
6. F. Quellette, “Fiber Bragg Gratings help WDM push limits of fiber capacity”, Laser Focus World, 83-89, March (1998).
7. A. D. Kersay, M. A. Davis, H. K. Patrick, M. LeBlanc, K. P. Koo, C. G. Askins, M. A. Putnam, “Fiber grating sensors”, Journal of Lightwave Technology, vol. 15, 1442-1463, (1997).
8. K. O. Hill, D.C. Johnson, F. Bilodeau, “Narrow bandwidth optical waveguide transmission filters: A new design concept and applications to optical fibre communication”, Electronics Letters, vol. 23, (1987).
9. T. Erdogan, “Fibre grating spectra”, Journal of Lightwave Technology, vol.15, no.8, 1277-1294, (1997).
10. A. Othonos and K. Kalli, “Fiber Bragg Gratings: Fundamentals and Applications in Telecommunications and Sensing”, Artech House, Inc., (1999).

11. K. Ennser, M. N. Zervas, R. I. Laming, "Optimization of Apodized Linearly Chirped Fiber Gratings for Optical Communications", IEEE Journal Of Quantum Electronics, vol. 34, no. 5, 770-778, (1998).
12. D. Pastor, **J.** Capmany, D. Ortega, V. Tatay, J. Marti, "Design of Apodized Linearly Chirped Fiber Gratings for Dispersion Compensation", Journal Of Lightwave Technology, vol. 14, no. 11, 2581-2587, (1996).
13. Y. Sun, C. Yun, J. Lin, Y. Qian, B. Bai, Y. Yang and W. Qiu, "Study on the apodized function of chirped fibre grating for dispersion compensation", Journal of Optoelectronics Laser, vol.10, no.3, 228-231,(1999).

VORONOI-BASED APPROACH FOR CONSTRUCTING CONNECTED COVER SET IN WIRELESS SENSOR NETWORKS *

JIE JIANG, ZHEN SONG, HEYING ZHANG AND WENHUA DOU

School of Computer Science,
National University of Defense Technology,
Changsha, P.R.China,
E-mail:{jiangjie,songzhen}@nudt.edu.cn

Reducing power consumption to extend network lifetime is one of the most important challenges in designing wireless sensor networks. One promising approach to reduce energy consumption is node scheduling, which keeps only a subset of sensor nodes active and puts others into low-powered sleep status. However, most of previous work on node scheduling considers only sensing coverage. In this paper, we consider the sensing coverage and communication connectivity simultaneously and address the issue of constructing a minimal connected cover set in wireless sensor network. We propose a centralized, Voronoi tessellation (CVT) based algorithm to select the minimum number of active sensor nodes needed to cover the region of interest (ROI) completely. The constructed sensor set is connected when sensor node's communication radius is at least twice of its sensing radius. For other situations where the CVT algorithm alone cannot maintain the network connectivity, we design a Steiner minimum tree (SMT) based algorithm to ensure the network connectivity. Finally, we evaluate the performance of the proposed algorithms through numerical experiments.

1. Introduction

Because of advances in micro-sensors, wireless networking and embedded processing, wireless sensor networks (WSN) are becoming increasingly available for commercial and military applications, such as environmental monitoring, biological attack detection, and battlefield awareness and surveillance, etc[1,2,3].

In large scale wireless sensor networks, energy is the most precious resource because of the following two factors. First, sensor nodes usually

*This work is supported by the National Natural Science Foundation of China under grant number 90104001.

operate on batteries with limited energy supply due to low cost and extreme small dimensions. Second, it is usually infeasible or even impossible to recharge or replace batteries due to the large number of sensor nodes in the network or the hazardous and hostile environment. So extending the network lifetime by carefully scheduling the activities of sensor nodes to save energy is the most concerned issue in wireless sensor networks.

One promising approach to realize the above object is node scheduling, which keeps only a subset of sensors active and puts other sensors into low-powered sleep status. While most of previous related work on node scheduling only considers the coverage requirement, we address the issue of selecting the minimal subset of active sensors while ensuring sensing coverage and network connectivity in this paper. For a given ROI, this problem is NP-hard. We propose a centralized Voronoi tessellation (CVT) based approximate algorithm to compute the near optimal cover set. In case of sensor's communication radius is at least twice of its sensing radius, the calculated cover set is connected. In other cases where the CVT algorithm alone cannot maintain the network connectivity, we design a Steiner minimum tree (SMT) based algorithm to ensure the communication connectivity. Finally, we evaluate the performance of the proposed algorithms through numerical experiments.

The rest of the paper is organized as follows. We review the related work in the literature in section 2 and formulate the problem in section 3. We propose centralized algorithms and present the experimental results in section 4 and section 5 respectively. Finally, we end with conclusion remarks in section 6.

2. Related Work

Slijepcevic and Potkonjak [4] propose a centralized heuristic solution for the Set K-Cover problem of finding the maximal number of disjoint sensor sets. Ye et al. [5] present a distributed, probing based algorithm to extend network lifetime. Tian et al. [6] propose a distributed sensor scheduling scheme that exploits the coverage overlap among neighboring sensors to prolong network lifespan. Chen et al. [7] propose a grid-based approach for selecting working nodes in sensor networks. Carbunar et al. [8] propose a distributed algorithm to improve energy efficiency while preserving the network's coverage. Yan et al. [9] address the issue of providing differentiated surveillance service for various target area. All aforementioned work only considers the sensing coverage when selecting working nodes.

3. Problem Statement

We consider static sensor networks in the 2D plane. We use "binary sensing model" to model sensor node's sensing capability. In this model, the coverage area of a sensor node s_i is a circle centered at s_i with radius R_s (sensing radius). The circular sensing/coverage area is called s_i's *sensing disk* and denoted by $S_i = \{p|p \in \mathbb{R}^2, d(p, s_i) \leq R_s\}$, where d is the Euclidean distance metric. Each senor node also has a limited communication range. We use $N(i) = \{s_j|d(s_j, s_i) \leq R_c, j \neq i\}$ to denote s_i's communication neighbor sets, where R_c is sensor node's wireless communication radius.

Definition 3.1. (Communication graph/path) Given a set of sensors S, the *communication graph* of the sensor network $G_c = (V_c, E_c)$ is an undirected graph, where $V_c = S$ and $e_{ij} = (s_i, s_j) \in E_c$ if $d(s_i, s_j) \leq R_c$. We say that the communication graph is induced by S. A *communication path* is a sequence of sensors where any two sequential sensors are communication neighbors. A communication graph is connected if there is a path between any two vertices of G_c.

Definition 3.2. (Connected cover set) A set of sensors S is a cover set for a ROI if each point in the ROI is covered at least by one sensor in S. If the communication graph induced by the cover set S is connected, set S is called a *connected cover set* (CCS) for the ROI.

Minimal Connected Cover Set (MCCS) Problem: Given a set of sensors S deployed in a ROI, the minimal connected cover set problem is to find a connected cover set $S' \subset S$ with the minimal cardinality.

The MCCS problem is NP-hard as the less general problem of covering points using line segments is known to be NP-hard. In the next section, we will propose algorithms for the MCCS problem.

4. Centralized Approximation Algorithm

When designing approximation algorithm, we assume that each sensor knows its coordinates. Many research efforts into the localization problem in wireless sensor network [10,11] make this assumption reasonable. As sensors are densely deployed, the original wireless sensor network is connected and can cover the ROI completely. Furthermore, all sensors have the same R_s and R_c, but the ratio of R_s to R_c is variable. Finally, we assume that the ROI is bounded and convex.

4.1. *Algorithm for Constructing the Minimal Cover Set*

4.1.1. *Identifying Redundant Sensors*

The minimal cover set can be obtained by turning off the maximal number of redundant sensors. A sensor is redundant if its sensing coverage is completely subsumed by other sensors. Turning off a redundant sensor will not leave sensing hole in the ROI.

Definition 4.1. (Sensing hole) A sensing hole in the ROI is a subarea of the ROI where points are not covered by any sensor.

According to definition 3.2 and 4.1, a ROI is completely covered by a sensor network is equal to there is no sensing hole in the ROI. The sensing hole is detected by utilizing the Voronoi tessellation [12] of the ROI. In general, the Voronoi polygon associated with node s_i is unbounded if s_i is on the boundary of the convex hull of S [12]. But when the ROI is bounded, the unbounded Voronoi polygons of sensors on the boundary of the convex hull of S will be bounded by the boundary of the ROI.

Definition 4.2. (Bounded Voronoi tessellation) A Voronoi tessellation with all Voronoi polygons bounded is called a bounded Voronoi tessellation.

Let $BVT\,(S, ROI)$ to denote the bounded Voronoi tessellation of the bounded ROI when taking S as the generator set, $BVC_i\,(S, ROI)$ to denote the bounded Voronoi polygon associated with sensor s_i, $BVV_i\,(S, ROI)$ to denote the set of vertices of $BVC_i\,(S, ROI)$ and $BVN_i\,(S, ROI)$ to denote s_i's Voronoi neighbors in $BVT\,(S, ROI)$. Since the Voronoi polygon is convex [12] and the ROI is also convex, all the Voronoi polygons in the bounded Voronoi tessellation are convex.

Theorem 4.1. *The ROI is completely covered by a sensor network consisting of a set of sensors S if and only if for each sensor $s_i \in S$, all the vertices of $BVC_i\,(S, ROI)$ are within s_i's sensing disk S_i.*

Proof: For any sensor $s_i \in S$, if all the vertices of $BVC_i\,(S, ROI)$ are within S_i, then $BVC_i(S, ROI) \subseteq S_i$. Since $ROI = \bigcup_{s_i \in S} BVC_i(S, ROI)$, we have $ROI = \bigcup_{s_i \in S} BVC_i(S, ROI) \subseteq \bigcup_{s_i \in S} S_i$. Therefore S is a cover set for the ROI.

If the ROI is completely covered by S, there must be no sensing holes in the ROI. If there is a sensor node whose sensing disk cannot cover all the vertices of its bounded Voronoi polygon, a sensing hole will inevitably occur. Suppose s_1 is such a sensor and its bounded Voronoi polygon is not completely covered by its sensing disk. Assume point $p \in BVC_1(S, ROI)$ is not covered by S_1, so $d(s_1, p) > R_s$. According to the definition of Voronoi tessellation, $d(p, s_j) \geq d(p, s_1) > R_s$ $(j \neq 1)$, which means that point p is not covered by any sensor in the network and a sensing hole occurs. This is contradictory to the precondition that the ROI is completely covered and there are no sensing holes in the ROI. ∎

Theorem 4.1 gives a method to judge whether a sensor node is redundant. Sensor node s_i is redundant if $S \backslash s_i$ is still a cover set for the ROI ($S \backslash s_i$ represents the set of remaining sensors after removing s_i from S). That is, for any sensor $s_j \in S \backslash s_i$, all the elements of BVV_j in $BVT(S \backslash s_i, ROI)$ are within S_j. Furthermore, we observe that only $BVC_j(S \backslash s_i, ROI), j \in BVN_i(S, ROI)$ may be different from $BVC_j(S, ROI)$. Other sensors' bounded Voronoi polygons will not change after excluding sensor s_i from the generator set because their Voronoi neighbors don't change. We conclude the above discussion as follows.

Coverage Redundant Condition: Given a bounded convex ROI and a sensor network consisting of a set of sensors S, sensor s_i is redundant if and only if for any sensor $s_j \in BVN_i(S, ROI)$, all the elements of BVV_j in $BVT(S \backslash s_i, ROI)$ are covered by S_j.

4.1.2. *Determining Active Sensor Set*

Definition 4.3. (Independently/Dependently redundant sensor) An independently redundant sensor is a redundant sensor whose Voronoi neighbors are all non-redundant. A dependently redundant sensor is a redundant sensor whose Voronoi neighbors include at least one redundant sensor.

Non-redundant sensors must be kept active and independently redundant sensors are safe to be turned off. If two dependently redundant sensors, which are Voronoi neighbors each other, are turned off simultaneously, an area between them may be left uncovered, thus a sensing hole will occur. So the problem of calculating the minimal set of the active sensors is equivalent to determining the maximal set of the dependently redundant sensors that can be turned off simultaneously. In our solution, we use Redundant Dependency Graph to resolve the dependency relationship.

Definition 4.4. (RDG graph) A Redundant Dependency Graph, $RDG = (V_r, E_r)$, is an undirected graph, where V_r is the set of all dependently redundant sensors and $\forall v_{ri}, v_{rj} \in V_r, (v_{ri}, v_{rj}) \in E_r$ if and only if v_{ri} and v_{rj} are Voronoi neighbors.

Then the problem of determining the maximal set of dependently redundant sensors that can be deactivated simultaneously is equal to the problem of calculating the maximal independent set (MIS) of the RDG graph. The CVT algorithm is presented in Figure.1.

4.2. *SMT Based Connection Algorithm*

It has been shown that the complete coverage of a convex region implies connectivity of the communication network induced by all active senor nodes if $R_c \geq 2R_s$ [13]. Therefore the cover set constructed by the CVT algorithm is connected if $R_c \geq 2R_s$. But when $R_c < 2R_s$, the communication connectivity of the cover set can't be ensured. In this subsection, we propose a Steiner Minimum tree (SMT) based connection algorithm to make the cover set connected if necessary.

Definition 4.5. (Primary/Assistant sensor) A sensor in the cover set is called a primary sensor. Otherwise it is an assistant sensor.

Definition 4.6. (Connected component) A connected component in the cover set is a connected subgraph of G_c whose vertices only involve primary sensors.

Suppose that sensors in the cover set constructed by the CVT algorithm form m separated connected components in G_c as shown in Figure.2. The connected component consists of only primary sensors (denoted by solid circular dots). These components are connected through assistant sensors (denoted by hollow circular dots). We abstract each connected component as one virtual vertex and use v_i to represent $comp_i$. Then we attach to v_i all edges in G_c that connect one primary sensor in $comp_i$ and another assistant sensor. After this conversion, we get an abstract communication graph G_c' (see Figure.3).

If we assign weight 1 to each edge in G_c', selecting the minimal number of additional sensors needed to connect the components in G_c is equivalent to solving the Steiner Minimum Tree problem in the 1-weighted graph G_c', where the virtual vertices representing components are considered as "terminals" and the needed assistant sensors are those "Steiner points" that are required to construct the Steiner Minimum Tree to connect all the terminals. We present the SMT-based connection algorithm in Figure.4.

Input: an initial set of sensors $IS = \{s_1, \ldots, s_n\}$ and the ROI
Output: a cover set (CS) for the ROI
Notations: IRS: Independently Redundant sensor Set; DRS: Dependently Redundant sensor Set; SS: Safe sensor Set; S: temporary sensor Set; MIS: Maximal Independent Set.

BEGIN

$SS = CS = \emptyset, S = IS$
if $ROI \not\subset \bigcup_{s_i \in S} S_i$ **then**
  Return $CS = \emptyset$
end if
while $S \neq \emptyset$ **do**
  $IRS = DRS = MIS = \emptyset$
  Identify all redundant sensor nodes in S
  for each redundant sensor $s_i \in S$ **do**
    if s_i is independently redundant **then**
      $IRS = IRS \bigcup \{s_i\}$
    else
      $DRS = DRS \bigcup \{s_i\}$
    end if
  end for
  if $DRS \neq \emptyset$ **then**
    Compute *MIS* of the RDG graph
    $SS = SS \bigcup IRS \bigcup MIS$
    $S = DRS - MIS$
  else
    $SS = SS \bigcup IRS$
    Break out the **while** loop
  end if
end while
$CS = IS - SS$

END

Figure 1. CVT Algorithm

5. Experimental Results

The region of interest is a square of size 400×400. The sensing model and communication model are described in section 3. The default sensing

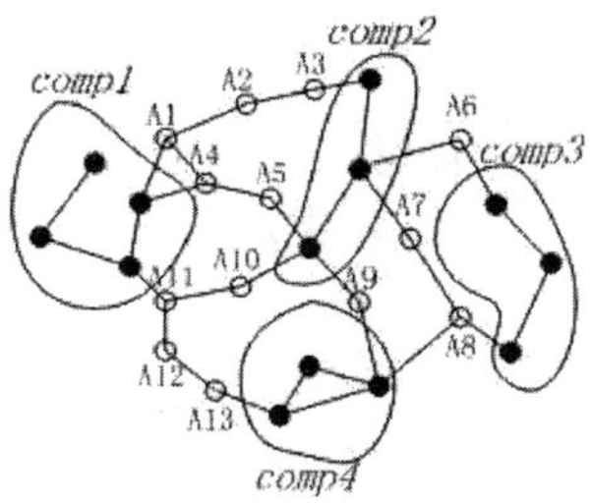

Figure 2. Connected Components in G_c

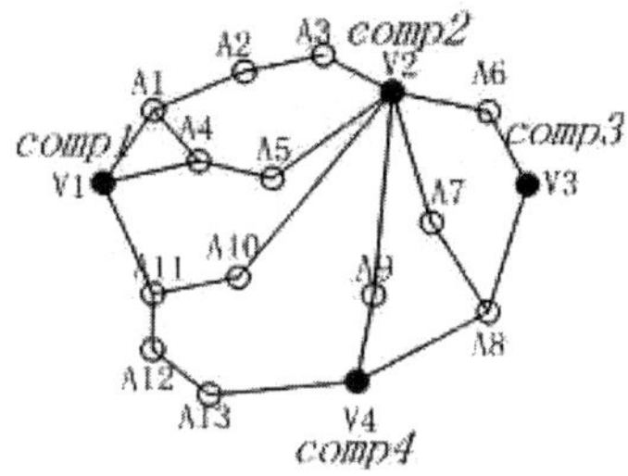

Figure 3. Abstract Communication Graph $G_c{}'$

BEGIN

1: Create the 1-weighted abstract communication graph $G_c{}'$ as described
2: Calculate the Steiner Minimum Tree (SMT) to connect all virtual vertices in $G_c{}'$.
3: Return all the assistant sensors corresponding to the Steiner points in the computed SMT.

END

Figure 4. SMT-based Connection Algorithm

radius is 30. To ensure the ROI is completely covered by the sensor network and the initial network is connected, we first divide the ROI into grid cells with dimension of 40 and deploy one sensor at the center of each grid cell. In this kind of node deployment, the minimal communication radius that can ensure the network connectivity is 40. When the sensing radius is 30, each sensor can only cover the grid where it is located. So we can expect the minimal size of the cover set is about 100 when the sensing range is 30. Besides the 100 fixed sensors, we also randomly deploy lots of sensors in this region.

Figure.5 shows how the number of the redundant sensors, the number of the sensors in the final CCS and the number of the sensors turned off vary with the number of deployed sensors when $R_c = 2R_s$. We note that the size of the CCS constructed by the CVT algorithm keeps constant when $R_c \geq 2R_s$ and is very close to the expected number of active sensors, i.e., 100. Note that these 100 sensor nodes are not the same as the 100 fixed sensor nodes. But when $R_c < 2R_s$, the size of the CCS is related to the ratio of R_s/R_c. In this case, the SMT algorithm is executed to calculate the

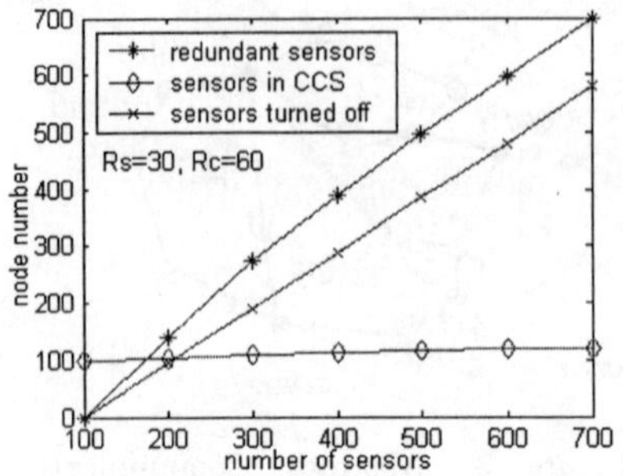

Figure 5. Solution Vs. node density ($R_c = 2R_s$)

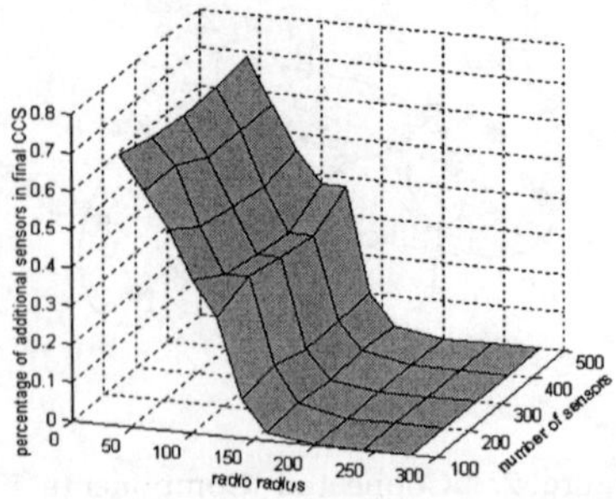

Figure 6. Percentage of assistant sensors in the final CCS

assistant sensor nodes needed to make the cover set connected. Figure.6 shows the 3D plot of the percentage of the additional assistant sensors in the final CCS when the total node number varies from 100 to 500. In this experiment, $R_s = 120$ and R_c varies from 40 to 280. We can see that the percentage of assistant sensors in the final CCS becomes very low (close to 0) when the ratio of $R_c/R_s \geq 4/3$. However, when the ratio of R_c/R_s is very small, the percentage is considerable, even more than 60%. So the SMT-based connection algorithm has further improvement room.

6. Conclusions

In this paper, we have addressed the minimal connected cover set problem in wireless sensor networks and designed centralized algorithms for this problem. The basic idea is to calculate the cover set firstly and then make it connected if necessary. We propose a centralized, Voronoi tessellation (CVT) based algorithm to calculate the near minimal cover set for the region of interest. The constructed cover set is connected if $R_c \geq 2R_s$. In case of $R_c < 2R_s$, we design a Steiner minimum tree (SMT) based algorithm to compute the minimal set of additional assistant sensors needed to make the cover set connected. And we evaluate the performance of the proposed algorithms via experimental results.

References

1. I. F. Akyildiz, W. Su, Y. Sankarasubramaniam and E. Cayirci, *Computer Networks (Elsevier)*, **38**,393-422 (2002).
2. J. Elson and D. Estrin, *Wireless Sensor Networks(Kluwer)*, 3-20 (2004)
3. A. Mainwaring, J. Polastre, R. Szewczyk and D. Culler, *Proceedings of the*

1st ACM International Workshop on Wireless Workshop in Wireless Sensor Networks and Applications (WSNA), 88-97 (2002).
4. S. Slijepcevic and M. Potkonjak, *Proceedings of IEEE International Conference on Communications (ICC)*, 472-476 (2001).
5. F. Ye, G. Zhong, S. Lu and L. Zhang, *Proceedings of the 23rd International Conference on Distributed Computing Systems (ICDCS)*, 28-37 (2003).
6. D. Tian and N. D. Georganas, *Proceedings of the 1st ACM Workshop on Wireless Sensor Networks and Applications (WSNA)*, 32-41 (2002).
7. H. Chen, H. Wu and N. Tzeng, *Proceedings of IEEE International Conference on Communications (ICC)*, **7**, 3673-3678 (2004).
8. B. Carbunar, A. Grama, J. Vitek and O. Carbunar, *Proceedings of the 1st IEEE Communications Society Conference on Sensor and Ad Hoc Communications and Networks (SECON)*, 377-386 (2004).
9. T. Yan, T. He and J. Stankovic, *Proceedings of the 1st International Conference on Embedded Networked Sensor Systems (SenSys)*, 51-62 (2003).
10. K. Romerm and E. Zurich, *Proceedings of the 1st International Conference on Moble Systems, Applications, and Services (MobiSys)*, 15-30 (2004).
11. T. He *et al*, *Proceedings of the 9th Annual International Conference on Mobile Computing and Networking (MobiCom)*, 81-95 (2003).
12. A. Okabe, B. Boots, K. Sugihara and S. N. Chiu, *Spatial Tessellations: Concepts and Applications of Voronoi Diagram*, (1999).
13. H. Zhang and J. C. Hou, *Theoretical and Algorithmic Aspects of Sensor, Ad Hoc Wireless and Peer-to-Peer Network*, (2004).

MESSAGES SCHEDULING OF CAN-BASED NETWORK FOR A HUMANOID ROBOT

J.-S. KONG
Industrial Automation Eng., Inha Univ., Yonghyun-dong, Nam-gu, Incheon, Korea

Y.-K. SUNG, J.-G. KIM
School of Electrical Eng., Inha Univ., Yonghyun-dong, Nam-gu, Incheon, Korea

B.-H. LEE
School of Electrical Eng., Semyung Univ., Shinwall-dong, Jecheon, Chungbuk, Korea

This paper deals with the messages scheduling of a CAN (Controller Area Network), which is based on the distributed control scheme to integrate actuators and sensors in a humanoid robot. For a humanoid robot to implement distributed processing, each control unit should have an efficient control method, and fast calculation and valid data exchange capabilities. A preliminary study revealed that CAN has better performance and is easier to implement than other networks such as FIP (Factory Instrumentation Protocol), VAN (Vehicle Area Network), etc. Since a humanoid robot has to process all the control signals from many actuators and sensors, communication time limitation is dependent on the transmission speed and data length of CAN. In this paper, the CAN message scheduling is proposed for a humanoid robot under the conditions of jitter-present message group, high load of messages over the network, and transmission errors. In addition, the worst-case response time was compared with the limitation time given by the simulation algorithm. The proposed message scheduling can guarantee the CAN limitation, and be used to generate the walking patterns for a humanoid robot.

1. Introduction

Humanoid robots, a kind of biped robots, have the shape and abilities of a human being. They are well suited for working with people in an environment originally designed for people. But biped robots are one of the hardest to control because of their instability, especially during dynamic walking. As such, there have been many studies on the challenging problem of biped robot control [1-4].

The ideal humanoid robots should be able to coexist and collaborate with humans and perform difficult and dangerous works that cannot be done by humans [5]. To carry out these tasks, humanoid robots must have autonomous system architecture [6]. To give the robot free mobility, their basic control system, servo system, communication system, and power supply system should be mounted on the body structure. The autonomous characteristic requires a high performance control system; that is, the autonomous robot becomes, in essence, a huge control system. Control units are difficult to install on the robot body because both the performance and structure of the control system must satisfy the robot specification. In this study, we propose a distributed control system [3, 7]. It gives an efficient control method, fast calculation and communication. We applied to the new distributed control system for a humanoid robot based on CAN.

Our robot system employs a wireless LAN to communicate with the remote robot controller and uses CAN with motor controllers in the body structure. Under this system structure, the time limitation and scheduling method of the CAN was verified, and simulated with valid samples related to a real humanoid robot.

2. Basic Configuration

Figure 1 shows the basic configuration of a designed humanoid robot with 21 DOFs, comprised of 6 DOFs in each leg, 3 in each arm, 1 in main body and 2 in head. Each of joints has its own control unit to drive the actuator, to acquire data from the sensors, and to communicate with the main controller.

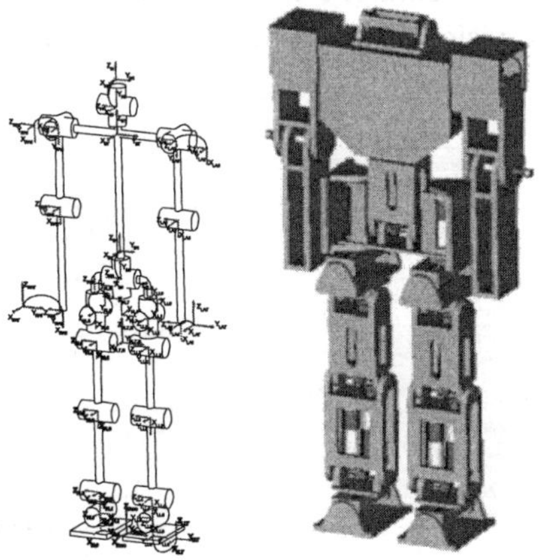

Figure 1. Coordination of a humanoid robot

To realize distributed control, two kinds of communication media were applied. One was the wireless LAN used to connect the PC simulator with the main controller in the robot body, and the other was the CAN employed to communicate with the main controller with joint controllers. Force sensors were mounted on the feet to measure the ground reaction force and then to calculate the actual ZMP (Zero Moment Point) position. A gyro-sensor was mounted at the robot's trunk to measure the robot's orientation. Table 1 shows the brief specifications of the humanoid robot used in this study.

Table 1. Basic Specification

Height	825mm	
Width	330mm	
Weight	6.84Kg	
Foot	135mm	
D.O.Fs	21	
Actuator	A-max26	Re-max 24
Power	18V, 11W	18V, 10W
Gear Ratio	190:1	231:1
Angular Velocity	240 deg/s	230deg/s

3. The Distributed Architecture

To achieve the autonomous walking, a humanoid robot should have modules: user interface, action, planner, vision and dynamics control of legs and arms, as shown in Figure 2.

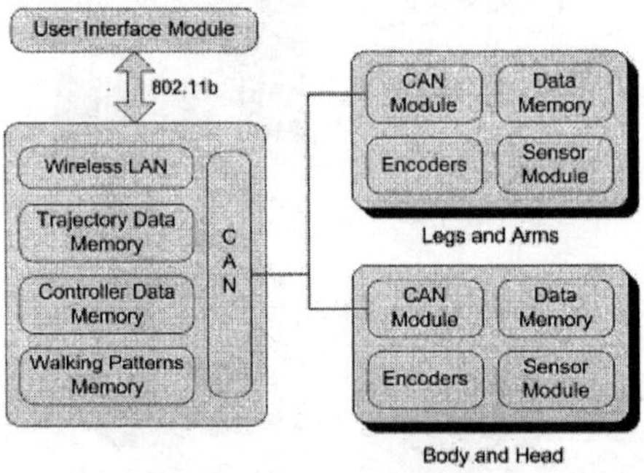

Figure 2. System architecture

If we use the central focusing control system, it has just all these modules in a main-controller, so the control system must be large and heavy system. It is possible to apply the distributed architecture to humanoid robots owing to high performance of microprocessors and the increased reliability for networks. Figure 2 shows the distributed system of our robot. Since all controllers are connected through network, the number of wire is significantly reduced with respect to the central architecture control system. The distributed controllers decreased in volume and weight lead to the reduction of energy consumption. So the distributed control architecture is well suitable for the autonomous humanoid robot.

3.1. Main Controller

Main controller contains three different types of CPU. 32-bit RISC CPU is used to control overall operation and its companion DSP processor is able to do fast computation in calculation of inverse kinematics and trajectory planning job, and also one CAN controller chip is mounted. Basically it has 64M SDRAM, additional memory can be extended using Multi Media Card. Host CPU and DSP use HPI (Host-Port Interface) protocol to transmit and receive data fast. To communicate with user interface module, main controller has wireless LAN, so user can send target position and data to a robot.

32. Local Controller

Local 32-bit DSP mounted control units have the ability to control their actuator. They also have the CAN module, A/D converter, PWM unit, and pulse encode unit, etc. Additionally it is equipped with interfacing circuit related with DC motor. The command data from main controller can be received through CAN and the local DSP controls its motor and sensors. Two or more local controller will have force sensors module and a gyro-sensor interface module.

33. Communication Method

As we know, there are two kinds communication media. One is the wireless LAN used between user interface module and a main controller, and the other is the local CAN. The user interface module consists of PC simulator based on windows system. To realize the straight walking, side walking and other posture, it generates the pattern data for actuators, and their data should be sent main controller using wireless LAN. If a humanoid robot has autonomous system to evaluate walking data, PC simulator only transmits via points or target point.

Main controller communicates with local controllers using CAN. Linux is running in the main control unit with an 80c91 CAN controller by Infineon and the device driver is also implemented. Since the local control units have the built-in CAN module, there is no use of loading other CAN controller. To increase the reliability of CAN, we arranged transmission speed, data length and other network conditions based on CAN. Generally there are several kinds of CAN specification such as standard or extend CAN, high speed or low speed and basic CAN or full CAN, and we select the standard, high speed and full CAN in our study.

4. Temporal Analysis of CAN

An analysis for the response time of messages is presented in the worst case for messages in real time, which is similar to the analysis by [8, 9], and some more aspects have been considered: the deadline of a message should not be larger than the period and the CAN controller should not transmit a message of low priority if exists a high priority message pending.

The CAN protocol uses a MAC (Medium Access Control) known as CSMA/NBA (Carrier Sense Multiple Access with Non-destructive Bit-wise Arbitration). The non-destructive bit-wise arbitration allows 100% utilization and message priority based on an 11-bit packet identifier in a standard CAN. In this protocol, any node can access the bus when it is idle. Similar to Ethernet, each node attempts to transmit when the bus is silent. Unlike Ethernet, there is no collision. If two or more nodes start transmitting simultaneously, bus conflict is resolved by bit-wise arbitration using the IDENTIFIER field. A "0" is dominant on wire and overrides a "1". When a node transmits a "1" but hears a "0". It immediately stops transmitting. The "winning"' node continues to transmit its message to completion. This mechanism guarantees that neither information nor time is lost. The value of the IDENTIFER defines priority during arbitration (lowest IDENTIFER "wins" arbitration). This means two nodes cannot share the same IDENTIFIER. All nodes check the consistency of the message being received and will acknowledge a consistent message and flag an inconsistent message in the ACK slot. The CAN provides automatic error detection, signalling and retransmission. The data portion of packet can be 0 to 8 bytes long. The CAN operates with a fixed priority scheduling policy, but does not support preemption of messages.

41. Analysis of CAN Response Time

According to [10 11], the transmission time of a message *i* in the worst case is given by:

$$R_i = J_i + w_i + C_i \tag{1}$$

The term R_i represents the biggest time required to transmit a message *i* over the physical bus. The CAN frame contains 47 bits of overhead and a bit-stuffing width of 5 bits. Only 34 of the 47 bits suffer stuffing. C_i can be expressed as:

$$C_i = ([34 + 8s_i / 5] + 47 + 8s_i)\tau_{bit} \tag{2}$$

The term s_i indicates the size of the message i in bytes and the term τ_i is the time spent to transmit a bit over the bus (for the 1Mbps bus it will be 1 μs). The term w_i in Eq. (1) represents the delay in the queue in the worst case (the biggest time spent between putting a message in a priority ordered queue and the beginning of the transmission) and is given by:

$$w_i = B_i + \sum_{\forall m \in hp(i)} \lceil (w_i + J_m + \tau_{bit})/T_m \rceil C_m \qquad (3)$$

where hp(i) is the set of messages in the system with higher priority than message i. The term B_i is the blocking time in the system with lower priority than message i and is given by:

$$B_i = \max_{\forall k \in lp(i)} (C_k) \qquad (4)$$

where lp(i) is the set of messages in the system with lower priority than message i. The term J_m is the jitter and T_m is the period of the set of messages with higher priority than message i. Since the term w_m appears in both sides of the equation, a recurrent solution is required, as shown bellow:

$$w_i^{n+1} = B_i + \sum_{\forall m \in hp(i)} \left| (w_i^n + J_m + \tau_{bit})/T_m \right| C_m \qquad (5)$$

Finally, the term J_i represents the message jitter (average waiting time of the message at the transmission queue before scheduling) and is empirically determined. We use the value 1ms.

42. Analysis of CAN Response Time under Error Conditions

Ken Tindell and Allan Burns proposed a model for the calculation of the worst-case response time of messages in CAN under error conditions [11]. The response time can be calculated as:

$$R_i = J_i + q_i + C_i \qquad (6)$$

The term q_m corresponds to the time spent by a message in the waiting queue under error conditions and is given by the following recurrent equation:

$$q_i^{n+1} = B_i + \sum_{\forall m \in hp(i)} \left\lceil \frac{q_i^n + J_m + \tau_{bit}}{T_m} \right\rceil C_m + E_i(q_i + C_i) \qquad (7)$$

$E_i(t)$ is a function of the error recovery overhead and gives the superior limit of all error recovery overheads that can occur in a time interval t. It is given by the following equation:

$$E_i(t) = \left(n_{error} + \left\lceil \frac{t}{T_{error}} \right\rceil - 1 \right) \left(29 + \max_{\forall k \in hp(i) \cup \{i\}} (C_k) \right) \qquad (8)$$

where n_{error} is the number of errors that can occur in a small arbitrary interval T_{error} is the period of error occurrence. The number of errors in an interval duration t is given by:

$$n_{error} + \left\lceil \frac{t}{T_{error}} \right\rceil - 1 \tag{9}$$

In every error, the error recovery overhead can be increased in 29 bits, followed by a message retransmission. Only messages with higher priority than message i can be retransmitted and cause a delay in messages i. The biggest of those messages is:

$$\max_{\forall k \in hp(i) \cup \{i\}} (C_k) \tag{10}$$

In the following section, the equations above will be used to calculate response time for messages of CAN with respect to a humanoid robot, considering the conditions of messages with jitter, presence of error and a very elevated message load in the network

5. Temporal Analysis of CAN

The control structure of our humanoid robot consists of one main controller and 14 local controllers. Each controller has the CAN, and its messages are presented in Table 2. All of the messages have the 20ms period and the 20ms deadline.

Table 2. Messages description of a humanoid robot

P	Message N [1~14]	Size	From	To
1~14	Motor N data	8 byte	Main	Module N
P	Message M [15~28]	Size	From	To
15~28	Motor M data	8 byte	Module M	Main

The communication data length between a main controller and local controller is defined as 2 bytes, and the standard CAN data length is 8 bytes data long, therefore it is efficient to define CAN messages containing 4 data. If sampling time is 10ms, the amount of 40ms data can be contained within one CAN messages. Main controller uses RTR (Remote Transmission Request) to acquire local controller data. If a robot requires more messages from the sensor, vision etc, the required time will be increased.

Table 3 shows the results of the scheduling test over the group of messages presented in Table 2, considering transmission rates 500kbps and 1Mbps. We guess the considered CAN have error conditions: $n_{error} = 5$ and $T_{error} = 10ms$ (error happens 6 times during 20ms), where P stands for priority, and therefore P28 is the lowest message. Message N means messages sent from main controller to local controller 1~14 and message M does from local controller 1~14 to main controller. The length of data is 8-byte and message jitter is 1ms. Transmission period of messages and deadtime is 20ms.

Table 3. Results of the scheduling test

	Response Time[ms]			Response Time[ms]	
Message	500kbps	1Mbps	Message	500kbps	1Mbps
1	3.3	2.3	15	6.8	4.1
2	3.6	2.4	16	7.3	4.2
3	3.8	2.5	17	7.6	4.4
4	4.1	2.7	18	8.0	4.6
5	4.3	2.8	19	8.4	4.8
6	4.6	2.9	20	8.7	5.0
7	4.9	3.0	21	9.1	5.2
8	5.1	3.2	22	9.5	5.3
9	5.4	3.3	23	9.8	5.5
10	5.6	3.4	24	10.2	5.7
11	5.9	3.6	25	10.6	5.9
12	6.2	3.7	26	10.9	6.1
13	6.4	3.8	27	11.3	6.3
14	6.7	4.0	28	11.7	6.5

>From the result, the response time satisfies the period and the deadline of the required specification. Humanoid robot using the speeds of 500kbps and 1Mbps can tolerate the presumed error rates, since the group of messages can be scheduled again. The message exchange time is simulated with ARENA. In the Table 4, the max time means the sum of response time for 14 data. The simulated result time is so different from the response time in Table 3.

Table 4. Response time of messages in the CAN using simulator (Unit: ms)

	500kbps			1Mbps		
Message	Ave	Min	Max	Ave	Min	Max
[1~14]	2.08	0.28	3.86	1.05	0.14	1.96
[15~28]	6.76	4.25	9.26	3.42	2.15	4.70

The reason comes from the existence of time of retransmission caused by errors. In this experiment we guess that the error happens 6 more times during 20ms than that without error, and also the error is generated randomly. By increasing the time of error occurrence, max time considering worst case will increase. Table 5 shows experimental response time of the messages.

Table 5. Response time of messages in experiment (Unit: ms)

P	500kbps	P	500kbps	P	500kbps	P	500kbps
1	0.24	8	1.80	15	3.39	22	5.00
2	0.46	9	2.02	16	3.62	23	5.20
3	0.69	10	2.26	17	3.85	24	5.43
4	0.91	11	2.48	18	4.07	25	5.66
5	1.13	12	2.70	19	4.31	26	5.88
6	1.35	13	2.93	20	4.54	27	6.12
7	1.58	14	3.17	21	4.76	28	6.35

In experiment, there was no error when the messages were transmitted. >From the results of Table 4 and Table 5, defined messages can be transmitted in 20ms using 500kbps speed. Therefore, it is possible to define more messages under the condition of 1 Mbps CAN transmission speed.

6. Conclusion

In this paper, we suggested the distributed CAN architecture for a humanoid robot. It consists of 3 controllers. A PC simulator generates all modules' angle data at remote side. Main controller receives all angle data from simulator and sends them local controllers. Each local controller commands module's motor and returns encoder data to main controller. Main controller and local controllers exchange their information such as motor control and monitoring values through CAN each other. In this case, the messages incline to meet the period of time limitation and the restriction caused by specification. We took a look the real response time of messages, found the appropriate time scheduling for our humanoid and verified it by simulator and experiment. In the future, we will focus on the realization this CAN scheduling at real humanoid.

References

1. K. Hirai and M. Hirose, The Development of Honda Humanoid Robot, *ICRA'98*(1998), 1321-1326
2. K. Hirai, The Honda Humanoid Robot: Development and Future Perspective, *Industrial Robot: An International Journal*, **Vol. 26, No. 4** (1999), 260-266
3. Y. Sakagami and R. Watanabe, The intelligent ASIMO: System overview and integration, *Proceedings of the IEEE Intl. Conference, 2002 Intelligent Robots and Systems* (2002), 2478 - 2483
4. M. Fujita and Y. Kuroki, A Small Humanoid Robot SDR-4X for Entertainment Applications, *Proceedings of the IEEE Intl. Conference, 2003 Advanced Intelligent Mechatroics*(2003), 938-943
5. N. Kanehira, T.U. Kawasaki, S. Ohta, T. Ismumi, T. Kawada, F. Kanehiro, S. Kajita, K. Kaneko, Design and experiments of advanced leg module (HRP-2L) for humanoid robot (HRP-2) development, *IEEE/RSJ International Conference on Intelligent Robots and System*, **Vol. 3** (2002), 2455-2460
6. M. Fujita and Y. Kuroki, Autonomous Behavior Control Architecture of Entertainment Humanoid Robot SDR-4X," *Proceedings of the IEEE Conference Intelligent Robots and Systems*(2003), 960-967
7. Shi. Zonging and Xu Wenli, Distributed Hierarchical Control System of Humanoid Robot THBIP-1, *Proceedings of the 4th World Congress Intelligent Control and Automation*(2002), 1265-1269
8. M. Farsi, K. Ratcliff, M. Barbosa, An overview of controller area network, *Computing & Control Engineering Journal*, **Vol. 10, Issue 3**(1999), 113–120
9. Ni Xiaodong and Zhang Yanjun, Determining message delivery delay of controller area networks, *Proceedings. 2002 IEEE Region 10 Conference on Computers, Communications Control and Power Engineering*, **Vol. 2**(2002), 767–771
10. Tindell, K., Burns, A. and Wellings, A., Calculating Controller Area Network (CAN) Message Response Time, *Control Engineering Practice*, **Vol. 3, No. 8**(1995), 1163-1169
11. Tindell, K. and Burns, A., Guaranteed Message Latencies for Distributed Safety Critical Hard Real Time Networks, *Technical Report YCS 229, Department of Computer Science, University of York, England*(1994)

Acknowledgements

This work was supported by Grant No. R01-2003-000-10364-0 from Korea Science & Engineering Foundation.

MORE EFFICIENT JAVA RMI FOR GPRS DEVICES

JALAL KAWASH, GHASSAN SAMARA, AHMAD EL-HALABI
Department of Computer Science, American University of Sharjah
Sharjah, P.O.Box 26666 , UAE

This paper introduces a new J2ME RMI package, which makes use of object compression in order to minimize the transmission time. The package also makes use of object encryption for secure channels. The currently used RMI package for wireless devices does not provide either of these features. Our package substantially outperforms the existing Java package in the total time needed to compress, transmit, and decompress the object for GPRS networks, even under adversary conditions. The results show that the extra time incurred to compress and decompress serialized objects is small compared to the time required to transmit the object without compression in GPRS networks. Existing RMI code for J2ME can be obliviously used with our new package.

1. Introduction

There is a constant increase in the proliferation of wireless handheld devices and in their computing capabilities. Wireless devices have limitations with processor power, memory space, and bandwidth. Sun Microsystems introduced Java 2 Micro Edition (J2ME) platform in order to cope with some of these limitations and to address the needs of a rapidly growing wireless technology market. About half a billion users currently carry handheld phones that can run J2ME and there are 150 mobile operators supporting Java [1]. Except for mobile gaming, this huge device population is not being taken advantage of.

Java Remote Method Invocation (RMI) allows programmers to rapidly create Java-to-Java distributed applications, without the need to reason about the complex message passing details. J2ME supports an RMI Optional Package (RMI OP) on some device families, and Java RMI on wireless devices offers a promising mechanism to address the need to build successful mobile and P2P applications. Many reasons lead us for this conjecture. These include Java's wide adoption, development convenience, cross-platform compatibility on a wide-rang of supporting devices, and an appealing security model.

Java objects are passed by value to remote methods through *serialization*, which is a mechanism of converting a set of objects into a linear stream of bytes. Because objects may contain references to other objects, serializing Java object converts them into linked structures and it also inflates their original size. Transmitting such large object graphs can consume a large chunk of network bandwidth and CPU time. In spite of low bandwidth and large transmission error rates in wireless networks, RMI OP does not try to compress serialized objects before transmitting them. Furthermore, RMI OP does not encrypt these objects before transmission. The programmers are left with the job of ensuring both efficient and secure transmission of Java serialized objects.

In this paper, we describe RMI EOP, a drop-in replacement for the RMI OP package that incorporates automatic compression and optional encryption for Java objects. Old code written using RMI OP is oblivious to the RMI EOP replacement. Our experimental results show that in spite of the extra time incurred by compressing and decompressing objects, RMI EOP transmits objects faster than RMI OP by a factor of 27% to 51% in GPRS networks.

Sun's original Java RMI implementation was slow and many enhancements and drop-in replacements have been suggested. Krishnaswamy et al. [2] proposed a better implementation of RMI that uses UPD instead of TCP and relies on caching. Thiruvathual et al. [3] and Philipsen et al. [4] suggested alternative object serialization mechanisms. Since serialization is the major performance inhibitor in RMI, Berg and Ploychronopoulos [5] implemented part of Java's serialization protocol in native code to make it faster. Other similar studies to improve RMI efficiency include Nester et al.'s [6] and Massen et al.'s [7]. The latter discussed a new implementation of RMI which uses static instead of just-in-time compiling. This allows the utilization of compile-time information to get better object sterilizations. The implementation also utilizes a faster protocol and communication. Their experimental results were obtained on multiprocessor machines with 16 or 32 processors. However, Nester et al. [6] show that faster RMI protocols can be implemented in Java and without native code. Kurzyniec et al. [8] tested different RMI protocol implementations. All of these studies are concerned with "full-size" Java Virtual Machines (JVMs) and do not apply to J2ME environments.

However, there is some (although very limited) related work in J2ME environments. P. C. Wei et al. [9] reported on RMI support and optimization for bluetooth environments. They developed a cost model for access patterns in RMI communication. This study is limited to bluetooth. Other related studies include memory management [10], garbage collection [11], and energy savings [12] for limited-memory environments. Optimizing Java-based cryptography applications to Kilobyte Virtual Machines is discussed in [13].

To the best of our knowledge, this is the first study that is concerned with developing a more efficient replacement of J2ME OP using serialized object compression. Our work also includes encryption for secure channel mechanisms.

2. Background

2.1 J2ME

The J2ME architecture involves *configurations*, *profiles*, and *optional packages*, which can be used by developers to construct a complete Java runtime environment that closely fits the requirements of a particular range of devices. Each combination is optimized for the memory, processing power, and I/O capabilities of a class of mobile devices. In J2ME, RMI is only [14] supported in the JSR36 Connected Device Configuration (CDC), which combines a Compact Virtual Machine (CVM) with selected library classes. CDC has many profiles and packages, including the JSR46 Foundation Profile (FP), JSR129 Basis Profile (PBP), JSR62 Personal Profile (PP) and RMI OP. The RMI OP reference implementation can be built with implementations of CDC/FP based profiles and PBP. RMI OP requires a minimum RAM of 512 KB.

The alternative configuration to CDC is the Connection Limited Devices Configuration (CLDC). However, RMI is not supported in CLDC.

2.2 Data Compression

Data compression is the process of encoding data so that its storage space or transmission time is minimized. There are two types of data compression algorithms depending on how they preserve data. *Lossy data compression* does not require the compressed data to be exactly the same as the decompressed data, but should be close enough in order to be useful in some way. Methods of this category are called *codecs* (coders/decoders) and are popular with streaming media and telephony applications [15]. Obviously, lossy compression algorithms are not suitable for compressing programs including Java objects, which require *lossless data compression*. This category prohibits any difference between de-compressed and compressed data [15].

Our RMI enhancement makes use of two lossless tools, which are Prediction by Partial Matching (PPM) [16] and GNU Zip (GZip) [17].

PPM is an adaptive statistical data compression technique based on context modeling and prediction. PPM tries to guess the nth symbol in a stream, after reading the preceding $n-1$ symbols. The probability distribution of making the correct guess determines the encoding of the next symbol [16]. PPM can be used with 16 different levels. Compression time and quality respectively increase and decrease with the compression level.

Gzip is an open-source replacement for the *UNIX compress* program. Gzip is based on the deflate algorithm, which is a combination of LZ77 and Huffman coding [17]. Its main advantages are much better compression rate and freedom from patented algorithms.

Our choice for these two tools is driven by a preliminary study of ours that compared the quality, time, and memory usage of six famous tools for compressing Java objects. These are PPM, GZip, BZip2, LZMA, LZO, and JXlib. It was determined that PPM generates a consistently high data compression ratio for small size and large size data objects as well. Other tools may exhibit inconsistency with the compression ratios for different object sizes. PPM, however, incurs a substantial running time cost. Since our objective is to minimize the data size transmitted over wireless network, we believe spending this extra time is essential. Nevertheless, to balance this choice, our solution can use GZip instead, which produces a lower compression quality, but in a substantially faster time. In our preliminary study, LZMA outperformed PPM in compression ratio as well as processing time. However, LZMA is not currently part of RMI EOP for reasons discussed in the conclusion.

3. RMI Enhanced Optional Package

Our protocol for RMI EOP consists of a revision of how RMI OP performs the *writing* of the serialized object to the "data block output stream" and consequently a revision of the *reading* operation from the stream. This requires the agreement between the remote object's skeleton and the client's stub on a new header format, implemented by our *construct header* operation. The protocol is size-dependent as implemented in the *operation mode* procedure, in order to prevent RMI EOP from making small objects become larger after compression. Each of these operations is briefly discussed next.

Writing and Reading: The writing operation is outlined in Figure 1. For small size (less than 32 bytes) serialized objects, compression is omitted, unless encryption inflates the object serialization to a size larger than 32 bytes. For larger objects, the procedure depends on the operation mode specified by the programmer. This mode affects the compression tool and level used. Regardless of the mode used, an appropriate packet header is generated (*Write Header* in Figure 1). The read operation is merely a reversed process for the write operation.

Operation Mode: There are three operation modes in RMI EOP: *medium*, *slow*, and *fast*. The medium mode is the default mode and it uses PPM with level 16 for medium size objects (between 32 and 256 bytes), and uses PPM level 8 for larger objects. The medium mode is suitable for high-end CDC devices (400Mhz processors and 128MB RAM). In the slow mode, PPM level 16 is used regardless of the size of the object. The slow mode is only suitable for full-blown server machines. Finally, the fast mode uses GZip for all objects. This mode is suitable for low-end CDC devices. These decisions are made on-the-fly based on the chosen mode.

Packet Header: The procedure Write Header is responsible for generating compatible packet headers between the remote object's skeleton and the client's stub. The header size varies with the object size. RMI EOP uses 3 header sizes, which can be determined by reading the first byte (called the *indicator*). For example, if the indicator includes a value less than 40Hex, the header is a 1-byte header. The headers are as follows:
1-byte header: four bits indicate the size of the object and an additional bit indicates if the object is encrypted or not.
4-byte header: The first byte is the indicator byte; the second byte is the operation mode; the third is the original object size (prior to compression and decryption); and the last is for the size after compression and encryption.
10-byte header: This header adds (to the 4-byte header) 3 bytes for the original size of the object and 3 bytes for the resulting size.

Encryption: Secure RMI is established by using symmetric-key cryptography. The symmetric key is valid for one RMI session and public key cryptography is used in order to exchange the session key.

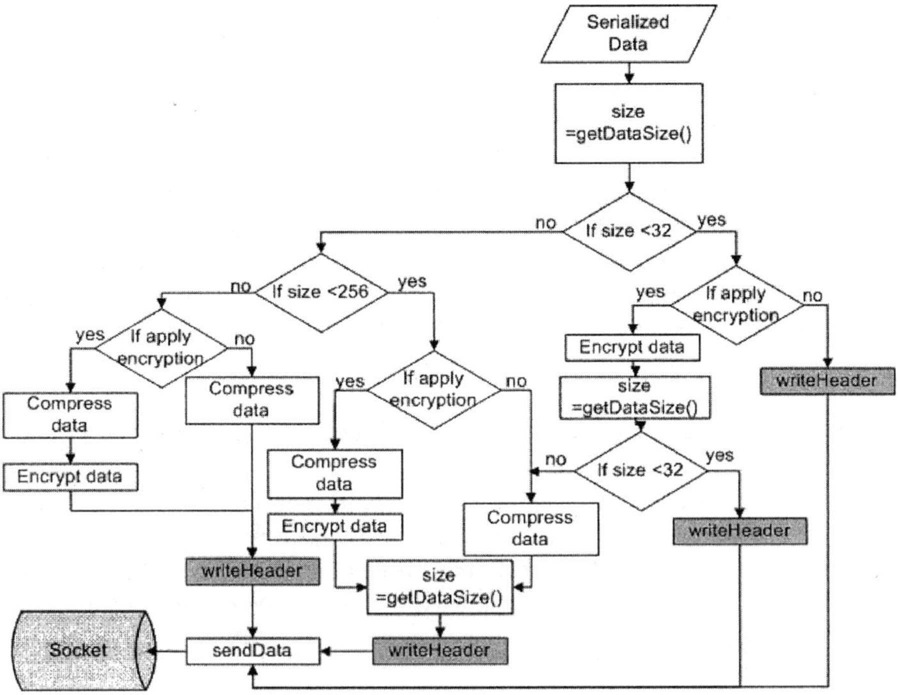

Fig. 1. A summary of the RMI EOP writing operation

Memory Requirements: On limited memory devices, PPM can be prohibitively expensive in terms of RAM usage. RMI EOP requires a minimum of 1MB of RAM for fast mode and 30MB for medium mode. Typical CDC devices are equipped with 32 to 128MB of RAM. For storing objects, RMI EOP makes use of chunking. It uses a 100KB buffer to store the compressed and encrypted object. When the buffer is filled, its contents are transmitted and a new chunk can be prepared in the buffer.

Using RMI EOP: The changes to existing Java RMI OP code are minimal. The programmer is required to make remote object types subclasses of `comUnicastRemoteObject`, instead of `UnicastRemoteObject`. A new overloaded constructor is provided in `comUnicastRemoteObject`, `super(port, mode)`, which allows the programmer to choose from eight operation `mode`s, combining compression, compression level, and encryption. All remaining code is oblivious to changes.

4. Experimental Analysis of RMI EOP

4.1 Java object benchmark

The benchmark introduced in [6] is not suitable for our purpose, since we are not testing different RMI protocols, and we are not aware of any other RMI benchmarks. In fact, both RMI OP and RMI EOP work using the same underlying RMI protocol and will both generate exactly the same communication patterns and number of messages. Since RMI EOP uses compression and encryption, we are obliged to verify how RMI EOP performs relative to RMI OP on different Java objects. So, our benchmarking is primarily concerned with using different object contents and sizes.

Test cases : Our benchmark contains objects that contain Java types (all primitive types plus some objects). These are: `boolean`, `byte`, `char`, `short`, `int`, `long`, `float`, `double`, `String`, `Vector`, and `HashTable`. The *base* class contains arrays of all of these types. All arrays of all members of one class have the same size, *ArraySize*, which is varied between experiments. *ArraySize* is one indicator of the object size. Variations on this base class are constructed by systematically removing a member of the largest type in size. This allows us to generate 550 different test case classes, with different contents and sizes.

Parameters and assumptions: RMI EOP incurs an additional cost for compressing the object by the sender and then decompressing it by the receiver. The time required to both compress and decompress an object is called *processing* time. So the total time required to send and receive an object between the calling object and the remote object in RMI EOP consists of processing time in addition to the *transmission* time. We assume that both ends in RMI communication (sender and receiver) are CDC devices (P2P environment). That is the time taken to compress and decompress an object is substantially larger than the case when one of the parties is a full-size server machine. Even with this assumption, we demonstrate that RMI EOP is appealing.

In RMI OP, only the transmission time need to be measured. The set up time is similar for both packages and is ignored. When secure channels are used the processing time for both packages includes the time required for encryption and decryption. Our analysis is based on GPRS wireless network technologies. The peak performance of GPRS is 53.6 Kilobit/second.

4.2 Development and Testing Environment

RMI EOP was developed using Nokia's Series 80 Developer Platform 2.0 SDK for Symbian OS – For Personal Profile, Version 1.0 [19]. The *running time* measurements reported in the next subsection are valid for devices with clock speed of 400 MHz and 128MB RAM, and RMI EOP is running in medium mode [18].

4.3 Summary Results

Even if GPRS operates at its peak, RMI EOP shows a total time savings over RMI OP of at least 27%, ignoring re-transmissions, and without encryption, as is shown in Figure 5 and Table 1. In Figure 2, the *x*-axis represents *ArraySize* (an indication of the object size). These numbers are even better for RMI EOP in the cases of faulty channels and secure channels. We only show the results for the base test class, which contains all of the Java types mentioned earlier.

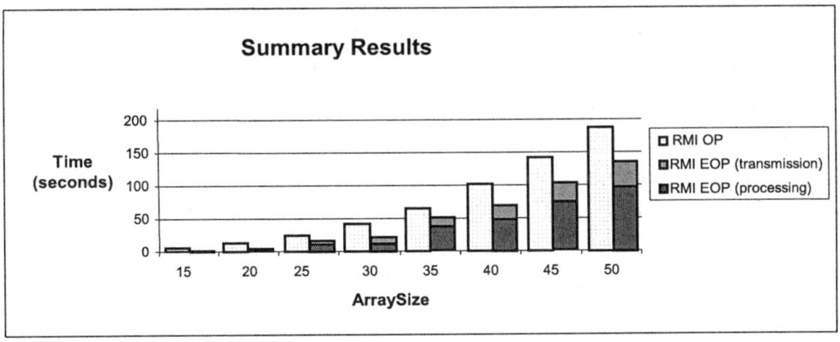

Fig. 2. Time for different ArraySizes in the base class

Table 1. Detailed results for selected array sizes in the base class

ArraySize	20	30	40	50
Original Object Size (Bytes)	88445	286855	686065	1263275
Compressed Object Size (Bytes)	20475.6	60868.6	140270	268334.6
RMI EOP Processing (Sec)	3.388	19.18	49.52	96.98
RMI EOP Transmission (Sec)	3.056	9.085	20.936	40.050
RMI EOP Total (Sec)	6.444	28.265	70.456	137.03
RMI OP (Sec)	13.201	42.814	102.398	188.549
RMI EOP Time Saving	51%	33%	31%	27%

Faulty Channels Effect: When channels are faulty (and this is typical in wireless networks), a retransmission of the serialized object will be required. The faulty channel effect on RMI EOP is minimal, but it has a high impact on RMI OP.
Secure Channels Effect: Encrypting serialized objects inflates their size and, therefore, makes their transmission time higher. Hence, the use of compression is even more urging when using secure channels. The benefits of using RMI EOP over RMI OP are magnified when objects of the base class are encrypted.
Bandwidth Loss Effect: When GPRS does not operate at its peak throughput, RMI EOP becomes even more attractive to use.
The full version of the paper discusses the experimental results for these three effects in detail [20].

5 Conclusions

We have introduced a new J2ME RMI package, which makes use of object compression in order to minimize the transmission time. The package, called RMI EOP, also supports secure channels. The currently existing RMI package (RMI OP) for wireless devices does provide either of these crucial features.
In GPRS networks, the total time needed in RMI EOP to compress, transmit, and decompress the object is substantially lower than the time required to transmit an uncompressed object using RMI OP. This conclusion is valid even under extreme conditions that favor RMI OP. These conditions are: (1) peak GPRS performance, (2) non-faulty channels, (3) insecure channels, and (4) both communication ends are CDC devices. When these conditions are relaxed, the results are more appealing.

References

1. Mobile Monday Web Site, April 2005. http://www.mobilemonday.com
2. Krishnaswamy V. *et al*, Efficient Implementation of Java RMI. In *Proc. Of the 24 USENIX Conference on Object-Oriented Technologies and Systems* (1998) pp. 19-27.
3. Thiruvathukal G. K., Thomas L. S., and Korczynski A. T., Reflective Remote Method Invocation. *Concurrency: Practice and Experience*, **10, 11-13** (1998) pp. 911-926.

4. Philippsen M., Haumacher B., and Nester C., More efficient Serialization and RMI for Java. *Concurrency: Practice and Experience*, **12,** 7 (2000) pp. 495-518.
5. Berg F. and Ploychronopoulos C. D., Java Virtual Machine Support for Object Serialization. In *Proc. of the ACM 2001 Java Grande Conference* (2001) pp. 173-180
6. Nester C., Philippsen M., and Haumacher, B., A More Efficient RMI for Java. In *Proc. Of the ACM 1999 Java Grande Conference* (1999) pp. 153-159.
7. J. Maassen, *et al*, Efficient Java RMI for Parallel Programming. *ACM Transactions on Programming Languages Systems*, **23, 6** (2001) pp. 747-775.
8. Kurzyniec D., Wrzosek T., and Slominiski A., Experiments with Multi-Protocol RMI in Java. In *Proc. of the ACM 2002 Java Grande Conference* (2002) pp 233.
9. Wei P. C., Chen C. H., Chen C. W., and Lee J. K., In *Proc. of the ACM 2002 Java Grande Conference* (2002) pp. 237.
10. Chen G. *et al*, Heap Compression for Memory-Constrained Java Envrironments. In *Proc. of the 18th Annual ACM Conference on Object-Oriented Programming, Systems, Languages, and Applications* (2003) pp. 282-301.
11. Chen G. *et al*, Tuning Garbage Collection in an Embedded environment. In *Proc. of the 18th Int'l Symposium on High-Performance Computer Architecture* (2002) pp. 92.
12. Chen G., Kandemir M., and Vijaykrishnan N., and Wolf W., Energy Savings through Compression in Embedded Java Environments. In *Proc. of the 10th International Symposium on Hardware/Software Codesign* (2002) pp. 163-168.
13. Matsuoka Y., Schaumont P., Tiri K., and Verbauwhede I., Java Cryptography on KVM and its Performance and Security Optimization using HW/SW Co-design Techniques. In *Proc. of International Conference on Compliers, Architecture, and Synthesis for Embedded Systems* (2004) pp. 303-311.
14. Java 2 Mirco Edition CDC v1.0a Specification, Retrieved September 14, 2004 from: http://jcp.org/en/jsr/detail?id=62
15. Data Compression, Retrieved October 1, 2004 from: http://www.bambooweb.com/articles/l/o/Lossless_data_compression.html
16. Crauser, A Prediction by Partial Matching. Retrieved October 1, 2004 from: http://www.algorithmic-solutions.info/leda/manual/PPMIICoder.html
17. Gailly J., The gzip homepage. Retreived October 1, 2004 from: http://www.gzip.org
18. i-mate Pocket PC. http://www.carrierdevices.com.au/products.php?id=3
19. Forum Nokia, Series 80 Developer Platform 2.0 SDK for Symbian OS – For Personal Profile User's Guide, July 6, 2004.
20. Kawash J., Samara G., and El-Halabi A., More efficient Java RMI for GPRS devices. Technical report, American University of Sharjah, UAE, July 2005.

IMPLEMENTATION AND PERFORMANCE ANALYSIS OF ISCSI-BASED VIRTUAL STORAGE SYSTEM WITH WIRELESS NETWORKS

HYOTAEK LIM AND SAEBOM CHOI

Department of Computer Engineering, Dongseo University
Busan, 617-716, Korea
htlim@dongseo.ac.kr, saebom@dongseo.ac.kr

DAEHUN NYANG

Graduate School of Information Technology and Telecommunication
Inha University, Inchon, 402-751, Korea,
nyang@inha.ac.kr

iSCSI(Internet Small Computer System Interface) is a block-oriented storage access protocol that enables a user to recognize a remote storage as their own local block device through general TCP/IP networks. Since iSCSI uses a standard ethernet switch and router for this kind of access, it can not only be applied to ethernet technologies, but can also be used to create a storage networking system without any distance restrictions that can equally be applied to a wireless network environment. Accordingly, focusing on this applicability, this paper presents an alternative approach to overcome the limited storage space of mobile devices based on the iSCSI initiator driver, which was originally designed for wired networks. Its potential with a wireless network is also evaluated.

1. Introduction

Mobile devices suffer from some basic physical limitations because of its aim at implementation of mobility, storage and power consumption. As a result, mobile devices have significant problems related to storage restrictions and limited computing resources. However, the demands on mobile devices are steadily increasing due to the rapid growth and implementation of mobile computing. As such, the most recent issues in mobile technology are focused not on the mobility function but rather on overcoming the present limitations. Therefore, a lot of research has been attempted to overcome the fundamental problems of mobile devices such as low power and small storage, which are the biggest complaints from end users. Therefore, vari-

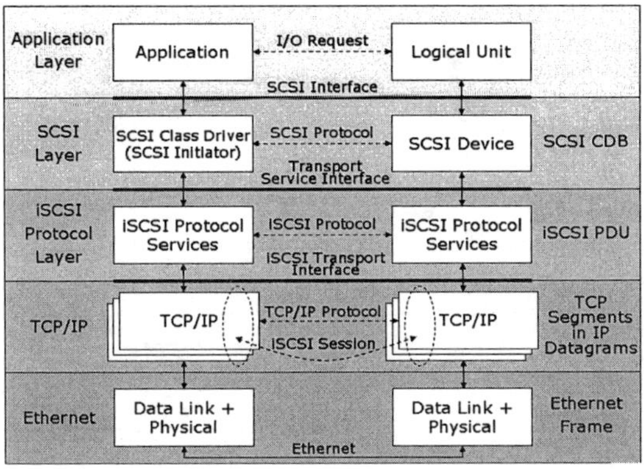

Figure 1. iSCSI Protocol Stack

ous storage devices such as CF (Compact Flash) and SD (Secure Digital) memory have been developed for mobile devices. Yet, these options are relatively expensive and their consumption of power is not ignorable. In particular, there are still clear storage limits when using multimedia data. Therefore, this paper focuses on a virtually mounted storage system based on a wireless network which is relatively cheap and able to supply a sufficiently large storage pool. The current research direction for storage systems based on wired networks is to physically separate the main computing system from storage device to offer more expandability and flexibility.

Therefore, in order to implement a block level I/O system for a mobile device, our study presents a wireless network-based virtual storage system using the iSCSI protocol that enables a block level I/O and high-capacity storage service over general IP networks. iSCSI protocol was designed to solve the problem using an existing IP network, and is now being used to extend the area of storage networking[3]. iSCSI, developed by the IPS(IP Storage) working group of IETF, encapsulates the SCSI CDB(Command Descriptor Block) in a serial stream and allows for the flexible deployment of shared storage resources. The serialized stream data is transferred over TCP/IP instead of over Fiber Channel networks[4]. The iSCSI protocol stack is shown in Fig. 1.

The data flow is started at a high layer position by the user, then the CDB is created according to the SCSI rules and the iSCSI PDU(Protocol Data Unit) is generated as the data structure for the session level. Finally, the storage data within the iSCSI PDU is transferred to the TCP/IP network. Basically, iSCSI is a session level protocol that uses a reliable TCP

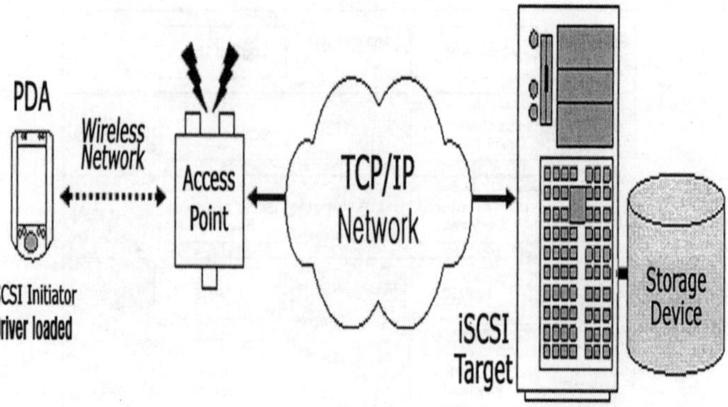

Figure 2. Remote Storage Access System on Mobile Device

connection, which supports built-in error detection and congestion control. However, the performance can deteriorate when network traffic occurs[5,6]. In this paper, the performance of iSCSI-based virtual storage system in wireless networks is evaluated using Bonnie and Tiobench in comparison with NFS.

2. Design and Implementation

2.1. *System Structure*

A PDA is used as the mobile device and an 802.11b network is used to access the remote storage. The iSCSI initiator and target driver is installed in the mobile device and server, respectively. We used the Linux environment as the development platform. Fig. 2 shows the general structure for approaching the remote storage system.

The iSCSI initiator driver uses LKM (Loadable Kernel Module) technology in the Linux system to support a block level I/O operation through the IP network. The driver module is dynamically supported in the Linux kernel. This is applied as shown in Fig. 3. Basically, the system is divided into the user and the kernel level. The iSCSI initiator driver in the PDA generates an iSCSI PDU for synchronization and encapsulation of the SCSI data from the user request. Next, the iSCSI PDU is transferred to TCP/IP over the target. Eventually, the mobile device can communicate with the remote iSCSI target server. Now, the user of the mobile device can recognize the remote storage device as its own local block device.

Usually, an mobile device does not need a SCSI driver and has a flash

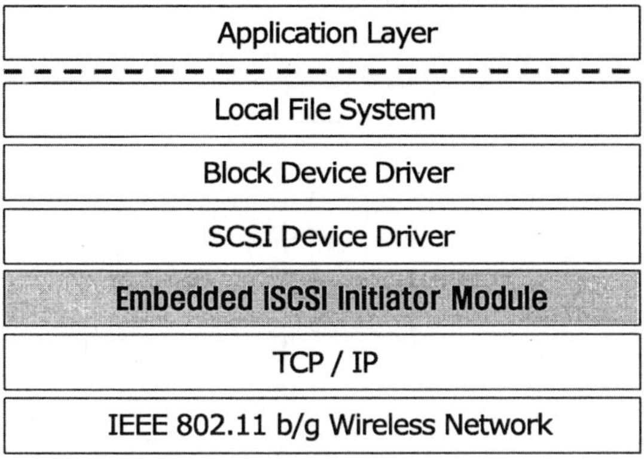

Figure 3. An Architecture Layer in Mobile Device

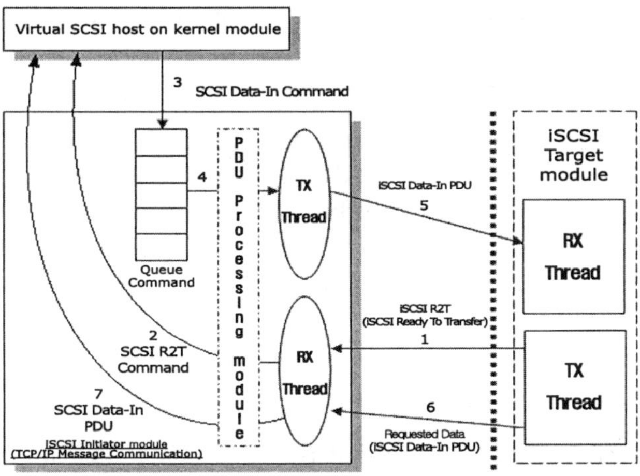

Figure 4. Fundamental Process of iSCSI Data-In Command

file system as a file system driver. Thus, to register a virtual SCSI host in the kernel, the SCSI dependant modules need to be loaded. When a virtual SCSI host is registered in the mobile device, it can perform a encapsulation and decapsulation of a SCSI command for an iSCSI operation.

2.2. *Data Transfer Procedure*

The iSCSI performs a real SCSI I/O over the TCP/IP. This process is almost the same as the iSCSI protocol in wired environment.

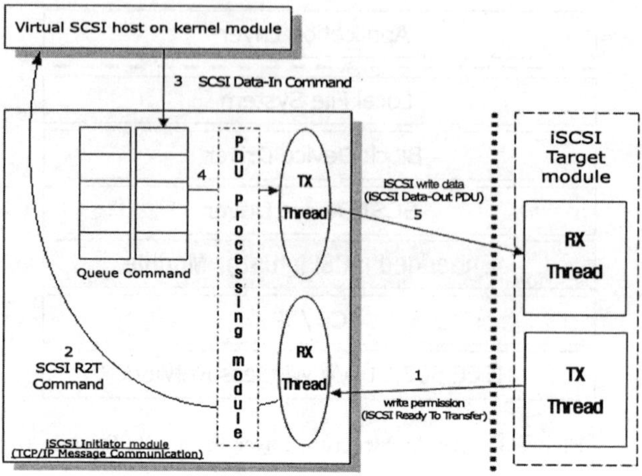

Figure 5. Fundamental Process of iSCSI Data-Out Command

2.2.1. *iSCSI Read Process*

When a user issues a read command, the virtual SCSI host in the mobile device creates a SCSI read command and sends it to the remote iSCSI target process through the wireless network. At this point, the iSCSI target replies to the requested command by sending an iSCSI R2T(Ready To Transfer), which means that the iSCSI target is ready to transfer. Fig. 4 describes this process.

2.2.2. *iSCSI Write Process*

After an iSCSI write request is sent by the iSCSI PDA, the target starts an iSCSI Data-out operation. Fig. 5 describes the iSCSI write process.

2.2.3. *User Interface*

It is easy to implement an iSCSI initiator based on a wireless network, since the basic process is almost the same as an initiator based on x86, except for the communication structure. The HPs iPAQ-h3850, selected as the target device, is a Strong-ARM (Advanced RISC Machine) system, so a Linux-2.4.19-rmk6-ppzal-hh30 kernel(version v7.0.2) was used.

As a result, a file system that can control the storage and an environment that can form a standard SCSI command set are well established. When the iSCSI initiator is loaded, the device is able to recognize the storage at

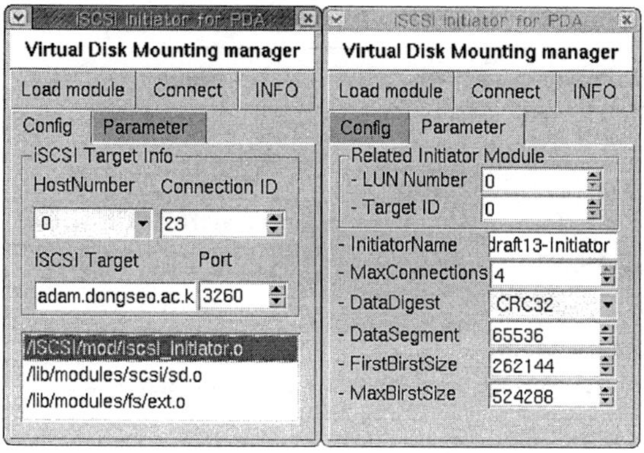

Figure 6. iSCSI Initiator Driver Control Application

a remote spot as a local SCSI disk. Also, the mobile device interface is made using an OPIE SDK based on QPE (Qt Palmtop Environment) that uses a Qt library, as described in Fig. 6, where the bottom left section shows the kernel module information of the mobile device for operating the application, and this is where the iSCSI Target IP domain and TCP port numbers can be set. The right tab is used to control a few parameters that are necessary for the session negotiation of the iSCSI.

3. Performance Evaluation

3.1. *Measurement environment*

The performance of the server was tested based on a campus wireless network, and the equipment used for the storage server is described in Table 1. We used the same environment to compare the performance of iSCSI and NFS.

The flow of data during the test started with the PDA asking for an I/O, which was then passed through the campus wireless network to the remote storage device, which was also on the campus (see Fig. 7). The test was performed on a mobile device like PDA. The campus wireless environment conforms to the IEEE 802.11b standard, and no particular security configuration was used during the test[9]. This is for comparison of NFS that operates based on file I/O and iSCSI that works on the basis of block I/O.

Table 1. Server Side Parameters for Mobile Device

Parameters	value
CPU	Intel Xeon 2.80GHz Dual CPU
OS / Kernel	Redhat Linux Fedora Core1 / 2.4.22-1.2174
SCSI Interface	Adaptec aic7899 Ultra160
Disk Model	COMPAQ BD072863B2
Disk capacity	73.4 GB
Rotational latency	2.99 msec (10,025 rpm)
iSCSI Target Driver	UNH-iSCSI(ref15)

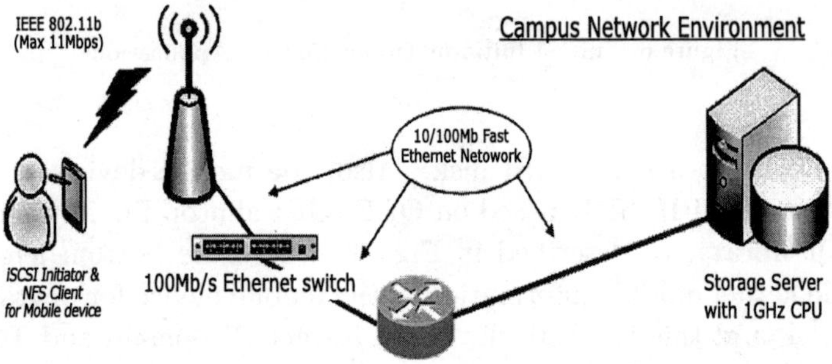

Figure 7. Testbed Environment for Performance Measurement of Mobile iSCSI

3.2. *Performance Analysis*

Considering the limited resources of mobile devices, the analysis was focused on the utilization of CPU according to the I/O operation and throughput of data. Two different analysis tools were used to confirm the results. The first tool was Bonnie, which measures the I/O data in a regular sequence, while the second one was Tiobench, which measures the I/O utilization using a multiple thread. As such, Bonnie was used to compare the throughput of a single data of a predetermined size, while Tiobench was used to measure the utilization of the mobile device CPU, response time, and throughput of data during an I/O. Table 2 shows the results measured by Bonnie. Here, the I/O operating results represent a single file, which shows the data access results in a regular sequence, and also shows the average random seek time. As regards the results measured for an I/O of a 100MB file, iSCSI outperformed NFS by 9% in an average advantage. Plus, it should also be noted that for the average seek time, iSCSI was superior to NFS. This was probably because iSCSI, unlike NFS, accesses the data based on an absolute block location value without passing the file system.

Table 2. Throughput Results of Particular File with Sequential I/O

File Size	50MB		100MB	
Configuration	NFS	iSCSI	NFS	iSCSI
Sequential Read (KB/s)	421	438	423	499
Sequential Write (KB/s)	537	589	546	616
Avg. Random Seek time(ms)	325	32.4	389	33.9

Next, the I/O ability was measured using Tiobench, and the results are described in Figs. 8, 9, and 10. At this time also, the NFS and iSCSI were measured and compared simultaneously. Thus, using two threads, two I/O operations were conducted at the same time. Fig. 8 shows the utilization of the mobile device CPU according to the I/O operation of iSCSI and NFS. Here, iSCSI had lower utilization than NFS had, and in the writing operation, iSCSI had higher utilization after 4Kbytes. It is supposed that this was due to the work-load of a contemporary I/O as the data size expanded. Considering the overall result, the utilization of the CPU in the mobile device was lower with iSCSI than with NFS. This was because the iSCSI initiator does not operate for a physical I/O at the remote storage, as the real SCSI host that exists at the target performs the operation instead. Plus, it was assumed that the result for the writing operation did not differ much between iSCSI and NFS, as the mobile device has to perform an additional operation to send the data in the file system to the iSCSI PDU.

Fig. 9 describes the average latency time of the data according to the size of the I/O. As expected from the results of the average seek time measured using Bonnie, the iSCSIs average latencytime was lower than tat of NFSs. The difference was insignificant at first when the data size was small, but as the data size grew larger the difference became noticeable. In all the results, the reading operation latency time was higher than the writing latency time, which seemed to have something to do with the ability of the mobile device. Fig. 10 describes the data throughput with regard to the I/O. There was no significant difference in the ability to manage the I/O, but iSCSI was superior to NFS in managing the data in general. Both methods had a higher data throughput for data reading than writing. However, interestingly, the writing operation ability with NFS increased as

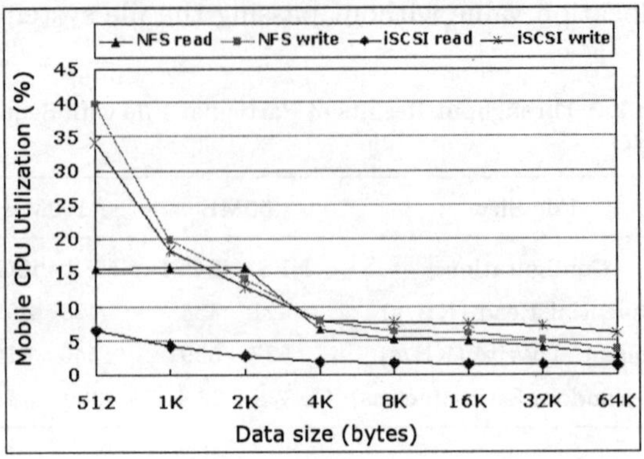

Figure 8. Result of CPU utilization measurement with Tiobench

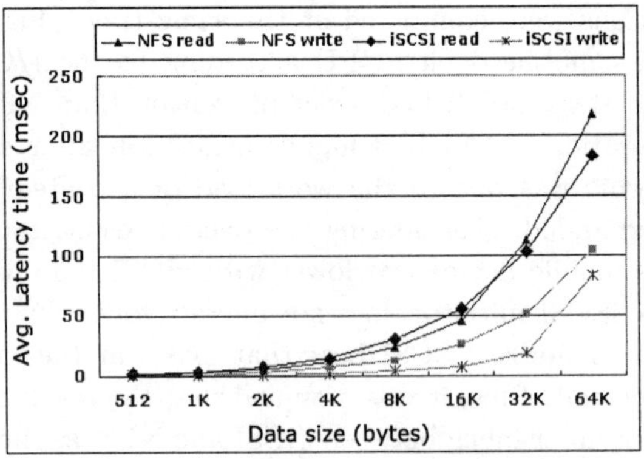

Figure 9. Result of average latency measurement with Tiobench

the data size grew larger. In contrast, the writing operation ability using iSCSI grew steadily. Although iSCSI has to convert the data to a packet to send the data through the network, after arriving at the remote storage, it can access the data using a low level block I/O, which means that it does not have to pass through the file system of the destination[10]. In contrast, NFS sends the I/O data through RPC(Remote Procedure Call) to the NFS destination. The daemon that receives the data sends the data again to the file system of the destination and then the file system sends the data to the block device inside. This difference seems to have caused the result in Fig. 10. Finally, the effect on reducing the power consumption was evaluated when operating an I/O in a mobile device. This was analyzed

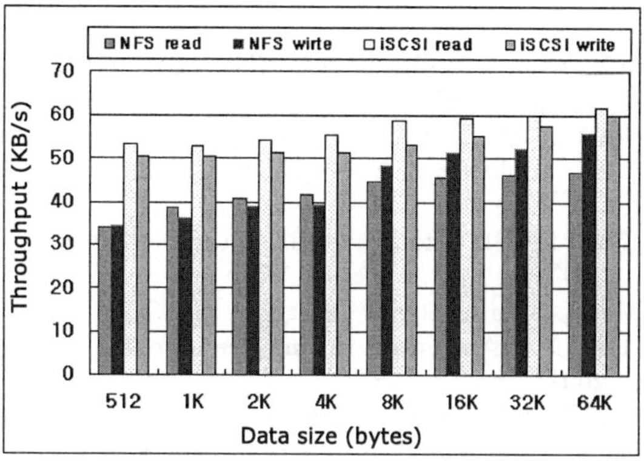

Figure 10. Result of I/O throughput measurement with Tiobench

by the CPU utilization of iSCSI, which was measured earlier, and it was found that a separate power source was not necessary for a physical data I/O in an actual mobile device. That is, iSCSI needs no additional power, except a little for the data I/O operation and use of the wireless network, thereby confirming that iSCSI can be an alternative approach to overcome the storage limitations of mobile devices and inefficient power.

4. Conclusion

We implemented an iSCSI initiator driver for a mobile device using embedded Linux, which is becoming more popular in the mobile market, and analyzed the iSCSI performance in wireless networks. Although the test was conducted in a limited wireless network environment, the proposed system exhibited a better ability than NFS as regards access to remote storage. In addition, the proposed virtual storage driver was applied to a campus IPv6 network. As the iSCSI initiator enables the PDA to have a sufficient storage area, it can be effectively used for multimedia devices. In conclusion, iSCSI would appear to be an effective alternative approach to overcome the current limitations to mobile devices with regard to reducing the power consumption and expanding storage, especially for a mobile environment that needs large storage space. Further research on logical volume separating methods is also needed to offer more efficient storage space, based on one huge remote storage system, to a high number of different kinds of mobile device.

References

1. Nat'l. Committee for Info. Tech. Stds. (NSITS), SAM2, SCSI Architecture Model 2, T10, Project 1157-D, Rev. 23, Mar. 16, 2002.
2. G. T. R. Khattar, M. Murphy and K. Nystrom, Introduction to storage area network, Redbooks Publications (IBM). Tech. Rep. SG24-5470-00, Sept, 1999.
3. John L. Hufferd, iSCSI, The universal storage connection, Addison Wesley Publication, 2003.
4. Kalman Z. Meth, Julian Satran, Design of the iSCSI Protocol, Proc. Of the 20th IEEE/11th NASA Goddard Conference on Mass Storage System and Technologies, 2003.
5. Stephen Aiken, Dirk Grunwald, Andrew R. Pleszkun, A Performance Analysis of the iSCSI Protocol, Proc. Of the 20th IEEE/11th NASA Goddard Conference on MMS, 2003.
6. Yingping Lu, David H. C. Du, Performance Study of iSCSI-Based Storage Subsystems, IEEE Communication Magazine, August, 2003.
7. Xubin He, Qing Yang, Ming Zhang, A Caching Strategy to Improve iSCSI Performance, Proc. Of the 27th Annual IEEE Conference on Local Computer Networks, 0742-1303/02, 2002.
8. David Woodhouse, JFFS : The Journalling Flash File system, Redhat Inc, 2002.
9. Shuang-Yi Tang, Ying-Ping Lu, David H.C. Du, Performance Study of Software-Based iSCSI Security, Proc. Of the First International IEEE Security in Storage Workshop(SISW02), 2003.
10. Kalman Z. Meth, Julian Satran, Features of the iSCSI Protocol, IEEE Communications Magazine, August 2003.

A ROBUST CLUSTER-BASED MULTI-HOP ROUTING ALGORITHM IN WIRELESS SENSOR NETWORKS*

XIAO CHEN, MINGWEI XU, YONG CUI

Department of Computer Science and Technology, Tsinghua University
Beijing 100084, P. R. China
E-mail: {csun, xmw, cy}@csnet1.cs.tsinghua.edu.c

A wireless sensor network (WSN) consisting of a large number of micro-sensors with low-power transceivers can be an effective tool for data-gathering in various environments. The energy constraint is the main challenge the WSN faces. Focusing on the characteristics of routing in WSN, we propose a novel Robust Cluster-based Multi-hop routing algorithm (RCM) that can save energy remarkably. The algorithm adaptively organizes sensors to multiple clusters, where each cluster includes a header and several members. The member takes charge of data collection and communication with header; while the header carries out data fusion and forwards the packet to the sink at cluster granularity. Furthermore, dynamic header rotation and node fail-to-resume mechanisms could balance the energy cost on every node and improve the robustness so as to prolong the lifetime of network. The simulation in ns2 demonstrates the advantages of the algorithm including energy efficiency, scalability and robustness.

1. Introduction

The advancements of Micro-Electro-Mechanical System (MEMS) technology, wireless communication and embedded processing have enabled the development of small-size, low-cost, low-power sensor nodes[1,2]. These sensor nodes, with functions of wireless communication, data sensing, processing and collaborative effort, are constructed to Wireless Sensor Networks (WSN) by self-organization.

Similar to that traditional networks (e.g. Internet, ad-hoc), the routing algorithm is still the core of WSN. Due to the unique features of WSN[3,4], it is difficult to transplant the existing routing algorithm to WSN. It is necessary to redesign it aiming at the characteristics of WSN. In WSN, the

*This work was supported by the Natural Science Foundation of China (No 60373010), National 973 Project Fund of China (No 2003CB314801).

energy of node is constrained and can not be recharged, so how to send data to the sink with the minimum energy is the main problem.

In this paper we propose the RCM as a novel routing algorithm in WSN. It is based on cluster model, which adopts multi-hop forwarding method at cluster granularity. In our cluster-based model, nodes are classified to *headers* and *members*. The algorithm organizes nodes to cluster by the way of self-organizing, in which members take charge of data collection and transmission to its header, while the header carries out data fusion and forwards that to the sink node through other cluster headers. Furthermore, there are several significant mechanisms including dynamic header rotation and node fail-to-resume mechanisms, which can average the energy consumption of each node, prolong the lifetime of the network and achieve high robustness. The design of the RCM algorithm guarantees below advantages: Energy Efficiency, Scalability, Robustness.

The remainder of the paper is organized as follows. Section 2 discusses the related work of routing algorithm; Section 3 describes the architecture of RCM algorithm, including the cluster construction phase and the data forwarding phase; Section 4 specifies the details of cluster construction and data forwarding; Section 5 evaluates the performance of the algorithm; and Section 6 concludes the paper.

2. Related Work

The fundamental and unique characteristics of routing algorithm in WSN attract attentions of lots of researchers, so many solutions are proposed. Generally, the routing algorithms can be classified into the plane routing[5–8] and the hierarchical routing[9–12].

Directed Diffusion[6] is a typical plane routing algorithm, which first sets up the appropriate gradient on every node and then forwards data to the sink hop-by-hop according to the gradient. Minimum Cost Forwarding (MCF)[7] establishes a cost field in WSN, which advocates that only nodes on optimal route can forward packets. The construction of cost field refers to the idea of DV routing protocol in Internet.

In plane routing algorithms, all the nodes are in the same layer with the same function. But in hierarchical routing algorithms, nodes are divided into different classes with different tasks each. LEACH[9,10] organizes the cluster dynamically using distributed algorithm, in which the cluster header collects the data from other nodes in the cluster and then directly forwards the data to the sink. LEACH algorithm is based on the analysis of wireless communication energy model, which considers multi-hop routing to be no better than that of single-hop in energy consumptions, even to result in more problems. In LEACH algorithm, the hierarchy and node classification can avoid the collision in data transmission and carry out efficient data fusion, both of which could reduce the energy cost. However, there are many defects and limitations in LEACH. For instance, as every node may become the cluster header, it potentially requires that every node can directly send packets to the sink, but this is impossible in large sensor networks.

3. Architecture

In order to sufficiently exert the advantages of hierarchical routing and avoid the unreasonable assumption of single-hop to the sink, we propose the RCM algorithm that is not only energy efficient but also with high robustness.

The algorithm has two phases: cluster construction phase and data forwarding phase. After all the nodes are deployed in the sensing area, the network undertakes an initialization procedure, namely cluster construction phase, which includes the election of header, communication slot allocation, etc. Afterwards, the network enters into the data forwarding phase to forward the data sensed by nodes to the sink at cluster granularity.

In the RCM, the backbone of the network is dynamically formed with cluster headers carrying out forwarding data, described in Figure 1. There are two layers based on cluster in WSN, including the real layer containing all the nodes and the forwarding layer only comprised of cluster headers. In the procedure of data forwarding, only headers are visible. In nature, it is an algorithm combining single-hop routing with multi-hop routing in order to avoid the unreasonable assumption of single-hop routing.

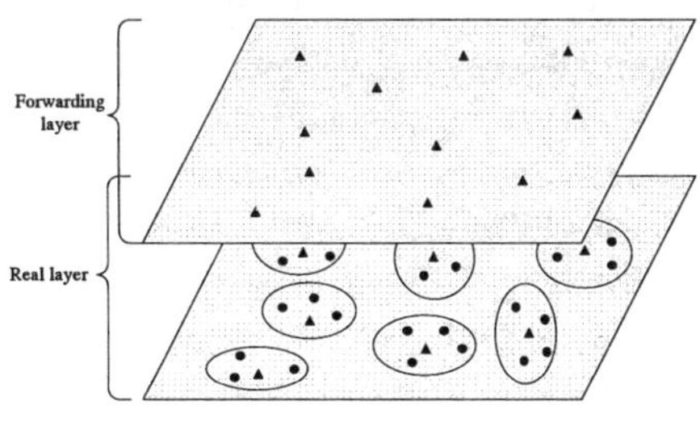

Figure 1. Cluster-based multi-hop routing algorithm.

3.1. *Cluster Construction Phase*

After the sensors are deployed in target area, the sink will send the initial control packet by flooding. Every node can get the distance value to the sink through the initial flooding and the value will be used to elect the header and organize the cluster.

Due to the large energy cost of headers for data-forwarding, it is necessary to design efficient dynamic header rotation mechanism to balance the energy consumption on every node. In the algorithm, the header attends its current energy level in real time. If the energy is lower than the designated threshold, the node will abandon the header role and hand it over to an-other node.

3.2. *Data Forwarding Phase*

In the data forwarding phase, the communication inside the cluster adopts TDMA mode that a member can send its data to the header only in the communication slot allocated in the cluster construction phase. In the rest of time, members could turn to the sleep state.

However, the data forwarding among clusters is another scenario. The cluster header will aggregate the data packets sent from members in a communication cycle, and then send the packet out. When some header receives packets from other headers, it needs to judge whether to go on forwarding the packets according to the algorithm.

4. Detail

In the above section we specify the architecture of the RCM , and then we will describe the details of the algorithm, including the cluster construction algorithm and the data forwarding algorithm.

4.1. *Cluster Construction Algorithm*

The cluster construction algorithm is the fundament of RCM, which takes charge of the construction and maintenance of cluster and the assurance the network connectivity. To describe the algorithm clearly, we define four types of control message.

The four types of control message are defined as follows:

(1) *ADV message* – the initial flooding message sent by the sink. It contains the distance value to sink node called *cost.*

(2) *HA message* – header advertisement message. It includes the hardware address of the header.

(3) *HS message* – header solidification message that requests to join the cluster, which is sent from members.

(4) *ACK message* – acknowledge message that contains the result of communication schedule.

4.2. *Initial Construction of Cluster*

There is an initialization of flooding in the cluster construction phase, to get the *cost* value and complete the construction of cluster. Firstly, the ADV message is flooded from the sink that initializes the *cost* as 0. Then the *cost* will increase with the ADV packet flooding gradually. In this way, every node will eventually get the *cost* value.

If the cost of a node is a multiple of 3 (denoted as *3i*), the node will become header and then broadcast the HA message after a short time. The node that could not be denoted as *3i* will start a timer for HA message after getting the *cost*. If it received the HA message before the time is out, it would set the source node as its header and send out HS message; else it would be advanced to header and send out HA message.

After the node has become cluster header, it will start a joining timer for collecting HS messages sent from neighboring nodes. When the joining timer expires, the header will allocate the communication slot for each member and then send the result to its members. So the members can acknowledge the joining successfully and get the communication slot. By far, the "3-way handshake" procedure of constructing cluster is done.

4.3. *Dynamic Header Rotation Mechanism*

In this mechanism, when a node became header, it should select the *successor* as quickly as possible. Once the energy of the header is lower than the designated threshold (called energy threshold α), the task of the header would be handed over to the successor.

In order to achieve the dynamic rotation, the member should be able to receive the control message sent from the header. So it must insert a member listening slot to the communication cycle in which members can receive the message from the header.

The data packet sent from the member must contain its current energy value, so the header could select the optimal successor through comparing energy values of the members. At the end of every communication cycle, the header will find the optimal member, and then inform it about its role of successor and the allocation information of communication slot. The successors selected in every cycle may be different, because the energy level of each member is changed in real time. At the same time of informing new successor, the old successor will be revoked. When the energy of a header is lower than the designated threshold α, the header rotation would be triggered actually. The header will send the control message of switching in the following member listening slot, informing the successor to take on the header task, so that rapid, seamless and dynamic header rotation can be achieved.

4.4. *Node Fail-to-Resume Mechanism*

Based on several methods described above, the problem of node failure can be solved gracefully. As impact of member failure is little, we can neglect this kind of situation that will not destroy the network.

The header failure may result in the disability of the whole cluster in some routing algorithm. But in RCM, the header should send message in member listening slot of every communication cycle. If the successor does not receive the message in several continuous listening slots, then the header is regarded as failed and the successor should become cluster header immediately. So the collapse of cluster resulting from the header failure can be avoided.

4.5. *Data Forwarding Algorithm*

The forwarding algorithm has two aspects: forwarding inside of cluster and forwarding among clusters. The former is very simple, in which members just send the data to its header in their slots. Here the multi-hop forwarding algorithm among clusters is the emphasis.

After the data packets sent from members are aggregated, the header will send the data processed to other headers for further forwarding. The data packet contains the expected distance value to the sink, which is initialized to the value of the *cost* of source header adding a non-minus offset. The expected distance value will be decreased by each hop. Broadcast is used in the forwarding procedure. A header sends a data packet, which can be received by all of the neighboring headers. The header that got the packet will compare the distance value with its *cost* if the packet is not duplicated. If the distance value is no bigger than the *cost*, the packet would be forwarded; or else the packet would be dropped. In this way the packet will eventually be forwarded to the sink at cluster granularity.

Since the distance value contained in packet is initialized to the cost plus a non-minus offset, there may exist multiple forwarding routes between the source header and the sink. Described as Figure 3, the expected distance value in the packet sent from header A is 45. Header B received the packet, in which the value is decreased to 42. Then the packet will be forwarded after comparison, and header C and D in the transmission range of B receive the packet with the value of 39 at this time. However, both header C and D can meet the forwarding condition, and will further forward data. So multiple forwarding routes appear.

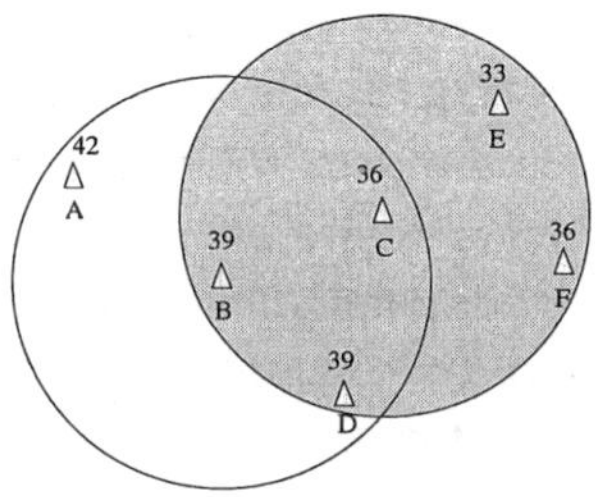

Figure 2. The data forwarding algorithm. The triangle denotes the header, and the figure on it denotes its cost. The member is invisible in the forwarding layer.

The multiple forwarding routes can bring the algorithm with higher robustness, but at the same time it results in a large amount of duplicate packets. So as to reduce the overhead, the algorithm inserts a random delay before forwarding. If the header receives the same packet from other header in the delay time, it will not forward the packet. So it can make the best of the broadcast medium. It restrains the forwarding of duplicate packets and thereby reduces the energy consumption. As described above in Figure 2, both header C and D can further forward the packet. We could assume that header C expires and then forwards the packet earlier than D does. As header D is in the range of C, it will not forward the packet because it knows that C has already forwarded the packet.

5. Performance Evaluation

5.1. *Experiment*

We simulate the RCM algorithm in ns2 environment. In the experiment, several important parameters are evaluated, such as the energy threshold α in dynamic header rotation and the offset in data forwarding algorithm.

There are 50 nodes deployed in the experiment, which are randomly distributed in the area of 500m * 500m. The bandwidth of wireless channel is 2 Mbps. The size of data packet is set to 500 Bytes, and control packet is 25 Bytes. The communication range of node is normally 100m, which increases to 300m when header forwards data among clusters. We assume that members perform sensing task continuously and send back the data packet in every communication cycle. The initial energy of node is set to 2J.

5.2. *Energy Threshold* α

As the header has to forward a large amount of data packets, it will consume much energy. Without efficient dynamic header rotation the network is prone to collapse. In the experiment, the number of data packets received at the sink and the number of nodes alive are considered as the metrics. Figure 4 verifies the effect of dynamic header rotation, and tries to find the approximate optimal value of the threshold. The green line denotes that α is 0, namely without header rotation. Figure 3(a) shows that the sink node can not receive any packet after a short time without the dynamic header rotation. It demonstrates that the network has almost collapsed. But we can find that there are still many nodes alive at that time in Figure 3(b). The reason is that the header failure would result in disability of the cluster. Though members still work normally, the data collected by them could not be sent to the sink.

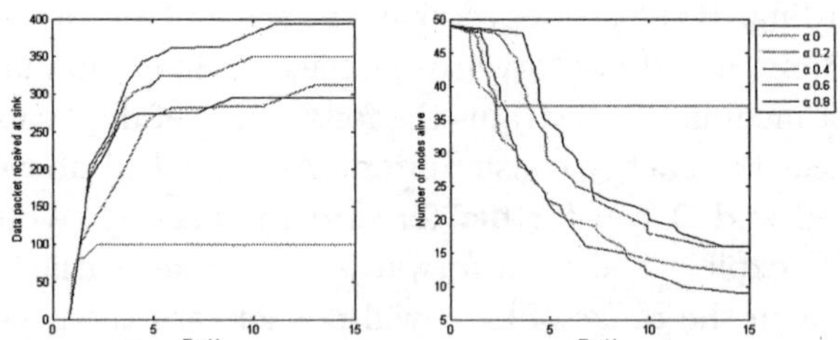

Figure 3. Impact of threshold α. The green line denotes the performance without dynamic header rotation.

With the dynamic header rotation mechanism, the performance is improved remarkably. Nevertheless, the value of energy threshold α can evidently influence the performance, as described in Figure 3. If the value is very small, the energy of the old rotated header will not be able to satisfy the requirements of member to collect and send data, which would depress the quantity and quality of sensing data. But if the value is too big, the initial construction of cluster will be changed after a short time, which would enlarge the energy consumption in following transmissions. So the number of packets received at the sink is decreased. From the figure we can find that 0.4J is an approximate optimal value of energy threshold in the situation that initial energy is 2J.

5.3. *Forwarding Offset*

As analyzed in the above section, the value of offset in data forwarding algorithm is important to the performance of algorithm. If the offset is specified too big, it will carry with a large amount of duplicate packets that result in excessive energy cost. But if the value is too small, the duplicate packets will decrease. However, it would appear that no route can be used to forward the packet, which cuts down the number of packet got at the sink. In Figure 4, we find that the optimal value of offset is 2.

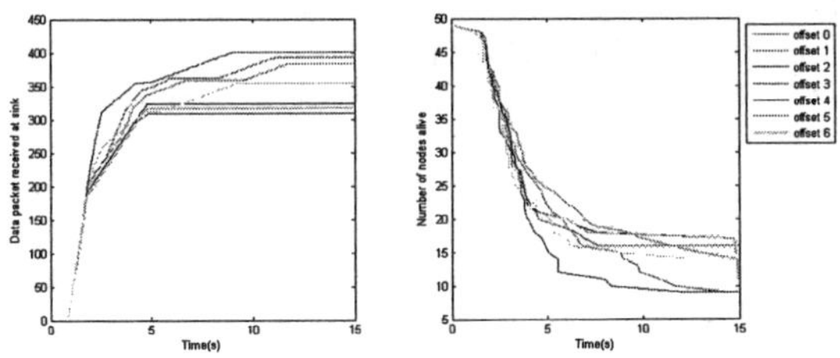

Figure 4. Impact of forwarding offset.

6. Conclusion

This paper studies the characteristics of routing algorithm in WSN, and proposes the RCM that is a novel cluster-based multi-hop routing algorithm. In the hierarchical model, sensor nodes are divided into two types: *headers* and *members*. The clusters are constructed by self-organizing method, in which the members take charge of collecting data and the header carries out data fusion and forwarding to the sink at cluster granularity. Furthermore, the dynamic header rotation and node fail-to-resume mechanisms are included in the algorithm. So the RCM algorithm provides many features including energy efficiency, scalability and high robustness. Through the simulating experiment in ns2 environment, we verify the correctness and effectiveness of the algorithm, and evaluate several important parameters on the performance, such as energy threshold and forwarding offset.

References

1. G. Pottie and W. Kaiser, Wireless Integrated Network Sensors, *Communication ACM*, **43** (2000) pp. 51-58.
2. P. Rentala, R. Musunuri, S. Gandham, U. Saxena, Survey on Sensor Networks (Technical Report, Univ. of Texas, 2002).
3. Ian F. Akyildiz, Weilian Su, Y Sankarasubramaniam, E. Cayirci, A Survey on Sensor Networks (IEEE Communication Magazine, 2002).
4. D. Estrin, R. Govindan,J. Heidemann, S. Kumar, Next Century Challenges: Scalable Coordination in Sensor Networks, *MobiCom* (1999), pp. 263-270.
5. K. Sohrabi, J. Gao, V. Ailawadhi, G. Pottie, Protocols for Self-Organization of a Wireless Sensor Network (IEEE Personal Communication, 2000).
6. C. Intanagonwiwat, R. Govindan, and D. Estrin, Directed diffusion: A Scalable and Robust Communication Paradigm for Sensor Networks, *MobiCom* (2000), pp. 56-67.
7. Fan Ye, A. Chen, Songwu Lu, Lixia Zhang, A Scalable Solution to Minimum Cost Forwarding in Large Sensor Networks (Proc. 10th Int. Conf. on Computer Communications and Networks, 2001).
8. D. Braginsky, D. Estrin, Rumor Routing Algorithm for Sensor Networks (WSNA, 2002).
9. W. Heinzelman, A. Chandrakasan, and H. Balakrishnan, Energy-Efficient Routing Protocols for Wireless Microsensor Networks (HICSS, 2000).
10. W. Heinzelman, A. Chandrakasan, H. Balakrishnan, An Application-specific Protocol Architecture for Wireless Microsensor Networks, *IEEE Transactions on Wireless Communications*, **1** (2002), pp. 660-670.
11. A. Manjeshwar, D. Agrawal, TEEN: A Routing Protocol for Enhanced Efficiency in Wireless Sensor Networks (Int. Proc. 15th Parallel and Distributed Processing Symposium, 2001).
12. S. Lindsey, C. Raghavendra, PEGASIS: Power-Efficient Gathering in Sensor Information Systems (Int. Conf. on Communications, 2001).
13. P. Rentala, R. Musunuri, S. Gandham, U. Saxena, Survey on Sensor Networks (Technical Report, Univ. of Texas, 2002).
14. A. Ahmed, Hongchi Shi, Yi Shang, A Survey on Network Protocols for Wireless Sensor Networks (ITRE, 2003).
15. A. Sinha, A. Chandrakasan, Dynamic Power Management in Wireless Sensor Networks (IEEE De-sign & Test of Computers, 2001).
16. M. Ettus, System capacity, latency, and power consumption in multihop-routed SS-CDMA wireless networks (RAWCON, 1998).
17. T. Shepard, A channel access scheme for large dense packet radio networks (In Proc. ACM SIGCOMM, 1996).

CLUSTER-BASED SECURITY MECHANISM FOR SENSOR NETWORK COMMUNICATION *

INSHIL DOH, HAYOUNG OH, KIJOON CHAE

Department of Ewha Computer Science & Engineering,
Ewha Womans University,
11-1 Daehyun-dong, Seodaemun-gu,
Seoul, 120-750, Korea
E-mail: isdoh@ewhain.net, hyoh@ewhain.net, kjchae@ewha.ac.kr

Security is a major concern in sensor networks, and key establishment is the basic element for secure communication. In this paper, we propose new pairwise key establishment mechanism based on clustering and polynomial sharing, and we also propose new authentication mechanism. Through analysis, we show that our key establishment mechanism achieves good performance, and our proposed authentication mechanism provides unicast and broadcast authentication.

1. Introduction

Distributed sensor networks have received a lot of attention recently due to its wide applications. Especially, as it is expected to provide the basic technique for ubiquitous computing, the development of cost effective and energy-efficient wireless sensor devices is getting more important. Sensor nodes are usually small, low-cost, battery powered, and highly resource constrained. And they can be used to gather a lot of information in various environment after being distributed in great scale. However, they may be deployed in hostile areas where communication is monitored and sensor nodes are subject to capture and manipulation by an adversary. These challenging operational requirements place equally challenging security constraints on distributed sensor network design[6]. Security services such as authentication and key management are critical to secure the communication between sensor nodes in hostile environments. In this paper, we propose cluster-based sensor network architecture and develop pairwise key

*This research was supported by University IT Research Center(ITRC) Project.

establishment and authentication mechanisms for secure sensor communication. Theses techniques are based on static sensor networks and exploit polynomial-based key predistribution scheme.

The rest of this paper is organized as follows. Section 2 gives an overview of basic key predistribution schemes and the problems of the techniques. Section 3 describes our proposal for key distribution and establishment. In section 4, we present authentication mechanism using pairwise keys established. Security analysis and performance evaluations are described in section 5. Section 6 concludes this paper and points out some future research directions.

2. Key management schemes in sensor networks

A fundamental security service is the establishment of a symmetric, pairwise key shared between two sensors, which is the basis of other security services such as encryption and authentication. Several key predistribution techniques have been developed recently to address this problem.

2.1. *Random key predistribution*

L. Eschenauer and V. Gligor proposed a random key predistribution scheme in which a random pool of keys is selected from the key space[1]. Each sensor node receives a random subset of keys from the key pool before deployment. Any two nodes able to find one common key within their respective subsets can use that key as their shared secret to initiate communication. Nodes can then set up path keys with nodes in their vicinity whom they did not happen to share keys with in their key rings. By doing this, two sensors can have a certain probability to share at least one key.

H. Chan, A. Perrig, D. Song proposed q-composite scheme. In the scheme, a pair of nodes sharing q keys can compute new key by applying hash function or XOR computation[2]. Q-composite scheme achieves significantly improved security under small scale attack.

However, these approaches still have some limitations. For the basic probabilistic and the q-composite key predistribution, a small number of compromised sensors may reveal a large fraction of pairwise keys shared between non-compromised sensors. Though the random pairwise keys scheme provides perfect security against node captures, the maximum supported network size is strictly limited by the storage capacity for pairwise keys and the desired probability to share a key between two sensors[3].

2.2. *Polynomial-based key predistribution*

Liu and Ning developed a framework to predistribute pairwise keys using bivariate polynomials and proposed two efficient schemes, a random subset assignment scheme and a grid-based key predistribution scheme, to establish pairwise keys in sensor networks[3]. A random subset assignment scheme can be considered as an extension to the basic probabilistic scheme in [5]. Instead of randomly selecting keys from a large key pool and assigning them to sensors, this method randomly chooses polynomials from a polynomial pool and assigns their polynomial shares to sensors. The scheme further differs from the previous scheme in which the same key may be shared by multiple sensors. In this scheme, there is a unique key between each pair of sensors. If no more than t shares on the same polynomial are disclosed, no pairwise keys constructed using Polynomial-based key predistribution this polynomial between any two non-compromised sensor nodes will be disclosed.

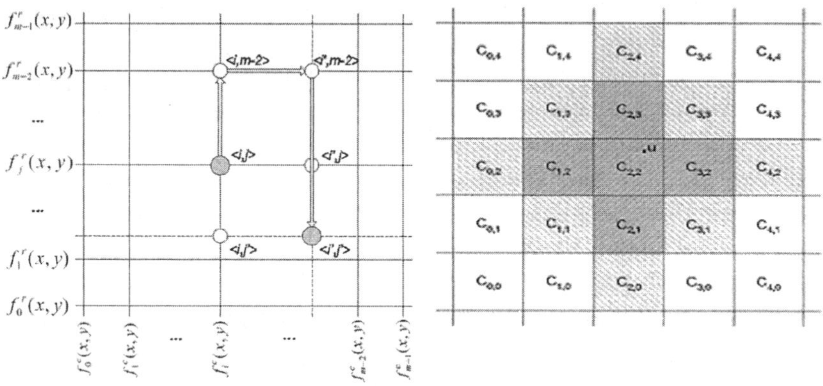

(a) Grid-based key predistribution (b) Location-based key predistribution

Figure 1. Polynomial-based key predistribution.

Grid-based key predistribution scheme by D. Liu, P. Ning generates and distributes polynomials from which keys can be derived[3]. If two sensor nodes share the same t-degree polynomial, they can derive common key values from the polynomial. As shown in Figure 1(a), each row j in the grid is associated with a polynomial $f_j^r(x, y)(0)$ and each column i is associated with a polynomial $f_i^c(x, y)$. The setup server assigns each sensor node in the network to a unique coordinate in this grid. For the node at the coordinate

$(i,\ j)$, the setup server distributes the polynomial shares of $f_i^c(x, y)$ and $f_j^r(x, y)$ to this node. As a result, sensor nodes on the same row or column can perform share discovery and path discovery based on this information.

D. Liu, P. Ning proposed another polynomial based key predistribution scheme which partitions the target field into small areas called cells, each of which is associated with a unique random bivariate polynomial[4]. The setup server distributes to each sensor a set of polynomial shares that belong to the cells closest to the one that this sensor is expected to locate in. Figure 1(b) shows an example partition of a target field. For each sensor, the setup server first determines its home cell($C_{2,2}$ for sensor u), and then discovers four cells adjacent to the sensors home cell, and finally distributes to the sensor its home cell coordinate and the polynomial shares of the polynomials for its home cell and the four selected cells. After deployment, if two sensors can find at least one such polynomial, a common pairwise key can be established directly using the basic polynomial-based key predistribution.

By using polynomial-based key predistribution scheme, instead of distributing pairwise keys, they assigned polynomial shares and enhanced security levels. However, even if we choose polynomials from a polynomial pool, the probability that common polynomial does not exist is high and the pool size affects the key establishment probability[1][3]. And in grid-based key predistribution scheme, when several polynomials are disclosed, all sensor nodes on the same row or column using the disclosed polynomials can be under attacks[3]. Location-based key predistribution scheme also has limitations that sensors located in five neighbor cells share the same polynomials and disclosure of a polynomial could lead to large fraction of sensor nodes are disclosed to attacks[4].

3. Cluster-based key predistribution

The main idea of our proposed mechanism is to combine clustering with the polynomial-based key predistribution technique[2]. In our mechanism, sensor nodes sharing the same polynomial are limited in one cluster, and even if the polynomial is disclosed, the effect could be confined in one cluster. And any pair of sensor nodes in the same cluster can setup pairwise key even if the polynomial pool size is small. In addition, by decreasing the amount of predistribution information, the key setup overhead also can be decreased. We describe the assumptions, network model, and the mechanism.

3.1. *Assumptions and Network model*

We assume that the sensor network field can be clustered as equal-sized hexagons and each cluster is associated with a unique random bivariate polynomial. Each cluster is composed of one clusterhead at the center and many sensor nodes. We predistribute pairwise keys to each pair of clusterheads and assign unique polynomial to each clusterhead before they are deployed. After they are deployed, all the clusterheads distribute polynomial shares to their own sensor nodes to make pairwise keys. We also assume that the clusterheads have stronger computational power and more storage than normal sensor nodes, and are safe during the key setup process.

3.2. *Key establishment mechanism*

Sensor nodes can generate pairwise keys with their own neighbors with the polynomial shares from their clusterheads. If two sensor nodes are located in a cluster, they can generate direct key with their polynomial shares and when they are located in each other's transmission range but in different clusters, they create path key.

3.2.1. *Key-related information pre-distribution*

Sensor network field s is partitioned as $s = n$ x n hexagonal clusters and clusterheads are located at the center of the clusters. As in figure 2, key setup server creates 6 pairwise keys for every clusterhead with the neighbor clusterheads and predistributes the keys. For example, for clusterhead *C6*, six pairwise keys $K_{C6,C1}$, $K_{C6,C2}$,$K_{C6,C5}$,$K_{C6,C7}$,$K_{C6,C9}$,$K_{C6,C10}$ are predistributed. Key setup server also generates a bivariate s t-degree polynomial $f(x,\ y)$ over a finite field Fq, where q is a prime number that is large enough to accommodate a cryptographic key, such that it has the property of $f(x,\ y) = f(y,\ x)$, and assigns unique polynomial to every clusterhead. After sensor nodes are depolyed, for each sensor i, the clusterhead distributes a polynomial share derived by polynomial $f_{Ci}(x, y)$. Polynomial share $f_{Ci}(Ni, y)$ is assigned for a sensor nodes Ni.

3.2.2. *Direct Key establishment*

After being deployed and distributed its own polynomial share, each sensor node broadcasts HELLO messages to its neighborhood. Every pair of sensor nodes including clusterhead in the same cluster can compute their own pairwise key using the assigned polynomial share and each other's id when they want to communicate with each other. For example, two sensor nodes *Ni, Nj* located in the same cluster can compute their pairwise key. *Ni*, with $f_{Ci}(Ni, y)$, computes the pairwise key by substituting y with *Nj*, and *Nj* does the same computation by substituting y with *Ni*. And according to the property of the polynomials, $f_{Ci}(Ni, Nj) = f_{Ci}(Nj, Ni)$, they can establish the same keys and use it as their pairwise key. Every pair of sensor nodes in the same cluster can establish its own pairwise key without exception because polynomial shares of the nodes are from the same polynomial.

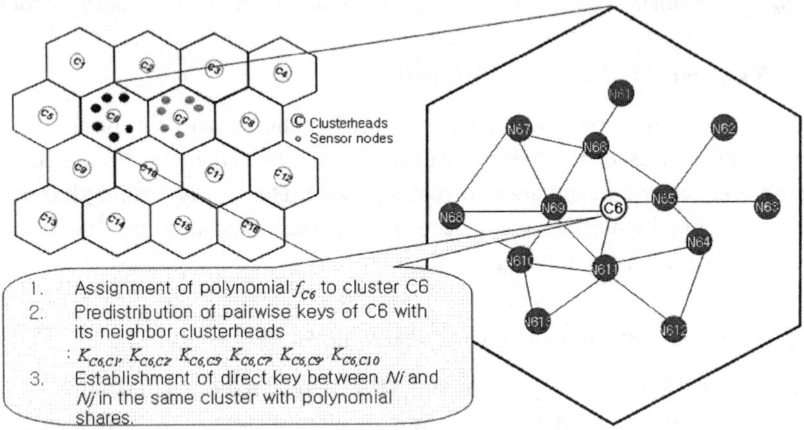

Figure 2. Direct Key Establishment.

3.2.3. *Path Key establishment*

When two sensor nodes wanting to communicate are each other's neighbors but are in different clusters, they establish path key. They cannot establish direct key because their polynomial shares are from different polynomials with each other. One sensor node generate a path key and delivers the key to the other sensor node through their clusterheads. The establishing steps are as follows.

◇ Steps for path key establishment between node *N61* and node *N71*

1. *N61* creates path key $K_{N61,N71}$ and path key establishment request message, encrypts the message with the pairwise key, $K_{N6,C6}$, and broadcasts the encrypted message.

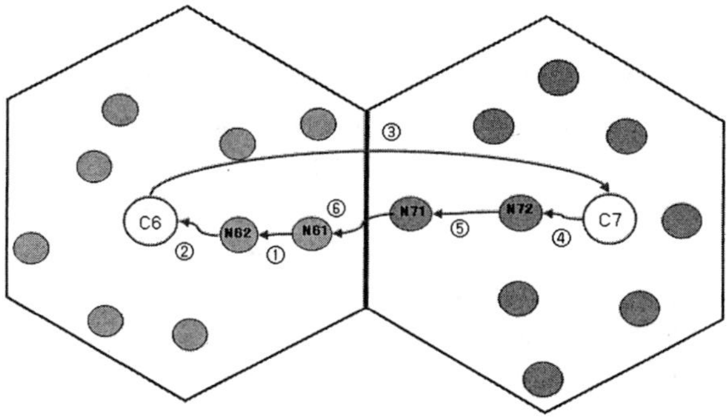

Figure 3. Path key Establishment.

2. Intermediate nodes rebroadcast the encrypted message upto the clusterhead C6.

3. Clusterhead *C6* for node *N61* decrypts the message, encrypts the path key with the pairwise key, $K_{C6,C7}$, and broadcasts the request message to target clusterhead *C7*.

4. *C7* decrypts the message, encrypts the path key with the pairwise key, $K_{C7,N71}$, and broadcasts the encrypted message.

5. Intermediate nodes rebroadcast the encrypted message.

6. *N71* decrypts the message with pairwise key, $K_{N71,C7}$, gets the path key, and sends confirm message to *N61*.

Our proposed mechanism establishes pairwise keys between sensor nodes through direct key and path key establishment process. Even though path key establishment has high overhead compared to direct key establishment, only nodes located near the cluster boundary need path key establishment, and path key establishment overhead can be decreased by meeting proper conditions such as cluster range, number of sensor nodes, sensor transmission range, sensor node density, and so on.

4. Cluster-based authentication mechanism

In this section, we propose authentication mechanism using pairwise keys between nodes established by proposed pairwise key establishment mechanism.

4.1. *Node-to-node authentication*

In our scheme, every message from one node to another node is authenticated in a hop-by-hop fashion using the pairwise keys established between the two neighboring nodes during its transmission. Thus, an unauthorized node cannot inject false data without it being detected. Moreover, when a node reports an event, it also needs to contain a timestamp, and an attack in which an outsider replays an old report will be detected. This hop-by-hop authentication increases the communication overhead, but it can provide strong integrity and authentication for important information.

4.2. *Broadcast authentication*

To authenticate a broadcast message from a sensor node, hop-by-hop authentication cannot be applied because of its delay and overhead. Perrig et al. presented $\mu TESLA$ for base station broadcast authentication, based on one-way key chains and delayed key disclosure[8]. But it assumes that only the base station broadcasts messages to all the sensor nodes because of the delay and the storage problem for key chains for each sensor node. For each node to broadcast messages to all over the network, we need another efficient broadcast authentication mechanism. In this subsection, we propose cluster-based broadcast authentication mechanism. In our mechanism, a sensor node broadcasts messages first, and then the clusterhead of the source sensor node delivers the key-related information to other clusterheads, and finally each clusterhead broadcasts the authentication information to its own member sensor nodes. We can further decrease the redundant traffic by limiting the broadcasting area in a cluster in the final step.

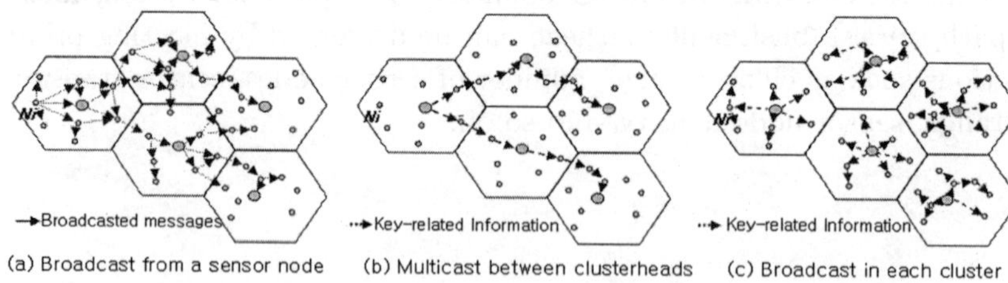

Figure 4. Cluster-based broadcast authentication mechanism.

For cluster-based authentication mechanism, we define group keys for each clusters. These group keys are generated before setting path keys between nodes from different clusters. After setting up direct pairwise keys, every clusterhead creates group key, encrypts it with pairwise keys with its neighbor node, and then delivers the encrypted group key to its neighbors. The neighbor nodes decrypt and relay the keys to its own neighbors by encrypting group key with its pairwise keys with neighbors. Because in this phase, path keys between clusters are not established, the group keys can be safely distributed only in each group. Figure 4 shows the three steps for broadcast authentication mechanism.

(a) When a node *Ni* has data to send, it broadcasts the message with MAC code in the network. The sensor node hashes its pairwise key with its own clusterhead and uses it as MAC key. All the receiving node cache this message.

$Ni \longrightarrow all : message, MAC(Hash(Key(Ni, CH)), message)$

(b) On receiving the broadcast message, the clusterhead recognizes the source node and computes the MAC key, verifies the message, and then encrypts the MAC key with its pairwise keys with other clusterheads and sends the encrypted key to the other clusterheads. If routing between clusterheads is setup at this stage, the message can be multicasted. Otherwise, broadcasting can be applied.

(c) All the other clusterheads decrypt the key value with its own pairwise key with the sending clusterhead and broadcasts the key values to its own member nodes using group key, and the member nodes verify the cached message with the MAC key.

Using this mechanism, we can provide efficient broadcast authentication, and decrease the delay for broadcast authentication. When the clusterhead identifies that the message was compromised, it filters the modified or forged message at the clusterhead level. This can decrease the useless traffic by not broadcasting the message in its cluster any further. In addition, we can maintain the data consistency if loose time synchronization is provided.

5. Performance Evaluation

In this section, we present security aspects against key disclosure, describe simulation model to evaluate the proposed mechanism and analyze the results.

5.1. *Security against Node Captures*

In this section, we analyze the security of our mechanism based on the approach of the analysis of location-based pairwise key establishment[4].

Table 1. Notations

dr	Transmission Range of a sensor node
m	Average number of nodes
a	Side length of a hexagonal cluster
N_s	Number of sensor nodes which share a unique polynomial in a cluster
$P_c(i)$	Probability that i sensor nodes are compromised sharing same polynomial
P_c	Probability that a polynomial is compromised
t	Degree of a polynomial

The density of the sensors in the network can be estimated by

$$D = m/(\pi\ dr^2)\,. \tag{1}$$

Clusters are hexagonal, and with side length a, the average number of sensors that are expected to be located in a cluster and share a polynomial can be estimated by $m(3\sqrt{3}a^2)/2)/\pi dr^2$. With the single range dr as the basic unit for distance measurement(dr=1), we have $m(3\sqrt{3}a^2)/2)/\pi$. We assume a fraction p_c of sensors in the network have been compromised by an attacker. Thus, among Ns sensors that have polynomial shares of a particular cluster, the probability that exactly i sensors have been compromised can be estimated by

$$p_c(i) = \frac{N_s!}{(N_s - i)!i!} p_c^i (1 - p_c)^{N_s - i}\,. \tag{2}$$

Thus, the probability of the bivariate polynomial for this cluster to be compromised is

$$p_c(i) = 1 - \sum_{i=0}^{t} p_c(i)\,. \tag{3}$$

And if we limit the number sensor nodes sharing same polynomial to t, our scheme proposed in this section can provide *perfect resistance against node captures.*

$$N_s = \frac{m * \frac{3\sqrt{3}a^2}{2}}{\pi} < (t+1)\,. \tag{4}$$

In addition, for our proposed mechanism, all sensor nodes located in a cluster can establish pairwise keys with each other with no relation to polynomial pool size, and even if a polynomial itself is compromised, the effect is limited in one cluster and we can decrease the key revision overhead.

5.2. *Simulation Results*

Our proposed mechanism can be affected by the number of path keys needed and the time for path key establishment. We show the efficiency of our mechanism by counting the path keys and estimating the path key establishment time. We used C for counting the number of keys and NS-2 on Linux 9.0 for estimating key establishment time[7]. We also showed the efficiency our mechanism over the location-based key predistribution scheme by simulating on broadcast-based routing mechanism. The parameters used for simulation is described in Table 2.

Table 2. Simulation parameters

Parameter	Values
Area	200m * 200m / 500m * 500m
RadioRange	10m, 20m, 30m
Placement	randomly
Movement	static
MAC	802.11
Numberofnodes	50 – 500
SimulationTime	150s

Figure 5 shows the influence of number of sensor nodes, sensor node transmission range, and cluster range on the number of path keys. We can see that number of path keys increases as sensor node transmission range is grows and approaches cluster range. This is because the number of path keys are needed when sensor nodes are in each other's range and but in different clusters, and the wider the cluster range is, the smaller the number of path keys. Usually because cluster area is much wider than a sensor's transmission range and covers many sensor nodes, even the number of sensor nodes increases, the number of path needed doesn't increase much.

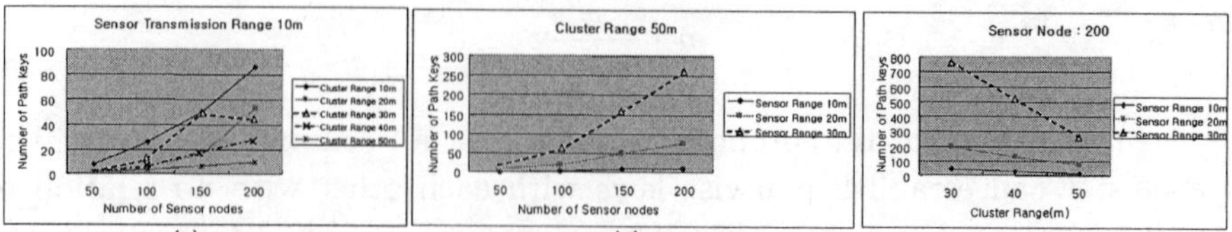

(a) (b) (c)

Figure 5. Number of Path Keys.

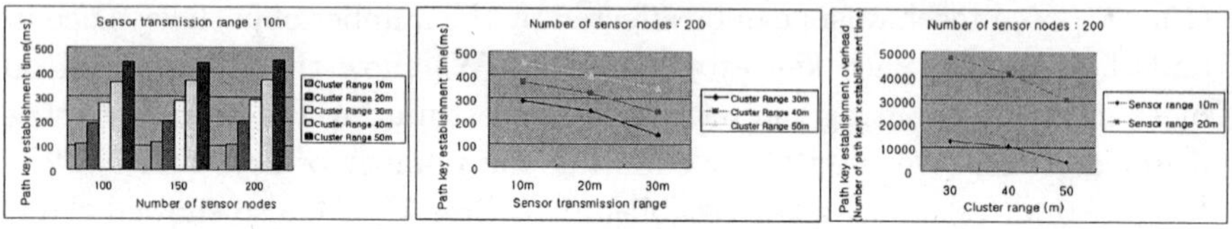

(a) (b) (c)

Figure 6. Path Key establishment key setup overhead.

Figure 6 shows the relationship between path key establishment time and the range. It indicates that the cluster range becomes wider, the time for path key establishment is long because path key request messages need to be relayed through many hops from initiating sensor node to destination sensor node through their own clusterheads. Figure 6(c) reflects the overhead for establishing path keys(number of path keys multiplied by time for establishment). As cluster range becomes wider, the number of path decreases and the time for path key establishment increases, and the result shows that the number of path key plays more important role in establishing path keys and the cluster range needs to be much larger than sensor node transmission range.

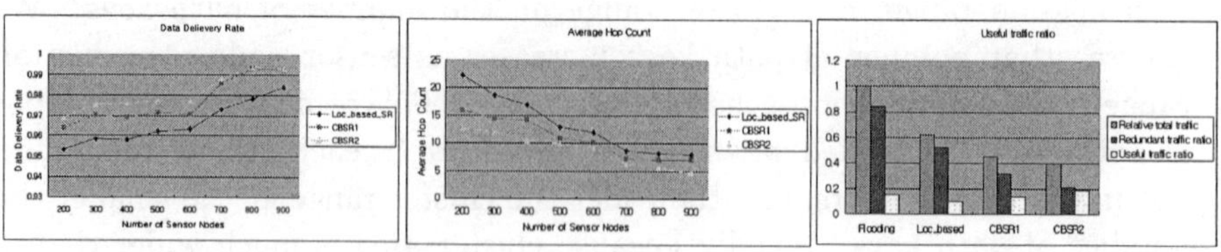

(a) *(b)* *(c)*

Figure 7. Comparision of proposed mechanism and location-based mechanism.

To show the efficiency of our mechanism, we also simulated routing performance based on broadcasting. To compare our mechanism with location-based key predistribution scheme, we assumed that our clusters are squares same as the cells in location-based scheme and increased the number of sensor nodes. Figure 7 shows the comparison of our proposal and location-based mechanism. CBSR1 is Cluster-Based Sensor Routing based on our proposal with clusterhead on random position, and CBSR2 is the one with the clusterhead at the center of the cluster. Figure 7(a) indicates that our proposal has better data delivery rate because packets can be routed diagonal direction while packets in location-based scheme can be routed only in horizontal or vertical directions. This is because, in location-based scheme, the sensors in each cells can establish pairwise keys with only the ones in 4 closest cells and it takes two hops to deliver packets to sensors in diagonal cell. Figure 7(b) shows the average hop count and the result can be explained from the same reasons. In both (a) and (b), as the network becomes denser, CBSR1 becomes closer to CBSR2. This is due to the fact that as more sensor nodes are deployed, even the clusterhead is not positioned at the center, other sensors node can be located around the center area and can play the similar role of relaying data packets. And finally, (c) shows the redundant and useful data traffic ratio compared with the data transmission through flooding mechanism, and it reflects that CBSR2 generates the least redundant data and can use energy more efficiently for useful data delivery.

5.3. *Analysis*

The polynomial-based key predistribution scheme can only tolerate no more than t compromised nodes, where the value of t is limited by the storage capacity for pairwise keys in a sensor. However, the larger a sensor network is, the more likely that an adversary compromises more than t sensors and then the entire network. Our mechanism can limit the number of sensor nodes located in a cluster less than t, and provide perfect resistance against node capture. In our mechanism, every pair of neighbor sensor nodes in a cluster can establish direct key, and this leads to strong probability for establishing pairwise keys. When two neighboring nodes cannot establish direct pairwise key because they are located in different clusters, they can setup path key through their clusterheads. Our proposal can enhance the security level and has many advantages if proper conditions such as cluster range, sensor transmission range, and the number of sensor nodes are met.

It further decreases the predistribution overhead because only clusterheads are assigned pairwise keys before deployment. The comparisons of our mechanism and other related schemes are in Table 3.

Table 3. Comparison with related works

Comparisons	Random key(pool-based)	Polynomial (pool-based)	Polynomial (grid-based)	Polynomial (location-based)	Proposed Mechanism
Probabilities of pairwise key establishment	0.99	0.99	1	1	1
Key derivation	key	Bivariate t-degree polynomials	Bivariate t-degree polynomials	Bivariate t-degree polynomials	Bivariate t-degree polynomials
Safety(Max number of disclosed keys)	1	$t+1$	$t+1$	$t+1$	$t+1$
Affected area by key disclosure	Sensors sharing same keys	Sensors sharing same polynomials	Column, row	Five clusters	One cluster
Key revocation overhead	Whole network	Whole network	Column, row	Five clusters	One cluster
Key predistribution	All sensor nodes	All sensor nodes	All sensor nodes	All sensor nodes	All clusterheads

6. Conclusions and Future work

To enhance the security of sensor network, efficient key establishment and authentication mechanism which costs less storage and computation is very important. We proposed a new secure and efficient pairwise key establishment and authentication mechanism. The main idea of the proposed technique is to combine the clustering scheme with the polynomial-based key predistribution technique. Using our proposed mechanism, every pair of neighbor sensor nodes can establish unique pairwise key for secure communication through their clusterheads. Specifically, our mechanism has high probability of establishing direct pairwise keys and provides better security and performance by reducing the overhead over the previous solutions. We also proposed efficient authentication mechanism for unicast and broadcast. In our proposal, sensor nodes only need to cache the broadcasted messages until verifying MAC, and it can decrease delay efficiently by delivering key-related information through their clusterheads. It also decreases useless redundant message by verifying at the clusterhead level and can provide data consistency.

For future research, we would like to investigate the authentication efficiency under various attacks and to propose secure routing using the pairwise keys established.

References

1. L. Eschenauer, V. D. Gligor : A Key-Management Scheme for Distributed Sensor Networks. Proc. of the 9th ACM conference on Computer and communications security, 41-47 (2002).
2. H. Chan, A. Perrig, and D. Song : Random Key Predistribution Schemes for Sensor Networks. IEEE Symposium on Security and Privacy, 197-213 (2003).
3. D. Liu and P. Ning : Establishing Pairwise Keys in Distributed Sensor Networks. Proc. of the 10th ACM Conference on Computer and Communications Security (CCS), 52-61 (2003).
4. D. Liu, P. Ning : Location-Based Pairwise Key Establishments for Static Sensor Networks. SASN'03 First ACM Workshop on the Security of Ad Hoc and Sensor Networks (2003).
5. C. Blundo, A. De Santis, Amir Herzberg, S. Kutten, U. Vaccaro, and M. Yung : Perfectly-secure key distribution for dynamic conferences. In Advances in Cryptology CRYPTO '92, LNCS 740, 471-486 (1993).
6. I. F. Akyildiz, W. Su, Y. Sankarasubramaniam and E. Cayirci : A Survey on Sensor Networks. IEEE Communications Magazine (2002).
7. The Network Simulator: ns-2. http://www.isi.edu/nsnam/ns.
8. A. Perrig, R. Szewczyk, V. Wen, D. Culler, and J. Tygar : SPINS: Security Protocols for Sensor Networks. Proc. of 7th ACM International Conference on Mobile Computing and Networks(Mobicom) (2001).

HTTP-MPLEX: AN APPLICATION LAYER MULTIPLEXING PROTOCOL FOR THE HYPERTEXT TRANSFER PROTOCOL (HTTP)

R. L. R. MATTSON AND S. GHOSH

La Trobe University,
Melbourne, Australia,
E-mail: {rlmattson,somnath}@cs.latrobe.edu.au

The Hypertext Transfer Protocol (HTTP) has progressively increased in sophistication and scope somewhat in parallel to growth of the Internet. HTTPs first incarnation allowed for only one transaction (request and retrieval) per connection, incurring a high overhead penalty for repetitive and laborious Transmission Control Protocol (TCP) connection management. Progressively HTTP was optimised through the inclusion of pipelined and persistent connections[1,2] to improve HTTPs non-optimal use of TCP. We introduce an application layer multiplexing adaptation to HTTP 1.1; HTTP-MPLEX for compressing GET requests and multiplexing responses. Our protocol is backwards compatible. It minimises verbose request header overhead, reducing the need for multiple server-client connections and allows prioritised object delivery with a companion response encoding scheme.

1. Introduction

The HTTP[2,3] specifications do not mandate the use of any specific transport protocol. Of the litany of transport protocols available only the User Datagram Protocol (UDP)[4] and Transmission Control Protocol (TCP)[5] are mandated transport layer protocols for Internet hosts[6]. However UDP does not provide ordered and guaranteed delivery, two necessary features of an HTTP transport protocol. TCP does provide such features and therefore is an obvious choice for maximizing the availability of HTTP and thus the web for Internet clients.

Historically, HTTP has not made efficient use of TCP. For each object that was to be retrieved using early implementations of HTTP a connection would be established and terminated. Connection lifetime was normally not long enough for TCP to achieve any throughput approaching the path bandwidth. Round trip time, transmission rate and other important state information[7,8] acquired and refined during the lifetime of a TCP connection (albeit short) would be discarded, often before a complete web page and its embedded objects are retrieved. The integration of pipelined and persistent connections[1] to HTTP has improved TCP utilization. Indeed, researchers have progressively recognized disproportionate bandwidth utilization among competing TCP sockets[9] and the importance of TCP's state information. HTTP 1.1 has increased the utilization of a single connection and thus increased its lifetime; improving the probability that TCP will achieve maximum throughput to reduce overhead and subsequent delay.

Most web-objects retrieved through the hypertext transfer protocol are not actually hypertext. Analysis of the 1998 soccer World Cup website[10] and of our faculty proxy logs show that 88% and 74.307% of requests respectivly are for non hypertext objects such as images, binary documents and multimedia content. This is partly a consequence of websites and web-content being designed by people unaware of underlying transport mechanisms. Considering not only the number of objects transferred, but the difference in size of hypertext documents and binary objects (often orders of magnitude) it is reasonable to conclude that HTTP is being used more as a file transfer protocol than purely for hypertext transfer. Perhaps the continuing evolution of the HTTP protocol should acknowledge the increasing number of referenced, large binary objects used to compose a web page.

A number of protocols have been developed that improve HTTPs utilisation of TCP: congestion manager[9], COrdinated Congestion CONtrol (COCCON)[11], Session Control Protocol (SCP)[12] and SMUX[13]. Congestion manager and COCCON are frameworks for coordinating the throughput of applications and transport protocols to collaboratively react to congestion and fairly allocate bandwidth. These protocols may require some limited re-implementation of TCPs at the operating systems level to facilitate the extended API. Applications that use TCP would also have to reapproach their use of the sockets to accommodate for the extended congestion management. SCP and SMUX are protocols that introduce a thin sub-application multiplexing layer. This layer simply couples multiple transport layer virtual connections into one TCP stream to consolidate congestion control, simultaneously render multiple objects and equitably distribute available bandwidth among competing connections.

We present an approach in this paper, by contrast, that is specific to the application layer. Observing the classic design principles that are at the heart of HTTPs success; ("speed (stateless, cacheable, few round-trips), simplicity, extensibility, data (payload) and independence"[14]) we describe an approach that is congruent with these principles. Our description is forward and backwards compatible, a server not compliant with the HTTP-MPLEX protocol, as specified below, would simply ignore HTTP-MPLEXs additional headers introduced by our proposed protocol and see only the initial request. The return of an HTTP 1.x response would indicate to a client non-compliance, thus the client is free to fall back to HTTP 1.x.

An important design consideration was the feasibility of a wide-scale, real world roll-out. We predict that a stable implementation of HTTP-MPLEX would require no more effort to introduce to the Internet community than that required for a software security update, a common and frequently occurring event. HTTP-MPLEX could be implemented as browser plug-ins or dynamically loaded shared object modules for Apache.

Our objective is to increase the efficiency of HTTP and reduce the rendering time of a page by improving HTTPs utilisation of TCP. We introduce in section 2 a simple object oriented compression scheme for HTTP. In section 3 we present an application layer multiplexing method for HTTP responses. We present our related work soon to be in progress at La Trobe University in section 5.

2. HTTP Request Compression

To improve TCP utilization and server response time, we can reduce the size and time of an HTTP interaction by combining the headers of multiple requests in such a way that we eliminate redundant (and often verbose) information.

HTTP requests are important and can be composed of standard[2] or non-standard headers. Requests specify not only the method, URI, protocol version, session persistent data (cookies) and host header but accommodate for content and connection modifiers. Connection modifiers are unique to a connection/hop coupling and content modifiers are establishing themselves as the most bloated part of an HTTP request. The use of content modifiers is steadily increasing as the number of unique devices and users with accessibility requirements increase in scope. They are used by the client to specify the client browser, its capabilities and version, the user's language preference, preferred file types, available plug-ins, response encoding and possibly any cookies.

We reviewed a number of HTTP transactions between a Mozilla 1.7.3 client and our university web server. One of the four transactions used for this paper is shown in Figure 1. Each of the four requests has a unique URI and one request has a conditional request header. Most of the content of

```
GET␣/ltu_assets/images/interface/home_logo.gif␣HTTP/1.1\r\n
Host:␣www.latrobe.edu.au\r\n
User-Agent:␣Mozilla/5.0␣(Windows;␣U;␣Windows␣NT␣5.0;␣en-US;
rv:1.7.3)␣␣␣␣Gecko/20040910\r\n
Accept:␣image/png,*/*;q=0.5\r\n
Accept-Language:␣en-us,en;q=0.5\r\n
Accept-Encoding:␣gzip,deflate\r\n
Accept-Charset:␣ISO-8859-1,utf-8;q=0.7,*;q=0.7\r\n
Keep-Alive:␣300\r\n
Connection:␣keep-alive\r\n
Referer:␣http://www.latrobe.edu.au/\r\n
Cookie:␣phpbb2mysql_data=a%3A0%3A%7B%7D;
␣␣␣␣ltusitevisitor=131.172.xx.xxx.319901096779449440\r\n\r\n
```

Figure 1. One of four requests to the La Trobe web server. (507 characters)

the request in Figure 1 was replicated among the other three requests and indeed throughout the wider client/server interaction. The User-Agent, Accept, Accept-Language, Accept-Encoding, Accept-Charset, Referer and Cookie headers are all repeated for each request and are somewhat redundant for the duration of interaction with the server.

We draw on two well established principles to define our header compression algorithm for HTTP-MPLEX. A HTTP axiom providing that "an implementation receiving a message header that it does not understand MUST ignore that header"[15] and we borrow from object oriented design and analysis[16,17] the tenants of inheritance and overriding. We infer by nesting a request within the scope of another request, that the nested request inherits the properties of its parent. This facilitates header reuse, which for large or commonly used headers enables us to minimise repetition thus conserving bandwidth. For headers that may not be required for a child request we provide a mechanism for selective inheritance and a mechanism for overriding headers and their values.

Figure 2 is the end result of following our compression algorithm described in Section 2.1 with our four observed requests, one of which is shown in Figure 1. A non MPLEX compliant implementation, upon receiving Figure 2 as a legitimate request would ignore the MPLEX headers and the request would be interpreted in the same way as Figure 1 would have been. Such a response would infer non-compliance and other requests can proceed without MPLEX compression. Such 'implicit detection' in-

```
GET␣/ltu_assets/images/interface/home_logo.gif␣HTTP/1.1\r\n
Host:␣www.latrobe.edu.au\r\n
GET1:␣/ltu_assets/images/interface/home_random3.jpg
{111111111}\r\n
GET2:␣/images2/home_campuspages.gif␣{111111111;
␣␣␣␣If-None-Match:␣"17b477-16ac-3fce87c2"}\r\n
GET3:␣/images2/text_00.gif␣{111111111}\r\n
User-Agent:␣Mozilla/5.0␣(Windows;␣U;␣Windows␣NT␣5.0;␣en-US;
rv:1.7.3)␣␣␣␣Gecko/20040910\r\n
Accept:␣image/png,*/*;q=0.5\r\n
Accept-Language:␣en-us,en;q=0.5\r\n
Accept-Encoding:␣gzip,deflate\r\n
Accept-Charset:␣ISO-8859-1,utf-8;q=0.7,*;q=0.7\r\n
Keep-Alive:␣300\r\n
Connection:␣keep-alive\r\n
Referer:␣http://www.latrobe.edu.au/\r\n
Cookie:␣phpbb2mysql_data=a%3A0%3A%7B%7D;
␣␣␣␣ltusitevisitor=131.172.xx.xxx.319901096779449440\r\n\r\n
```

Figure 2. An MPLEX compliant, compressed series of transactions from Figure 1. (705 characters)

flicts a certain delay (1 x RTT) in determining if the server is compliant. Of course, the client should be aware of the servers MPLEX compliance before its initial request to avoid unnecessary round trips. The server can advertise compliance through its "Accept-Encoding:" response to the initial request for an index document, or through a specific type of DNS entry. These two methods would rule out unnecessary round trips that waste time.

2.1. *Header Compression Algorithm*

We keep as many HTTP semantics as possible to maintain consistency: records are separated by \r\n. [0x0d , 0x0a] and HTTP headers are terminated with \r\n\r\n [0x0d , 0x0a , 0x0d , 0x0a]. The algorithm we used for compression is as follows:

(1) From the queue of pending requests at the client, select the request that has the most headers in common with the other requests. This will serve as our parent request (or super-class in object-oriented terminology). It may be acceptable to stall the transmission of

requests to increase the number of potential candidates for compression.

(2) For each request to be multiplexed into the parent, append a 'GET⟨int⟩:' header after the mandatory HTTP 1.1 host header, where ⟨int⟩ is a serialised integer incrementing from 1. We refer to this collection of headers as child-requests. By nesting a request as a child of the parent request, we infer the child inherits properties from the parent as controlled by the bitmap discussed in point 3.

(3) If a child request is nested into a parent request and any header cannot be inherited or should be overridden, we provide a mechanism for selective inheritance and overriding. Optionally, the URI of a child can be followed by a parenthesised expression containing inheritance caveats. Elements of the parenthesis are separated by semi-colon. Literal semi-colons are escaped with a backslash. Absence of the parenthesised expression infers complete inheritance. The general form of the parenthesis is;

{ [BITMAP] [; ⟨overriding header⟩: ⟨overriding value⟩]* }

(a) The BITMAP is a string of ASCII characters either '1' or '0' ([0x31] or [0x30]). The character in the first position corresponds to the first header of the parent request; the second character corresponds to the second header and so on. A '1' forces inheritance and a '0' prevents inheritance. The number of bits in the bitmap may be less than the number of headers in the parent request, bits not present infer inheritance. A pure white space bitmap infers total inheritance. Excess bits are ignored.

(b) A parent request header can be overridden or if absent declared for a child in the parenthesis. Headers are included verbatim; with the exception that the white space normally used to separate headers is replaced with a semi-colon. Semicolons are escaped with a backslash should it be required.

Headers present for the parent request are appended after the serialised 'GET⟨int⟩' headers.

Considering the size in magnitude of HTTP headers as overhead relative to that of the objects transported, the relative benefit of compressing headers may not make an incredible improvement particularly when transferring anything larger than a modest sized object, or 'average' web page. The form of an HTTP-MPLEX request lends itself quite well to what we might expect a request for a multiplexed response would look like. We correlate the client assigned request identifiers from the integer part of 'GET⟨int⟩' header and use them to identify channels in a multiplexed response, linking the compressed request to the multiplexed response.

This compression algorithm infers that a concrete relationship exists between a header and its relative position in the request. This is at odds with the HTTP 1.1[2] specification. Agents honoring the HTTP-MPLEX specification must maintain the relative position of request headers, or upon modifying the request maintain the accuracy of the bit-masks.

3. HTTP-MPLEX Response Encoding

Browsers use multiple (by default four[18]) TCP connections to download and retrieve embedded objects referenced in an HTML document. On receiving a MPLEX encoded request, we propose that a server should send a multiplexed response conforming to the specification outlaid below, for the following reasons:

- Increasing the use of a single TCP connection reduces competitive overhead from multiple connections and improves the probability of TCP reaching and maintaining a high throughput.
- MPLEX allows a more complete page to be rendered earlier as image dimensions (typically stored at the start of a graphics file) are retrieved in the first or second round of a multiplexed response. We would also expect that images retrieved in a multiplexed response would be rendered at the same rate in very similar proportions.
- MPLEX provides the ability for web servers to prioritize the transmission of specific objects by weighting queues in the round robin. For example; advertisement graphics, style sheets and JavaScript. Other multiplexing protocols do not facilitate prioritisation.
- To a limited extent prolonging a period of transmission would reduce the 'burstyness'[1] of traditional HTTP data by sustaining a longer period of response traffic.

Multiplexing HTTP connections over a single TCP connection is not a new notion; SCP 1.0[12] to SCP 2.0 and subsequently W3C's SMUX specification[13] explore the idea of encapsulating HTTP sessions through a session multiplexing protocol. These specifications focus on the use of session level management to reduce or eliminate excess connection overhead. Session management introduces a limited level of complexity even through it is only implementing light-weight connection management. Although the argument that supports the existence of both MPLEX and SCP/SMUX are close, the two solutions are fundamentally different. SCP is a transport layer solution intended to allow for the co-existence of multiple virtual channels. It does not infer that there should be any cooperative interaction at the application layer among processes.

An obvious disadvantage of a single TCP connection is delay caused by loss; should the multiplexed connection be subject to a loss close to, or at the end of the TCP congestion window at the end of a response (such that a duplicate acknowledgment is not sent and a fast transmit does not occur) the stream would be delayed by the TCP retransmit timer.

The SMUX specification uses a credit based flow control and deadlock avoidance scheme to prevent clients being 'overrun' with data. We believe that it is satisfactory for our adaptation to rely on TCPs receiver advertised congestion window for flow control. If a device has insufficient resources to handle MPLEX communication a client could limit the number of objects requested in an MPLEX request or the server could fall back to HTTP 1.1.

A HTTP agent on receiving an MPLEX compliant request has four response options:

(1) An Error. The server may encounter an internal or other error; the server should return the appropriate HTTP 1.x error code.
(2) Non-compliant response. An agent not-compliant with HTTP-MPLEX simply ignores the augmented 'GET⟨int⟩' headers, responding to the parent request only, returning a 200 response code.
(3) Conventional response. The agent de-multiplexes the request header, responding to each request individually as though the requests were HTTP 1.x compliant. Each individual response has a code of 210, a successful serialised response to an HTTP-MPLEX request. Responses are identical to a code 200 response.
(4) A HTTP-MPLEX compliant response as described in Section 3. I with a response code of 211.

3.1. *The format of an MPLEX compliant response;*

An HTTP-MPLEX response is a normal HTTP response with a response code of 211 and a content-type header set to "HTTP/MPLEX". The response body is the encoded multiplex stream.

On receiving an MPLEX request, the serving agent de-compresses the nested requests from the parent request (maintaining the identifier allocated by the client) and passes those requests in parallel to an available HTTP process. The data (header and message-body) returned from the HTTP processes are treated as data for the purposes of multiplexing and are multiplexed using the format described below.

We propose two possible queuing methods. Firstly by breaking responses into chunks the size of *ChunkSize*, the value of which may be dependent on the objects to be transmitted and the network environment. We allow for it to be configuration dependent (we are experimenting with 1–10kb). The responses to be transmitted are queued and multiplexed by round robin. If a response has less than the prescribed *ChunkSize* to be multiplexed, no chunk will be multiplexed larger than that queue for one round. If there is more data than the configured *ChunkSize* but less than *ChunkSize + 2 * sizeof(ChunkHeader)*, all remaining data from that response queue is sent. The multiplexing methodology then returns to round robin. A second possible methodology for multiplexing is to use fraction based chunk sizes. A queuing methodology such as this would be a good choice for many relatively similar sized responses, when the queue size is finite and when the ratio of overhead to data is low. The size for the chunk is not selected by a constant threshold but selected as some configured and relative fraction of the queued responses.

4. Content Response Encoding Scheme

The structure of multiplex stream Protocol Data Units (PDU's) are defined thus;

4.1. *mplexHdr*

The multiplex preamble.
Mplex_Definition - An array of characters identifying the version of the multiplexing protocol. By default set to "MPLEX/1".
NumStreams - The number of streams multiplexed.
ChunkSize - The preferred size of each chunk. This information is not strictly necessary, however may help the de-multiplexer allocate buffers.

4.2. *mplexChanHdr*

The channel preamble. The presence of a channel/HTTP response is signaled by this header, one channel per response.
NameSize - The size in characters of the string pointed to by FileName.

```
struct mplexHdr{
  char Mplex_Definition[10];
  u_int NumStreams;
  u_short ChunkSize;
};
```

```
struct mplexChanHdr{
   char NameSize;
   char ChanName[];
   u_int ChunkID;
   u_int CheckSum;
   u_int FileSize;
 };
```

```
struct mplexChunkHdr{
  u_int int ChunkID;
  u_int EOF : 1;
  u_int ChunkLength : 31;
};
```

Figure 3. MPLEX stream PDU's.

ChanName - An array of characters identifying the file identified by ChunkID.
ChunkID - A sequentially allocated numerical identifier, unique for each channel. This identifier corresponds to the numerical identifier allocated by the client, zero is for the parent request, one is for the first child request and so on.
CheckSum - A 32-bit Cyclic Redundancy Check (CRC) of the channel data before multiplexing.
FileSize - The size, in bytes of the pre-multiplexed file.
CheckSum and FileSize may be set to zero for dynamically generated content.

4.3. *mplexChunkHdr*

The chunk preamble.
ChunkID - The chunks corresponding mplexFileHdr identifier.
EOF - A single bit. When set to 'On' indicates that this chunk is the last chunk of the stream.
ChunkLength - The length of the file chunk.

5. Future Work

We are working on an experimental implementation of HTTP-MPLEX, HTTP 0.9 and 1.1. It is our intention to conduct and publish our analysis of the network performance of HTTP-MPLEX relative to past implementations. We expect that we will establish HTTP-MPLEX as a possible step in the continuing evolution of Internet protocols.

This work does not explicitly provide for compatibility with proxies, as the host header is not well catered for. Future provisions of the protocol will allow for multiple messages destined for different web sites to be multiplexed and sent to the same proxy server in the same connection. We intend to explore the possible benefit of a proxy server multiplexing requests from autonomous clients to common origin-servers. This may further improve and emphasize the benefits of using HTTP-MPLEX.

Our experimentation with the HTTP-MPLEX protocol is ongoing. We predict a reduced capacity for HTTP-MPLEX to improve retrieval of objects should object references be sparsely distributed in HTML. Under such an environment, the request queue may not grow large enough for many objects to be queued and therefore compressed and multiplexed. We propose that it may be advantageous to prototype references in HTML/XHTML at the beginning of a document. Prototyping references notifies a client as early as possible of the embedded objects and enables a request to be sent as early as possible both for HTTP 1.1 and HTTP-MPLEX. Co-locating references to embedded objects should maximise the ability of HTTP-MPLEX to compress requests.

We briefly address in this paper the problem of deadlock avoidance with respect to HTTP-MPLEX. It should be possible for clients with limited resources to use our protocol without falling back to HTTP 1.x. We are investigating the impact of a client proposing a ChunkSize that is more appropriate to the limitations of an embedded system.

References

1. H.F. Nielsen, J. Gettys, A. Baird-Smith, E. Prud'hommeaux, H.W. Lie and C. Lilley, Network performance effects of HTTP/1.1, CSS1, and PNG. In ACM. Computer Communication Review, vol.27, no.4, Oct. (1997). USA. 155–66
2. R. Fielding, J. Gettys, J. Mogul, H. Frystyk, L. Masinter, P. Leach and T. Berners-Lee, Hypertext Transfer Protocol – HTTP/1.1, RFC 2616. Internet Engineering Task Force (1999)
3. T. Berners-Lee, R. Fielding and H. Frystyk, Hypertext Transfer Protocol – HTTP/1.0, RFC 1945. Network Working Group (1996)
4. J. Postel, User Datagram Protocol, RFC 768. Internet Engineering Task Force (1980)
5. J. Postel, Transmission Control Protocol, RFC 793. Defence Advanced Projects Research Agency (1981)
6. R. Braden, Requirements for Internet Hosts – Communication Layers, RFC 1122. Internet Engineering Task Force (1989)

7. V. Jacobson and M. Karels, Congestion avoidance and control, SIGCOMM '88 Symposium: Communications Architectures and Protocols. Stanford, CA, USA. ACM. 16-19 Aug. (1988)., Communication Review, vol.18, no.4, Aug. 1988, pp.314-29. USA. (1988) Lawrence Berkeley Lab. California Univ., Berkeley, CA, USA.
8. W. Stevens, TCP Slow Start, Congestion Avoidance, Fast retransmit, and Fast Recovery Algorithms, RFC 2001. Network Working Group (1997)
9. H. Balakrishnan, H. S. Rahul and S. Seshan, An integrated congestion management architecture for Internet hosts, ACM SIGCOMM Computer Communication Review **29** (1999) 175–187
10. M. Arlitt and T. Jin, A workload characterization study of the 1998 world cup web site. IEEE Network **14** (2000) 30 – 37
11. Y. Gao, H. Guanghui, J. Hou and S. Paul, COCOON: An alternative scheme for end-point congestion management, http://stat.bell-labs.com/who/yuangao/papers/cocoon.pdf, (2000).
12. S. Spero, Session control protocol (SCP), http://www.w3.org/Protocols/HTTP-NG/http-ng-scp.html
13. J. Gettys, F.H. Nielsen, SMUX protocol specification (1998), http://www.bilkent.edu.tr/pub/WWW/Protocols/HTTP-NG/mux/simplemux.html
14. R. Fielding, Representational state transfer: An architectural style for distributed hypermedia interaction (1998)
15. J. Mogul, R. Fielding, J. Gettys and H. Frystyk, Use and Interpretation of HTTP Version Numbers, RFC 2145. (1997)
16. P. Coad, E. Yourdon, Object-Oriented Design. 2 edn. Prentice-Hall, Englewood Cliffs, NJ (1991)
17. P. Coad, E. Yourdon, Object-Oriented Analysis. Prentice-Hall, Englewood Cliffs, NJ (1991)
18. W. Stevens, TCP/IP, Illustrated, Volume 3: TCP for Transactions, HTTP, NNTP and the UNIX Domain Protocols. Addison-Wesley, Massachusetts (1996)

A NEW APPROACH TO DETECT DDOS ATTACKS USING SUPPORT VECTOR MACHINE*

JUNGTAEK SEO AND CHEOLHO LEE
National Security Research Institute
KT 463-1 Jeonmin-dong, Yuseong-gu, Daejeon, 305-811, Republic of KOREA
E-mail: seojt{chlee}@etri.re.kr

TAESHIK SHON AND JONGSUB MOON
CIST, KOREA University 1-Ga, Anam-dong, Sungbuk-Gu, Seoul, Republic of KOREA
E-mail: 743zh2k{jsmoon}@korea.ac.kr

The current Internet infrastructure is suffering from various types of Distributed Denial of Service (DDoS) attacks. Internet worms are one of the most crucial problems in the field of computer security today. Worms can be propagated so fast that most Internet services over the world may be disabled by DDoS effects from the self-propagation. In our earlier research, we presented Traffic Rate Analysis (TRA) to analyze the characteristics of network traffic for DDoS attacks. In this research, we propose Support Vector Machine (SVM) approach with TRA to automatically detect DDoS attacks. Experimental results show that SVM can be a highly useful classifier for detecting DDoS attacks.

1 Introduction

As we can see in the incidents of Distributed Denial of Service (DDoS) attacks against commercial web sites such as *Yahoo, e-Bay*, and *E*Trade*, computing resources connected to the Internet are vulnerable to DDoS attacks [3,5,11]. DDoS attacks can temporarily disable the network services or damage systems by flooding a huge number of network packets for several minutes or longer.

Since these DDoS attacks are harmful to almost all networked systems which have limited computing resources (e.g. network bandwidth, memory, CPU, etc), these attacks are regarded as a serious problem, and thus much research is in progress to detect and prevent them [4,6,7].

In our earlier research, we presented Traffic Rate Analysis (TRA) to analyze the characteristics of network traffic for the DDoS attacks [9,12]. TRA is a network traffic analyzing method which examines the occurrence rate of a specific type of packet within the stream of monitored network traffic and is composed of a TCP flag rate and a Protocol rate. The result of analyzing network traffic using TRA showed us that there are distinct and predictable differences between normal traffic and DDoS attack traffic. In addition, we were able to automatically generate DDoS

* This work was supported by the Ministry of Information Communications, Korea, under the Information Technology Research Center Support Program supervised by the IITA.

detection rules by compiling the experimental results with SVM [1,2]. Our detection method showed a high degree of performance, and detected various DDoS attacks successfully.

We introduce related research in section 2, and explain TRA and SVM in section 3. In section 4, the experimental environment and the detection performance of SVM is explained. Lastly, we mention the conclusion of this research and the direction of future work in section 5.

2 Related Work

Almost DDoS attackers use IP spoofing to hide their real IP addresses and locations. Since spoofed IP addresses are generated randomly, this characteristic of randomness may be used to reveal the occurrence of DDoS attacks. Kulkarni et al [7] presents DDoS detection methods based on this characteristic. This method uses *Komogorov complexity metrics* to measure the randomness of source IP addresses in network packet headers [10]. Gil and Poletto [4] examine the disproportion between *to-rate* of the network traffic flows to a specific subnet and *from-rate* of the network traffic flowing from a specific subnet. This method also characterizes the randomness of source IP addresses. When DDoS attacks occur, a large mismatch is observed between *to-rate* toward the victim and *from-rate* flowing to the outside from the victim.

However, these approaches are based on the effect of IP spoofing and may not work properly if the attackers don't spoof the IP addresses or change the level of spoofing in their attacking network packets.

On the other hand, our own detection method proposed in the earlier research [12] is expected to efficiently detect DDoS attacks without regard to IP spoofing.

3 Overview of Traffic Rate Analysis and Support Vector Machine

3.1 Definition of Traffic Rate Analysis

Traffic rate analysis was defined as measuring packet traffic in a network [9]. It examines the occurrence rate of a specific type of packets within the stream of monitored network traffic, and is composed of TCP flag rate and Protocol rate. TCP flag rate is defined in the following equation.

$$R_{td}[F\,i \mid o] = \frac{\sum flag(F)\ in\ a\,TCP\ header}{\sum TCP\ packets} \tag{1}$$

TCP flag rate means the ratio of the number of a specific TCP flag to the total number of TCP packets. In the equation (1), a TCP flag *'F'* can be one of *SYN, FIN, RST, ACK, PSH, URG,* and *NULL*, and *'td'* is the time interval used to calculate the value. The direction of network traffic is expressed as *'i'* (inbound) and *'o'* (outbound). For example, $R_1[Si]$ means the occurrence rate of *SYN* flags within TCP packets when measuring inbound network traffic (toward the monitored network) during interval 1.

$$R_{td}[[TCP|UDP|ICMP]i\,|\,o] = \frac{\sum[TCP|UDP|ICMP]packets}{\sum IP\ packets} \tag{2}$$

Protocol rate is defined in equation (2). It means the ratio of specific Transport-Layer protocol (e.g. TCP, UDP, and ICMP) packets to total Network-Layer (IP) protocol packets. For instance, $R_1[TCPi]$ means the occurrence rate of TCP packets within IP packets when measuring outbound network traffic (from the monitored network) during interval 1.

3.2 SVM for Categorization

In this section we review some basic ideas of SVM. Given the training data set $\{(x_i, d_i)\}_{i=1}^{N}$ with input data $x_i \in R^N$ and corresponding binary class labels $d_i \in \{-1,1\}$, the SVM classifier formulation starts from the following assumption. The classes represented by the subset $d_i = 1$ and $d_i = -1$ are linearly separable, where $\exists w \in R^N$, $b \in R$ such that

$$\exists w, b \quad s.t \quad \begin{Bmatrix} w^T x_i + b > 0 & for & d_i = +1 \\ w^T x_i + b < 0 & for & d_i = -1 \end{Bmatrix} \tag{3}$$

The goal of SVM is to find an optimal hyperplane for which the margin of separation, ρ, is maximized. ρ is defined by the separation between the separating hyperplane and the closest data point. If the optimal hyperplane is defined by $(w_0^T \cdot x) + b_0 = 0$, then the function $g(x) = w_0^T \cdot x + b_0$ gives a measure of the distance from x to the optimal hyperplane.

Support Vectors are defined by data points $x^{(s)}$ that lie the closest to the decision surface. For a support vector $x^{(s)}$ and the canonical optimal hyperplane g, we have

$$r = \frac{g(x^s)}{\|w_0\|} = \begin{Bmatrix} +1/\|w_0\| & for & d^{(s)} = +1 \\ -1/\|w_0\| & for & d^{(s)} = -1 \end{Bmatrix} \tag{4}$$

Since, the margin of separation is $\rho \propto \frac{1}{\|w_0\|}$. $\|w_0\|$ should be minimal to achieve the maximal separation margin. Mathematical formulation for finding the canonical optimal separation hyperplane, given the training data set $\{(x_i, d_i)\}_{i=1}^{N}$, solves the following quadratic problem

$$\left\{\begin{array}{c} \min \tau(\omega,\xi) = \frac{1}{2}\|w\|^2 + C\sum_{i=1}^{l}\zeta_i \\ s.t \quad d_i(w^T x_i + b) \geq 1 - \zeta_i \quad for \quad \zeta_i \geq 0, \quad i = 1,\dots,l \end{array}\right\} \tag{5}$$

Note that the global minimum of above problem must exist, because $\Phi(w) = \frac{1}{2}\|w_0\|^2$ is convex in w and the constrains are linear in w and b. This constrained optimization problem is dealt with by introducing Lagrange multipliers $a_i \geq 0$ and a Lagrangian function given by

$$L(w,b,\zeta,a,v) = \tau(w,\zeta) - \sum_{i=1}^{l} a_i\left[d_i(w_i^T x_i + b) - 1 + \zeta_k\right] - \sum_{i=1}^{l} v_i\zeta_i \tag{6}$$

which leads to

$$\frac{\partial L}{\partial w} = 0 \quad \Leftrightarrow \quad w - \sum_{i=1}^{l} a_i d_i x_i = 0 \quad (\therefore w = \sum_{i=1}^{l} a_i d_i x_i) \tag{7}$$

$$\frac{\partial L}{\partial b} = 0 \quad \Leftrightarrow \quad \sum_{i=1}^{l} a_i d_i = 0 \tag{8}$$

The solution vector thus has an expansion in terms of a subset of the training patterns, namely those patterns whose a_i is non-zero, called Support Vectors. By the Karush-Kuhn-Tucker complementarity conditions, we have,

$$a_i\left[d_i\left(w^T x_i + b\right) - 1\right] = 0 \quad for \quad i = 1,\dots,N \tag{9}$$

by substituting (7),(8) and (9) into equation (6), find multipliers a_i for which

$$\max \Theta(a) = \sum_{i=1}^{l} a_i - \frac{1}{2}\sum_{i=1}^{l}\sum_{i=1}^{l} a_i a_j d_i d_i \langle x_i \cdot x_j \rangle \tag{10}$$

$$s.t. \quad 0 \leq a_i \leq c, \quad i = 1,\dots,l \quad and \quad \sum_{i=1}^{l} a_i y_i = 0 \tag{11}$$

The hyperplane decision function can thus be written as

$$f(x) = \text{sgn}\left(\sum y_i a_i \cdot (x \cdot x_i) + b\right) \quad (12)$$

where b is computed using (9). To construct the SVM, the optimal hyperplane algorithm has to be augmented by a method for computing dot products in feature spaces nonlinearly related to input space. The basic idea is to map the data into some other dot product space (called the feature space) F via a nonlinear map Φ, and to perform the above linear algorithm in F, i.e nonseparable data $\{(x_i, d_i)\}_{i=1}^{N}$, where $x_i \in R_N$, $d_i \in \{+1, -1\}$, preprocess the data with,

$$\Phi : R^N \rightarrow \Theta(x) \quad where \quad N << \dim(F) \quad (13)$$

Here w and x_i are not calculated. According to Mercer's theorem,

$$(\Phi(x_i) \cdot \Phi(x_j)) = K(x_j, x_j) \quad (14)$$

and $K(x, y)$ can be computed easily on the input space. Finally the nonlinear SVM classifier becomes

$$f(x) = \text{sgn}\left(\sum_{i=1}^{l} a_i d_i K(x_i \cdot x) + b\right) \quad (15)$$

4 Experiment

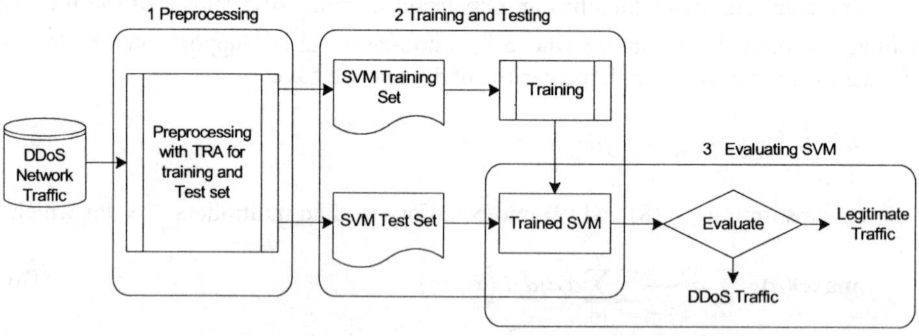

Figure 1. Overall composition of DDoS detection process

Figure 1 shows the overall composition of our DDoS detection process. First, we capture raw network traffic from both DDoS and legitimate network traffic and extract features from the captured raw network traffic by the scheme of proposed by TRA for each training and test set. A set of training and testing is used by machine learning tool; mySVM [14]. mySVM is a training and testing tool for SVM. We evaluate machine learning algorithm by calculating detection performances for given testing sets.

4.1 *Experimental Environment*

Our traffic monitor was developed with the network packet capturing library *libpcap* [8]. It can be divided into two modules. One is the module for capturing network traffic and calculating TCP flag rate and protocol rate from the monitored network, and the other is the intrusion detection module for detecting DDoS attacks by the detection machine tuned by the support vector machine. The TRA analyzer is located on the adjacent site of a target Web server and captures both inbound and outbound network traffic packets through an Ethernet hub, and then calculates TCP flag rate and protocol rate every second.

Web clients are composed of four hosts using *SPECweb99* to generate normal web traffic toward an *Apache* web server [15]. *TFN2K* is use to generate DDoS attack traffic toward the web server [13]. *TFN2K* can generate various DDoS attacks such as TCP/SYN flooding attacks, UDP flooding attacks, ICMP flooding attacks and so on. All hosts in the simulated environment are Linux machines (Linux 2.4.18).

4.2 *Feature Extraction*

In this research, we used mySVM [14] for training and testing. We made two classes, *attack (-1)* and *normal (+1)* for classifying input packets. Normal web traffic was categorized as *normal*, and the various DDoS attack traffic was categorized as *attack*. We collected network traffic for 100 seconds during training and testing. Web clients continually generated normal web traffic toward the web server, and various DDoS attacks occurred between the 25th and 75th seconds. For both training and testing, we used 10 features: $R_1[S_i]$, $R_1[F_i]$, $R_1[R_i]$, $R_1[A_i]$, $R_1[P_i]$, $R_1[U_i]$, $R_1[N_i]$, $R_1[TCP_i]$, $R_1[UDP_i]$, and $R_1[ICMP_i]$.

4.3 *Detection Performance*

4.3.1 Training Set and Test Set

Table 1 shows the composition of the training set. The sizes of training sets were 400, 2,000, 4,000, 6,000, 8,000, 10,000, 12,000, 14,000, 16,000, and 18,000 for each feature. Each attack set was comprised of 5 different types of DDoS attacks (SYN, UDP, ICMP, TARGA3, MIX). For instance, in the case of T4, the *attack (-1)* class contained 60 traffic data for each type of DDoS attack, and 300 traffic data comprised the *normal (+1)* class. The number of test sets for performance testing was 10. Each test set contained 100 data, 50 *attack* and 50 *normal.*

Table 1. The composition of training set

Name	T1	T2	T3	T4	T5	T6	T7	T8	T9	T10
Attack	200	1,000	2,000	3,000	4,000	5,000	6,000	7,000	8,000	9,000
Normal	200	1,000	2,000	3,000	4,000	5,000	6,000	7,000	8,000	9,000
Total Size	400	2,000	4,000	6,000	8,000	10,000	12,000	14,000	16,000	18,000

4.3.2 Results of Testing

For each training set, we used dot and polynomial kernel with epsilon 0.01. The detection performance using SVM is shown in Figure 2.

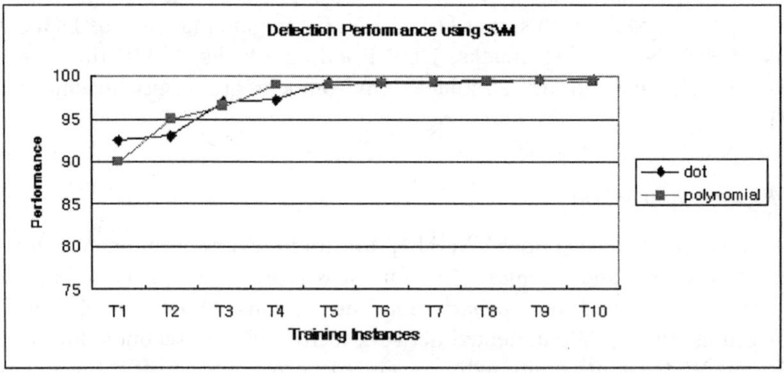

Figure 2. Detection Performance using SVM. Polynomial kernel performed better than dot kernel. Overall performance was 99.5%

As we can see in Figure 2, SVM shows higher performance in attack detection. In Figure 2, the polynomial kernel performed better than the dot kernel and the overall detection performance is almost 100%. We used 1000 as capacity parameter and +0.01 as epsilon parameter which represents insensitivity value that prediction can deviate from the functional value without being penalized for both dot and polynomial kernel and degree 3 for polynomial kernel. Table 2 shows performance of each training set with polynomial kernel.

In case of false alarm, our proposed scheme showed small number of false rate (below 0.5%).

Table 2. Performance of each training set with polynomial kernel

Name	T1	T2	T3	T4	T5	T6	T7	T8	T9	T10
Accuracy	0.950	0.965	0.990	0.990	0.991	0.992	0.994	0.995	0.993	0.994
Precision	0.978	0.969	0.994	0.993	0.997	0.995	0.996	0.998	0.998	0.998
Recall	0.920	0.960	0.985	0.986	0.985	0.988	0.991	0.991	0.998	0.990

5 Conclusion

In this research, we utilized a Traffic Rate Analysis method proposed in earlier research as feature extraction method of machine learning algorithm and adopted Support Vector Machine (SVM) to automatically compile detection rules. As a result, SVM showed higher performance (99.5%). Furthermore we determined that a polynomial kernel performed better than a dot kernel. We expect that our approach will be useful in providing early detection of DDoS attacks against Internet infrastructure and eventually be helpful in keeping the Internet society healthy. However, our machine learning scheme does not have unsupervised feature but supervised feature. It may mean sometimes if our scheme meet a kind of unexpected situation, it is difficult it can work well or not. Thus, we need additional work using unsupervised learning method without pre-existing knowledge. In our future work, we will test other machine learning algorithm (e.g., CN2, C4.5, and Bayesian) and kernel function methods of SVM. Moreover, we are going to focus on detecting and defending against other types of attacks like worms.

References

1. Burges. C.: LA Tutorial on Support Vector Machines for Pattern Recognition, Data Mining and Knowledge Discovery, Boston, 1588.
2. Cristianini, N., Shawe-Taylor, J.: An Introduction to Support Vector Machines, Cambridge University (2000).
3. Garber, L.: Denial-of-Service Attacks Rip the Internet, IEEE Computer, vol. 33(4), (2000) pp. 12-17.
4. Gil, T.M, and Poletto, M.: MULTOPS: a data-structure for bandwidth attack detection, In Proceedings of the 10th USENIX Security Symposium, (2001) pp. 23-38.
5. Houle, J.K., and Weaver, M.G.: Trends in Denial of Service Attack Technology, CERT Coordination Center, (2001).
6. Householder, A., Manion, A., Pesante. L., and Weaver. M.G.: Managing the Threat of Denial-of-Service Attacks, CERT Coordination Center, (2001).
7. Kulkarni, A.B., Bush, S.F., and Evans, S.C.: Detecting Distributed Denial-of-Service Attacks Using Kolmogorov Complexity Metrics. Technical report 2001CRD176, GE Research and Development Center, (2001).

8. Lawrence Berkeley National Labs Network Research Group. Libpcap
9. Lee, C., Noh, S., Choi, K., and Jung, G.: Characterizing DDoS Attacks with Traffic Rate Analysis, In *Proceedings of the IADIS e-Society*, vol. 1, (2003) pp. 81-88.
10. Li, M., and Vitanyi, P.: An Introduction to Kolmogorov Complexity and Its Applications, Springer-Verlag, Section 7.6, (1997) pp. 506-509.
11. Moore, D., Voelker, G.M., and Savage, S.: Inferring Internet Denial-of-Service Activity. In Proceedings of the 10th USENIX Symposium, (2001) pp. 9-22.
12. Noh, S., Lee, C., Choi, K., and Jung, K.: Detecting Distributed Denial of Service (DDoS) Attacks through Inductive Learning, Lecture Notes in Computer Science(LNCS), Springer-Verlag, vol. 2690, (2003) pp. 286-295.
13. Packet Storm. Tribe Flood Network 2000 (TFN2K) DDoS tool, available on-line: http://packetstormsecurity.org/distributed/ TFN2k_Analysis-1.3.txt.
14. Ruping S.: mySVM – a Support Vector Machine, University of Dortmund (2004).
15. Standard Performance Evaluation Corporation. SPECweb99 Benchmark, available on-line: http://www.spec.org/osg/web99.

PERFORMANCE EVALUATION OF END-TO-END SECURITY IN WIRELESS APPLICATIONS USING WTLS HANDSHAKE PROTOCOL

BURAK BAYOGLU

TUBITAK – UEKAE, National Research Institute of Electronics and Cryptology, Gebze, TR-41470, Kocaeli, Turkey

ALBERT LEVI, ERKAY SAVAS

Sabanci University, Fac. of Eng. & Nat. Sci., Orhanli, Tuzla, TR-34956, Istanbul, Turkey

In this paper we analyze the performance of end-to-end security in wireless applications. WTLS (Wireless Transport Layer Security) handshake protocol is used as the key security protocol. Several scenarios and different cryptosystems are considered. We took an experimental approach and implemented the protocols and necessary crypto primitives in both wireless handheld device and server. Tests are performed over a GSM provider network. Processing, queuing and transmission delays are considered in the analysis. Results are interpreted from both client and the server points of view. Not only the key sizes proposed by the WTLS standard, but also stronger key sizes are tested. Results show that (i) Elliptic Curve Cryptosystems (ECC) perform better than RSA cryptosystem, and (ii) it is possible to use ECC key sizes larger than the ones proposed in the WTLS standard without significant performance degradation. In our tests, GSM CSD and GPRS bearers are taken into account. Another interesting result is that the these two bearers perform close to each other in WTLS handshake protocol because of similar and significant traversal delays in both bearers.

1. Introduction

Mobility requirements for today's daily life have brought up an increasing demand on Internet services in mobile devices. Security is very important in these applications. Because of the insecurity of the hybrid communication media, end-to-end security mechanisms play a significant role. SSL (Secure Socket Layer) [4] provides end-to-end security to TCP/IP applications. However the resource constrained handheld devices used in mobile Internet access make the SSL quite costly to provide end-to-end security. The main reason behind this fact is the high computational power and memory requirements of cryptographic operations (especially public-key cryptography) needed in SSL. WTLS (Wireless Transport Layer Security) [2] is proposed as a lightweight protocol alternative to SSL. Actually WTLS is part of the WAP (Wireless Access Protocol) [1] protocol suite that is promoted as an enabling technology to bring Internet applications to resource constrained handheld devices. Although it may be argued that WAP falls short to deliver its promises, the consistent wide gap between the computational power and memory of handheld devices and desktop computers signifies a continuous need of a light end-to-end security protocol, like WTLS, to be used in handheld devices. That is why the analysis performed in the paper would be still valuable even if WAP was discontinued.

WTLS operates between a mobile client and a server, which is also called as WAP gateway (the terms server and gateway will be used interchangeably throughout the paper). WTLS addresses confidentiality, integrity and authentication of the information flow between the mobile client and the gateway. It is possible to provide end-to-end security using WTLS by putting the content server and the WAP gateway on the same machine.

Public key cryptosystems are extensively used in WTLS Handshake protocol. The key sizes offered by the WTLS standard are not large enough to meet today's security requirements. Considering the low processing power of the handheld devices, it may be reasonable to restrict the key sizes. However, the standard makers do not seem to rely on a serious cryptographic research while recommending the key sizes in the WTLS standard [2]. Therefore, a performance evaluation of the WTLS Handshake Protocol for different key exchange suites is valuable. Especially a feasibility study on the use of stronger key sizes that have not been offered by the standard yet will put a light on the future progress of the WTLS and similar standards.

There is a limited study in the literature about the performance of end-to-end security protocols. Levi and Savas [8] have proposed a limited analytical performance model for WTLS handshake protocol. Apostolopoulos et al. [9, 10] take a close look at the SSL protocol, the ancestor of WTLS, with an eye on performance. Herwono and Liebhardt [11] have presented simulation-based performance measurements of the WTLS protocol, and analyzed the correlation between the crypto processing times and the network throughput.

In this paper, a more realistic performance evaluation of the WTLS Handshake Protocol is performed. Performance model considers the client and server processing times, server queue delay and the data transmission time over the channel as bottleneck candidates of the handshake operation. Processing times and data transmission times are measured by performing the tests over a GSM service provider network, not through off-line simulations, in order to practically assess the effect of underlying bearer in the performance of the protocol. Queue delay performance is modelled analytically. In our tests, elliptic curve and RSA cryptosystems are taken into account.

The rest of this paper is organized as follows: Background information about WTLS handshake protocols is given in Section 2. WTLS handshake protocol performance evaluation including processing time analysis, transmission time analysis, queue delay analysis and total handshake time analysis is given in Section 3. Section 4 discusses the conclusions reached by this study.

2. Background

In WTLS handshake protocol, public-key cryptosystems are used for securely exchanging secret keys between the client and the server. Use of public-key certificates in WTLS also requires public-key cryptosystem based signature and verification operations. RSA (Rivest-Shamir-Adleman) [5] and ECC (Elliptic Curve Cryptography) [6] are the most widely used public key cryptosystems in WTLS Handshake Protocol.

Lenstra and Verheul have compared the cryptographic key sizes of RSA and ECC cryptosystems in [7] as given in Table 1. We consider these three cryptographic strength levels in this study. Three different types of ECC curves have been taken into account: prime, Koblitz, and random curves. Level 1 and 2 curves are offered by the WTLS standard [2]. Level 3 is not offered in the WTLS standard but we are going to analyze its feasibility in this paper.

Table 1. RSA and Elliptic Curve Cryptosystems cryptographic strength level comparison

Cryptographic Strenght Level	ECC	RSA
1	160 bit Prime, 163 bit Koblitz, 163 bit Random	1024 bit
2	224 bit Prime, 233 bit Koblitz, 233 bit Random	2048 bit
3	56 bit Prime, 283 bit Koblitz, 283 bit Random	3072 bit

2.1 WTLS Handshake Protocols

In WTLS protocol, although there are more efficient handshake alternatives, the peers should perform a full handshake at the beginning to agree on the cryptographic parameters and master secret. In this paper we deal with two types of WTLS full handshake protocols. These are Server-Authenticated WTLS Full Handshake, and Mutual-Authenticated WTLS Full Handshake.

Mutual-authenticated WTLS Full Handshake requires both the client and the server have valid certificates for the selected key exchange suite. These digital certificates are used through the key exchange process to compute the premaster secret. RSA or ECDH_ECDSA key exchange suites can be used in mutual-authenticated WTLS full handshake.

This protocol is shown in Figure 1. First, client and server send their hello messages by which (i) they agree on the cryptographic mechanisms, and (ii) exchange random values to be used in the rest of the protocol.

Client		Server
ClientHello	→	
	←	ServerHello
	←	Certificate
	←	CertificateReq
	←	ServerHelloDone
Certificate	→	
ClientKeyExch*	→	
CertificateVerify*	→	
ChangeCipherSpec	→	
Finished	→	
	←	ChangeCipherSpec
	←	Finished
Application Data	↔	Application Data

encrypted (client side, from ChangeCipherSpec on); encrypted (server side, from ChangeCipherSpec on)

* If using RSA key exchange method

Figure 1. Mutual-authenticated WTLS full handshake message flow

Client		Server
ClientHello	→	
	←	ServerHello
	←	Certificate
	←	ServerHelloDone
ClientKeyExch	→	
ChangeCipherSpec	→	
Finished	→	
	←	ChangeCipherSpec
	←	Finished
Application Data	↔	Application Data

encrypted (client side, from ChangeCipherSpec on); encrypted (server side, from ChangeCipherSpec on)

Figure 2. Server-authenticated WTLS full handshake message flow

Server-Authenticated WTLS Full Handshake, which is depicted in Figure 2, requires only the server to have a valid certificate for the selected key exchange suite. Therefore, the protocol is shorter than the mutual-authenticated one. However, in this protocol, the server does authenticate the client; only client authenticates the server. RSA or ECDH_ECDSA key exchange suites can be used in server-authenticated WTLS full handshake.

This protocol is the same as the mutual-authenticated one up to and including the server hello done message. After that, the client sends the client key exchange message for premaster secret exchange.

3. WTLS Handshake Protocol Performance Evaluation

In this section, performance evaluation of WTLS handshake protocols is given. We consider three main factors on WTLS Handshake Protocol performance. These are, processing times at both client and server sides, server queue delay, and handshake data transmission time over the network.

Timing measurements were performed using a handheld device with Symbian 6.1 operating system, 104 MHz ARM-9 CPU, and 4 MB RAM, as the client and open-source Kannel gateway running on Cygwin as the WAP gateway. Crypto primitives and the WTLS Handshake Protocol are implemented using C++. Microsoft Visual Studio 6.0 has been used as the development environment for both client and server sides, where Nokia's Symbian 6.1 SDK was used to build the code for the ARM processor of the handheld device. The gateway (server) operating system was Microsoft Windows 2000 Advanced Server SP4 running on an Intel P4 2.4 GHz CPU and 1GB DDR RAM.

Performance analysis is done for 24 mutual-authenticated and 24 server-authenticated WTLS handshake test cases. Each test case differs by the CA and peers' certificate public key parameter specifiers. Due to space limitations only half of these cases are presented in this paper. These cases include client and server certificates from all possible cryptographic strength levels described in Table 1. CA signatures over these certificates have the strongest cryptographic strength level (level 3). For the entire analysis, the readers may refer to [14].

3.1 Processing Time Analysis

For the test cases considered, client and server processing times are given in Figures 3 and 4 respectively. Our test results show that ECC curves perform better than the RSA cryptosystems in WTLS Handshake Protocol.

Client processing times of RSA handshakes always have the highest value, where the Koblitz curve handshakes have the lowest client processing times. Prime curves (denoted with suffix p) have the highest client processing time among the other ECDH_ECDSA key exchange suites.

Prime curves are always faster than Koblitz and random curves at the server side. Koblitz curves are the second but random curve processing times are generally similar to the Koblitz curves at the server side. Server processing times for both mutual-authenticated and server-authenticated WTLS handshake using prime curves are always less than the half of the Koblitz and random curve server processing times.

In mutual-authenticated handshake, increase in the client processing time is negligible for ECDH_ECDSA key exchange suites. On the other hand, there is a significant increase in the client processing time for the RSA key exchange suites. The reason is that, for mutual-authenticated ECDH_ECDSA key exchange suites, clients do not perform an extra operation except sending the client certificate to the server; whereas in the RSA key exchange suites, clients need to perform a private key operation which is significantly costly in time, to generate the CertificateVerify message.

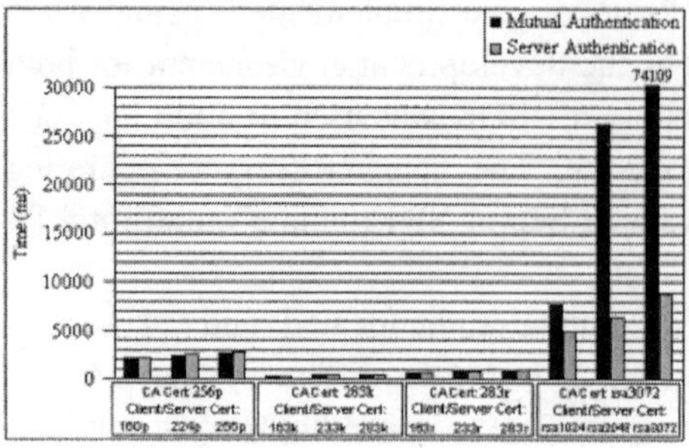

Figure 3. Client processing times

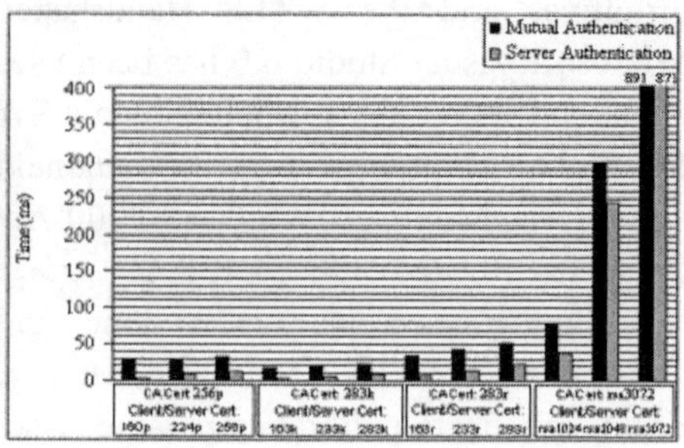

Figure 4. Server processing times

3.2 Transmission Time Analysis

Data transmission time modeling is the most complex part of the WTLS handshake protocol performance analysis due to the different characteristics of available data bearer types and existing of intermediate systems such as BTS (Base Transceiver Station), BSC (Base Station Controller), MSC (Mobile Services Switching Center), SGSN (Serving GPRS Support Node), and GGSN (Gateway GPRS Support Node) servicing between the gateway and client.

Typically the data transmission time T_{TD} can be computed by a simple formula given below:

$$T_{TD} = \frac{Data \quad length}{Channel \quad transmission \quad rate} \tag{1}$$

This equation is not sufficient for the WAP access transmission time computation because it does not consider the extra time cost due to the data bearer type. Several studies [12, 13] have shown that the traversal delay of the GSM network is significant on data transmission time. The duration between the transmission of the data packet and receipt of the required ACK packet is defined as RTT (Round Trip Time). The RTT value a very important parameter that must be considered in our transmission time modeling.

The RTT value contains the data transmission time in addition to the traversal delay of the GSM network. The traversal delay varies for different data bearer types. Overall transmission delay is modeled as follows:

$$T_{TD} = \frac{L}{R} + 2 \times N_{msg} \times T_{traversal} \tag{2}$$

Where; L is the total data length (in bits) including all the handshake messages and their corresponding ACK packets, R is the channel transmission rate (bit/s), T_{TD} is the data transmission time (s) and N_{msg} is the number of messages exchanged during the WTLS protocol.

Data transmission time analysis is performed for two data bearer systems. These are GSM CSD (Global System for Mobile Communication Circuit Switched Data) and GPRS (General Packet Radio Service) data bearers. Using the timings obtained from our experiments and eq. 2, we calculate the traversal delay of the GSM CSD network as 391.3 ms, which causes the major component of the overall transmission time. As a result of the significant effect of the traversal delay, we observe that the data transmission time of the different test cases do not differ too much although they differ in total data transmitted. Number of handshake messages, which is multiplied by the traversal delay in the data transmission time, is the most important parameter. Data transmission times for each test case of GSM CSD bearer are given in Table 2.

Table 2. Transmission delays for GSM CSD bearer (ms)

CA Cert.	Client/Server Cert.	Mutual Auth.	Server Auth.	CA Cert.	Client/Server Cert.	Mutual Auth.	Server Auth.
256p	160p	5121.5	5164.2	283r	163r	5039.5	4905.6
256p	224p	4906.5	5144.9	283r	233r	6750.7	5023.4
256p	256p	5242.1	5133.6	283r	283r	4966.5	5451.0
283k	163k	5164.5	4930.2	rsa3072	rsa1024	5149.1	4499.5
283k	233k	5247.3	4926.8	rsa3072	rsa2048	5327.2	5103.4
283k	283k	5054.2	5138.2	rsa3072	rsa3072	5008.4	4930.3

It is also observed that the transmission delay coming from the traversal delays of the network is 76% of the overall data transmission time on the average. This supports the idea that the number of handshake messages for a given key exchange suite is more significant than the data size, on the overall handshake duration for GSM CSD data bearer systems.

Our performance tests over GPRS bearer also show that the traversal delay has the most important effect. In general, GPRS data rates are higher than GSM CSD.

However, this data rate advantage cannot be utilized for the WTLS handshake protocol. This is because of the high valued network traversal delay for GPRS bearers. High data rate is an advantage when downloading large volumes of data, but there is only a slight effect in the data transmission time for WTLS handshake protocol due to the small sized handshake messages.

Traversal delays for both bearer types are compared in Table 3. Variance of traversal delay is an important factor that effects the total transmission time in a counter-intuitive way. For example, in 283r CA certificate values of Table 2, one would expect that the transmission time should increase as the client certificate size increases. It, however, does not because of the variance in the traversal delay. Moreover, as Table 3 shows clearly, traversal delays are similar for both data bearer types, but GPRS suffers from variance more than GSM CSD does.

Table 3. Comparison of traversal delays for GSM CSD and GPRS bearers

Bearer	Mean Value (ms)	Standard Deviation (ms)
GSM CSD	391.3	90.0
GPRS (worst case)	398.4	213.9
GPRS (average case)	376.1	141.2
GPRS (best case)	351.4	120.1

3.3 Total Handshake Time Analysis

Figures 5 shows the total handshake times for mutual-authenticated and server-authenticated WTLS handshakes for the selected test cases. Total handshake time is the sum of processing and transmission times. As discussed in Section 3.2, although there is a significant data rate difference between GSM CSD and GPRS bearers, the overall handshake data transmission time is not very different for these bearers because of the similar network traversal delay characteristics. Therefore only one of these bearers, namely GSM CSD, is taken into consideration for total time analysis.

Data transmission time is the biggest portion of the total handshake time for ECDH_ECDSA key exchange suites. When RSA is used, especially in mutual-authenticated WTLS handshake, processing time becomes effective on the total handshake time.

By analyzing Figure 5, we can easily say that the fastest RSA choice performs worse than slowest ECC choice. Moreover, considering the mutual-authenticated case, it is possible to reach level 3 security at both client and server parts under 10 seconds of handshake time using ECC, whereas the same level requires about 80 seconds using RSA. However, it is feasible to use RSA in server-authenticated handshake protocols although it performs worse than ECC.

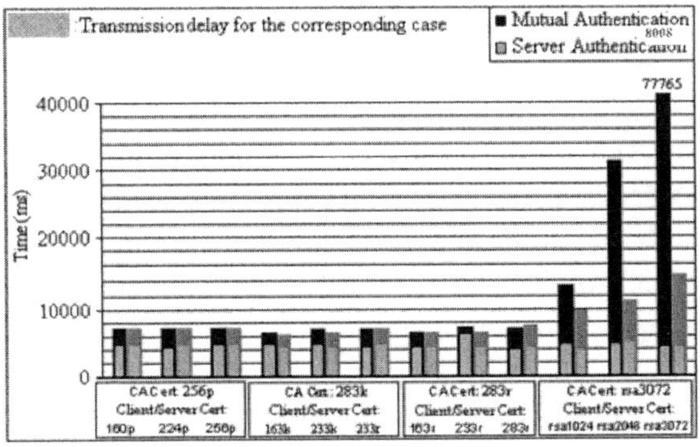

Figure 5. WTLS handshake total handshake times

3.4 *Queue Delay Analysis*

Queue delay is the time that a WTLS handshake message has to wait for being served in the server. Generally the queue delay depends on the number of servers, average service time, and arrival rate. The server is analytically modeled as an M/G/1 queue (poisson arrivals, general service time, one server). Server processing times of Section 3.1 are used in the analysis. In order to simulate the real behavior of a server, we have employed a mix strategy where the server processes several handshake requests at different key sizes. Simulations are performed using Matlab 6.0.

Due to the low server processing times of ECC certificates and ECDH_ECDSA key exchange suites, the system has an acceptable queue delay performance; as a worse case scenario and with group 3 elliptic curves. On the other hand, queuing delay performance of RSA key exchange suites is not as good as ECC cases. The queue delay asymptotically increases for higher arrival rates. As an expected result, the case that uses purely 3072 bit RSA server certificates has the worst queue delay performance. Due to space limitations, we do not give all of the analyses in this paper. The reader may refer to [14] for more details about queue delay analysis.

4. Conclusions

In this paper, WTLS handshake protocol performance is evaluated by modeling the different components of the protocol and by analyzing the implementation results parallel to the performance model. The performance model considers three main components that may cause bottleneck in the protocol. These are client and server processing times, server queue waiting time and handshake data transmission time over the channel. The data needed for processing time and the transmission time analyses are obtained by literally running the protocol over a GSM provider network and by using real handheld devices and gateway platform. Performing the tests over a real GSM service provider network comes with the advantages of reflecting the network specific operational costs and message parsing costs to the total handshake time.

As an expected result, both client and server processing times increase as the key size increases for the same public key cryptosystem. However, increase in the processing time is much more significant for RSA key exchange suites. We see that increasing the security level has a significant effect on the handshake processing time for RSA key exchange suites, where the increase is tolerable for ECDH_ECDSA key exchange suites.

Our results show that server queue delay may be a source of bottleneck in the WTLS handshake protocol execution. Average waiting time in the server queue is negligible when using ECDH_ECDSA key exchange suites for server-authenticated WTLS handshake. This is due to the low processing times of ECDH_ECDSA key exchange suites' handshake messages. On the other hand, server queue delay must be considered when using RSA.

Handshake data transmission time is an important concern for the total handshake time. It is obvious that the data transmission time depends on the transmission rate of the data bearer used. However, another characteristic to consider is the traversal delay of the network. This delay is added to the RTT (Round Trip Time) regardless of the data size sent. Measurements show that the traversal delay of the network is much more significant on the transmission time then the data transmission rate for both GSM CSD and GPRS data bearer types. There is no significant difference between the data transmission time over GSM CSD and GPRS for small data sizes. This is due to the similar traversal delay characteristics for both carrier systems. Therefore, the number of handshake messages becomes the most important parameter that affects the WTLS handshake data transmission time.

In consideration of overall end-to-end delay, our analysis shows that RSA performs always worse than ECC in WTLS handshake protocol. For large key sizes at cryptographic level 3 of Table 1, RSA key exchange suites are infeasible to use in mutual-authenticated WTLS handshake protocol. However, ECDH_ECDSA can be used at this level. These level 3 curves are not offered by the WTLS standard [2], but our analysis showed that they could be used at a cost of minimal increase in latency.

References

1. WAP Forum, "Wireless Application Protocol Architecture Specification, WAP-100-WAPArch-19980430-a", WAP Forum Specifications 30-Apr-1998 version
2. WAP Forum, "Wireless Application Protocol Wireless Transport Layer Security Specification, WAP-199-WTLS-20000218-a", WAP Forum Specifications 18-Feb-2000 version
3. T. Dierks and C. Allen, "The TLS Protocol – Version 1.0", January 1999, IETF RFC 2246
4. A. Frier, P. Karlton, and P. Kocher, "The SSL 3.0 Protocol", Netscape Communications Corporation, Nov. 1996
5. R. Rivest, A. Shamir, and L. Adleman, "A Method for Obtaining Digital Signatures and Public Key Cryptosystems", *Communications of the ACM*, vol. 21, no. 2, pp. 120-126, February 1978
6. N. Koblitz, "Elliptic Curve Cryptosystems", *Mathematics of Computation*, 48(177):203-209, January 1987
7. A. K. Lenstra, E. R. Verheul, "Selecting Cryptographic Key Sizes", *Proceedings of the Public Key Cryptography*, January 2000
8. A. Levi, and E. Savas, "Performance Evaluation of Public-Key Cryptosystems Operations in WTLS Protocol", *Proceedings of the Eight IEEE International Symposium on Computers and Communication (ISCC'03),* 2003
9. G. Apostolopoulos, V. Peris, and P. Pradhan., "Securing Electronic Commerce: Reducing the SSL Overhead", *IEEE Network*, (14)4: 8-16 July/August 2000
10. G. Apostolopoulos, V. Peris, and D. Saha, "Transport Layer Security: How much does it really cost?", *Proceedings of IEEE Infocom'99*, pp. 717-725, March 1999
11. I. Herwono, and I. Liebhardt, "Performance of WTLS and its Impact on an M-Commerce Transaction", *ICICS 2001 – Proceedings of the Third International Conference on Information and Communications Security*, Nov. 2001, pp. 167-171, Xi'an, China
12. G. Xylomenos, G. Polyzos, P. Mahonen, and M. Saaranen, "TCP Performance Issues over Wireless Links", *IEEE Communications Magazine*, Volume 39, No. 4, 2001, pp.52-58
13. R. Ludwig, and B. Rathonyi, "Link Layer Enhancements for TCP/IP over GSM", *IEEE Infocom'99*, March 1999
14. B. Bayoglu, Performance Evaluation of WTLS Handshake Protocols Using RSA and Elliptic Curve Cryptosystems, M.S. Thesis, Sabanci University, 2004.

INTEGRATING SEMANTIC CONTEXT MODEL INTO ADAPTIVE MIDDLEWARE FOR UBIQUITOUS COMPUTING *

QING WU, ZHAOHUI WU AND JIE SUN

College of Computer Science, Zhejiang University,
Hangzhou, Zhejiang, China, 310027
E-mail: {*wwwsin, wzh, sunjie*}*@cs.zju.edu.cn*

Ubiquitous computing aims at pursuing naturalness, harmony and adaptation. We think that "semantic" is the key aspect in co-operations and communications of people, devices and smart devices. This paper presents a semantic context model for an adaptive middleware. We emphasize on the fusion of semantic context information in smart vehicle space for ubiquitous computing. Semantic web technology and web ontology language are used to build the ontology of the smart vehicle space. In addition, we propose an application scenario and a prototype system. The contribution is twofold. First, we present the architecture of semantic context model. Seconde, we have built the ontology of smart vehicle space, with which we make context fusion and inference for middleware adaptation.

1. Introduction

In 21st century, a new computation model called "ubiquitous computing" [1] goes into our life. People, smart devices and environment are three elements of this novel computation model. In order to co-operate with each other naturally, harmoniously and adaptively, multifarious technologies are synthesized. Therefore, to realize the ideas of ubiquitous computing, it requires to integrate many research methods such as software architecture, middleware platform, languages design, distributed systems, artificial intelligence, vision recognition, user interfaces and biology authentication. Currently, a lot of related academic research efforts and commercial realities are made for ubiquitous computing. They focus on some active and smart spaces (e.g., Intelligent home, Easy meeting room, and Smart museum). In smart spaces, according to the changes of people, smart devices and environment,

*This work is supported by 863 National High Technology Program under Grant No. 2003AA1Z2080, 2003AA1Z2140 and 2002AA1Z2308.

the computation should self-adjust based on the strategies automatically to a new balanceable state for better cooperation and communication. Therefore, it poses a large number of new challenges for software architecture and middleware technology for above attractive goals. However, the traditional software middlewares do not adapt to ubiquitous computing environment. [2] As a result, the novel middleware architecture is needed. To solve this problem, we think the key issue is "semantic". There are too many different and hierarchical contexts of people, smart devices and environment. Nevertheless, they should be understood and used correctly and effectively. Semantic information can provide an infrastructure for context awareness and adaptation.

Nowadays, vehicles have played an important role in our daily life. People require more safety, comfort and facilities in vehicles. We select the vehicle space as a representative scene to research on ubiquitous computing. We have developed a ScudWare [3] middleware for smart vehicle space[4], which is a context-aware and adaptive middleware platform based on semantic information. In this paper, we detail the semantic context model, which is integrated in the ScudWare middleware. In addition, we use semantic web technologies and web ontology language to build and use the ontology of smart vehicle space.

The structure of the paper is as follows. Section 2 presents the ScudWare middleware overview, including smart vehicle space and its hierarchy architecture. In section 3, we give the framework of semantic context model, comprising semantic view for context, ontology of smart vehicle pace and its architecture. Following this, section 4 gives an application scenario and a prototype system. Then some related works are presented in section 5. Finally, section 6 summarizes the discussions and introduces some areas demanding further investigation.

2. ScudWare Platform

In order to implement smart vehicle space naturally and adaptively, we have built a ScudWare middleware that is an adaptive middleware platform. This section introduces the smart vehicle space and the ScudWare architecture.

2.1. *Smart Vehicle Space*

In recent years, a lot of developers have applied embedded, AI and biology authentication technologies to vehicles. The drive capability, dependability, comfort and convenience of the vehicle are improved greatly. When people go into smart vehicle space, they will find many intelligent devices and equipments around them. They communicate with these tools naturally and friendly. It forms a harmonious vehicle space, where people, smart devices and environments co-operate with each other adaptively.

Smart vehicle space has four parts and is defined as SVS=(CA, CR, AC, CP). CA is a context acquisition system providing hardware infrastructure. $CA = ((\Delta State(pe, de, en), (sen, cam, sou))$ aims at sensing status changes of people, devices and environments in the vehicle, including sensors, cameras and sound receivers. CR is a context repository reasoning system. CR=(context, ontology, domain, inference) uses correlative context and application domain ontology to make manipulating strategy for adaptation. AC is an auto controlling system. AC=(ste, com, ent, nav, sec) consists of steering, communication, entertainment, navigation and security subsystem. CP is a centralized processing system. Particularly, CP is the kernel of smart vehicle space, which controls above third parts co-operating effectively.

2.2. *ScudWare Architecture*

ScudWare architecture consists of six parts, defined as SCUDW = (SOSEK, ACE, ETAO, SCUDCCM, SVA). SOSEK denots SMART OSEK [5], an operating system of vehicle conformed to OSEK specification developed by us. ACE denotes the adaptive communication environment, providing high-performance and real-time communications. ACE uses inter-process communication, event demultiplexing, explicit dynamic linking and concurrency. Therefore, ACE simplifies the development of object-oriented network applications and services. In addition, ACE automates system configuration and reconfiguration by dynamically linking services into applications at run-time and executing these services in one or more processes or threads. ETAO extends ACE ORB and is designed using the best software practices and patterns on ACE in order to automate the delivery of high-performance and real-time QoS to distributed applications. ETAO includes a set of services such as persistence and transaction services. In addition, we have developed adaptive resource management service, semantic context service and notification service. Specially, the semantic context service is based on the semantic context model. SCUDCCM is conformed to CCM specification and consists of adaptive component package, assembly, deployment and allocation at design time. Besides, it comprises component migration, replacement, updating and variation at run-time. SVA denotes semantic virtual agent[6] and aims at dealing with application tasks. Each SVA presents one service composition, comprising a number of meta objects. During the co-operations of SVA, the SIP(Semantic Interface Protocol) set is used including sva discovery, joining, lease and self-updating protocols. Due to the limited space, we don't detail SVA in this paper.

3. Semantic Context Model Framework

There are many kinds of contexts in smart vehicle space, which are hierarchical, inhomogeneous and dynamic. For context acquisition, presentation and usage, we present semantic context model for ScudWare middleware. During its implementation, we use semantic web technologies and web ontology language to build the ontology of smart vehicle space. First, this section presents the semantic view for context. Second, we details the ontology built and its usage in smart vehicle space. Finally, the architecture of semantic context model is proposed.

3.1. *Semantic View for Context*

Context[7] is any information that can be used to characterize the status of an entity. An entity may be a person, place or object that is considered relevant to the interaction between a user and an application, including the user and application themselves. The widely used context consists of location, identity, time, temperature and activity. We consider special objects in environments are all context. In addition, context-aware is an ability to sense and use different context. Context-aware computing is the ability of computing devices to detect, interpret, and respond to the changes of environment and system. Any application that takes advantage of context is a context-aware application.

However, the presentation, sharing and reasoning of contexts is very difficult. In smart spaces, context is very complicated and hard to understand and well use. It demands a method with strong expression ability and easy sharing. Because the semantic information of contexts is essential for dealing with the complex tasks in ubiquitous computing environments, we think the semantic web technologies and web ontology language can be used to solve above problems.

As Tim Berners-Lee [8] described, semantic web is an extension of the current web where information is given well-defined meaning, and better enabling people to co-operate with computers. In addition, semantic web provides an infrastructure that makes not just web pages, but databases, services, programs, sensors, personal devices and even household appliances to both consume and produce data on the web easily. On the other hand, W3C organization has specified a language OWL that is based on DAML and OIL for semantic web, which is more expressive than RDF and RDF-S. The OWL language builds on XML's ability to define customized tagging schemes and RDF's flexible approach to represent data. As a result, the semantic web technologies and OWL language is suitable for dealing with context.

As a whole, the semantic view of context is to use above semantic technologies to manage the context. By this means, we can share the common vocabularies and use OWL as standard syntax to present context information and inference more effectively and adaptively.

3.2. *Ontology in Smart Vehicle Space*

Ontology[9] is an agreement about shared conceptualization, which includes conceptual frameworks for modelling application domain knowledge, content-specific protocols for communication among interacting agents and agreements about the representation of specific domain theories. The common understanding of ontology is on two different levels: (a) It is a vocabulary, which uses appropriate terms to describe entities and relationships between entities. (b) It is a knowledge base for a specific domain. We think that ontology describes the domain knowledge in a general way and provides consistent understanding for one application domain. As following, we introduce the ontology build and usage in smart vehicle space.

3.2.1. *Ontology Build*

Because the smart vehicle space is a special environment, we examine characteristics from the view of semantic context and aim at some special applications. To build the ontology in smart vehicle space easily, we give two principles: (a) We emphasize on the contexts inside the vehicle, because space inside vehicle is relatively confined and the devices inside it are limited and fixed. (b) We need not concern all dynamic changes, though environments outside of vehicle change continually. What we need is only those can influence our special applications.

In terms of above two principles, we have built the ontology of smart vehicle space $Ontology_{svs} = \{O_{Vehicle}, O_{Environ}, O_{People}\}$. $O_{Vehicle}$ is a set of the vehicle contexts, including the status and attribute of the devices inside the vehicle, such as air-condition, wiper, light, engine, ABS, and seat. $O_{Environ}$ is a set of environment contexts, comprising the environmental elements that may influence driving, such as weather information, road status and signal lamps. O_{People} is a set of driver context, including (a) status of the driver, such as the suitability and ability to driving; (b) physiological parameters, such as alcohol density and pupil diameter.

3.2.2. *Ontology Usage*

Based on above ontology and knowledge base, the system deals with context acquisition, representation and fusion automatically. We filter the context scenario and specify the concrete point that should be responded. Once the system meets the situation defined, the context reasoning subsystem will be triggered and operates, then some actions will be done.

We use the ontology of people to monitor the status of the driver, such as the level of tiredness or ebriety. Importantly, we specify several situations of driver. Each one corresponds to different physiologic parameters. According to the different danger levels, system takes various actions. For example, if the driver is unable to continue driving when the danger level is high, the system will force to stop and call for help. If the situation is not very serious, the system just park to the nearest safe location. The ABS of the vehicle will be start up in case of the friction is too little or other emerge situation occurs. As a result, in terms of this ontology, the system can deal with different problems adaptively.

3.3. *Semantic Context Model Architecture*

According to semantic view for context and ontology of smart vehicle space, we present a semantic context model and integrate it into ScudWare middleware, which is responsible for context adaptive management including context acquisition, representation, and fusion. Specially, semantic context model is based on semantic information using semantic web and ontology technologies. In addition, semantic context model can cooperate with semantic virtual agent on multi-agent level in semantic web. The structure of semantic context model is shown in figure 1. We introduce three functional modules of this model as following.

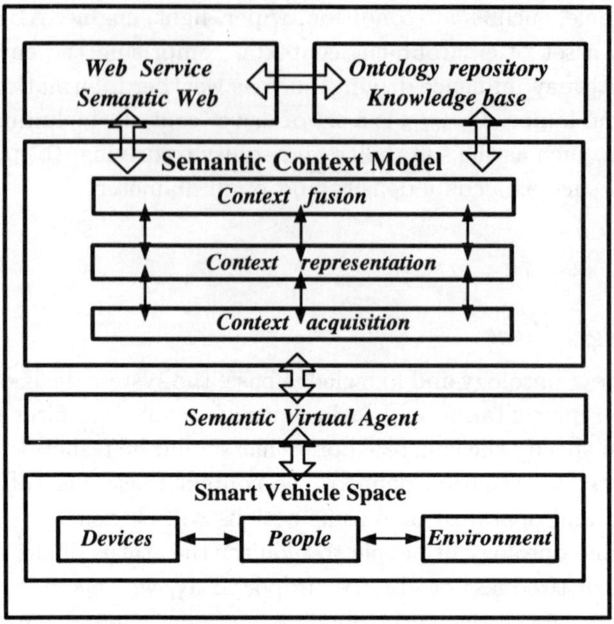

Figure 1. Semantic Context Model Architecture

3.3.1. *Context Acquisition*

It is the low module of the model. Many kinds of sensors such as temperature, speed and humidity sensors are used to obtain the low-level and coarse sensing data for further processing. For example, the temperature sensor can get the temperature inside or outside the vehicle. In addition, the digital cameras, microphone and physiologic sensors are used to get the status of people. For instance, the alcohol sensor is used to decide whether the driver is drunk. Specially stated, the data from this part has low semantic meaning and is not to share and use. Therefore, this data need to be well represented.

3.3.2. *Context Representation*

In order to well share and use the low-level context data from context acquisition part, we need to deal with these data well understood. For high-level semantic abstraction, we use semantic web language and OWL language to represent these data in terms of the ontology associated with smart vehicle space. The ontology repository is built for representing and understanding these data better. For example, we can represent the speed of the vehicle, driver's tiredness level and road surface status for easily understanding and using based on the ontology.

3.3.3. *Context Fusion*

Based on the semantic context information from context representation, the problem of context sharing and well understood is solved. However, these contexts should be further processed including fusion and inference to decide which actions will be taken. In this part, the useless contexts are removed and the useful information is for reasoning based on the knowledge base. After the context fusion, some control decisions are made and some actions are executed. Specially, the context information is dynamic and hierarchical.

4. Smart Vehicle Space Scenario

ScudWare middleware has integrated the semantic context model and applied it into smart vehicle space. To demonstrate applications in smart vehicle space, we give the following application scenario. Besides, one primary implementation prototype is introduced.

Dr. Wang stayed up all night for one project yesterday. It is 8 o'clock and he should go to work now. He carries his palm, walks out his home and comes in front of his "intelligent vehicle". The palm connects with the control system in vehicle through wireless network. After the system authenticates and confirms him a valid host, the door of vehicle is open. At the same time, semantic context service begin to run. A voice "Good morning, Dr. Wang" comes from the speaker. He enters the vehicle and sits down. When the sensor finds he is ready, the system closes the door automatically. During his driving, context acquisition module is running all along and gets the work status of equipments in vehicle, road surface and Dr. Wang's face status, etc. Then context representation module uses semantic web technologies and OWL language to represent these data and stores them into the control system. In addition, context fusion module analyzes these semantic information and decides what to do. After ten minutes, he feel a little tired and current status of road surface is not good. The control system alarms and warns him to slow down and pay attention to the road status. As a result, the safety and adaptation of smart vehicle space are improved greatly.

According to above application scenario, we have developed a prototype for smart vehicle space based on ScudWare middleware. By this prototype system, we can get required information about drivers, environments and vehicles. In terms of the semantic context model, the control system manages smart vehicle space automatically and adaptively.

5. Related work

In the past, a number of system architectures integrating the context model have been developed to support ubiquitous computing. CoBrA [10] describes a new approach that explores the use of semantic web languages in building an architecture for supporting context-aware systems. Context toolkit framework [11] presents a toolkit that supports the development of context-enabled applications. The context toolkit was inspired by the success of GUI toolkits. CARISMA [12] is a mobile computing middleware which exploits the principle of reflection to enhance the construction of adaptive and context-aware mobile applications. The middleware provides software engineers with primitives to describe how context changes should be handled using policies. RCSM [13] is a middleware designed to facilitate applications that require context-awareness or spontaneous and ad hoc communication. CARMEN [14] is a middleware for context-aware resource management, capable of supporting the automatic reconfiguration of wireless internet services in response to context changes without any intervention on the service logic. Comparing to above systems, our work focuses on smart vehicle space and emphasizes on the semantic view for context-aware middleware. We have integrated semantic context model into ScudWare middleware for smart vehicle space. Semantic web technologies and OWL language are used to build the ontology in our application domain.

6. Conclusions and Future Work

This paper proposes a semantic context model of ScudWare middleware for exploring ubiquitous computing in smart vehicle space. First, we give an overview of smart vehicle space and a ScudWare middlware framework. Second, we focus on semanitc view for context and use semantic web technologies and OWL language to build ontology of smart vehicle space. Then we propose the semantic context model. Finally, from a practical point of view, an application scenario and a prototype system in smart vehicle space are given.

However, this is a preliminary design of semantic context model in smart vehicle space for ubiquitous computing. The performance of this model need to be tested fully. Our future work includes: (a) Improving the ontology for special applications in smart vehicle space; (b) Improving the context fusion method.

References

1. Weiser M, The Computer for the 21st Century, *Scientific American.* (1991) pp.94-100
2. Anand Tripathi, Next-Generation Middleware Systems Challenges Designing, *Communications of the ACM* 45 (2002) pp. 39-42
3. Zhaohui Wu, Qing Wu, Jie Sun, Zhigang Gao, Bin Wu, and Mingde Zhao, ScudWare: A Context-aware and Lightweight Middleware for Smart Vehicle Space, *In proceeding of the first International Conference on Embedded Software and System* (2004) pp. 178-183
4. Qing Wu, Zhaohui Wu, Bin Wu, and Zhou Jiang, Semantic and Adaptive Middleware for Data management in Smart Vehicle Space, *In proceeding of the fifth Advances in Web-Age Information Management* (2004) pp. 107-116
5. Mingde Zhao, Zhaohui Wu, Guoqing Yang, Lei Wang, and Wei Chen, SmartOSEK: A Dependable Platform for Automobile Electronics, *In proceeding of the first International Conference on Embedded Software and System* (2004) pp. 355-365
6. Qing Wu and Zhaohui Wu, Semantic and Virtual Agents in Adaptive Middleware Architecture for Smart Vehicle Space, *In proceeding of the 4th International Central and Eastern European Conference on Multi-Agent Systems* (2005) to be appeared
7. Anind K. Dey, Providing Architectural Support for Building Context-Aware Applications, *PhD thesis, Georgia Institute of Technology* (2000)
8. Tim Berners-Lee and Mark Fischetti, Weaving the web: The original design and ultimate destiny of the world wide web by its inventor (2001)
9. B. Chandrasekaran, John. R Josephson, and Richard V. Benjamins, What Are Ontologies, and Why do We Need Them? *IEEE Transactions on Intelligent Systems* (1999) pp. 20C26
10. Harry Chen, Tim Finin, Anupam Joshi, A Context Broker for Building Smart Meeting Rooms, *American Association for Artificail Intelligence* (2004)
11. Daniel Salber, Anind K. Dey and Gregory D. Abowd, The Context Toolkit: Aiding the Development of Context-Enabled Applications, *In proceedings of CHI'99, ACM Press* (1999)
12. Licia Capra, Wolfgang Emmerich, and Cecilia Mascolo, CARISMA: Context-Aware Reflective mIddleware System for Mobile Applications, *IEEE Transactions on software engineering* 29 (2003)
13. Stephen S. Yau, Fariaz Karim, Yu Wang, Bin Wang, and Sandeep K.S, Gupta: Reconfigurable Context- Sensitive Middleware for Pervasive Computing, *Pervasive computing* (2002)
14. Paolo Bellavista, Antonio Corradi, Rebecca Montanari, and Cesare Stefanelli, Context-Aware Middleware for Resource Management in the Wireless Internet. *IEEE Transactions on software engineering* 29 (2003)

AN INFRASTURCTURE FOR CONTEXT-AWARE AUTHORIZATION IN UBIQUITOUS COMPUTING ENVIRONMENTS

YOUNG-CHUL SHIM
Hongik University, Department of Computer Engineering
72-1 Sangsudong, Mapogu, Seoul, Korea

Context-awareness and security are critical issues in ubiquitous computing. In this paper we present a framework for context-aware authorization in ubiquitous computing environments. We present an architecture consisting of authorization infrastructure and context infrastructure. The authorization infrastructure makes decision to grant access rights based on both contexts and policies specified with a flexible language. The context infrastructure provides contexts at various levels of abstraction and enables context users to acquire contexts by submitting a query or using an event notification mechanism. The policy specification language allows one to authorize, prohibit, delegate, and revoke access rights. It also has constructs to package policies, resolve conflicts among policies, and specify the interaction with the context infrastructure.

1. Introduction

In ubiquitous computing environments nearly everything is connected to the network in order to provide service and information on anything, anywhere, anytime. This poses a serous security issues and the success of ubiquitous computing environments depends on our ability to secure them. We have to ensure that access to service and information is permitted only to authorized users. Moreover in many cases the decision to grant access rights can be dependent on contexts such as location, time, etc.

In this paper we present a framework for context-aware authorization in ubiquitous computing environments. We present an infrastructure for context-aware authorization that consists of an authorization infrastructure and a context infrastructure. The authorization infrastructure allows the enforcement of access control policies based on not only the requesting user and the requested operation as in traditional authorization systems but also various context information and the authentication method used by the requesting user. The context infrastructure provides necessary context information. Contexts can be dynamic ones obtained from sensors or static ones stored in database. These basic contexts can be composed into high-level contexts. Context users can obtain contexts by either submitting queries or requesting the detection and notification of events that they are interested in.

We also propose an authorization policy specification language with which one can authorize or prohibit access requests and initiate/terminate management actions. One can also delegate its access rights to other users and later revoke them. Meta policies enable one to specify constraints holding among multiple policies. The language also provides mechanisms to package policies and resolve various kinds of conflicts among policies.

Many researchers have studied a context infrastructure for context-aware applications[1,2]. Within a Gaia project, an infrastructure for context-aware security services, called Cerberus, was proposed[3]. Its authorization infrastructure is similar to ours but its context infrastructure is primitive and the interaction between these two infrastructures is not clearly explained. There have been many studies on policy specification in the security and network management areas[4,5]. But most of them are either too narrow-scoped or too complex for practical uses. One of the most comprehensive and practical policy languages is Ponder[6]. We base our policy language on Ponder and extend it so that the context constraints and the interaction with the context infrastructure can be specified.

The rest of the paper is organized as follows. Section 2 describes both authorization and context infrastructures. Section 3 presents the authorization policy specification language and is followed by the conclusion in Section 4.

2. Context-Aware Authorization Infrastructure

Figure 1 shows the overall architecture of the authorization infrastructure. A ubiquitous application that wants to access a resource sends its access request to the authorization service module to get the authorization. When the application sends the request, it sends not only the basic information on the request such as the subject(requesting user), object(target resource), operation type, and operation parameter values but also other security related information about the subject such as what kind of authentication method has been used, what kind of encryption and/or integrity method has been used, etc. We call this security-related information to be the security information of the session in which the requesting user is running the application and submitting the access request. The authorization service module consults the inference engine to determine whether to permit the access request or not and returns the result to the application. The inference engine makes its decision

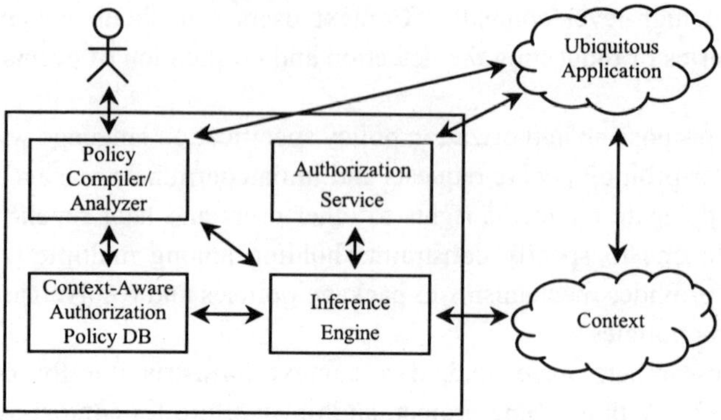

Figure 1. Authorization Infrastructure

based on the authorization policies stored in the policy database. Because the authorization policies are written in terms of not only the request information and the session security information but also the context information, the inference engine consults the context infrastructure to retrieve necessary context information. The context-aware authorization policies can be added/deleted/modified by human operators, the inference engine, or ubiquitous applications. When a new policy is to be added to the policy database, the policy compiler/analyzer checks its syntactic/semantic correctness and analyzes whether its addition will cause any conflicts with existing policies in the database. When a conflict is detected, either the addition of the new policy is rejected or some conflict resolution methods that will be explained in the next section may be taken.

Figure 2 shows the overall architecture of the context infrastructure. The infrastructure provides two kinds of contexts: dynamic contexts and static contexts.

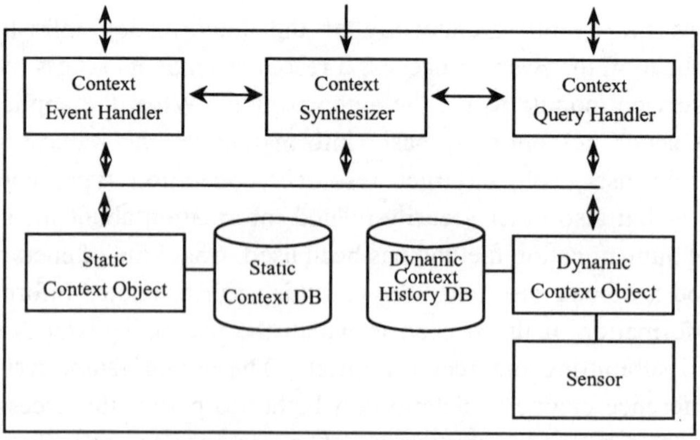

Figure 2. Context Infrastructure Overview

User location and temperature are examples of dynamic contexts that can change over the time and are collected by sensors. Contexts such as a building layout and a person's phone number are fairly static and stored in a database. There are two methods by which context consumers, that include applications and the inference engine in Figure 1, can obtain contexts. In the first method, context consumers send queries and get contexts that they are interested in. In the second method, context consumers request to be notified when the contexts they are interested in become true. Now we explain the components of the context infrastructure in more detail.

- Dynamic Context Object: provides object-oriented abstraction of a sensor. It encapsulates the attributes (Type, Id, Location, InstallationTime, Resolution, SamplingInterval, Value) and operations (Start, Stop, Test, Report, ChangeResolution, ChangeSamplingInterval) defined on a sensor. In addition to the general attributes such the type, id, location, installation time of a sensor, resolution and sampling interval attributes are defined. It defines the resolution with which the sensor collects data such as the location of an automobile. If the ChangeResolution operation is defined, the resolution of the sensor can be changed. If a sensor collects data by periodic sampling, the SamplingInterval attribute defines how frequently the data should be gathered. If the ChangeSamplingInterval operation is defined, the sampling interval can be changed. The value attribute represents the collected sensor data. A sensor value can be associated with three meta-attributes: time, resolution, and sampling interval. They define when the sensor data was gathered and what the resolution and the sampling interval of the sensor were at that time, respectively. The value attribute can have not only the current sensor data but also previous data. The past sensor data are stored in the dynamic context history database.
- Static Context Object: provides the object-oriented abstraction of static context information. In its object definition, only attributes need to be defined. The actual data are stored in the static context object.
- Context Synthesizer: The context objects provide only low-level context information. The context synthesizer allows that high-level context can be inferred using the low level contexts. As an example, let's assume that context objects provide low-level contexts such as how many people are in a certain room, what kinds of applications are running on the computer in that room, whether a beam projector is used in that room, etc. From these low-level contexts the context synthesizer can infer whether the room is idle, showing a movie, or used for presentation. The synthesizer infers these high-

level contexts using rules as will be explained in the later section. The rules are added either manually or automatically by applications.

- Context Query Handler: allows context consumers to send queries to get the contexts they want. By using the well-defined APIs of the context query handler, context consumers can send not only simple queries but also complex queries. It answers queries by using contexts stored in dynamic/static context objects and the context synthesizer. It also provides APIs that enable context consumers to change the resolution and sampling interval of a sensor.
- Context Event Handler: allows context consumers to be notified when the context that they are interested in becomes true. A context consumer registers the specification of the context in the context event handler. The handler detects when that context becomes true and notifies the consumer. This functionality is useful for not only applications but also the context-aware authorization service as will be explained in the next section.

3. Authorization Policy Specification

In this section we present the language for specifying authorization policies. We took the Ponder specification language as the basis and modified it to make it more suitable for context-aware authorization.

3.1. Basic Policies

There are 6 basic policy types in the proposed language. They are **authorize**, **prohibit**, **initiate**, **terminate**, **delegate**, and **revoke**.

An authorize policy allows a subject to perform operations on a target and a **prohibit** policy forbids a subject to perform operations on a target. Their syntaxes are as follows.

```
policy ( authorize | prohibit ) policy-Name "{"
   subject   object-Expression ;
   target         object-Expression ;
   operation      operation-Expression ;
   [ when         constraint-Expression ;]
   [ while        constraint-Expression ;]
   [ entry        action-Expression ;]
   [ exit         action-Expression ;] "}"
```

Boldfaced words are keywords in the specification language. Selections are enclosed in the matching parentheses separated by |, options are specified with square brackets [], and repetition is specified with braces {}. We explain the above syntax with an **authorize** policy. When an authorization request is made, the constraint expressions in the **when** and **while** clauses are evaluated and the requested operations are permitted only if both evaluation results are true. The constraint expression in the **while** clause should remain true, while the authorized operations are being executed. Otherwise the operations should be terminated. When the authorization request is made, actions in the **entry** action clause are executed. When the authorized operation is completed, actions in the **exit** action clause are executed. The **entry** and **exit** action clauses are included for house-keeping purposes such as recording logs. In case of a prohibit policy, while and exit clauses are not used. Now we give a simple example of an **authorize** policy. We want to allow students to use department printers only on weekends. We can specify this as follows:

```
policy authorize usingDeptPrinter {
   subject        student ;
   target         departmentPrinter ;
   operation print ;
   when           weekend ; }
```

An **initiate** policy dictates that a subject should perform operations on a target while a **terminate** policy specifies that operations that a subject is performing on a target should be terminated. These policies are activated when the occurrence of the specified event is detected and their syntaxes are as follows.

policy (**initiate** | **terminate**) policy-Name [reuse-Flag] "{"
   [**subject** object-Expression ;]
   target object-Expression ;
   operation operation-Expression ;
   on event-Expression ; "}"

When an **initiate/terminate** policy is stored in the policy database, the event expression in the on clause is registered in the event hander in the context infrastructure. An event expression can be a constraint expression, a simple event specification, or any logical combination of them. When the constraint expression becomes true or the occurrence of the event is detected, the event handler notifies of the inference engine so that the corresponding **initiate/terminate** policy can be activated. If the reuse flag is not set, the policy is deleted from the policy database after the policy gets activated. Although **initiate/terminate** policies are general purpose, they can be used to implement certain features of **authorize** policies. For example, when an authorize policy with a **while** constraint-Expression is successfully applied, the following **terminate** policy is added to the policy database.

```
policy terminate terminateOperation {
    subject object-Expression ;
    target          object-Expression ;
    operation       operation-Expression ;
    on              NOT ( constraint-Expression ) ; }
```

The object expressions and operation expressions are actual values when the **authorize** policy was applied. The constraint expression is copied from the **authorize** policy.

To transfer access rights to some other subjects, a **delegate** policy is used. Its syntax is as follows.

```
policy delegate policy-Name [ forwardable-Flag ] "{"
    grantor   object-Expression ;
    grantee   object-Expression ;
    target          object-Expression ;
    operation       operation-Expression ;
    [ when          constraint-Expression ; ]
    [ while         constraint-Expression ; ]
    [ entry         action-Expression ; ] "}"
```

It allows the grantor to delegate to the grantee the right to perform the specified operation on the target if the constraints in the **when** and **while** clauses are satisfied. Of course, the grantor should have the same access right on the specified target. If the constraint in the **while** clause becomes false after the right has been delegated, the right should be revoked. If the forwardable flag is set, the grantee receives also the right to delegate the same access right to some other subject. If the grantor wants to revoke the access rights that it has delegated to the grantee, it uses the revoke policy of the following format.

```
policy revoke policy-Name "{"
  grantor   object-Expression ;
  grantee   object-Expression ;
  target              object-Expression ;
  operation           operation-Expression ;
  on                  event-Expression ; "}"
```

3.2. Meta-Policies

Meta-policies are policies on other policies and used for specifying constraints on a policy or a set of policies. They have the similar syntax as in [6] as follows.

```
metaPolicy meta-Policy-Name
           exception exception-Name [ "(" parameters ")" ] "{"
 policy-Exception-Expression "}"
```

If a policy or policies satisfy the policy exception expression, an exception with the name of exception-Name is raised. The names of the policies that cause the exception to be raised are returned in the parameters. Using this syntax the example in [6] can be specified as follows.

```
metaPolicy budgetDutyConflict
           exception conflictInBudget (policy1, policy2) {
    (and   (Intersect policy1.subject policy2.subject)
           (Intersect policy1.target policy2.target)
           (Include policy1.operation "submit")
           (Include policy2.operation "approve")) }
```

This meta-policy causes an exception to be raised when the same person both submits and approves a budget and returns the names of these two policies.

3.3. Structuring Policies and Resolving Conflicts

We use the **package** construct to group a set of related policies and specify the hierarchical relationship among policy groups. The syntax of the **package** construct is as follows.

package package-Name "{"
{ policy-Directives }
{ basic-Policy-Definition }
{ meta-Policy-Definition }
{ package-Definition } "}"

A directive is used to specify who can manage the policies within the package. A user who is defined to be the manager of the package can add, delete, and modify any basic polices and meta-policies in the package. If one wants to give a management right of a policy to a certain user other than the manager, it can be defined with an authorize policy with the name of the managed policy in the **target** line. A directive is also used to specify what can be done when an **authorize** policy conflicts with a **prohibit** policy. Default is a negative mode where a **prohibit** policy overrides the conflicting **authorize** policy. But when the positive mode is defined using a directive, an **authorize** policy overrides the conflicting **prohibit** policy.

A package definition can include other package definitions to define the hierarchical relationship among them where the enclosed packages become the children of the enclosing package. When a policy conflicts with other policy in an ascendant package, the latter has precedence over the former. Conflicts in policies in a package can be resolved by associating priority values with conflicting policies.

4. Conclusion

Capturing context information and adapting its behavior according to contexts are an important issue in ubiquitous computing. Security is also a critical issue in ubiquitous environment that is a massively distributed computing system. In this paper we presented a framework for context-aware authorization in ubiquitous computing environment. The proposed framework consists of an authorization infrastructure and a context infrastructure. The authorization infrastructure makes decisions to grant access rights based on context information and policies written in a flexible language. The context infrastructure provides both static and dynamic contexts at various levels of abstraction and enables context users to acquire contexts by submitting a query or using an event notification mechanism. It also enables one to control the resolution of sensors that collect dynamic contexts. The policy specification language is designed based on Ponder and enables one to specify policies to authorize or prohibit access requests, initiate or terminate management actions, and delegate or revoke access rights.

References

1. J.I. Hong & J.A. Landay, An Infrastructure Approach to Context-Aware Computing, HCI Journal 16(2-3), 2001.
2. G. Judd & P. Steenkiste, Providing Contextual Information to Pervasive Computing Application: IEEE PerCom'03, 2003.
3. J. Al-Muhtadi et al, Cerberus: A Context-Aware Security Scheme for Smart Spaces, IEEE PerCom'03, 2003.
4. J.A. Hoagland et al, Security Policy Specification using a Graphical Approach, Technical Report CSE-98-3, UC Davis Computer Science Dept., July 1998.
5. R. Ortalo, A Flexible Method for Information System Security Policy Specification, ESORICS'98, 1998.
6. N. Damianou et al, The Ponder Policy Specification Language, LNCS 1995, 1995, 18-39.

Acknowledgements

This research was supported by University IT Research Center Project of the Ministry of Information and Communication in Republic of Korea.

PERFORMANCE CONSIDERATIONS FOR ELLIPTIC CURVE CRYPTOGRAPHY IN COMMUNICATIONS

ÖMER ÖZGÜR BOZKURT

Yildiz Technical University, Computer Engineering Department
34349, Istanbul, Turkey
ozgur@ce.yildiz.edu.tr

Elliptic Curve Cryptography is one of the emerging public key cryptography algorithms to provide communications security. Providing security means a decrease in performance and this decrease should be kept minimal in order to make the security algorithm attractive. Contemporarily, internet communications and sensor networks found a broad usage and research interest. In this paper, the performance of most dominant internet security protocol, Secure Sockets Layer, and TinySec, the link layer security mechanism for sensor networks, which are both enhanced by Elliptic Curve Cryptography, are studied.

1 Introduction

Whatever the type of the online transaction over the Internet is, security is the first in demand. During a transaction, both sides should be sure about not only the identity of the correspondent, but also the integrity and confidentiality of the data being transmitted. Secure Sockets Layer (SSL) [7] mostly fulfils those Internet user demands. SSL Protocol is an application independent protocol. SSL runs over a reliable transfer protocol such as TCP and is used to encapsulate various higher level protocols such as HTTP, TELNET, FTP, etc. SSL Protocol provides a private and reliable connection over an insecure, public network and the peers' identity can be authenticated using either symmetric or public-key cryptography. SSL is mostly used to secure the main protocol of the Internet, HTTP Protocol which is also referred to as HTTPS. However, the use of SSL reduces the web server throughput and causes slower response times. A benchmark study shows that using SSL may reduce the web pages that can be accessed up to 85 percent. [3] This means that web servers running SSL may respond almost 9 times slower.

SSL Protocol involves two components; Handshake protocol and Record Layer protocol. The Handshake protocol lets the peers negotiate a common cipher suite, authenticate each other and establish a shared secret. The Record Layer is then used to derive symmetric keys from the shared secret; and encryption and authentication of data transferred is performed with symmetric key algorithms. The main overhead of the SSL is from the public key cryptographic operations which require processing of very large integers. Once a connection is established, the shared secret may be reused, so that no more public-key cryptography is required. Symmetric key algorithms are faster and do not require large overhead data.

Sensor networks are being used for a vast number of different purposes, ranging from home automation to military surveillance. Devices used in sensor networks are mostly limited in power, computational capacities and memory [1]. This nature of the wireless sensor network makes traditional protocols and algorithms inapplicable. To overcome these limitations special protocols and algorithms are developed for sensor networks and most of those were examined in [1]. However, effort is mostly to provide more effective use of the limited resources of the devices and to provide more reliable communication within the network.

Currently, TinySec [12], the security component of TinyOS [15] provides symmetric cryptography for securing data. However, the schema depends on 80 bits SKIPJACK algorithm and cryptographic keys are written to the devices before they are deployed. After the deployment there is no way to change the keys other than collecting the devices to re-write the keys, despite the fact that TinySec provides ability to change the cryptographic keys.

Elliptic Curve Cryptography (ECC) was first proposed by Victor Miller [18] and Neal Koblitz [13] independently in 1985. ECC can be used to provide both a digital signature scheme and an encryption scheme and operates over points on an elliptic curve defined over a finite field. It relies on the assumed difficulty of the elliptic curve discrete logarithm problem (ECDLP). This property of ECC makes it superior to the traditional public-key cryptosystems, since ECDLP has exponential running time while the others have sub-exponential running times. [24]

In this study, elliptic curve cryptography is used for distribution of keys using the facilities provided by TinySec and for public key cryptographic operations of SSL.

2 Public Key Cryptosystems

Public-key cryptographic algorithms are designed so that the key used for encryption is different from the key used for decryption. Furthermore, having the encryption key in hand does not make it possible to calculate the decryption key in a reasonable amount of time. The algorithms are called public-key, because, encryption key can be made public. Anyone can encrypt a message using the encryption key, but, only a specific person holding the corresponding decryption key can decrypt the message. The strength of the public key cryptosystems depends on the mathematical problem that the algorithm depends on. [22]

2.1 Integer Factorization Problem

Given a positive integer, n, it is hard to compute prime factors of n especially if n has large prime factors. Many cryptographic algorithms, including RSA depend on integer factorization problem (IFP). The best method known for factorization problem is number field sieve factoring [25] which has a sub exponential running time.

2.2 Discrete Logarithm Problem

Given a cyclic group G of order n, generator of G, p and an element of G, q; it is hard to find an x where $p = qx$ mod n. Many cryptographic algorithms, including Diffie-Hellman (DH) key exchange, depend on discrete logarithm problem (DLP). The index-calculus algorithm is the most powerful method known for computing discrete logarithms [25]. This technique does not apply to all groups, but when it does, it gives a sub exponential-time algorithm.

2.3 *Elliptic Curve Discrete Logarithm Problem*

Given an elliptic curve E, generator point P, and a point Q on E, it is hard to find x, such that $P=xQ$. The best general algorithm known to date for ECDLP is Pollard-rho algorithm, which has a fully exponential running time. However, for some special class of elliptic curves, called supersingular curves, and F_q-anomalous curves, ECDLP can be reduced to DLP. Those curves are not recommended for ECC.

3 Digital Signature Algorithm

When a message is received, the recipient may desire to verify that the message has not been altered in transit. Furthermore, the recipient may wish to be certain of the originator's identity. Both of these services can be provided by a digital signature algorithm. A digital signature is an electronic analogue of a written signature in that the digital signature can be used in proving to the recipient or a third party that the message was, in fact, signed by the originator.

A digital signature algorithm is used by a *signatory* to generate a digital signature on data and by a *verifier* to verify the authenticity of the signature. Each signatory has a public and a private key. The private key is used in the signature generation process and the public key is used in the signature verification process. An adversary, who does not know the private key of the signatory, cannot generate the correct signature of the signatory. In other words, signatures cannot be forged. However, by using the signatory's public key, anyone can verify a correctly signed message. [21]

4 Diffie - Hellman Key Exchange

DH key agreement algorithm is the first practical solution to the key distribution problem, allowing two parties to establish a shared secret by exchanging messages over an open channel. The security rests on the intractability of the DH problem and the related problem of computing discrete logarithms. The basic version provides protection in the form of secrecy of the resulting key from passive eavesdroppers, but vulnerable to man-in-the-middle attack. There is no way to assure the identity of the source message, or the receiver of the message. Algorithm is as follows [17]. A and B send one message to each other over an open channel and both parties get the shared secret k as a result.

1. One-time setup. An appropriate prime p and generator α of Z_p ($2 \leq \alpha \leq p-2$) are selected and published.
2. Protocol messages.

   $A \rightarrow B : \alpha^x \bmod p$ (M*i*)

   $A \leftarrow B : \alpha^y \bmod p$ (M*ii*)

3. Following steps are performed each time a shared key is required:
   (**a**) A chooses a random secret x, $1 \le x \le p-2$, and sends B message (M*i*).
   (**b**) B chooses a random secret y, $1 \le y \le p-2$, and sends A message (M*ii*).
   (**c**) B receives α^{x} and computes the shared key as $k = (\alpha^{x})^{y} \bmod p$.
   (**d**) A receives α^{y} and computes the shared key as $k = (\alpha^{y})^{x} \bmod p$.

5 Elliptic Curve Cryptography

ECC operates over a group of points on an elliptic curve defined over a finite field, unlike the conventional public-key cryptosystems which operates directly on finite fields. To use an elliptic curve for cryptographic operations, a base point G for the curve should be defined. Base point is a point on the curve which can generate most of the points with scalar multiplication.. Scalar multiplications of any point on the curve, except the point at infinity, O, gives another point on the curve. Given the base point G, and the point P, which is $P = kG$, it is hard to find k.

There are two distinct, non-interoperable types of elliptic curve cryptography. The elliptic curve can be either odd characteristic (also called modulo p or prime characteristic) or even characteristic (also called characteristic 2).

Studies show that, the use of elliptic curve cryptographic techniques provide greater security using fewer bits, resulting in low computational overhead. Table 1 shows the required key sizes for desired level of security. [14]

Table 1. Key sizes for equivalent security levels

Symmetric	DH/DSA/RSA	ECC
80	1,024	163
112	2,048	224
128	3,072	256
192	7680	384
256	15360	521

5.1 Elliptic Curve Digital Signature Algorithm

The Elliptic Curve Digital Signature Algorithm (ECDSA) is the elliptic curve analogue of DSA. ECDSA was first proposed in 1992 by Scott VanStone [26] in response to NIST's request for public comments on their first proposal for digital signature Standard (DSS).

5.2 Elliptic Curve Diffie-Hellman

In ECDH key exchange, the two communicating parties A and B agree beforehand to use the same curve parameters and a base point G. They each generate their private keys a and b randomly, and compute the public keys, aG and bG. Both A and B can compute abG, which is the shared secret. Third parties cannot determine this secret key from either the elliptic curve parameters, or the public keys.

6 Secure Sockets Layer Protocol

The primary goal of the SSL Protocol is to provide privacy and reliability between two communicating applications. The protocol is composed of two layers. At the lowest level, layered on top of some reliable transport protocol (e.g., TCP), is the **SSL Record Protocol**. The SSL Record Protocol is used for encapsulation of various higher level protocols. One such encapsulated protocol, the **SSL Handshake Protocol**, allows the server and client to authenticate each other and to negotiate an encryption algorithm and cryptographic keys before the application protocol transmits or receives its first byte of data. One advantage of SSL is being application protocol independent. A higher level protocol can layer on top of the SSL Protocol transparently.

```
Client                                      Server

ClientHello          ------>
                                       ServerHello
                                      Certificate*
                                ServerKeyExchange*
                               CertificateRequest*
                     <-------      ServerHelloDone
Certificate*
ClientKeyExchange
CertificateVerify*
[ChangeCipherSpec]
Finished             ------->
                                [ChangeCipherSpec]
                     <-------             Finished
Application Data     <------>     Application Data

* Indicates optional or situation dependent
messages that are not always sent.
```

Figure 1. SSL Handshake Operation

There are two cases of SSL handshake operation: Only the server is authenticated or both client and server are authenticated as shown in Figure 1. In the first case some data is encrypted by the server and decrypted by the client. In the latter case, both sides require encryption and decryption. With RSA, in case of server authentication only, client performs one RSA public key operation to verify server's certificate and one to encrypt the pre-master secret key with server's public key. The server only performs one RSA private key operation to decrypt the ClientKeyExchange message and recover the pre-master secret key. Client authentication additionally requires an RSA private key operation to create CertificateVerify message on the client side and two RSA public key operations (to verify the client's certificate and to verify the client's signature in the CertificateVerify message) with a private key operation to decrypt the pre-master secret [5].

6.1 *Elliptic Curve Based Secure Sockets Handshake*

With ECC, if client authentication is not performed, the client verifies server's certificate by an ECDSA verification operation and then computes the shared pre-master secret using its ECDH private key and the server's public ECDH key. On the server side only an ECDH operation is carried out to arrive at the same secret. In case of client authentication, the type of the client's certificate (ECDSA or ECDH), results in two different scenarios. If the client is using ECDH certificate, an ECDSA verification operation is performed on both sides to verify the other's certificate and an ECDH operation is carried to compute the pre-master secret. If the client is using an ECDSA certificate, the client performs an ECDSA verification of the server's certificate and an ECDH operation to compute the pre-master secret, followed by another ECDSA operation to generate the certificate verify message. On the server side, one ECDH operation to compute the pre-master secret and two ECDH operations to verify the client's certificate and *CertifyVerify* message are performed [9].

7 Sensor Networks

The limited computational power of current sensor devices make public-key cryptographic primitives too expensive in terms of system overhead. Key-establishment techniques need to scale to networks with hundreds or thousands of nodes. The simplest solution for key establishment is using a network wide shared key. One step further is to use a single shared key to establish a set of link keys, one per pair of communicating nodes, then erase the network wide key after setting up the session keys. However, this variant of the key-establishment process does not allow addition of new nodes after initial deployment [20]

8 Implementation

8.1 *Elliptic Curve Cryptography Enhanced Secure Sockets Layer*

The main purpose of the evaluation was to study the performance impacts of replacing RSA with ECC in the SSL protocol. Experiment focused mainly on the handshake portion of the SSL protocol. As explained in Section 1, the main overhead involved in SSL operations is caused by the public key operations and especially with session reuse, public key operations are carried once per session, then the agreed private keys are used during the communications.

To compare the performance of the cryptographic algorithms, various curves suggested by NIST [19] and SEC working group [24] are implemented and different key sizes are tried. OpenSSL 0.9.7b is tailored to include ECC operations. ECC digital certificate creation is also added. For speed measurement speed utility is modified. Experiments are run on an Intel Pentium III 733 MHz computer with 256 MB of main memory running Red Hat Linux 9 operating system.

8.1.1 Results

Table 2. RSA performance measurements

	Sign(ms)	Verify(ms)
RSA 1024 bit	9.7	0.6
RSA 2048 bit	57.8	1.8

Table 3. DSA performance measurements

	Sign(ms)	Verify(ms)
DSA 1024 bits	4.9	5.9
DSA 2048 bits	16.2	20.1

Table 4. ECDSA performance measurements

	sign(ms)	verify(ms)
160 bit ECDSA	1.3	5.9
224 bit ECDSA	1.7	8.3

Table 5. ECDH performance measurements

	Op (ms)
160 bit ECDH	4.9
224 bit ECDH	7.1

In case of server authentication is not performed, for RSA, client performs one RSA sign and one RSA verify operation which results in 10.3ms on the client side, and 9.7 ms on the server side for decryption. While client authentication requires additional DSA sign; that is 4.9ms, on the client side and 2 RSA verify operations, 1.2ms on the server side, resulting a total of 15.2ms on the client side and 10.9ms on the server side.

While using ECC, in case of server authentication only, client performs one ECDSA verify and one ECDH operation, 10.8ms, and server has only ECDH operation that is 4.9ms. If client authentication is required, one ECDSA verify and one ECDH operation, a total of 10.8 on the client side and the server side, since the same operations are performed.

The values given above are for 1024 bit RSA and 160 bit ECC. 2048 bit RSA and 224 bit ECC results are given in Table 6. 1024 bit RSA performance and 160 bit ECC performance seems to be almost equal, however, when the key size is increased, ECC performance overwhelms the performance of RSA. The decrease of RSA performance when increasing key size seems to be multiples of that of ECC. Therefore, it can be concluded that, for larger keys, performance difference would be more noticeable.

Table 6. Comparison of cryptographic protocol performance

	1024 bit RSA	160 bit ECC	2048 bit RSA	224 bit ECC
Client side without client authentication	9.7ms	10.8ms	59.6ms	15.4ms
Server side without client authentication	10.3ms	4.9ms	57.8ms	8.3ms
Client side with client authentication	15.2ms	10.8ms	77.9ms	15.4ms
Server side with client authentication	10.9ms	10.8ms	61.4ms	15.4ms

8.2 Key Distribution Using Elliptic Curve Cryptography in Sensor Networks

Providing physical security of the sensor network devices seems unfeasible since their lifetime is usually limited by the lifetime of their batteries. In such an environment, seizure of a single node, may reveal the secret key of the whole network. Using different keys between any pair of devices may provide higher security, however, this requires, n^2 80 bit keys to be stored on each device if there are n devices on the network. Making use of symmetric key changing capability provided by TinySec seems to be a good solution. Since it is impossible to collect the devices to re-write the keys, public key cryptography should be used for distributing the keys.

Among the public key cryptography algorithms, DH key exchange is the most suitable one for this purpose. STS (station-to-station) protocol [6], a variant of DH key exchange applied to sensor networks, allows the use of public key cryptography between sensor nodes. The main trouble is to distribute the 80 bit symmetric keys in the same security level. 80 bit symmetric cryptographic security can only be provided by 1024 bit public key cryptography. 160 bit operations on 1024 bit values are out of acceptable boundaries by using 8 bit processors. At this point ECC which can provide same security level by 163 bits seems more feasible.

Elliptic curves are examined in two distinct classes as mentioned earlier. Both, prime characteristic or characteristic 2 can be used for implementation, however, elliptic curves of characteristic 2 are preferred since, as opposed to prime characteristic, there are many reasons why finite fields of characteristic 2 are attractive for implementation [4]:

- The arithmetic is carry free in characteristic 2 curves since we are dealing with essentially those polynomials of which the coefficients are always mod 2.
- There are many types of basis (e.g. polynomial or normal), which can be used to represent the points on the curve.
- To achieve sub second performance with prime characteristic, a crypto coprocessor is generally required which can increase the over all cost of the product.
- Point compression required negligible computation in characteristic 2 while it may need considerable resources in prime characteristic curves.

- It is easier to get the y coordinate of a point, given its x coordinate, in characteristic 2 with a single additional bit of extra information.

Furthermore, Koblitz Curves, a special subset of elliptic curves is preferred for implementation since some operations are especially optimized on Koblitz Curves.

Applying the optimizations in [2] to our ECC library prepared for a PhD Thesis, and using the curve parameters suggested by [19] it is shown that, ECC based key distribution on sensor networks is possible even with limited sources of the nodes.

Implementation requires 36 KB of ROM for instructions and slightly less than 2 KB of RAM for execution. Public key generation requires 52 seconds and private key generation requires 380ms in average. Power consumption and processor utilization is not examined.

Experiment results may seem discouraging, however, key distribution is not a frequent operation, and therefore, this overload may be accepted to provide security.

9 Conclusion

The above results show that ECC cipher suites can increase the performance of SSL protocol while increasing the security provided. Considering the trend that, more and smaller devices are using networking, ECC gains more significance by the smaller key sizes and faster operations. The performance impacts of ECC were also studied by [8], [10] and the results confirm each other. It is also shown that, to distribute symmetric keys using ECC in sensor networks is feasible. Prime characteristic curves may give better results with good optimizations. Malan et al have slightly better results in [16] and suggest further optimizations to improve the performance.

References

1. Akyildiz, I.F. Su, W. Sankarasubramaniam, Y. and Cayirci, E: “Wireless Sensor Networks: A Survey”. Computer Networks, Elsevier Science (2002) 38
2. Aydos, M. Sunar, B. Koc, C.K: “An Elliptic Cryptography based Authentication and Key Agreement Protocol for Wireless Communication”, in Proceedings of 2nd International Workshop on Discrete Algorithms and Methods for Mobile Computing and Communications, Dallas, TX (1998) 1-12
3. Badia, L: “Real World SSL Benchmarking” Rainbow Tech. Whitepaper (2001) http://www.rainbow.com/insights/whitePDF/RealWorldSSLBenchmarking.pdf
4. Certicom Corp: “The Elliptic Curve Cryptosystem for Smart Cards”, www.certicom.com/resources/w_papers.
5. Dierks, T. Rescorla E: “The TLS Protocol Version Version 1.1” IETF Internet draft <draft-ietf-tls-rfc2246-bis-06.txt>
6. Diffie, V. van Oorschot P.C. and Viener, M.J: “Authentication and Authenticated Key Exchanges” Designs, Codes and Cryptography, Kluwer Academic Publishers, (1992) 107-125
7. Freier, A. Karlton P.and Kocher P.: “ The SSL Protocol Version 3.0” IETF internet draft <draft-freier-ssl-version3-02.txt>

8. Gupta, V. Gupta, S. and Chang S.: "Performance Analysis of Elliptic Curve Crptography for SSL" ACM Workshop on Wireless Security (WiSe) (2002)
9. Gupta, V. Blake-Wilson, S. Moeller, B. Hawk C: "ECC Cipher Suites for TLS", IETF internet draft <draft-ietf-tls-ecc-05.txt> (Jan. 2004)
10. Gupta, V. Stebila, D. Fung S: "Speeding up Secure Web Transactions using Elliptic Curve Cryptography." The 11th Annual Network and Distributed System Security (NDSS) Symposium, San Diego, (Feb. 2004)
11. Hankerson, D. Hernandez, J. L. Menezes, A: "Software Implementation of Elliptic Curve Cryptography over Binary Fields", LNCS 1965, S. Verlag (2000)
12. Karlof, C. Sastry N. and Wagner, D: "TinySec: A Link Layer Security Architecture for Wireless Sensor Networks", In *Proceedings of the 2nd Int. Conf. on Embedded Networked Sensor Systems (SenSys'04)*, ACM Press, Baltimore, (2004)
13. Koblitz, N: "Elliptic Curve Cryptosystems" Mathematics of Computation. 48. (1987) 203-209
14. Lauter, K: "The Advantages of Elliptic Curve Cryptography for Wireless Security", IEEE Wireless Communications, IEEE Press, (2004)
15. Levis, P. Lee, N. Welsh M. and Culler, D: "TOSSIM: Accurate and Scalable Simulation of Entire TinyOS Applications", In *Proc. of the 1st Int. Conf. on Embedded Networked Sensor Systems (SenSys'03)*, ACM Press, LA (2003)
16. Malan, D. Welsh, M. and Smith, M. D: "A Public-key Infrastructure for Key Distribution in TinyOS Based on Elliptic Curve Cryptography". In 1st IEEE Int. Conf. on Sensor and Ad Hoc Communications and Networks (SECON 2004)
17. Menezes, A. van Orschot P. C. and Vanstone, S. S: "Handbook of Applied Cryptography", CRC Press, (1996)
18. Miller, V: "Uses of Elliptic Curves in Cryptography" Crypto 1985, LNCS 218: Advances in Cryptology. Springer-Verlag, (1986) 417-426
19. NIST: "Recommended Elliptic Curves For Federal Government Use" http://csrs.nist.gov/ CryptoToolkit/ dss/ecds/NISTReCur.pdf (1999)
20. Perrig, A. Stankovic, J. and Wagner, D: "Security in Wireless Sensor Networks" Communications of the ACM (June 2004) vol 47 num. 6 53-57
21. Rivest, R.L. Shamir, A. Adleman L.M: "A Method for Obtaining Digital Signatures and Public-key Cryptosystems". Communications of the ACM, V.21, n:2, (Feb 1978). 120-126
22. Schneier B: "Applied Cryptography, Second Edition: Protocols, Algorithms, and Source Code in C". John Wiley and Sons, Inc. (1996)
23. Schroeppel, R. Orman, H. O'Malley S. and Spatscheck O: "Fast Key Exchange with Elliptic Curve Systems", Advances in Cryptology – LNCS: 963, pp. 43-56, Springer-Verlag, (1995)
24. Standarts for Efficient Cryptography Group: "SEC1: Elliptic Curve Cryptography" Certicom Resarch, (2000)
25. Stinson D: "Cryptography: Theory and Practice" CRC Press. (1995)
26. Vanstone, S. "Responses to NIST's Proposal" Communications of the ACM, 35, July 1992, 50-52

MINIMUM POWER MULTICASTING WITH DELAY BOUND CONSTRAINTS IN AD HOC WIRELESS NETWORKS

O. E. KUNDAKCIOGLU, K. BULBUL, T. ÜNLÜYURT, K. KILIC AND O. ERCETIN

Sabanci University,
Orhanlı, Tuzla, 34956, Istanbul, Turkey
Email: {*erhunk@su., bulbul@, tonguc@, kkilic@, oercetin@*}*sabanciuniv.edu*

In this paper, we design a new heuristic for an important extension of the minimum power multicasting problem in ad hoc wireless networks [20,21]. Assuming that each transmission takes a fixed amount of time, we impose constraints on the number of hops allowed to reach the destination nodes in the multicasting application. This setting would be applicable in time critical or real time applications, and the relative importance of the nodes may be indicated by these *delay bounds.* We design a filtered beam search procedure for solving this problem. The performance of our algorithm is demonstrated on numerous test cases by benchmarking it against an optimal algorithm in small problem instances, and against a modified version of the well-known Broadcast Incremental Power (BIP) algorithm [20] for relatively large problems.

1. Introduction

In this study, we consider the minimum power multicasting (MPM) problem with delay bounds in ad hoc wireless networks. In this setting, a designated source node sends the same information to a subset of the nodes of the network (destination nodes) by possibly using the rest of the nodes as relay nodes. In addition, for each destination node, we impose a delay bound indicating the maximum number of nodes that the information goes through before reaching that node.

Many new multimedia applications, e.g., video streaming and multimedia conferencing, involve dynamic multiple participants, have stringent end-to-end delay requirements and consume large amount of network resources.

We select a set of nodes and their transmission powers (coverage). Each node transmits at the same transmission rate. A node that receives a packet waits until the completion of the transmission, checks if the packet can be decoded correctly, and then starts transmitting to its children if selected. Thus, a slotted system architecture can be assumed with a slot length equal to the transmission delay. The propagation delay is neglected. There are no MAC layer collisions, since the same packet is transmitted throughout the network. By using a short and known pilot tone before the transmission of a packet, each receiving node can determine the channel parameters between the transmitter and itself. This information is then used to remove the negative effects of simultaneous transmissions of the same packet.

Unlike in wired networks, wireless multicast sessions may reach several nodes with a single transmission. Assuming omnidirectional antennas, all nodes that are within the maximum range of a node receive the same information when the node transmits. The maximum range depends on the the power level of the transmitting node and the channel dependent exponent.

Given a fixed network topology, a designated source node and a set of destination nodes along with their delay bounds, our goal is to construct a multicast tree where the sum of the power levels for all nodes is minimum. This problem is $\mathcal{NP}$-complete even without the delay bounds, e.g., see [4,3]. In this paper, we develop a heuristic algorithm based on filtered beam search and report computational results. We benchmark our proposed algorithm against the optimal solution for small problems and against a modified version of the Broadcast Incremental Power (BIP) algorithm proposed in [20] for the broadcasting problem without delay bounds.

Numerous papers have been published on the broadcasting/multicasting problem. Since all different versions of the problem are $\mathcal{NP}$-complete [4,3,22], in almost all these papers heuristic algorithms are proposed. These papers can be classified along several dimensions. First, different solution approaches for broadcasting/multicasting are required in link-based wired and node-based wireless networks [20]. Second, some papers consider the problem with delay bounds [14] while others do not incorporate any such constraints [15]. Among those that consider delay bounds, some use the maximum number of relay nodes [6], and others use a function of the distance between the destination node and the source node in the tree [14] as the maximum possible delay. Third, different objective functions are considered, such as minimizing the total power allocation [15], maximizing the life time of the system [19] or minimizing the maximum power assigned to the nodes of the network [6].

In the literature, different variations of the wired case have been considered with and without delay bound constraints. Typically, for such problems, shortest path, minimum spanning tree, Steiner tree based algorithms are proposed [14,15,1]. Some of these algorithms can be implemented in a distributed manner [2,7,8]. A genetic algorithm is proposed in [18] whereas a branch and cut algorithm is developed in [16]. A polynomial time approximation scheme is presented in [22] for a restricted version of the problem.

The line of research that considers the wireless case is limited. Alternate integer programming formulations are provided in [5] for finding the optimal broadcast/multicast tree. In [13], the problem of minimizing the maximum power is considered, and some special cases are solved optimally in polynomial time. In [10], mixed integer programming models are presented as well as valid inequalities to solve the problem exactly whereas in [9,17], various heuristics are proposed. To the best of our knowledge, there is only one published paper for wireless ad hoc networks with delay bounds [23] which provides heuristic algorithms for a special case. A recent general review of optimization issues in broadcasting and multicasting problems is provided in [11].

We have several contributions in this paper. First, we extend the multicasting problem in ad hoc wireless networks to include delay bound constraints. Second, in Sect. 2 we provide substantial improvements to an integer programming formulation that was given in [5]. Third, we design a scalable heuristic to solve our problem for practical network sizes. In particular, we apply a general heuristic framework to this multicasting problem that was developed in the context of machine scheduling problems [12].

2. Problem Formulation

2.1. *Terminology*

We assume a fixed network topology with N nodes where V and D represent the set of all nodes and the set of destination nodes in the multicast application, respectively. Without loss of generality, node 1 is the source node, and it sends a message to all nodes in the set $D \subseteq V$. Each node may receive the multicast message either directly from the source or over a *relay* node that is retransmitting the message. Any node may transmit the message at most once, and such nodes are called *hop* nodes, including the source node. Note that several hop nodes may transmit simultaneously. *Leaf* nodes receive the message, but do not retransmit it. The number of hops from node 1 to node i is defined as the delay of node i. Our objective is to construct a multicast tree with minimum total power consumption such that no delay bound constraint is violated.

The power required to transmit a message from node i to node j in the network is proportional to d_{ij}^{α} where d_{ij} is the Euclidean distance between nodes i, j, and α is a constant that depends on the channel medium. In general, α is assumed to be between 2 and 4. Note that the locations of the nodes are fixed and known, and we let P be an $N \times N$ matrix in which P_{ij} denotes the minimum transmission power required to reach node j from node i.

A single transmission may reach several nodes in a wireless network, and in order to construct a multicast tree with minimum power consumption, we must keep track of all nodes that are covered by a single transmission $m \rightarrow n$ from node m to node n. Note that the multicast tree is not necessarily a spanning tree because some non-destination nodes may never be reached. Following the terminology in [5], we define an $N \times N$ reward matrix R in which the entry R_{mn} is a binary $N-$vector that specifies all nodes reached by the transmission $m \rightarrow n$. If $R_{mn}(p)$, the pth element of R_{mn}, is equal to 1, then we have $d_{mp} \leq d_{mn}$, and the message sent from m to n does also reach node p. Otherwise, we have $R_{mn}(p) = 0$. Note that the reward matrix may not be symmetric, i.e., the vector R_{mn} is not necessarily equal to the vector R_{nm}.

Let X_{ijk} be a binary variable that assumes the value 1 if the kth transmission in the multicast tree is $i \rightarrow j$, and zero otherwise. These binary variables are necessary to ensure the precedence relationships between the wireless links in the multicast tree, and to incorporate the delay bound constraints. The entry l_i in the delay bound vector $L = [l_1, \ldots, l_N]^T$ denotes the maximum number of hops allowed in order to reach node i from node 1. For $i \notin D$, $l_i = \infty$. Since each node may transmit at most once, a node $i \in D$ must receive the multicast message in at most $N-1$ hops, and we define $k^{\max} = \min(N-1,\ \max_i(l_i))$ as the maximum number of hops allowed to reach all nodes in set D.

2.2. *IP Formulation*

One of our main contributions in this paper is improving an integer programming (IP) formulation that was proposed in [5] for solving the minimum power broadcasting/multicasting problem in the absence of delay bound constraints. The IP formulation below is adapted from Formulation A in [5] by removing the redundant variables and constraints in that formulation as explained later in this section, and by adding the delay bound constraints (6). This formulation is used for benchmarking our heuristics against the optimal solution in small problem instances in Sect. 5.

$$\min \sum_{i=1}^{N} \sum_{\substack{j=1 \\ j \neq i}}^{N} \sum_{k=1}^{k^{max}} P_{ij} X_{ijk} \tag{1}$$

$$\sum_{j=2}^{N} X_{1j1} = 1 \tag{2}$$

$$\sum_{i=1}^{N} \sum_{\substack{j=1 \\ j \neq i}}^{N} X_{ij1} \leq 1 \tag{3}$$

$$\sum_{\substack{j=1 \\ j \neq i}}^{N} X_{ijk} - \sum_{p=1}^{k-1} \sum_{m=1}^{N} \sum_{\substack{n=1 \\ n \neq m}}^{N} R_{mn}(i) X_{mnp} \leq 0 \qquad \forall i \neq 1,\ 2 \leq k \leq k^{\max} \tag{4}$$

$$\sum_{p=1}^{k-1} \sum_{m=1}^{N} \sum_{\substack{n=1 \\ n \neq m}}^{N} R_{mn}(i) X_{mnp} + \sum_{m=1}^{N} \sum_{\substack{n=1 \\ n \neq m}}^{N} X_{mnk} \geq 1 \qquad \forall i \in D,\ 2 \leq k \leq k^{\max} \tag{5}$$

$$\sum_{p=1}^{l_i} \sum_{m=1}^{N} \sum_{\substack{n=1 \\ n \neq m}}^{N} R_{mn}(i) X_{mnp} \geq 1 \qquad \forall i \in D \tag{6}$$

$$X_{ijk} \in \{0, 1\} \qquad \forall i, j,\ i \neq j,\ \forall k \tag{7}$$

The objective function (1) minimizes the total power consumption. Only the source node transmits in the first hop as ensured by the constraints (2)-(3), and a node $i \geq 2$ cannot transmit in hop $k \geq 2$ unless it has been reached by the first $k-1$ transmissions by the constraints (4). Constraints (5) ensure that there is *at least* one transmission in hop $k \geq 2$ if there is at least one node $i \in D$ that has not been reached by the first $k-1$ transmissions. A node $i \in D$ must be reached after l_i transmissions as enforced by the delay bound constraints (6). Note that a node $i \notin D$ may act as a relay node in this model.

In our preliminary computational experiments, we observed that our formulation is able to solve significantly larger models than Formulation A in [5] although we do not report detailed results here.

Theoretically, both our IP formulation and Formulation A in [5] include $O(N^2)$ constraints[a] and $O(N^3)$ variables assuming k^{max} is $O(N)$. Therefore, even our formulation does not scale well when the number of nodes in the network increases, and heuristics are required for networks of practical size. We propose an effective heuristic for the minimum power multicasting problem with delay bounds in the next section.

---

[a]In [5], the authors make an incorrect assertion that their formulation has $O(N^3)$ constraints.

3. Filtered Beam Search

Filtered Beam Search (FBS) first proposed in [12] for machine scheduling problems is essentially an *approximate* Branch and Bound (B&B) method. It partially inherits the power of B&B to search the feasible space systematically while also limiting the computational time. An example of a search tree for our multicasting problem with $N = 7$, *filter width* $f = 4$ and *beam width* $b = 2$ is presented in Fig. 1. The root node represents the partial multicast tree with only the source node before any transmission, and the nodes at level 1 represent the possible multicast trees after the source transmits its information. In general, we find the multicast trees after k transmissions at level k of the search tree. Some of these may be infeasible, and the rest are either complete or partial. The key to FBS is the two parameters *filter width* f and the *beam width* b. At each level of the tree, we follow a two-stage process to determine which partial multicast trees are likely to provide good solutions when they are completed. First, all nodes corresponding to partial multicast trees are evaluated for their quality by a local evaluation function (LEF) which is called *filtering*. The best f nodes are considered for a thorough investigation by a global evaluation function (GEF). Among these f nodes the best b are retained in the search tree for *beam* construction and the rest of the partial multicast trees are discarded permanently. Typically, GEF requires that we construct a complete solution starting with the partial solution represented by the current node. Thus, it provides a "global view" of the node. Unfortunately, such a thorough analysis for all nodes at each level may be computationally prohibitive for large problems. This is why we need the filtering process based on a "local view". Later in this section, we discuss the specific local and global evaluation functions employed in this study. In Fig. 1, nodes 2 and 7 are pruned by LEF, and nodes 3 and 4 are pruned by GEF. Nodes 5 and 6 are retained for beam construction. At a node at level k of the

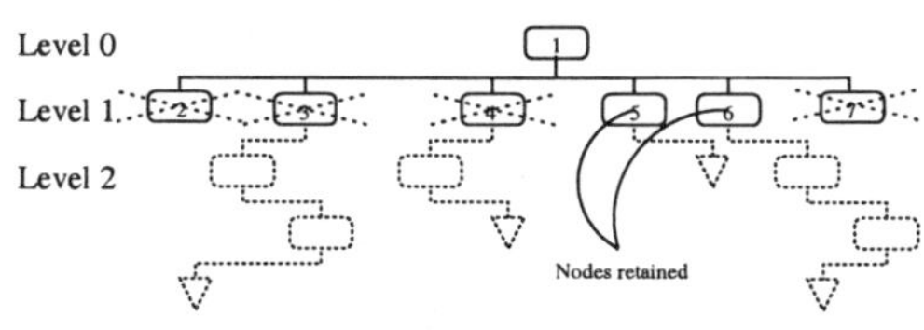

Figure 1. Broadcast tree with centralized algorithm

search tree, we keep track of the following information: the current set of transmissions $T^k = \{i_0 \rightarrow i_1,\ i_1 \rightarrow i_2, \ldots, i_{k-1} \rightarrow i_k\}$, the set of covered nodes C^k that have already received the information, the set of uncovered nodes $NC^k = V \setminus C^k$, the set of nodes NA^k that have already transmitted once and are not allowed for another transmission, and the delay vector $Q^k = [q_1^k, q_2^k, \ldots, q_N^k]$ given the current set of transmissions T^k. For a node $i \in C^k$, q_i^k is the actual delay and for a node $i \in NC^k$, q_i^k is a lower bound on the delay of the node as we discuss later. We initialize $T^0 = \emptyset$, $C^0 = \{1\}$, $NC^0 = V \setminus \{1\}$, $NA^0 = \emptyset$ and $Q^0 = [0, -1, \ldots, -1]$.

In order to pass from level k to $k+1$ of the search tree, we consider all transmissions $i_k \rightarrow i_{k+1}$ for all partial multicast trees in the beam at level k so that $i_k \in C^k \setminus NA^k$ and $i_{k+1} \in NC^k$. Given a transmission $i_k \rightarrow i_{k+1}$, the delays are updated as:

$$q_p^{k+1} = q_p^k \qquad \forall p \in C^k \tag{8}$$

$$q_p^{k+1} = q_{i_k}^k + 1 \qquad \forall p \in NC^k \text{ and } R_{i_k i_{k+1}}(p) = 1 \tag{9}$$

$$q_p^{k+1} = \min_{i \in C^{k+1} \setminus NA^{k+1}} q_{i_k}^{k+1} + 1 \qquad \forall p \in NC^{k+1}. \tag{10}$$

The delays of the nodes that are covered by the first k transmissions are not affected by the transmission $i_k \rightarrow i_{k+1}$ as given in (8). The delays of the nodes that are not covered by the first k transmissions and are covered by $i_k \rightarrow i_{k+1}$ are updated in (9). For the rest of nodes that are still not covered after the transmission $i_k \rightarrow i_{k+1}$ we can only specify lower bounds on their potential delays. For any such node, the delay is at least one more than the minimum delay of a node that is covered and has not transmitted yet as given in (10). After the updates (8)-(10), if $q_p^{k+1} > l_p$ for some node p, then the transmission $i_k \rightarrow i_{k+1}$ leads to an infeasible multicast tree, and the corresponding node at level k of the search tree is fathomed. Otherwise, given a partial multicast tree at level k and a feasible transmission $i_k \rightarrow i_{k+1}$, $T^{k+1} = T^k \cup \{i_k \rightarrow i_{k+1}\}$, $C^{k+1} = C^k \cup \{p \mid R_{i_k i_{k+1}}(p) = 1\}$, $NC^{k+1} = V \setminus C^{k+1}$ and $NA^{k+1} = NA \cup \{i_k\}$ is obtained at level $k+1$ of the search tree.

If a feasible transmission $i_k \rightarrow i_{k+1}$ added to a partial multicast tree at level k results in a complete multicast tree such that $D \subseteq C^{k+1}$, then this multicast tree is saved as one of the solutions of FBS. The FBS algorithm terminates when there are no more partial multicast trees to consider in the search tree, and the complete multicast tree with the minimum total power requirement is the solution found by FBS.

In this paper, we implement a slight variation of FBS, and we apply the filtering procedure separately to each of the b nodes in the beam at level k of the search tree. In other words, given a partial multicast tree at level k, all possible feasible partial multicast trees at level $k+1$ are evaluated according to LEF, and the best f are retained to be evaluated by GEF. Therefore, when we move from level k to $k+1$ of the search tree we initially have at most $b \times f$ partial multicast trees at level $k+1$ to be evaluated by GEF. After the evaluation by GEF, only b of the partial multicast trees at level $k+1$ are kept for beam construction, and the rest are discarded permanently. We also introduce a *child width* c for ensuring the diversification of the search and restrict the number of children of any node in the beam to at most c.

Suppose that we consider adding a feasible transmission $i \rightarrow j$ to a partial multicast tree T^k at level k, and we define a priority function Γ_{ij}^k for this transmission as specified in (11). This priority function, for which higher values are preferred, is our local evaluation function. In addition, in order to evaluate $i \rightarrow j$ globally, starting with $i \rightarrow j$ we keep adding feasible transmissions with the highest Γ_{ij}^k values to T^k until we obtain a complete multicast tree. The total power requirement of this complete multicast tree is the global evaluation function for the transmission $i \rightarrow j$. The function Γ_{ij}^k is simple and fast to compute which is important because up to $f \times b$ partial multicast trees must be evaluated globally at each level of the FBS tree.

$$\Gamma_{ij}^k = \pi^{\alpha/2}\left(\frac{|\{p \mid R_{ij}(p)=1\} \setminus C^k|}{\pi d_{ij}^2}\right)^{\alpha/2} = \frac{|\{p \mid R_{ij}(p)=1\} \setminus C^k|^{\alpha/2}}{P_{ij}} \quad (11)$$

The term in parentheses is the density of the previously uncovered nodes that are covered by the transmission $i \rightarrow j$. The priority function does also account for previously uncovered nodes that are not in the destination set because these may act as relay nodes. Finally, observe that the power consumption for reception and processing for nodes within the range of $i \rightarrow j$ can easily be incorporated into (11) by adding these quantities into the denominator of Γ_{ij}^k.

4. Modified BIP Algorithm with Delay Bound Constraints

The Broadcast Incremental Power (BIP) algorithm was introduced in [20], and its improved performance against other proposed heuristics was demonstrated computationally. Also, a Multicast Incremental Power (MIP) algorithm was developed in [20] by removing the unnecessary transmissions in a complete broadcast tree obtained by BIP. The BIP algorithm is a greedy construction algorithm. At each iteration, it considers all possible transmissions from the set of covered nodes to the set of uncovered nodes. The transmission with the minimum incremental cost is added to the partial broadcast tree until all nodes are covered. Note that if a node i is already transmitting to a node j, then its incremental power consumption to cover an additional node k is $P_i' = P_{ik} - P_{ij}$. We modify the BIP algorithm to incorporate delay bound constraints and compare its performance to that of the filtered beam search in Sect. 5.

In the modified BIP (ModBIP) algorithm for our problem, the initializations of the sets T, C, NC and the delay vector Q are identical to those in FBS, i.e., $T = \emptyset$, $C = \{1\}$, $NC = V \setminus \{1\}$ and $Q = [q_1, q_2, \ldots, q_N] = [0, -1, \ldots, -1]$. At each iteration, we consider all transmissions $i \to j$ so that $i \in C$, $j \in NC$ and $q_i + 1 \leq l_j$, and the transmission $i' \to j'$ with the minimum incremental cost is added to the multicast tree. We obtain $T = T \cup \{i' \to j'\}$, $C = C \cup \{p \mid R_{i'j'}(p) = 1 \text{ and } q_{i'} + 1 \leq l_p\}$, $NC = V \setminus C$. The delays are updated as:

$$q_p = \min(q_p,\ q_{i'} + 1) \qquad \text{if } R_{i'j'}(p) = 1 \text{ and } p \in C \tag{12}$$

$$q_p = q_{i'} + 1 \qquad \text{if } R_{i'j'}(p) = 1,\ p \in NC \text{ and } q_{i'} + 1 \leq q_p. \tag{13}$$

We continue to iterate until all destination nodes are covered. In the final complete multicast tree some transmissions may be redundant. Therefore, a *sweep* operation [20] is applied to the final multicast tree to check whether the transmission power of any node can be decreased without violating the feasibility of the multicast tree. In particular, we sort the nodes in non-increasing order of their transmission powers and apply a sweep operation to each node starting at the head of the list. The sweep operation is applied to the final solutions of both ModBIP and FBS.

5. Computational Results

The algorithms for FBS and ModBIP are implemented in C++, and the IP formulation in Sect. 2.2 is solved by ILOG OPL Studio 3.7 and CPLEX 9.0. All computations are performed on an Intel Xeon 2.00 GHz PC with 1 GB of memory.

In all experiments, the nodes are distributed randomly in a 10×10 grid, and the channel loss component α is equal to 4. In order to test to impact of the tightness of the delay bounds, we generate uniformly distributed delays $U(1, \lceil \log_2 N \rceil)$ and $U(1, N-1)$. Each node is selected as a destination node with probability $p = 0.5$, 0.75 or 1 where $p = 1$ corresponds to broadcasting instances. For each combination of parameters, 50 problem instances are generated randomly for $N = 10$, 20, 30, 40, 50. For small problem instances with $N = 10$ and $N = 20$, we compare the performances of FBS and ModBIP against the optimal solution. For larger problems, the heuristics are benchmarked against each other. After preliminary experiments, the filter, beam and child widths in FBS are set to $f = 0.3N$, $b = 0.2N$ and $c = 0.1N$, respectively.

In each cell of Table 1, the number in the first row is the number of optimal solutions obtained, and the numbers in parentheses are the average and maximum optimality gaps, respectively. We observe that as the number of nodes increases, the performance of FBS improves relative to that of ModBIP in terms of both the number of optimal solutions obtained and average optimality gaps.

N	$p = 0.5$			
	$l_i \sim U(1, N-1)$		$l_i \sim U(1, \lceil \log_2 N \rceil)$	
	ModBIP	FBS	ModBIP	FBS
10	29 (0.28, 3.74)	30 (0.14, 1.67)	24 (0.45, 3.11)	36 (0.13, 1.41)
20	10 (1.02, 8.61)	18 (0.34, 3.84)	7 (0.67, 4.97)	38 (0.09, 1.19)

N	$p = 0.75$			
	$l_i \sim U(1, N-1)$		$l_i \sim U(1, \lceil \log_2 N \rceil)$	
	ModBIP	FBS	ModBIP	FBS
10	23 (0.33, 3.01)	30 (0.09, 1.52)	20 (0.44, 3.18)	41 (0.05, 0.89)
20	11 (0.80, 12.48)	27 (0.08, 0.76)	14 (0.31, 3.05)	34 (0.05, 0.77)

N	$p = 1$			
	$l_i \sim U(1, N-1)$		$l_i \sim U(1, \lceil \log_2 N \rceil)$	
	ModBIP	FBS	ModBIP	FBS
10	20 (0.17, 1.35)	37 (0.06, 1.19)	21 (0.32, 2.67)	45 (0.04, 0.72)
20	6 (0.64, 5.74)	26 (0.10, 1.38)	15 (0.10, 0.90)	39 (0.02, 0.63)

In each cell of Table 2, the number in the first row is the number of times FBS(ModBIP) performs better than ModBIP(FBS), and the numbers in parentheses are the average and maximum gaps with respect to the best solution found by either heuristic, respectively. The results indicate that FBS obtains significantly better solutions as the delay bounds get tighter and the problem size increases. In addition, in both Tables 1 and 2 the performance of ModBIP improves as p increases.

Tighter problems are solved by an order of magnitude faster by FBS and ModBIP as the feasible space is reduced significantly for such problems. For problem instances with $N = 50$, FBS requires less than 5 seconds on average. However, ModBIP requires an order of magnitude less computation time than FBS in general.

6. Conclusions and Future Work

In this paper, we consider the minimum power multicasting problem in ad hoc wireless networks with delay bound constraints. A combinatorial search algorithm FBS is developed and benchmarked against a modified version of a well-known heuristic developed originally for minimum power broadcasting. Our initial computational results are promising for FBS.

The performance of our search algorithm depends critically on a local priority rule, and we plan to devise more effective rules. In addition, power consumption for reception and processing may be incorporated for a more realistic model as we indicate in Sect. 3. Other important extensions in-

N	$p = 0.5$			
	$l_i \sim U(1, N-1)$		$l_i \sim U(1, \lceil \log_2 N \rceil)$	
	ModBIP	FBS	ModBIP	FBS
10	14 (0.25, 3.74)	16 (0.12, 1.67)	7 (0.39, 3.11)	22 (0.08, 1.36)
20	15 (0.80, 7.27)	29 (0.19, 3.84)	1 (0.52, 4.97)	42 (0.01, 0.58)
30	14 (0.93, 6.32)	32 (0.16, 2.65)	2 (0.38, 4.34)	37 (0.01, 0.40)
40	12 (0.98, 10.93)	29 (0.09, 1.00)	3 (0.41, 4.85)	41 (0.01, 0.48)
50	7 (1.58, 16.88)	42 (0.04, 1.02)	2 (0.36, 4.45)	38 (0.01, 0.31)

N	$p = 0.75$			
	$l_i \sim U(1, N-1)$		$l_i \sim U(1, \lceil \log_2 N \rceil)$	
	ModBIP	FBS	ModBIP	FBS
10	9 (0.27, 3.01)	22 (0.05, 1.52)	3 (0.40, 3.18)	28 (0.01, 0.52)
20	9 (0.70, 11.36)	33 (0.03, 0.50)	2 (0.24, 1.93)	34 (0.01, 0.66)
30	12 (0.72, 5.42)	37 (0.06, 0.98)	3 (0.24, 4.10)	31 (0.01, 0.29)
40	8 (0.82, 8.26)	39 (0.05, 0.64)	1 (0.12, 0.76)	42 (0.00, 0.07)
50	7 (1.13, 7.34)	40 (0.05, 1.14)	1 (0.10, 0.75)	38 (0.00, 0.00)

N	$p = 1$			
	$l_i \sim U(1, N-1)$		$l_i \sim U(1, \lceil \log_2 N \rceil)$	
	ModBIP	FBS	ModBIP	FBS
10	6 (0.15, 1.35)	26 (0.04, 1.19)	1 (0.27, 2.67)	28 (0.00, 0.04)
20	2 (0.46, 3.36)	42 (0.01, 0.23)	4 (0.09, 0.85)	32 (0.01, 0.56)
30	5 (0.74, 6.94)	44 (0.01, 0.14)	1 (0.24, 2.21)	41 (0.01, 0.69)
40	6 (1.05, 6.68)	43 (0.04, 0.66)	4 (0.10, 0.88)	37 (0.02, 0.60)
50	4 (0.74, 10.53)	44 (0.03, 1.05)	2 (0.11, 0.74)	37 (0.00, 0.07)

clude designing a distributed algorithm and exploring the trade off between transmission rates and delays.

References

1. M. Aissa and A. Ben Mnaouer. A new delay-constrained algorithm for multicast routing tree construction. *Internatinal Journal Of Communication Systems*, 17(10):985–1000, 2004.
2. F. Bauer and A. Varma. Distributed algorithms for multicast path setup in data networks. *IEEE-ACM Transactions On Networking*, 4(2):181–191, 1996.
3. M. Hubaux Cagalj and C. C. JP Enz. Energy-efficient broadcasting in all-wireless networks. *Wireless Networks*, 11(1-2):177–188, 2005.
4. X. Z. Cheng, B. Narahari, R. Simha, M. X. Y.Cheng, and D. Liu. Strong minimum energy topology in wireless sensor networks: Np-completeness and heuristics. *IEEE Transactions On Mobile Computing*, 2(3):248–256, 2003.
5. Arindam K. Das, Robert J. Marks, Mohamed El-Sharkawi, Payman Arabshahi, and Andrew Gray. Minimum power broadcast trees for wireless networks: Integer programming formulations. In *Proceedings of IEEE Infocom*, 2003.
6. X. Jia, D. Li, and D. Du. Qos topology control in ad hoc wireless networks. In *Proceedings of IEEE Infocom 2004*, 2004.
7. X. H. Jia, Y. C. Zhang, N. Pissinou, and K. Makki. A distributed multicast routing protocol for real-time multicast applications. *Computer Networks*, 31(1-2):101–110, 1999.
8. C. P. Low and Y. J. Lee. Distributed multicast routing, with end-to-end delay and delay variation constraints. *Computer Communications*, 23(9):848–862, 2000.
9. Robert J. Marks, Arindam K. Das, Mohamed El-Sharkawi, Payman Arabshahi, and Andrew Gray. Minimum power broadcast trees for wireless net-

works: Optimizing using the viability lemma. In *Proceedings of the IEEE International Symposium on Circuits and Systems*, Scottsdale, Arizona, 2002.
10. R. Montemanni and L. M. Gambardella. Exact algorithms for the minimum power symmetric connectivity problem in wireless networks. *Computers and Operations Research*, 32(11):2891–2904, 2005.
11. C. A. S. Oliveira and P. M. Pardalos. A survey of combinatorial optimization problems in multicast routing. *Computers and Operations Research*, 32(8):1953–1981, 2005.
12. P. S. Ow and T. E. Morton. Filtered beam search in scheduling. *International Journal of Production Research*, 26:35–62, 1988.
13. I. Papadimitriou and L. Georgiadis. Energy-aware broadcast trees in wireless networks. *Mobile Networks and Applications*, 9(6):567–581, 2004.
14. G. N. Rouskas and I. Baldine. Multicast routing with end-to-end delay and delay variation constraints. *IEEE Journal On Selected Areas In Communications*, 15(3):346–356, 1997.
15. H. F. Reeves Salama and Y. D. S. Viniotis. Evaluation of multicast routing algorithms for real-time communication on high-speed networks. *IEEE Journal On Selected Areas In Communications*, 15(3):332–345, 1997.
16. C. S. Sung and J. M. Hong. Branch-and-price algorithm for a multicast routing problem. *Journal Of The Operational Research Society*, 50(11):1168–1175, 1999.
17. B. Wang and S. K. S. Gupta. S-remit: A distributed algorithm for source-based energy efficient multicasting in wireless ad hoc networks. In *Proceedings of IEEE Globecom*, 2003.
18. B. Wang and S. K. S. Gupta. Extending the lifetime of multicast trees in wanets. *Journal of Information Science and Engineering*, 20:425–447, 2004.
19. Z. Y. Wang, B. X. Shi, and E. Zhao. Bandwidth-delay-constrained least-cost multicast routing based on heuristic genetic algorithm. *Computer Communications*, 24(7-8):685–692, 2001.
20. J. E. Wieselthier, G. D. Nguyen, and A. Ephremides. On the construction of energy-efficient broadcast and multicast trees in wireless networks. In *Proceedings of IEEE Infocom*, pages 585–594, March 2000.
21. J. E. Wieselthier, G. D. Nguyen, and A. Ephremides. Resource-limited energy-efficient wireless multicast of session traffic. In *Proceedings of 34th International Conference on System Sciences*, January 2000.
22. G. L. Xue and W. Xiao. A polynomial time approximation scheme for minimum cost delay-constrained multicast tree under a steiner topology. *Algorithmica*, 41(1):53, 72 2005.
23. W. L. Yang. Constructing energy-efficient multicast trees with delay constarints in wireless ad hoc networks. In *Proceedings of IEEE AINA 2005*, 2005.

VIDEO SEGMENTATION WITH BLOCK BASED CHANGE DETECTION USING NUMEROUS PRECEDING IMAGE FRAMES

O. URHAN, S. ERTÜRK

Electronics and Telecommunications Engineering Department, Veziroglu Campus, University of Kocaeli, 41040, Kocaeli, TR.

&

LATARUB Research Centre, University of Kocaeli, Kocaeli, 41380, TR.

This paper presents a robust video segmentation method particularly aimed at videophone and videoconference type video sequences containing slow moving objects. Classical change detection approaches based only on the frame difference of two successive image frames usually result in incorrect segmentations for video sequences containing slow motions or temporary poses. The video segmentation approach presented in this paper carries out block based change detection using numerous preceding image frames to accomplish successful segmentation in the presence of slow motions and temporary poses.

1. Introduction

Segmentation of digital video plays an important role for content based multimedia applications. The new video coding standard MPEG-4 for instance relies on the decomposition of image sequence frames into semantically meaningful video objects (VO) to provide content based functionalities. These content based functionalities allow separate coding and encoding of objects and permit the manipulation of the original scene by simple operations on the bit stream [1]. In this case, each object in an image frame is represented as a video object plane (VOP) with contour, motion and texture information being coded in a separate VOP-layer in the MPEG4 visual coding standard.

Moving object segmentation techniques can be separated into motion-based methods and spatio-temporal methods [2]. Motion based methods can be classified as 2D [3-7] and 3D techniques. 2D motion based methods have usually a relatively low computational complexity and facilitate simple implementation, but generally lack robustness. 3D methods have a relatively high computational load but are generally more robust. Change detection has been proposed to obtain temporal information for the extraction of VOPs from image sequences [8-10]. Change detection based methods proposed so far have employed frame difference information of two successive frames (the current and the previous frame) only. An algorithm based on change detection using a special relaxation algorithm which increases noise strength has been proposed in [8]. In this case a memory is used for change detection masks in order to improve temporal coherency of the resulting object masks. *Neri et al.* in [9] proposed an algorithm based on change detection which separates potential foreground regions employing a higher order statistics (HOS) significance test to inter-frame differences. A pixel based background registration technique, which uses a change detection mask, is proposed to obtain reliable background information in [10]. This technique compares each incoming frame with the background image to decide whether a pixel corresponds to the background or a foreground object, however time consuming morphological filters are used to construct the final complete object mask. The advantage of change detection based approaches is the low computational load and system complexity enabling real-time applications. Because only frame by frame differences are monitored in the methods proposed so far, a moving foreground is required for successful segmentation, failing at slow movements and temporary poses of objects.

2. The Proposed Segmentation Algorithm

The flow diagram of the proposed segmentation algorithm is shown in Figure 1. One of the original aspects of the proposed segmentation algorithm is that block based change detection is utilized instead of the classical pixel based change detection approaches. Therefore the image frame is initially divided into image blocks. A background image is employed, similar to [10], however in this case resolved background information is stored on a block basis with a background block mask indicating whether the background information is available for any block or not. The utilized block based change detection approach computes pixel-by-pixel differences and then obtains the block average and decides on the situation of the block using the block average. This approach introduces robustness against pixel noise as noise effects are largely dissolved within the block average.

If the background information of any block is already available in the background image, the situation of the block is simply decided using the corresponding average block difference result between the current frame and the background image. If the block average is below a certain threshold the block in the current frame is assigned as background, otherwise it is assigned as foreground.

If the background information of any block is not available, the situation of the block is decided according to block based frame differences using numerous preceding frames. This novel approach of employing past frame differences, instead of computing the difference with respect to the previous frame only, enables the detection of slow object movements and temporary object poses and therefore, facilitates correct segmentation for sequences showing such features. Furthermore the efficiency of background registration is improved, as erroneous update of the background image, i.e. the background image being updated with foreground information, is avoided. Block based morphology is applied to fix the status of any blocks that might incorrectly be assigned as background although they are located in between foreground blocks. This process facilitates additional robustness against slow movements and temporal poses. As morphology is utilized on a block basis the procedure is considerably less time consuming than pixel based morphology.

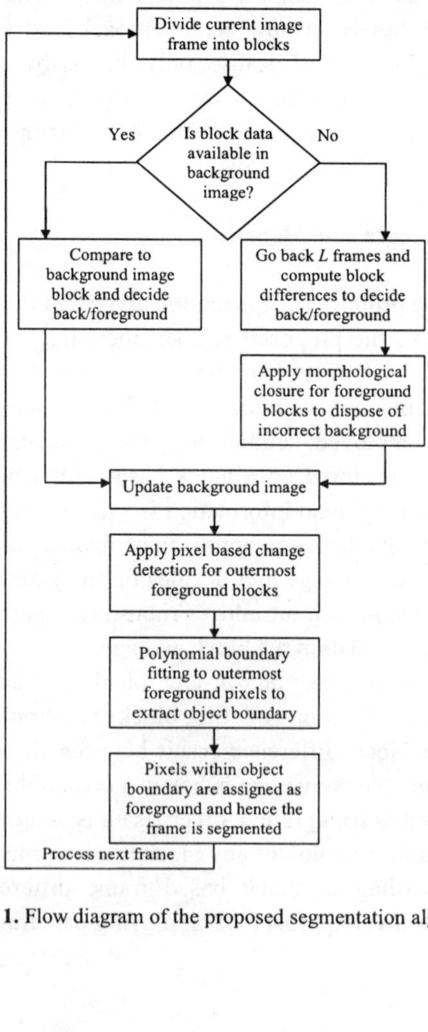

Figure 1. Flow diagram of the proposed segmentation algorithm

After a decision on whether the block corresponds to foreground or background is given for all blocks in the current image frame, the background image (and background image mask if necessary) is updated to take latest background information into account. Note that fine-tuning is required in order to have segmentation results approach object borders and avoid blockiness. For this reason additional pixel based change detection is carried out at the outermost foreground blocks to ensure that object borders are approached. The pixel based change detection decides on the status of a pixel according to differences computed using numerous preceding frames. After pixel based change detection, polynomial boundary fitting at the outermost detected foreground pixels is employed to eliminate incorrectly detected pixels. The polynomial fitting produces a smooth object boundary. Finally pixels within this boundary are assigned as foreground and pixels outside the boundary are assigned as background to complete the segmentation process.

2.1. Block Based Change Detection

Segmentation techniques based on change detection commonly obtain the pixel based difference between consecutive frames and utilize thresholding to detect changes. Figure 2 (a) and (b) show an example of pixel based change detection with two different threshold values, for two succeeding frames of the "Claire" sequence. Because object motion in the corresponding sequence is relatively restricted, low threshold values detect objects movements more accurately but can cause detection noise in the background region. Comparably higher thresholds can be utilized to avoid detection noise, however object segmentation accuracy is degraded.

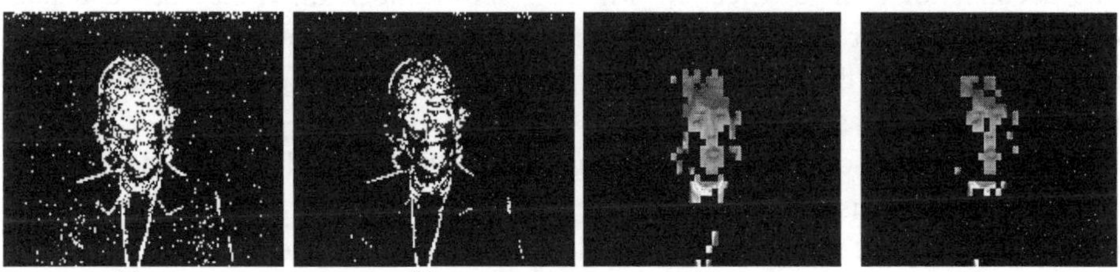

(a) (b) (c) (d)

Figure 2. Pixel based change detection. (a) Difference image (threshold=2) (b) (threshold=3). Block based change detection (difference images for Claire #120, #119 displaying image blocks above the threshold). (c) Threshold=2, (d) Threshold=3.

Block difference based change detection, instead of a pixel difference based change detection process is proposed in this paper to overcome the encountered noise problem. For this purpose, image frames are initially divided into non-overlapping blocks. The block difference measure is obtained by averaging pixel-by-pixel differences of all pixels within the corresponding block so that a single difference measure is obtained for each block. This averaging enables pixel based noise effects to be dissolved within the block. Figure 2 (c) and (d) show the block based change detection results for two succeeding frames of the "Claire" sequence. It is seen that incorrect detection in the background region (detection noise) is successfully avoided even for lower threshold values.

If objects within a scene move at slow rates or temporarily cease moving, the difference between the current and the previous frame will be too small, preventing accurate segmentation. Although slow movements might be detected with a relatively low threshold, in this case the detection noise will be severe, and segmentation is out of the question. Furthermore, temporary poses cannot be detected by any means using only the difference of current and previous image frames. This is for instance the case for well known head-and-shoulder sequences, where the head displays reasonable movements whereas the body is relatively still, and in this case only the head is segmented while the body is assigned as background [11]. Figures 2 clearly displays that the head region can successfully be segmented because evident motion is encountered, while the body of the person is missed due to indistinct movements. In this case, the threshold is adjusted to eliminate detection noise, resulting in the loss of shoulder information.

It is proposed in this paper to utilize several past frames for sequences that contain slow movements or temporary poses. Considering the computational load it is practical to use only several past frames for change detection. For instance, for the segmentation of frame n, it is possible to take image frames n-1, n-5, n-10, and n-25 into account for change detection. Figure 3 shows block difference based change detection results for the "Claire" sequence using several past frames. It is clearly seen that by taking the past frames into account it becomes possible to detect slow movements as well as temporary poses.

In the proposed segmentation algorithm, block based change detection is applied simultaneously with respect to numerous past image frames. For instance, denoting the current frame as frame n, block based change detection is evaluated for frame pairs (n, n-1), (n, n-5), (n, n-10), and (n, n-25); and segmentation decision is established taking all change detection results simultaneously into account. An image block is assigned to correspond to the background, only if a background decision is given for all differences, i.e. block differences of the corresponding block for all considered past frames are below the threshold. If any block difference result is above the threshold, indicating that movement is present in the block, the corresponding block is assigned as foreground. Figure 4 (a) and (b) show the segmentation results for the "Claire" and "Grandma" sequences, with segmentation carried out on a block-by-block basis, with block difference based change detection employing several past image frames. It can be seen that although numerous preceding frames are utilized, some blocks within the object boundary are still classified as background due to slow movements that do not introduce substantial spatial change within the object region. Nonetheless object regions are segmented in the overall sense, and it becomes possible to deal with the small number of incorrect classifications by block based morphology.

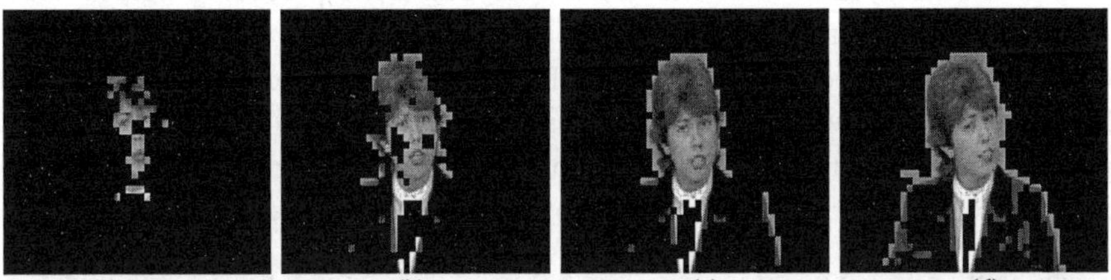

(a) (b) (c) (d)

Figure 3. Block difference based change detection. (a) Block based difference image (Claire frame #120, #119). (b) Block based difference image (Claire frame #120, #115). (c) Block based difference image (Claire frame #120, #110). (d) Block based difference image (Claire frame #120, #095).

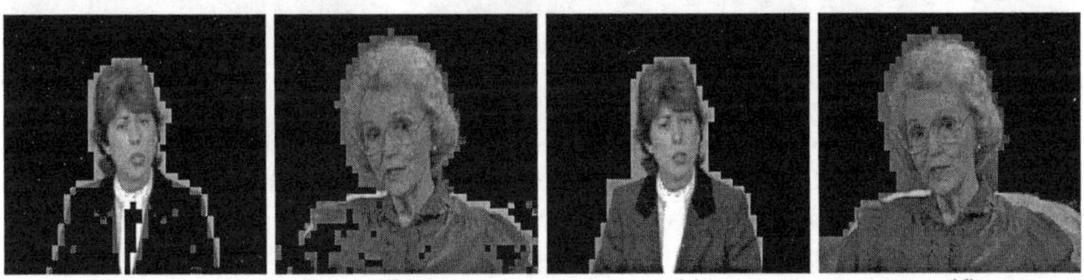

(a) (b) (c) (d)

Figure. 4. Block based change detection (difference images for Claire #120, #119 displaying image blocks above the threshold). (a) Threshold=2, (b) Threshold=3.
Output images after block based morphological operation. (c) Claire #120 after block based morphology. (d) Grandma #700 after block based morphology.

Block based morphological closing operation on blocks classified as foreground, enables blocks that actually belong to the foreground but are misclassified as background to be recovered. This procedure also ensures that the background image used for registration is not updated with any foreground data which would cause problems in upcoming frames. As morphology is applied on a block basis, the overall computational load is significantly reduced compared to pixel based morphology. Figure 4 (c) and (d) display segmentation results for the "Claire" and "Grandma" sequences after block based morphology has been applied.

2.1. Object Boundary Construction

Segmentation accomplished by block based change detection results in blocky images, visually unpleasant as well as slightly off the correct object boundary. In order to have segmentation results approach the object boundary, pixel based change detection is employed at the outermost blocks only. The preceding frames used in block based detection are also used for pixel based change detection in order to account for slow movements and poses. The pixel is assigned as background if all differences are below the predefined threshold. Figures 5 (a) and (b) show the segmentation results for the "Claire" and "Grandma" sequences after pixel based change detection at the outermost blocks of the block based segmentation results.

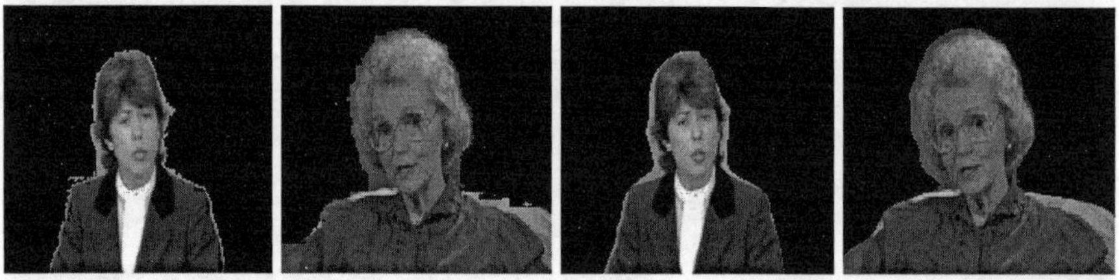

Figure 5. Output images after pixel based change detection at outermost blocks of the block based segmentation results. (a) Claire #120 after pixel based change detection. (b) Grandma #700 after pixel based change detection. Output images after polynomial boundary fitting. (c) Claire #120 after polynomial boundary fitting. (d) Grandma #700 after polynomial boundary fitting.

Once more it is possible to encounter misclassifications, now pixel based, which is particularly obvious for the "Claire" result shown in Figure 5 (a). Although it is once more possible to utilize morphological operations for correction, this is not desired due to the relatively high computation load which would be introduced by pixel based morphology. Instead of morphological correction, it is proposed to fit a low-order polynomial to the object boundary detected after pixel based change detection, so as to construct the smooth object boundary correctly. For each pixel obtained to correspond to the object boundary after pixel based change detection (i.e. outermost pixels), sliding low-order polynomial fitting is carried out taking surrounding boundary pixels into account. The resultant object boundary is then used to define the foreground region, and pixels within this boundary are included to correspond to the foreground object, while pixels outside this boundary are classified as background. Figure 5 (c) and (d) show the results for the "Claire" and "Grandma" sequences after the final segmentation process.

3. Experimental Results

If the image sequence contains only an ignorable amount of noise, which for instance is typically the case for the "Akiyo" sequence, change detection based segmentation can easily be accomplished to obtain successful results. The segmentation results for the "Akiyo" sequence with the proposed segmentation algorithm, shown in Figure 6, confirm successful segmentation. For the "Akiyo" sequence successful head-and-shoulder segmentation results are obtained going only back up to 25 frames for the proposed change detection process. In this case the threshold values can conveniently be decided due the lack of background noise.

If the image sequence contains a considerable amount of noise, which for instance is typically the case for the "Claire" sequence, it is still possible to obtain successful segmentation results as shown in Figure 6. Successful segmentation results are obtained for the "Claire" sequence, going again only back up to 25 frames for the preceding frames based change detection process. However different threshold values have to be employed to cope with the considerable noise amount.

Sequences that not only contain a considerable amount of noise but also very slow movements and temporary poses at all or part of the object, such as the "Grandma" sequence, are very difficult to segment with change based detection techniques. While many methods reported in literature have avoided using such sequences, others were only successful in segmenting the faster moving facial regions. For instance, [11] reports that only the head of the "Grandma" sequence could be segmented successfully, loosing the shoulders to background. Although it is required to go further back to successfully segment sequences displaying slow movements or temporary poses, Figure 6 shows that the sequence can successfully be segmented with the proposed technique. In this case segmentation results are obtained by going back up to 100 frames for the proposed change based detection process, to take poses into account (note that the difference is not computed with all past 100 frames, but only with several frames with certain distances to each other). In the future it is aimed to automatically determine the necessary thresholds and the number of required preceding frames making use of the histogram information of successive frame difference images.

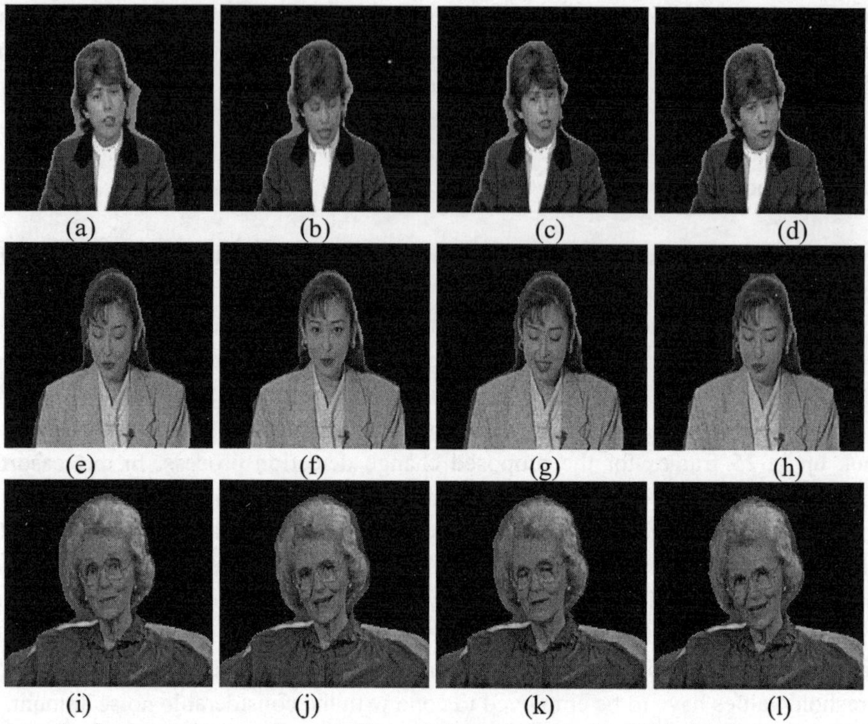

Figure 6. Segmentation results. (a) Claire #075, (b) #150, (c) #200, (d) #250, (e) Akiyo #050, (f) #100, (g) #150, (h) #200, (i) Grandma #150, (j) #200, (k) #250, (l) #300

Note that alike common change based segmentation algorithms the proposed technique relies on a stable background. If the camera is displaying global movements it is possible to incorporate global motion compensation.

4. Conclusions

A novel video segmentation algorithm based on change detection has been presented in this paper. The proposed algorithm constitutes of block based change detection including numerous past frames and object boundary construction which is carried out by pixel based change detection at outermost foreground blocks followed by low order polynomial boundary fitting. It is shown that the proposed segmentation algorithm gives successful results even for sequences containing a considerable amount of noise and slow movements or temporary poses, for which previously reported techniques fail. The proposed method is particularly suitable for image sequences displaying slow movements, such as videophone type head-and-shoulder sequences, and can be incorporated into MPEG 4 systems, that support video objects and sequence classification, to segment appropriate sequences.

References

1. Sikora T., *The MPEG-4 Video Standard Verification Model* (IEEE Trans. on Circuits and Systems for Video Technology), **7(1)**, 1997, 19-31.
2. Zang D.S. and Lu G., *Segmentation of Moving Object in Image Sequence: A Review* (Circuits, Systems and Signal Processing (Special Issue on Multimedia Services)), **20(2)**, 2001, 143-183.
3. Kim M., Choi J.G., Kim D., Lee H., Lee M.H., Ahn C., Ho Y-S., *A VOP Generation Tool : Automatic Segmentation of Moving Objects in Image Sequences Based on Spatio-Temporal Information* (IEEE Trans. on Circuits and Systems for Video Technology), **9(8)**, 1999, 1216-1226.
4. Park H.W., Schoepflin T., Kim Y., *Active Contour Model with Gradient Directional Information: Directional Snake* (IEEE Trans. on Circuits and Systems for Video Technology), **11(2)**, 2001, 252-256.
5. Gatica-Perez D., Gu C., Sun M-T., *Semantic Video Extraction Using Four-Band Watershed and Partition Lattice Operators* (IEEE Trans. on Circuits and Systems for Video Technology), **11(5)**, 2001 603-618.
6. Kim C. and Hwang J-N., *Fast and automatic video object segmentation and tracking for content-based applications* (IEEE Trans. on Circuits and Systems for Video Technology), **12(2)**, 2002, 122-129.
7. Kim B-C. and Park R-H., *A fast automatic VOP generation using boundary block segmentation* (Real-Time Imaging), **10(2)**, 2004, 117-125.
8. Mech R. and Wollborn M., *A Noise Robust Method for 2D Shape Estimation of Moving Objects in Video Sequences Considering a Moving Camera* (Signal Processing), **66(2)**, 1998, 203-217.
9. Neri A., Colonnese S., Russo G., Talone P., *Automatic moving object and background separation* (Signal Processing), **66(2)**, 1998, 219-232.
10. Chien S-Y., Huang Y-W., Hsieh B-Y., Ma S-Y., Chen L-G., *Fast video segmentation algorithm with shadow cancellation, global motion compensation, and adaptive threshold techniques* (IEEE Trans. on Multimedia), **6(5)**, 2004, 732-748.
11. Meier T. and Ngan K.N., *Video segmentation for content based coding* (IEEE Trans. on Circuits and Systems for Video Technology), **9(8)**, 1998, 1190-1203.

AN ETHERNET-ORIENTED RECEIVER-INITIATED RELIABLE MULTICAST PROTOCOL WITH AN EARLY MESSAGE LOSS DETECTION SCHEME

YILMAZ KEMAL YUCE

Department of Biostatistics and Medical Informatics, Akdeniz University, Akdeniz Universitesi Dumlupinar Bulvari 07070 Antalya, Turkey
E-mail: ykyuce@akdeniz.edu.tr

ALEXANDER KOSTIN AND ERHAN BASRI

Department of Computer Engineering, Eastern Mediterranean University, Magusa, via Mersin 10, Turkey
E-mail: {alexander.kostin, erhan.basri} @emu.edu.tr

In reliable multicast systems with receiver-oriented reliability approach, the reliability mechanism works based on detection of communication failures by the receivers themselves. Such mechanisms imply that a receiver can detect that it has missed one or more messages by means of a successful receipt of a subsequent message. However, in case some receivers miss the last message and if there is no subsequent message for a relatively long period of time, then the receiver group gets into an undesirable state in which the violation of "all or none" semantics, i.e. atomicity, occurs. This paper proposes a mechanism to prevent such a scenario by introducing a new reliable multicast protocol called RDDP-LAN that provides a loss-tolerant, totally ordered and atomic reliable multicast service for LANs of Ethernet type. To evaluate the system, a prototype of the protocol has been implemented in a Linux environment and investigated. Throughput performance results and the cost of the early message loss detection mechanism are presented.

1 Introduction

As the demand on and widespread use of distributed applications arise in many fields, reliable multicast (RM) as a communication paradigm in which data packets from a source (sender) are guaranteed to arrive error and duplication-free to all targeted destinations (receivers) with intended order of delivery [12], has received a great deal of attention. Applications that can take advantage of such a service include but not limited to distributed Interactive Simulation (DIS), Computer Supported Cooperative Work (CSCW), Distance Education, Distributed Operating Systems and Stock Market Applications [11].

Together with topology and scalability, the extent and nature of reliability, which differs from application to application, has resulted in the development of many different RM systems with different reliability mechanisms [2,4,6,10].

In receiver-initiated reliability mechanisms, which have been developed and considered as an alternative to a sender-initiated approach [7], data loss detection and signaling are responsibilities of recipients. The protocols with this type of mechanisms perform better than the ones with sender-initiated mechanisms in terms of throughput [7], but since they assume an infinite buffer size theoretically as their operation principle, they face message buffer size limitation problem in practice [5].

Such systems also suffer from a more serious problem. The operation principle of receiver-initiated mechanisms may lead to the violation of the atomicity property. When all group members are silent for a relatively long period of time, it is generally not possible to detect whether a message loss has occurred or not at any recipient related with the last sent message, until a change occurs in the dynamics of the group or the next multicast message is sent.

For a reliable multicast protocol that is not capable to prevent such a condition, it means that protocol is neither robust nor correct since the atomicity feature of reliability could not be preserved. On the other hand, from the perspective of an application, such a situation might lead to many unexpected results. Depending on the type and domain of the application, the results may even cause a disaster.

In this paper, we propose a new approach for early detection of lost messages to prevent such situations to occur, together with a new loss-tolerant, totally ordered, atomic and LAN-oriented reliable multicast protocol called Reliable Data Dissemination Protocol for LANs (RDDP-LAN).

Architecturally, RDDP-LAN adopts a centralized architecture and a receiver-initiated reliability technique, which was originally proposed by M. Franz Kaashoek and Andrew S. Tanenbaum [4,12] to realize reliability properties. Basically, the reliability mechanism uses a control parameter that is the time necessary to complete a multicast or the time that passes between the beginning and the end of the multicasting process for a single message. The protocol uses this parameter, based on an adaptive reliability scheme with timers, to make members be aware of potential message losses in advance to preserve atomicity and to detect node failures earlier. In other words, the protocol's reliability scheme acts depending on the performance of the underlying topology, i.e. LAN of type Ethernet, for future loss recovery.

The remaining parts of this paper are organized as follows. Section 2 introduces the basic assumptions and design choices made for the development of the protocol. In Section 3, the basic protocol operation with the new acknowledgement scheme and the control parameter, a multicast completion period, will be explained together with the scheme for early message loss detection. Next, Section 4 will present the experimental results on throughput performance and cost of the early message loss detection mechanism. Finally, Section 5 concludes the paper.

2 Basic System Design and Assumptions

RDDP-LAN is an application level protocol that provides a reliable multicast service on top of unreliable data transmission protocols, i.e. IP Multicasting and UDP, in LANs of Ethernet type. The protocol inherits some design properties from the group communication protocol developed for Amoeba Distributed OS [4]. However, the proposed protocol differs from its ancestor in many respects, due to assumptions made and its unique reliability approach. The main difference between RDDP-LAN and its ancestor is that RDDP-LAN is not implemented as part of a microkernel [3,4,9] but as a stand-alone library of group communication primitives, to be used by applications.

2.1 Basic Assumptions and Design Choices

2.1.1 Basic Assumptions

The system is intended to be deployed in a LAN of type Ethernet and it works on top of UDP and IP Multicast [1]. The protocol makes use of these best-effort transmission protocols for (i) unreliable transmission of data to group members and for (ii) reliability and error recovery mechanisms. It is assumed that the underlying network supports hardware multicast, e.g. Ethernet multicast, and has a procedure for mapping IP group addresses to Ethernet multicast addresses [1].

2.1.2 Design Choices

For a reliable multicast service, the design criteria set defines the communication aspects (characteristics) supported by the service for application implementation. Many different applications require different communication characteristics and it is hard to support all of them in a single protocol.

Addressing

In RDDP-LAN, groups are addressed by using a (IPv4 Multicast Address, Port) pair. An IPv4 IP multicast address is the IP host group address defined to be a Class D IP address, i.e. those IP addresses with "1110" as their high order bits, reserved for IP multicast [1]. Together with a port number, an IP host group address may be referred to as a group identifier.

Ordering

The protocol is assumed to support total ordering. To guarantee total ordering, the protocol uses a centralized logical structure per group, called a sequencer. The purpose of the centralization node is to make sure that all multicasts are done from the same node (or group member)[4,12].

Reliability

The reliability scheme works based on a "two-phase operation" mechanism. The first phase, the traditional error recovery phase, works when the group is busy multicasting messages and there are still messages to multicast. The sequencer initiates the second phase whenever it detects that there are two messages left to be multicast for a period of time. Within the first phase, reliability is ensured using Automatic Repair reQuests (ARQs). ACKs are used to prevent a specific scenario of atomicity violation. Whenever the second phase starts within a group, it is checked, if there is any message loss experienced by any group member after the last message multicast, based on a probabilistic measurement called "multicast completion period", which gives a result of the current condition of the LAN at that moment.

Delivery Semantics

This design aspect defines how a message is considered successfully delivered to a group. The proposed protocol supports the atomic delivery, which implies that a multicast is successful if and only if all group members have received the message; else no member should assume it is delivered.

Group Structure

Two important properties of a group are defined with this design criterion. The first one is being an open or closed group. An open group is the one that allows non-members to send messages to the group. In RDDP-LAN, a closed group structure is chosen and implemented, i.e. a non-member is not allowed to send messages to a group directly. However, it is still possible for a non-member to send messages to a group by asking a member of that group to send its messages to the group using a unicast link and a basic protocol that could be embedded into RDDP-LAN.

The second property defines membership dynamics of a group. A group is said to be static if it does not allow joining that group, once the group is formed before the multicast session. On the other hand, a dynamic group is the one to which it is possible to join or leave at any instant of communication. RDDP-LAN supports only static group structure. Such two design choices eliminate complications of keeping and changing state information and ease the implementation.

2.2 Protocol Entities

Basically, the proposed protocol is built on the existence of two types of entities: a sequencer and a group member. Each entity type has its own operation principles and implementation architecture.

2.2.1 Sequencer

As the type of entity with the highest workload, a sequencer has many tasks to carry out. The sequencer is responsible for (i) to guarantee reliable delivery of messages, (ii) to retransmit lost messages, and (iii) to handle multicast requests. Although the sequencer seems to be a dedicated process, it is also an ordinary group member. Due to its wide range of tasks, the sequencer is implemented as a two-threaded process, with the main thread and the multicast request service thread, in the prototype implementation of the proposed protocol. Each thread has been intended to manage task-related components, e.g. communication endpoints and queues, and to carry out an individual task or a collection of tasks.

The multicast request service thread, as the name implies, controls the sequencer's multicast request endpoint to which group members send the messages they want to be multicast, and hence, it handles the first phase of multicast completion process (see Section 3). Therefore, the main function of the multicast request service thread is to receive the messages to be multicast and store them in the order they arrive in the "multicast request queue".

The main thread is the central functional unit that handles a collection of tasks. Its major duty is to realize multicast service and to guarantee reliability. Thus, the main thread uses multicast service and acknowledgement endpoints. To make a multicast, at first, it simply accesses the multicast request queue to fetch the next message. After it makes sure that multicast is completed successfully by aggregating acknowledgements, it writes that message into its history buffer, to access and send it whenever a retransmission request arrives for that message from some member. Hence, the main thread also has the control over retransmission service and its endpoint.

2.2.2 Group Member

As the building blocks of a logical group structure, the proposed protocol needs members to be uniquely identified. For this purpose, members are assigned a unique identification number during the group formation stage starting from 0. In the prototype implementation of the proposed protocol, an ordinary group member has been implemented as a single-threaded process. This single thread will be created by an application whenever a membership operation is requested by making a call to *joinGroup ( )*. Member thread manages all the structures needed, i.e. retransmission and multicast service endpoints and message queues, and handles all related operations like buffering received multicast and retransmitted messages, generating and sending multicast requests to sequencer whenever the application makes a call to *sendToGroup ( )* and delivering the next message to the application from the received multicast message buffer, when it makes a call to *receiveFromGroup ( )* library functions.

3 Description of the Proposed Protocol and Its Schemes

3.1 Basic Protocol and Story of a Multicast Message in the System

The protocol deals with "multicasting a message" in the form of a three-phase procedure. The first phase covers the point-to-point transmission of message M from a group member to the sequencer with a request to multicast it. The second phase involves two parts. The first part handles the transmission of message M to the group by the sequencer. During the second part, the sequencer makes certain that message M is received by at least *r* group members. Finally in the third and last phase, the sequencer announces that message M is accepted and can be delivered to the applications.

A message's life begins at a group member. The application makes a call to the library function *sendToGroup ( )* to send message M. This call blocks the caller application and passes M to the member thread. The member thread immediately generates a request to multicast and encapsulates M into this point-to-point request message.

Thereafter, the member sends its request to the sequencer and starts to wait for an acknowledgement from it. The group member waits for a period of time to receive the acknowledgement. The length of this period depends on the measurement called multicast completion period, which will be discussed in Section 3.2. In case the member does not receive an acknowledgement, the member thread sends its request again. This procedure is repeated a number of times determined in the call to *joinGroup ( )* as a parameter of communication, which is called successive check.

When the sequencer receives such a request, at first, it sends a point-to-point acknowledgement to the sender of the request, and then it stores the message in its multicast request queue. When message M becomes the first message in the multicast request queue, the sequencer fetches M, encapsulates it in a multicast message with the next sequence number *s*, and multicasts the packet.

Subsequently, like its ancestor protocol [4], the proposed protocol employs an acknowledgement scheme to prevent violation of atomicity in case of member failures. In other words, the scheme guarantees that all surviving members receive all messages that were multicast before a member crashes. For this purpose, the sequencer makes sure that at least r group members have successfully received and buffered message M, where $0 < r <=$ (group size) and is called group resiliency.

Therefore, right after multicasting message M, the sequencer starts to collect acknowledgements from a subset of group members notifying successful receipt of message M. The cardinality of the subset of acknowledgers depends on the application requirements and should be selected carefully.

3.2 *The Acknowledgement Scheme and Multicast Completion Period*

3.2.1 The Acknowledgement Scheme

During a communication session, there is always a possibility for parties to experience crashes. In reliable multicast, such an incident may lead to the violation of the "all-or-none" semantics. For the proposed protocol, the violation of atomicity may occur as a result of a specific scenario. In this scenario, a member sends a multicast request to the sequencer. The sequencer receives the member's request and then multicasts its message, but all the group members miss the multicast, except the sender of the request and the sequencer. Then they pass that message to their application upon its receipt and both crash [4]. The occurence of such a scenario must be avoided. The ancestor of the proposed protocol deals with this special case of atomicity violation by using an acknowledgement scheme. The system employs an acknowledgement summon mechanism using a parameter called group resiliency or resilience degree , *r* [4]. According to this scheme after each multicast, the sequencer must collect *r* acknowledgements from *r* members of the group.

The use of this scheme with parameter *r* guarantees there will always be at least one member alive that has the multicast history and hence, atomicity will be preserved by retransmitting the lost messages if necessary.

RDDP-LAN inherits the same approach with a small but important change. In the original protocol in Amoeba, the set of acknowledgers are determined as the those having member identifiers smaller than *r*. This set is static. That is, during a multicast session it is always the same set of group members that must send acknowledgement for every message multicast, unless a crash is experienced. However, RDDP-LAN uses a simple, dynamic scheme to distribute acknowledgement responsibility among members. According to the proposed scheme, any group member will acknowledge the receipt of *r* multicast messages out of *n* messages, where *n* is equal to the group size, *r* represents the resiliency degree, $0 < r <= n$. Basically, after receiving a multicast message, all group members first check if they are one of the *r* members that must acknowledge that message. Hence, the scheme specifies the set on a per message basis. For a group G with *n* members and resiliency *r*, the set of member identifiers of those members who must acknowledge the receipt of message M with sequence number *s* is defined as

$$K = \{ i \mid i = [(s + t) \% n], for\ t = \{ 0, 1, ..., r - 1 \} \}$$

3.2.2 Multicast Completion Period

From the described procedure, it is obvious that a multicasting process for message M begins and ends at different points in an ordinary group member and the sequencer. In other words, they have distinct perceptions of a multicast process. This distinction arises from different assumptions of process initiation and completion.

That is, the sequencer considers the moment it multicasts the acceptance message for message M as the end of the multicast process for M. However, a group member perceives that the multicast is completed for message M and it can be delivered to the application when it receives the acceptance message for it. The same applies to the beginning of the process. Although such a difference exists, all group members including the sequencer measure the time that passes between the beginning and the end of a multicasting process. This measurement is called a "Multicast Completion Period" and it is a crucial parameter to the operation of the proposed protocol since it is used both for reliability and adaptability reasons.

According to the protocol, all the members of a group measure the multicast completion period, and calculate and keep track of its mean and standard deviation for different message sizes, with intervals of 20 octets. For this purpose, every group member (including the sequencer) maintains a vector called a "System Condition Vector" shown in Fig. 1.

Mean and Std. Dev. for messages of size 0-19 octets	Mean and Std. Dev. for messages of size 20-39 octets	....	Mean and Std. Dev. for messages of size 1440-1459 octets	Mean and Std. Dev. for messages of size 1460-1479 octets

Figure 1. System Condition Vector.

The upper limit for message size is defined as 1480 octets depending on two basic assumptions: (i) an Ethernet frame can carry a maximum of 1500 octets of data and out of these 1500 octets, 20 octets are reserved for packet headers, and (ii) messages having a size larger than 1500 octets would cause fragmentation in the data link layer, which in turn may affect the system throughput. Hence, using application level framing principle, the messages are split into chunks, each of which fits an Ethernet frame.

The protocol entites use system condition vector for reliability and adaptability. As soon as the sequencer multicasts a message, it sets a timer and starts to collect acknowledgements during 2 * (sum of multicast completion period mean and standard deviation for that message size) microseconds. The factor of 2 is for the fluctuation margin. In case this period is exceeded during the multicasting process of message *M*, then the sequencer assumes there is a serious fluctuation in the LAN and sets the mean for that message size equal to the multicast completion period for message *M*. Also, the standard deviation is calculated as if only 2 multicasts have been completed, but not *m*, where *m* is equal to the number of messages with a specific message size interval which were multicast until that moment. Similarly, an ordinary group member uses multicast completion period in case it does not receive an acceptance for an already multicast message. This measurement also constitutes a fast way of detecting processor failures or checking if group members are alive.

Aside from these cases, the protocol makes use of this measurement in the early loss detection mechanism.

3.3 *Early Message Loss Detection Scheme*

The basic principle of message loss detection in a receiver-oriented reliability mechanism relies on the fact that a receiver (a group member) can detect if it has missed one or more messages by means of a successful receipt of another message multicast in the system.

This principle works well with the basic assumption of existence of another message multicast after each message. However, it might be the case that there will be no message multicast for a period of time. In such a situation, the receivers will not be able to detect if they have missed, for example, the last message multicast until the next message is transmitted. If there are members that did not receive the last message, the situation will yield the temporary violation of "all-or-none" semantics. To preserve atomicity in such cases, the proposed protocol employs an early message loss detection mechanism as part of the reliability scheme. This mechanism works based on two independent complementary phases: (i) a preliminary detection phase and (ii) a posterior detection phase.

3.3.1 Preliminary Detection Phase

The first phase is triggered whenever the sequencer realizes that there are exactly two messages left to be multicast in its multicast request queue. While generating the multicast packet for the first message, the sequencer writes the size of the message that will be multicast next into a special field in the header of that packet. In this way, the sequencer helps the members to discover that there will potentially be an open ended time interval during which no multicast will take place. Also, learning the size of the next message, group members know approximately when this period will begin by accessing their system condition vector. After receiving a message, a member checks if the "next message's size" field contains a valid value. If so, it immediately accesses the system condition vector and gets the mean and standard deviation of multicast completion periods for the received message and the next message using their sizes. Subsequently, it starts a timer and waits for the next message to be multicast. In case the member receives neither the next message itself nor the acceptance for it within $2 * (a + b)$ microseconds, where a is equal to the sum of mean and standard deviation for the message just received and b is equal to the sum of mean and standard deviation for the next message, it assumes that the open ended period has already begun. Consequently, it generates a retransmission request with the encapsulated sequence number of the message it has received last. The factor 2 in the waiting period takes into account the fluctuation in the message propagation time.

3.3.2 Posterior Detection Phase

This phase is initiated by the sequencer whenever its multicast request queue becomes empty. After announcing the acceptance of the last multicast message, the sequencer starts a timer and waits for a while to receive new multicast requests from group members before taking an action. The duration of this waiting period is equal to the minimum of the sums of means and related standard deviations of multicast completion period in the system condition vector. At the end of this period, if no multicast requests have arrived, the sequencer multicasts a control message called CHECK_SEQ_NUMBER_REQ with the sequence number of the last multicast message that will make the group members check if they have experienced message losses and detect it.

The described two phases act as the complementary for each other. The factor 2, in waiting period length for self-loss detection of a member at the preliminary detection phase, is actually a parameter of their cooperation. The preliminary detection phase operates and makes a member to send a retransmission request, if and only if the posterior detection phase could not make that member to detect the loss. Otherwise, the member stops the timer of the preliminary detection phase and checks if a loss has occured. If so, it sends a retransmission request to the sequencer.

4 Performance and Cost Analysis

In order to evaluate the performance of the proposed protocol experimentally, its prototype version has been implemented using C language in Linux Mandrake Distribution. An experimental environment was setup that consisted of 4 PCs connected to the 10 Mbps Ethernet, each with an Intel Celeron 333 MHz processor, 64 MB RAM, 4 GB HDD and a 10 Mbps Realtek Network Interface Card.

4.1 Throughput Performance

The protocol was tested for a varying group size, number of senders, resilience and message size. Throughout the experiments, groups of 2, 3 and 4 members were used, with resilience and the number of senders assigned the same value (group size – 1). The only group member that was not used as a sender is the sequencer. This is to allow the sequencer to deal with its main task and, hence, to obtain the maximum throughput of the proposed protocol with high resilience. The protocol performance for message sizes that would require fragmentation at the Ethernet layer was not tested. The measurements were done at the application layer, and throughput was expressed in messages per second and KBps/member.

The results depicted in Figure 2, correspond to the experiments when, (group size – 1) members of the given group continuously make consecutive calls to *sendToGroup ( )* and *receiveFromGroup ( )* primitives. The maximum throughput was found as 479 256-octet long messages per second.

Generally, the protocol throughput (messages/second) decreases, for a fixed group size, as the message size increases. On the other hand, this throughput has a tendency to increase with the increase of the group size, for a fixed message size. Only, for 256-octet long messages, the system shows throughput degradation, when group size increases. This is also reflected in Figure 3. This means that RDDP-LAN does not perform well with groups of size 2.

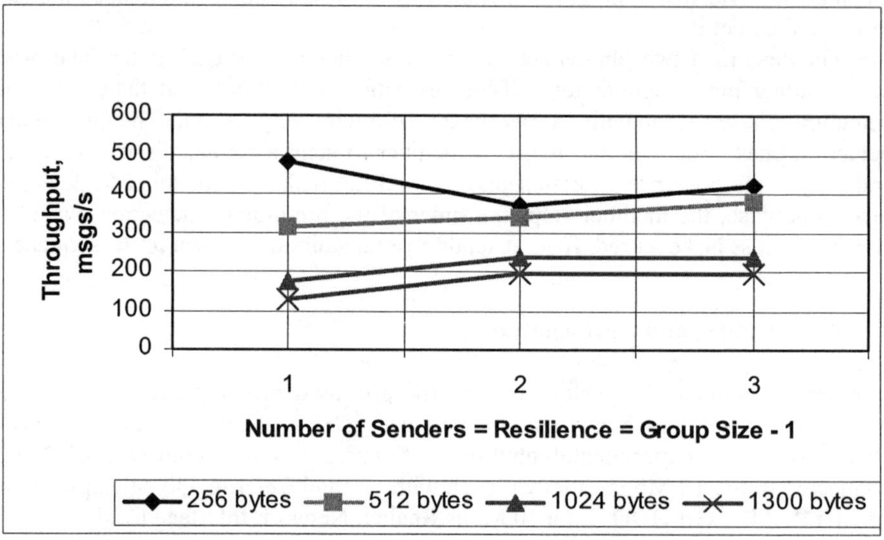

Figure 2. Throughput for different message sizes of the proposed protocol.

4.2 *Cost of the Early Message Loss Detection*

To analyze the cost of the early message loss detection, another series of experiments for groups of 2, 3 and 4 members with resilience 1 was conducted. In order to eliminate the start -up effects, a preliminary run was done before each test.

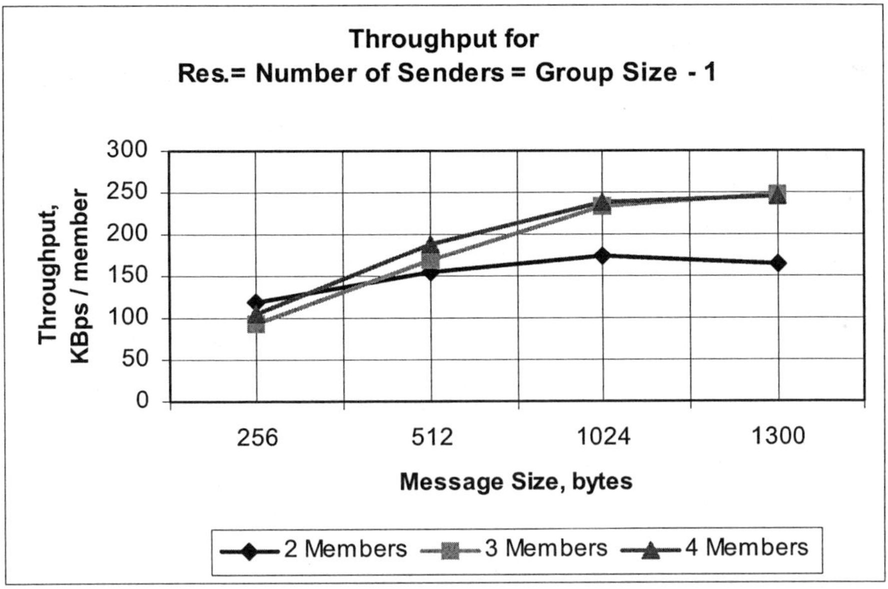

Figure 3. Throughput of the protocol in KBps / member, for different group sizes.

The early message loss detection in the proposed protocol has a small cost for relatively large group sizes. For example, for groups of 3 and 4 members, with resilience 1 and a single sender, the sequencer unnecessarily interrupted the communication by generating and multicasting 2 or 3 CHECK_SEQ_NUMBER_REQs in a session of 81920 multicast messages with a single sender that requests consecutive multicasts. This shows that, the fluctuation tolerance approach works well under such circumstances.

However, for a group of size 2, the protocol behavior is not satisfactory. In Figure 4, the number of CHECK_SEQ_NUMBER_REQ multicasts for a group of size 2, with resilience 1 is presented for different message sizes. For each experiment shown in Figure 4, 81920 multicast messages were transmitted. With this group size, almost after every message multicast, the sequencer generated a CHECK_SEQ_NUMBER_REQ. This means that a redundant message is sent almost after every multicast of a group size 2 with resilience 1. This is a costly side effect that might have a serious impact on the throughput capacity of the protocol with groups of size 2.. That is, RDDP-LAN is not suitable for using in groups consisting of only 2 members. For such a small group, multicast can be easily replaced by unicast communication.

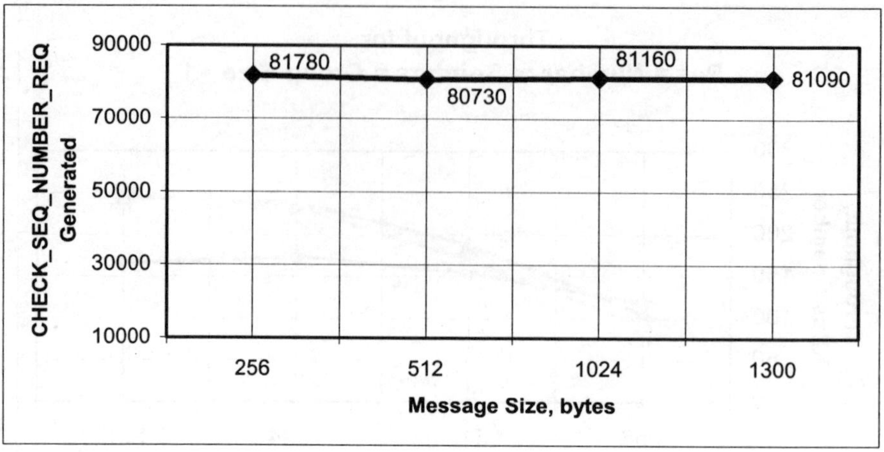

Figure 4. The cost of the early loss detection for the group size 2 and resilience 1.

5 Conclusion

In this paper, a new reliable multicast protocol, RDDP-LAN, with a new scheme for early message loss detection is proposed. The design properties of the protocol were explained together with the basic assumptions. The performance study of a prototype implementation of the protocol was carried out and the cost of the new scheme was estimated in experiments.

References

1. Deering S., RFC1112, Request For Comments 1112 Host Extensions for IP Multicasting, August 1989
2. Floyd S., Jacobson, V. McKanne, S. Liu C-G, and Zhang L., A Reliable Multicast Framework for Lightweight Sessions and Application Level Framing. IEEE/ACM Transactions on Networking, vol. 5 no. 6 (1997) 784-803.
3. Kaashoek F., Renesse R.V., Staveren H.V., and Tanenbaum A.S., FLIP: An Internetwork Protocol for Supporting Distributed Systems, Technical Report (1994).
4. Kaashoek F., Tanenbaum A.S., Group Communication in the Amoeba Distributed Operating System. Proc. of the IEEE 11th Int'l Conference on Distributed Computing Systems, 222-230 (1991).
5. Levine B.N., and Aceves J.J. G-L, A Comparison of Reliable Multicast Protocols. ACM Multimedia Systems Journal, vol. 6 no. 5 (1998) 334-348.

6. McKinley P.K., Rao R.T., and Wright R.F., H-RMC: A Hybrid Reliable Multicast Protocol for the Linux Kernel. Proc. of the IEEE SC99: High Performance Networking and Computing Conference (1999).
7. Pingali S., Towsley D., and Kurose F., A Comparison of Sender-Initiated and Receiver-Initiated Reliable Multicast Protocols. IEEE Journal on Selected Areas in Communications, vol. 15 no.3 (1997) 398-406.
8. Stevens W.R., Unix Network Programming v1, Networking APIs and XTI, 2nd ed., Addison-Wesley.
9. Tanenbaum A.S., Renesse R.V., Staveren H.V., Sharp G.J., Mullender S.J., and Rossum G.V., Experiences with the Amoeba Distributed Operating System. Communications of the ACM, vol. 33 no. 12 (1990) 46-63.
10. Whetten B., Montgomery T., and Kaplan S., A High Performance Totally Ordered Multicast Protocol (Reliable Multicast Protocol-RMP). Proc. of the Int'l Workshop on In Theory and Practice in Distributed Systems, Springer Verlag LCNS, (1994) 33-57.
11. Maxemchuk N.F., and Shur D., An Internet Multicast System for the Stock Market. ACM Transactions on Computer Systems, vol. 19 no. 3, (2001) 384-412.
12. Kaashoek F., Efficient Reliable Group Communication for Distributed Systems. PhD Dissertation, Vrije Universiteit (1992).

A DYNAMIC ROUTE OPTIMIZATION TO SUPPORT NETWORK MOBILITY BY USING HMNR SCHEME

MOON-SANG JEONG, JONG-TAE PARK, AND YEONG-HUN CHO

School of Electronic and Electrical Engineering, Kyungpook National University
1370, Sankyuk-Dong, Buk-Gu, Daegu, Korea 702-701
E-mail: {msjeong, jtpark, yhcho}@ee.knu.ac.kr

The IETF NEMO working group proposed the basic support protocol for the network mobility to support the movement of a mobile network consisting of several mobile nodes. However, this protocol has been found to suffer from the so-called 'dog-leg problem', and despite alternative research efforts to solve this problem, there are still limitations in the efficiency for real time data transmission and intra-domain communication. Accordingly, this paper proposes a new route optimization methodology that uses unidirectional tunneling and a tree-based intra-domain routing mechanisms which can significantly reduce delay in both signaling and data transmission

1 Introduction

As the technology related to the wireless and mobile network environments is rapidly being developed, it increases the necessity for research about network mobility that could support the mobility of not only a single mobile node but also the movement of a mobile network which consists of several mobile nodes [1]. The most representative work is that of the IETF (Internet Engineering Task Force) NEMO (Network Mobility) working group. The IETF NEMO working group has proposed several Internet drafts [2], [3], [4].

The NEMO basic support protocol defines a methodology for supporting network mobility by using bi-directional tunneling between the home agent and the MR(Mobile Router). It extends binding messages of Mobile IPv6 and the data transmission of a mobile network can be achieved by using the MR which is the egress interface of a mobile network. In other words, only the MR is involved in the acquisition of CoA (Care of Address) according to a handover of the mobile network. A MNN (Mobile Network Node) which is connected to the MR can maintain their home network address. The NEMO basic support protocol defines basic procedures to support network mobility of a mobile network, but excludes route optimization, multi-homing, and other issues. These issues are examined in the extended network mobility support part. In particular, the basic support protocol has a serious problem called dog-leg problem; that is, all traffic to or from the MNN of the nested mobile network passes through the HAs (Home Agents) of all preceding mobile networks.

To solve this problem, various methodologies have been proposed [5], [6], [7]. However, these ideas are still inefficient for real time data transmission and they remain as the optimal route because they are based on bi-directional tunneling between the root-MR and HA of the nested mobile network. Furthermore, direct message exchange between the MNNs within the same root-MR, which is called intra-domain communication, is not supported and the root-MR can experience a very heavy load because it must maintain full paths for all nested MRs. If there are frequent movements of mobile networks, and intra-domain communication is large, these methodologies are very inefficient. Thus, most previous methods have limitations with regard to signaling overhead, concentrated traffic and load in the root-MR, and packet-header overhead due to multiple encapsulations.

Accordingly, this paper proposes a new route optimization methodology for the efficient support of network mobility based on unidirectional tunneling between the HA of a nested mobile network and the root-MR, and the use of a tree-based intra-domain routing mechanism. The use of unidirectional tunneling facilitates more optimized route construction. When using tree-based routing for intra-domain communication and binding procedures, a hierarchical mobile network routing is more efficient and faster than previous tunneling mechanism for signaling and data transmission.

2 Previous Work

The IETF NEMO working group has defined a basic protocol operation to support the network mobility of a mobile network based on Mobile IPv6. There have already been several Internet drafts related to the goals, requirements, terminology, and basic support protocol for network mobility. Network mobility is essentially defined as Nemo basic support and Nemo extended support, where the purpose of Nemo basic support is to preserve session continuity in a mobile network, while Nemo extended support provides more optimal routing for a nested mobile network [4]. The goal of the Nemo basic support protocol is to support network mobility and backward compatibility by extending Mobile IPv6. As such, its definition of the MR extends the MN of Mobile IPv6, where the MR performs internal routing and external data transmission for an MNN, which moves with the MR. Data transmission between the MNN and the CN is performed using bi-directional tunneling between the HA and the MR. All traffic passes through the HA, and IPSec is used for secure signaling between the MR and the HA [4].

In a mobile network on a visited link, a bi-directional tunnel is created between the HA and the MR for data transmission. Thus, data transmission by a mobile network is achieved using the MR, which is the egress interface of the mobile network. In other words, since only the MR is involved in the acquisition of a CoA in a mobile network handover, an MNN behind the MR can maintain its home network address. For the construction of a bi-directional tunnel, the basic support protocol extends the binding message of Mobile IPv6. The extended BU(Binding Update) message contains a network prefix instead of a home address, and the egress interface address of the MR as the CoA. Thus, by using these extensions, network mobility can be supported without changing the addresses of the MNNs in the mobile network.

The Nemo basic support protocol defines the minimal procedures and extensions required to support network mobility, as such it does not cover route optimization, multi-homing, and so on. In the basic support protocol, the tunnel of a nested mobile network is constructed through all preceding mobile network tunnels, and all the traffic of the nested mobile network passes through the HAs of all preceding mobile networks, thereby causing a serious problem called the 'dog-leg problem'. Figure 1 shows an example of the dog-leg problem in the basic support protocol.

Recently, a lot of research has focused on solving the dog-leg problem, including route optimization of the basic support protocol [5], [7], [9]. Several previous studies on route optimization have used bi-directional tunneling between the HA of the nested mobile network and the root-MR, where two bi-directional tunnels are made between the HA of the nested mobile network and the root-MR, and between the root-MR and the MR of the nested mobile network. By using direct tunneling between the HA of the nested mobile network and the root-MR, the dog-leg problem is solved. Yet, an extended RA(Router Advertisement) message that includes an address of the root-MR egress interface is required to discover and notify the root-MR address to the nested MRs.

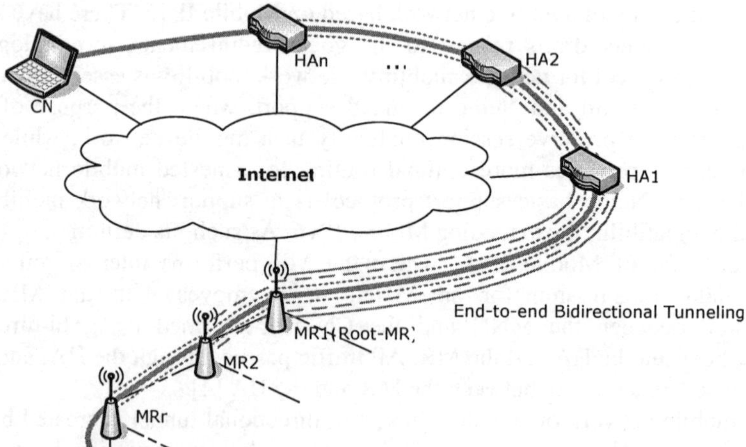

Figure 1. Dog-leg problem in Nemo basic support protocol

Most of previous works in route optimization have used bidirectional tunneling. The methods using bidirectional tunneling has some drawbacks for real-time data transmission. Since these methods have more complex signaling than the basic support protocol. Because if the root-MR moves along with the nested mobile network, the nested mobile network must re-establish the tunnel since the root-MR address was changed. In addition, these methods do not support intra-domain communication, because all traffic passes through either the HA of the nested mobile network or at least the root-MR. The root-MR must maintain full paths for the MRs of all nested mobile networks. If there are frequent movements of mobile networks, these methods become very inefficient due to the large signaling overhead, large data transmission delay, traffic concentration in the root-MR, and packet header overhead resulting from multiple encapsulations. Therefore, a new route optimization methodology is needed to support efficient signaling and optimized routes.

3 Hierarchical Mobile Network Routing Scheme

3.1 Basic Operation of HMNR

To solve the problems as stated above, this paper proposes a HMNR(Hierarchical Mobile Network Routing) scheme consisting of intra-Nemo routing and extra-Nemo tunneling, where tree-based routing is used for intra-domain data transmission and signaling, while unidirectional tunneling is used for data transmission to or from the external network. Figure 2 shows the operation of the HMNR scheme for route optimization. As shown in Figure 2, an MNN behind the MR cannot receive data from the CN directly since a mobile network uses the network prefix of the home network. However, data from an MNN can be directly transmitted to the CN using a normal routing scheme. In other words, although a tunnel is required for data transmission from the HA to the MR, the other tunnel from the MR to the HA does not need to be established to optimize the route. As a result, the MNN can communicate with the CN using only a unidirectional tunnel from the HA to the MR. Similarly, route optimization for a nested mobile network can be achieved using unidirectional tunneling from the HA of the nested mobile network to the root-MR by binding the network prefix to the CoA of the root-MR. Only the root-MR can perform decapsulation of the packets from the CN.

The direct tunneling between the HA of the nested mobile network and the root-MR requires the additional handover procedure because the binding address of the mobile network needs to be changed for the root-MR movement along with the nested mobile network. Thus, the handovers are divided into three cases: inter-Nemo, intra-Nemo and root-MR handover. In the vehicular environments, the root-MR handover frequently occurs and it accompanies with the mass signaling for all nested mobile networks, and the root-MR suffers from the large processing load, bottleneck and the service discontinuity.

To satisfy the requirements, this paper proposes the HMNR scheme with two operating modes for the signaling efficiency and route optimization respectively: the basic mode and the extended mode. In the extended mode, the route optimization is performed by using the direct tunneling from the HA to the root-MR. On the other hands, the MR in the basic mode binds its network prefix to the HoA of the root-MR, thus the data from the CN to the MNN passes through both HAs of the MNN and of the root-MR. By using this mechanism, the MR is independent of the root-MR handover. Moreover, the route is more optimal than the one of the basic support protocol with same signaling complexity because the HMNR scheme has only two intermediate HAs regardless of the nested level of the mobile network. Each operating mode is dynamically switched by sending the BU message including the HoA or CoA of the root-MR for the binding address. Thus the MR decides the basic mode for the vehicular environment with low data traffic, and it can switch into the extended modes if the data traffic or inter-Nemo handover is increased.

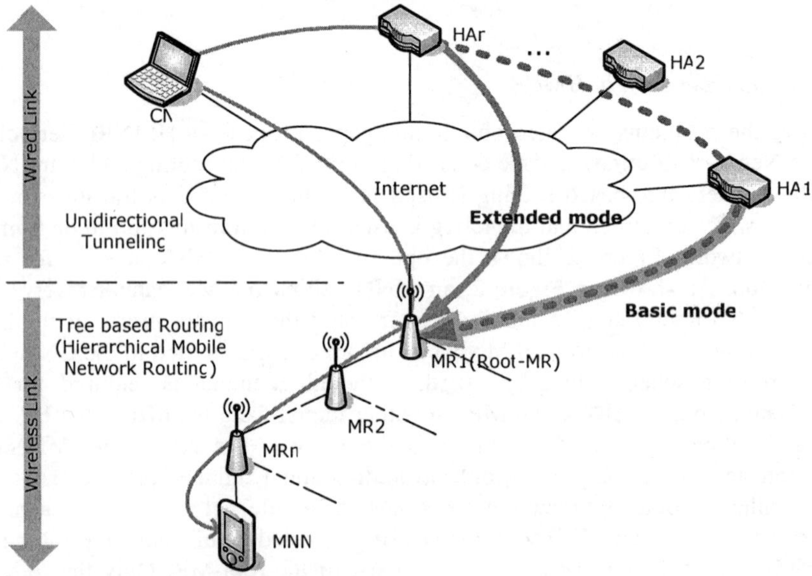

Figure 2. HMNR Scheme for Route Optimization

3.2 *Routing & Handover Procedures*

Mobile networks are composed of a tree topology from the root-MR to the MRs of each nested mobile network, where only the root-MR has an egress interface for transmitting data to or from the external network. Thus, a new routing mechanism based on a tree topology is needed where the root-MR is the root of the tree and the nested MRs are the tree nodes. In a tree-based routing scheme, each MR contains a parent-MR address as a default route entry and maintains a routing table that consists of a mobile network prefix and next hop address pairs for each nested mobile network. In this case, the traffic from the root-MR to the CN is transmitted using the default route entry of the root-MR, that is, an AR(Access Router) instead of tunneling. The routing process is completed by updating the routing entry, which consists of a mobile network prefix and new MR's CoA pair, to the parent-MR, then the parent-MR updates its routing entry and resends the RU message to its parent-MR recursively. At this time, the RU message from the parent-MR has a new next hop address as the CoA of the parent-MR. If an RU message reaches the root-MR or a crossover MR that contains the same routing entry in the RU message, the routing update procedure is completed. The proposed HMNR scheme can also support intra-domain data communication without passing through the HA, because the MR maintains the routing information while providing a routing for transmitting data from MNNs. Traffic can also be transmitted to its destination without passing through the root-MR, if a crossover MR exists which contains a routing entry to the destination.

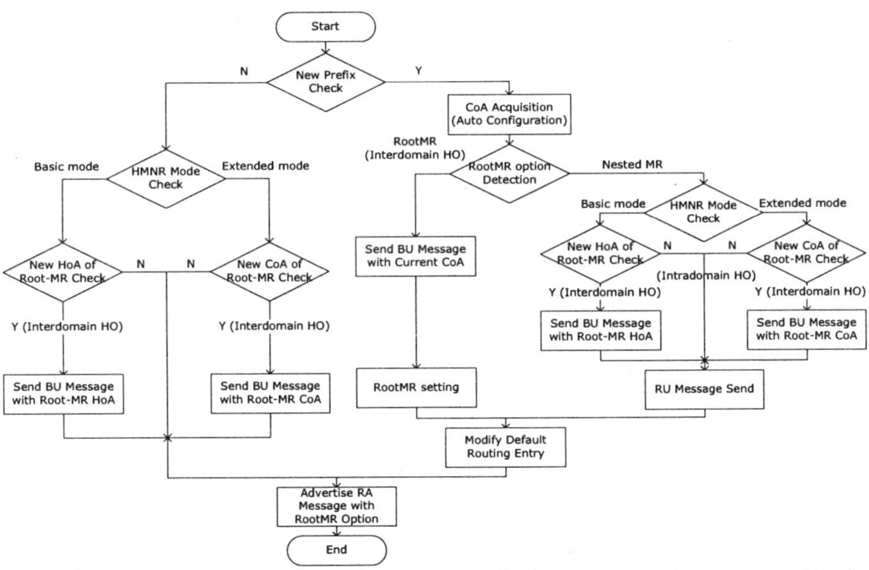

Figure 3. RA Message Handling Procedures for supporting Inter-domain and Intra-domain Handover

To support the binding and routing of HMNR, an RA(Router Advertisement) message extension is needed to discover the root-MR and advertise its information. The HMNR also requires a Root-MR Option, which contains the CoA and HoA of the root-MR, and an RA message with the Root-MR Option is used to advertise the addresses of the root-MR.

When a mobile network detects movement, the MR sends an RS(Router Solicitation) message to acquire a network prefix for the foreign network. If an RS message is received, the parent-MR or access router then responds to the MR with an RA message and Root-MR Option. As such, the handover procedures can be decided using an RA message. Figure 3 shows the RA message handling procedures for supporting an inter-domain and intra-domain handover. An inter-domain handover includes two cases where the mobile network obtains a new root-MR address: inter-Nemo handover or root-MR handover.

In the former case (*inter-Nemo handover*),

(1) The MR obtains a new CoA
(2) The MR processes a binding procedure between the HA and the root-MR using the address for the root-MR obtained by exchanging RS and extended RA messages with a Root-MR Option.
(3a) The MR sends an RU message with its own network prefix and CoA to the parent-MR for intra-Nemo data transmission.
(4a) Finally, the MR advertises the root-MR address to the nested mobile network by using an RA message with a Root-MR Option.
(3b) Conversely, if the MR receives an RA message without a root-MR address option, this means that the MR is directly connected to the AR, in which case, the MR does not perform a routing procedure, but rather sets itself up as the root-MR
(4b) The MR advertises an RA message with its CoA to the nested mobile network.

In the latter case (*Root-MR handover*),

(1) The preceding MR obtains a new CoA
(2) The preceding MR performs a handover procedure similar to the former case
(3) Then it advertises a new root-MR address to the nested mobile network. If a mobile network receives an RA message with a new root-MR address
(4) If the MR uses the HMNR extended mode then, the MR reestablishes the unidirectional tunnel between the HA and the new root-MR CoA
(5) Finally, the MR advertises the root-MR address to the nested mobile network.

Meanwhile, an intra-Nemo handover occurs when a mobile network moves within the root-Nemo domain, that is, the root-MR address is not changed. In this case, the MR does not need to update the binding to the HA and only performs a routing procedure.

4 Performance Analysis

This section presents a comparison of the following network mobility support protocols: Basic support protocol (BASIC)[2], route optimization method using bi-directional tunneling (TLMR)[4], and HMNR schemes (HMNR-B and HMNR-E).

Table I shows the characteristics of these methods regarding the support of network mobility. The Nemo basic support protocol and HMNR-B Scheme have the least amount of signaling overhead, as they do not need to perform binding procedures when root-MR handover occurs. Therefore, they have the advantages in terms of both signaling complexity and scalability. However, the basic support protocol has drawbacks in terms of the signaling latency, handover delays, and data transmission delays due to the dog-leg problem. In particular, the proposed scheme has several advantages compared with previous methodologies. It has smallest delay in both data transmission and signaling. Moreover, intra-domain handover and communication are well supported, and micro-mobility can be well supported without the need for an additional extension.

Table 1. Characteristics of various network mobility support protocols.

	BASIC	TLMR	HMNR-B	HMNR-E
Signaling Amount	Small	Large	Small	Medium
Signaling Latency	Large	Medium	Medium	Small
Signaling Complexity	Small	Large	Small	Medium
Handover Delay	Large	Medium	Medium	Small
Transmission Delay	Large	Medium	Medium	Small
Intra-domain Data Transmission	N/A	Possible	Support	Support
Scalability	Large	Medium	Large	Medium
Micro-mobility	N/A	Possible	Support	Support

Figure 4 shows the performance analysis of the inter-domain and intra-domain signaling completion time (dotted lines) and data transmission delay (solid lines). In the inter-domain communication environment, the signaling delay for the route optimization methodologies was shorter than that for the basic support protocol, plus the handover delays were minimal. Furthermore, the data transmission delay for the HMNR-E scheme was shorter than that for the TLMR scheme, because the data from the CN was directly transmitted to the root-MR. Meanwhile, in the intra-domain communication environment, the signaling completion times were all constant when the depth of the mobile network remained constant (at 6), and the HMNR scheme had the shortest signaling completion time. The data transmission delay was also minimal. Therefore, the proposed scheme was found to provide the optimal intra-domain communication for a mobile network.

Figure 4 (d) and (e) shows the average packet header overhead resulting from tunneling and the average processing load of the root-MR in relation to signaling the nested mobile networks. The packet header overhead was determined by measuring the average packet size over the signaling procedure. As the depth of the mobile network increased, the overheads for the basic support protocol and TLMR scheme increased, as they used multiple encapsulations.

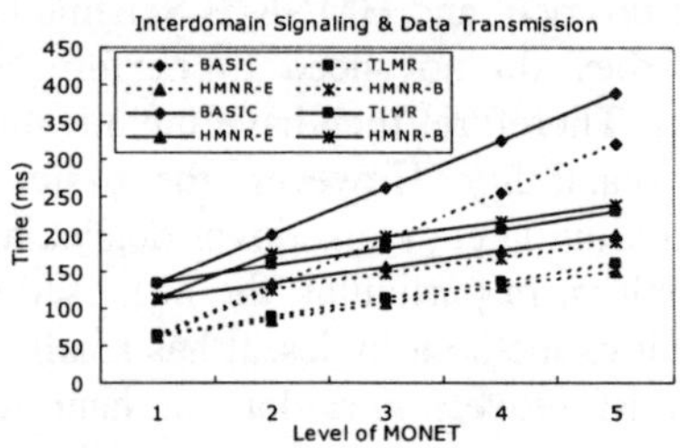

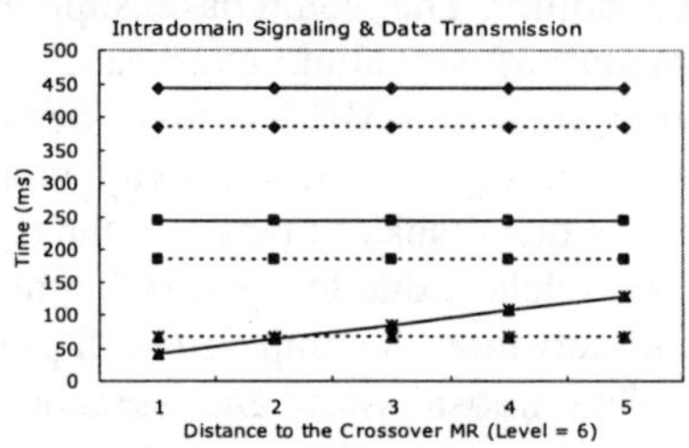

(a) Inter-domain Signaling & Data transmission Delay (b) Intra-domain Signaling & Data transmission Delay

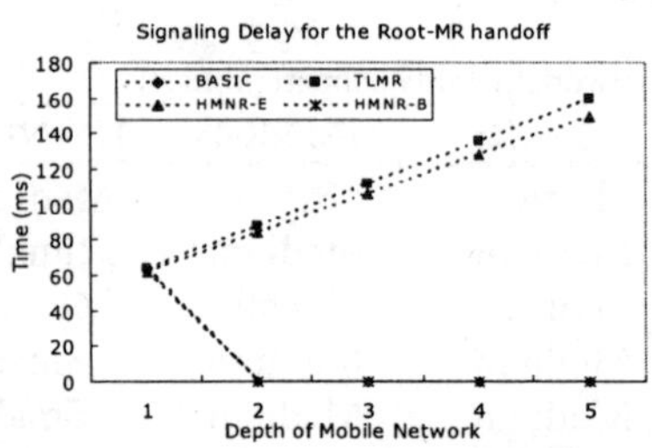

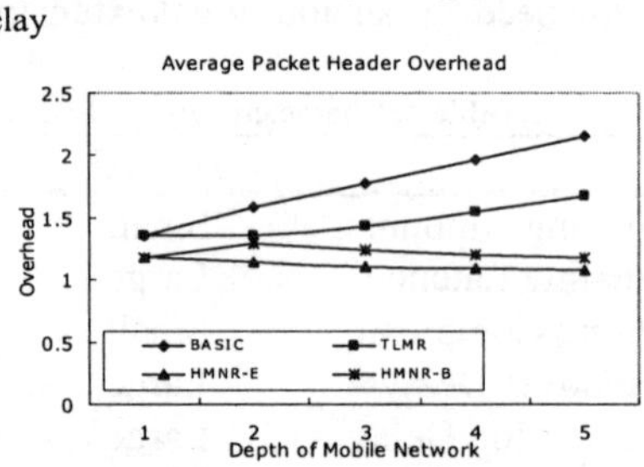

(c) Signaling Delay for the Root-MR Handover (d) Average Packet Header Overhead

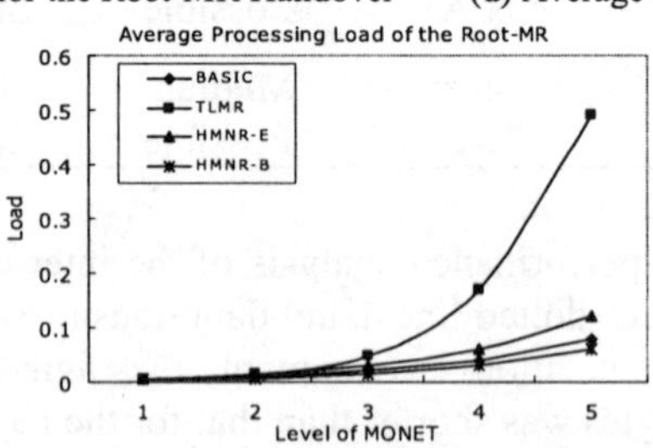

(e) Average Processing Load of the Root-MR for Signaling

Figure 4. The Performance Analysis for the Hierarchical Mobile Network Routing Scheme

In the analysis of the processing load, the basic support protocol and HMNR-B had the least amount of signaling, resulting in a lower signaling complexity and average processing load. With the TLMR scheme, the processing load increased, because the root-MR performed extensive tunneling processes. Meanwhile, since the HMNR scheme minimized the role of the root-MR and the nested MR shared the signaling role, it produced similar results to the basic support protocol.

5 Conclusion

This paper has comparatively analyzed the characteristics of various approaches on network mobility. We have proposed a new hierarchical mobile network routing scheme for efficient route optimization in a mobile network. The proposed hierarchical mobile network routing scheme improves the performance of the route optimization by using unidirectional tunneling and tree based hierarchical routing techniques. The proposed scheme can be used in various mobile environments, such as WPAN, ubiquitous computing, and VNE.

References

1. Hong-Yon L., Christophe J, and Alexandru P., Network Mobility in Beyond-3G Systems, *IEEE Communications Magazine* **41** (2003) pp.52-57.
2. Thierry E., Network Mobility Support Goals and Requirements, *IETF Internet-Draft* (2003)
3. Thierry E. and Hong-Yon L., Network Mobility Support Terminology, *IETF Internet-Draft* (2003)
4. Vijay D., Ryuji W., Alexandru P., and Pascal T., NEMO Basic Support Protocol, *IETF Internet-Draft* (2003)
5. P. Thubert, M. Molteni, and C. Ng, Taxonomy of Route Optimization models in the Nemo Context, *IETF Internet-Draft* (2003)
6. H.S. Kang et al,, Route Optimization for Mobile Network by Using Bi-directional Between HA and TLMR, *IETF Internet-Draft* (2003)
7. H. Ohnishi, K. Sakitani, and Y. Takagi, HMIP based Route Optimization method in a mobile network, *IETF Internet-Draft* (2003)
8. Hyunsik K. et al, Route Optimization for Mobile Network by Using Bi-directional Between Home Agent and Top Level Mobile Router, *IETF Internet-Draft* (2003)

PREDICTION ACCURACY STUDY OF AN ADAPTIVE ALGORITHM IN CLUSTER-BASED NETWORK SERVERS WITH RESOURCE ALLOCATION

KATJA GILLY AND SALVADOR ALCARAZ

Universidad Miguel Hernández, Departamento de Física y Arquitectura de Computadores, Avda. de la Universidad, s/n, 03202 Elche (Spain).
Email: {katya,salcaraz}@umh.es

CARLOS JUIZ AND RAMON PUIGJANER

Universitat de les Illes Balears, Departament de Ciències Matemàtiques i Informàtica, Ctra. de Valldemossa, km 7.5, 07122 Palma de Mallorca (Spain).
Email: {cjuiz,putxi}@uib.es

Prediction is one of the most important factors that prevents a Web system from collapsing when high intensity of transactional traffic arrives to it. It is necessary to ensure the quality of prediction is good enough in order to maintain under control the correct utilization of the Web system by allocating its resources among different types of incoming traffic that can reach the system and by controlling bursty transaction arrivals to the system. We have developed an algorithm that resides in a Web switch and distributes the workload among a set of servers following a resource allocation policy based on quality of service (QoS) attributes. The algorithm includes a *reward* scheme to control the accuracy of the predictions on real time.

1 Introduction

The Internet community is continuously growing and the need of performance studies in this field is becoming crucial to obtain better service response times for the web users. Within the parameters to be controlled in order to avoid web system congestion, some of them are related to traffic arrival attributes at web servers. If the web system is receiving arrivals that follow a constant distribution, then the situation is simplified considerably. Unfortunately this is not applicable on web. The problem is that Internet traffic's behaviour is based on bursty patterns, therefore a control of burstiness in arrival rate is necessary to ensure a good response from the system. On the other hand, it is necessary also to control the web server's utilization level continuously to ensure that user' requests with high SLA (*Service Level Agreement*) are attended faster than others with a lower SLA and to reject requests when the servers are overloaded. We have focused our research on web performance by proposing an enhanced solution for a web switch algorithm based on throughput prediction of a set of web servers that compose a cluster. Our dispatching algorithm selects the server that is going to attend the following requests and includes a resource allocation policy based on the utilization of servers among the different types of users that can reach the system. It also controls the arrival rate pattern to detect when burstiness appears and therefore, to prepare the system for it. The architecture of the system we have considered is depicted in figure 1.

The dispatching algorithm is mainly composed by two phases: the *transient* phase and the *computation* phase, organised in a variable slotted time schedule. The web switch is always executing the *transient* phase that attends incoming requests and process outgoing responses, and balances the load among the servers of the system. *Computation* phase is executed concurrently to *transient* phase when each slot is near to be finished. The content of this paper is focused in the *computation* phase that prepares the system for the following slot.

Adaptiveness is an attractive feature that is being considered more and more by researchers to be necessarily included in systems that are exposed to external factors that can make them unstable, to avoid unexpectedly situations that may result in the fall of the complete system. In fact some of works have recently appeared relating adaptive mechanisms to distributed systems [2, 11] and web services [1, 3, 6, 7, 12]. Aron et al. [1] proposes an optimization algorithm to determine the cluster reserve during execution that implies a high computational cost for the front end node and that requires significant changes in the operating system kernel of all nodes of the system for customizing resource scheduling. Li et al. [6] implement a thin layer between Ethernet driver and IP layer. Some works [7, 12, 3] based their study on a load model that do not consider bursty arrivals. We propose a modification of code just in the Web switch, leaving the server's operating system untouched.

The remainder of this paper is organized as follows: section 2 presents the adaptive features of the algorithm. Section 3 introduces the throughput predictors used in the algorithm. The statistic used to know the quality of forecast measurements and the forecast control are described in section 4. Experimental results are depicted in section 5. Finally some concluding remarks can be found in section 6.

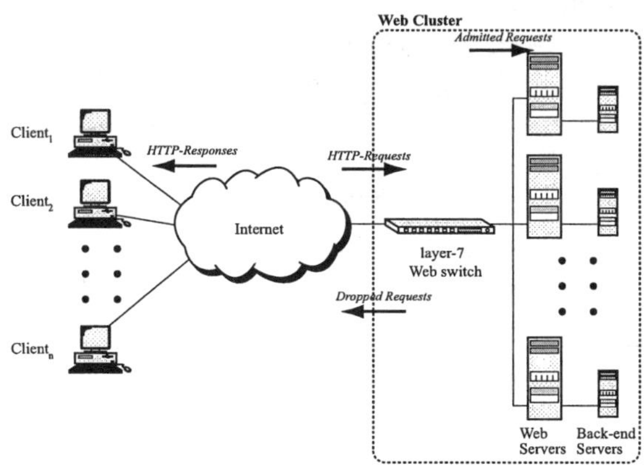

Figure 1. Web cluster architecture

2 Adaptiveness

Our proposal is called *adaptive* because it reacts to several circumstances and modifies the behaviour of the system trying to obtain the best results in terms of performance. One of these adaptive features is related to incoming traffic by using a variable slotted checking time. We also implement some QoS requirements in the dispatching algorithm; therefore adaptiveness refers, in this case, to the allocation of the resources for each type of users. Both are explained in next subsections.

2.1 Burstiness control and variable slotted scheduling time

The mean arrival rate of http transactions for each server *i* during the whole measurement interval is noted as $\overline{\lambda}_i$ For each slot *k* and each server *i*, $\lambda_{k,i}$ is the corresponding arrival rate. If $\lambda_{k,i} > \overline{\lambda}_i$ then the slot is considered as a "bursty" slot. Given *m* slots, *burstiness factor* is defined as the relation between the cumulative number of slots that satisfy $\lambda_{k,i} > \overline{\lambda}_i$, called k_i^+ [9]:

$$b_{k,i} = \frac{k_i^+}{k}, \qquad k = \{1, 2, \ldots, m\} \tag{1}$$

When the algorithm detects traffic transaction peaks (*burstiness*) arriving to the system, it reacts by checking the status of the servers in a shorter period of time than previous one. If no burstiness is detected among the cluster of servers, then the following testing period will be longer than previous. Let's consider the observation time *T*, divided into several slots of variable duration. Therefore the number of slots during running time is also variable and it is calculated at the end of previous slot, e.g., slot *k*, then we define e_{k+1} as the number of slots we propose for the slot *k*+1. At the end of slot *k*, the number of slots that will be considered to obtain the duration of slot *k*+1 is calculated as expression (2), considering maximum and minimum burstiness, $\widehat{b}_k$ and $\breve{b}_k$, respectively, detected in servers in slots *k* and *k*-1 [5]:

$$\begin{aligned}
e_{k+1} &= e_k + \breve{b}_k \cdot e_k && \text{if } \widehat{b}_k - \widehat{b}_{k-1} > 0 \\
e_{k+1} &= e_k - \widehat{b}_k \cdot e_k && \text{if } \begin{cases} \widehat{b}_k - \widehat{b}_{k-1} \le 0 \\ \text{and } \widehat{b}_k \ne 0 \end{cases} \\
e_{k+1} &= e_k / k && \text{if } \widehat{b}_k = \breve{b}_k = 0
\end{aligned} \tag{2}$$

and the duration of the slot *k*+1, named D_{k+1}, is obtained as follows:

$$D_{k+1} = \frac{T}{e_{k+1}} \tag{3}$$

2.2 *Resource allocation based on server's utilization level*

Incoming http requests can be generated by two types of users; we call the *first-class* (*class-1*) users and *second-class* (*class-2*) users. The *service level agreement* (SLA) for *class-1* users is more exigent than the one for *class-2*; hence http requests for the first one should be attended mainly by the best performing servers while *class-2* user's requests have to be served by the rest of the servers. Initially the users have available a fraction of the web server's utilization. This allows servers to process an amount of http requests from both types of users that changes over the time depending on the best and worst server for each type of users' traffic obtained on the basis of throughput forecasting. The selection of the best and worst performing servers is explained later.

The servers are organized in two symbolic *Round Robin* (RR) queues, one for each traffic class. When a server reaches its utilization limit for a traffic class, then it should not receive more https requests of that traffic class until the utilization comes down, so the algorithm removes it from the corresponding RR queue until the next checking time (*computation* phase). When the RR queue of a traffic class is empty, then requests of this class are rejected because all servers have reached their maximum utilization levels permitted to attend that kind of incoming traffic.

We define a constant *weighting index* of class j as c_j, representing the user's relative utilization specifications [5]. For our simulations we have used c_1=0.5 and c_2=0.3, both are normalised in the interval [0, 1] to be comparable to utilization level values. On the basis of this index, we calculate a variable *weighting index,* $c'_{k,i,j}$, in each slot k for each server i and for each traffic class j depending on best and worst performing tactics that consist on maximizing and minimizing a factor $q_{k,i,j}$ that is explained in next section.

$$\left.\begin{aligned} c'_{k+1,i,1} &= c'_{k,i,1} + \alpha \cdot N \cdot c_1 \\ c'_{k+1,i,2} &= c'_{k,i,2} - \alpha \cdot N \cdot c_2 \end{aligned}\right\} \quad \begin{aligned} &\textit{if } \max\{q_{k+1,i,1}\} \textit{or } \min\{q_{k+1,i,2}\}, \\ &\qquad i \in \{1,..,N\} \end{aligned}$$

$$\left.\begin{aligned} c'_{k+1,i,1} &= c'_{k,i,1} - \alpha \cdot N \cdot c_1 \\ c'_{k+1,i,2} &= c'_{k,i,2} + \alpha \cdot N \cdot c_2 \end{aligned}\right\} \quad \begin{aligned} &\textit{if } \max\{q_{k+1,i,2}\} \textit{or } \min\{q_{k+1,i,1}\}, \\ &\qquad i \in \{1,..,N\} \end{aligned} \qquad \textbf{(4)}$$

$$c'_{k+1,i,1} = c'_{k,i,1} \qquad \textit{otherwise}$$

We have introduced a new factor α that is obtained from the number of servers, N divided by a reducing factor, ε.

3 Throughput Predictors

Our previous work [4] compares results obtained by several predictive techniques tested in our algorithm and supports the election of a combination of *Filter Predictor* and *Burst Predictor* as the best option. The main effect of the first predictor is smoothing traffic peaks to hold an accurate performance estimation of the servers in the long run. The role of the second one is to prevent the servers' performance computation degeneration caused by incoming traffic that shows bursty behaviour. A more detailed description of both predictors can be found in [5].

Filter predictor forecasts the throughput that servers will have in the following slot by this expression:

$$\widetilde{X}^{I}{}_{k,i,j} = A_k \cdot \widetilde{X}^{I}{}_{k-1,i,j} + (1 - A_k) \cdot \frac{X_{k,i,j} + X_{k-1,i,j}}{2} \tag{5}$$

Being A_k a probability that balances the weight of the expression in function of the number of slots considered; hence it depends indirectly on burstiness:

$$A_k = \frac{2 \cdot e_k - 1}{2 \cdot e_k + 1} \tag{6}$$

Burst predictor uses a *Locking Indicator* that factorizes the tendency of burstiness during the last two periods with the variation of throughput.

$$\beta_{k,i,j} = \left(b_{k,i} - b_{k-1,i}\right) \cdot \left|X_{k,i,j} - X_{k-1,i,j}\right| \tag{7}$$

Therefore, this indicator is multiplied by the utilization of the server i attending requests of type j, $U_{k-1,i,j}$, to scale the increase or decrease of throughput prediction.

$$\widetilde{X}^{II}{}_{k,i,j} = \widetilde{X}^{II}{}_{k-1,i,j} - \left(\beta_{k,i,j} \cdot U_{k-1,i,j}\right) \tag{8}$$

We compute the *Euclidean distance* from both throughput estimations of server candidates to the origin (0, 0). The selected "best" server for traffic class j is the one that maximizes this distance among the n servers that belong to the set at slot k for traffic class j. The more distance from the origin to the two-dimension estimation point, the faster is the considered web server. The "worst" server minimizes it.

$$q_{k,i,j} = \sqrt{\left(\widetilde{X}^{I}{}_{k,i,j}\right)^2 + \left(\widetilde{X}^{II}{}_{k,i,j}\right)^2} \tag{9}$$

It is important to consider that when a server is dropped from one of the RR queues because it has reached its utilization limit, then it will not receive any request of that type of traffic during the following slot. Thus it is necessary to modify the values of the predictors because the server's throughputs will only depend on the length of the queue of requests that are waiting to be attended, Q_i and the response time of one request (W_i). We introduce t, $0 \le t \le T$ as the current time instant.

$$\widetilde{X}^{I}{}_{k+1,i,j} = \frac{X_{k,i,j} \cdot t + \frac{Q_i}{W_i} \cdot D_{k+1}}{t + D_{k+1}}; \qquad \widetilde{X}^{II}{}_{k+1,i,j} = \frac{X_{k,i,j} \cdot t + \frac{Q_i}{W_i} \cdot D_{k+1}}{t + D_{k+1}} \tag{10}$$

Finally, the resource allocation has to be performed only on active servers, which are included in the *Round Robin* queues. The resource allocation cannot be done when a single server is in a RR queue, because the same server would act as the best and the worst one. Thus, when two or more servers are in the RR queue, the resource allocation is recomputed so throughput predictors for the best and the worst performing servers need to be adjusted again.

We define $\vartheta_{k+1,i,j}$ as the factor that modifies the already calculated throughput predictions of servers:

$$\vartheta_{k+1,i,j} = \frac{\alpha' \cdot c'_{k+1,i,j}}{\sum c'_{k,i,j}} \qquad \textbf{(11)}$$

We rewrite expression (4) including the new values of the predictors:

$$\left.\begin{array}{l} c'_{k+1,i,1} = c'_{k,i,1} + \alpha \cdot N \cdot c_1 \quad ; \quad c'_{k+1,i,2} = c'_{k,i,2} - \alpha \cdot N \cdot c_2 \\ \widetilde{X}^{v}_{k+1,i,1} = \widetilde{X}^{v}_{k+1,i,1} + \vartheta_{k+1.i.1} \cdot \widetilde{X}^{v}_{k+1,i,1}; \\ \widetilde{X}^{v}_{k+1,i,2} = \widetilde{X}^{v}_{k+1,i,2} - \vartheta_{k+1.i.2} \cdot \widetilde{X}^{v}_{k+1,i,2}; \end{array}\right\} \begin{array}{c} \text{if } \max\{q_{k+1,i,1}\} \text{ or } \min\{q_{k+1,i,2}\}, \\ i \subset RR(1), \\ v = \{I, II\} \end{array}$$

$$\left.\begin{array}{l} c'_{k+1,i,1} = c'_{k,i,1} - \alpha \cdot N \cdot c_1 \quad ; \quad c'_{k+1,i,2} = c'_{k,i,2} + \alpha \cdot N \cdot c_2 \\ \widetilde{X}^{v}_{k+1,i,1} = \widetilde{X}^{v}_{k+1,i,1} - \vartheta_{k+1.i.1} \cdot \widetilde{X}^{v}_{k+1,i,1}; \\ \widetilde{X}^{v}_{k+1,i,2} = \widetilde{X}^{v}_{k+1,i,2} + \vartheta_{k+1.i.2} \cdot \widetilde{X}^{v}_{k+1,i,2}; \end{array}\right\} \begin{array}{c} \text{if } \max\{q_{k+1,i,2}\} \text{ or } \min\{q_{k+1,i,1}\}, \\ i \subset RR(2), \\ v = \{I, II\} \end{array} \qquad \textbf{(12)}$$

$$c'_{k+1,i,1} = c'_{k,i,1} \qquad \textit{otherwise}$$

4 Forecast accuracy

4.1 Theil's U statistic

Prediction techniques may be used to guarantee the accuracy of the particular forecasting method for a given data set. This means how well the forecasting model is able to reproduce the data that are already known, in our case we are interested in the *future* forecast.

We are going to base our forecast accuracy measurement on Theil's U statistic [8] because it is almost immediate to obtain, which is shown in equation (13). We rename U to Z to avoid confusion with utilization metrics. This statistic allows a relative comparison of formal forecasting methods with naïve approaches that consists on using the most recent observation available as a forecast.

$$Z = \sqrt{\frac{\sum_{t=1}^{n-1} (FPE_{t+1} - APE_{t+1})^2}{\sum_{t=1}^{n-1} (APE_{t+1})^2}} \qquad \textbf{(13)}$$

$$FPE_{t+1} = \frac{F_{t+1} - Y_t}{Y_t}; \quad APE_{t+1} = \frac{Y_{t+1} - Y_t}{Y_t},$$

Where FPE_{t+1} is the forecast relative change and APE_{t+1} is the actual relative change. F_t is the forecasting value for time t and Y_t is the observed value for time t.

The most interesting feature of this statistic is that it has an intuitive interpretation. If the resulting value of Z is lower than 1, it means that the forecasting technique used is better than the naïve method, but if Z=1 it means that the naïve method is, at least, as good as the forecasting technique being evaluated and, if Z>1, the forecasting technique employed is useless, the naïve method would produce better results.

4.2 *Forecast Control in the algorithm*

In order to test the quality of the forecasting, we are going to make our algorithm self-detecting when a prediction is not good enough in one slot and to correct it on the following slot. The quality of the forecasting based on Theil's U-statistic at the end of slot k depends on the condition of the if sentence. If the condition is TRUE, then the corresponding prediction is worst than taking the previous observation value of throughput, so it has to be corrected in slot k+1. Obviously, in this case, a bad prediction was already done and could have caused a mistaken decision in the best and worst performing servers. We are going to control also all the wrong decisions our algorithm takes to know the accuracy of it. The correction of the prediction consists on an alteration of the prediction for slot k+1.

In the case of a bad prediction detected the *Filter Predictor*:

if $\widetilde{X}^{I}_{k,i,j} - X_{k,i,j} > X_{k,i,j} - X_{k-1,i,j}$

then
$$\widetilde{X}^{I}_{k+1,i,j} = P_e \cdot \widetilde{X}^{I}_{k,i,j} + (1 - P_e) \cdot \frac{X_{k,i,j} + X_{k-1,i,j}}{2} \quad \textbf{(14)}$$

And in the case of the *Burst Predictor*:

if $\widetilde{X}^{II}_{k,i,j} - X_{k,i,j} > X_{k,i,j} - X_{k-1,i,j}$

then
$$\widetilde{X}^{II}_{k+1,i,j} = P_e \cdot \widetilde{X}^{II}_{k,i,j} + (1 - P_e) \cdot X_{k,i,j} \quad \textbf{(15)}$$

In both cases the value of $P_e = 0.1$, so only a residual fraction of previous wrong prediction is carried in the historical of the forecasting, while the main part of the prediction, i.e. 90%, depends on the throughputs of the Web servers.

Figure 2 represents a complete flow chart of the *Computation* phase.

5 Experimental results

The workload and testbed used to stress the Web cluster system in the experiments are described in [5]. A simulation model of complete web cluster system has been constructed using QNAP2 [10]. We have run simulations starting from an arrival rate that makes servers reach 5% of its utilization level until an arrival rate that supposedly stresses servers to 125% of its utilization level (obviously rejection of requests take place). We compare the results obtained with this work to previous ones achieved with the algorithm **APRA1** (Adaptive-Predictive with Resource Allocation v.1) that we have already contrasted to other schemes and showed the best behaviour in [4] and that is described in detail in [5]. The algorithm developed in this paper is called **APRA2.**

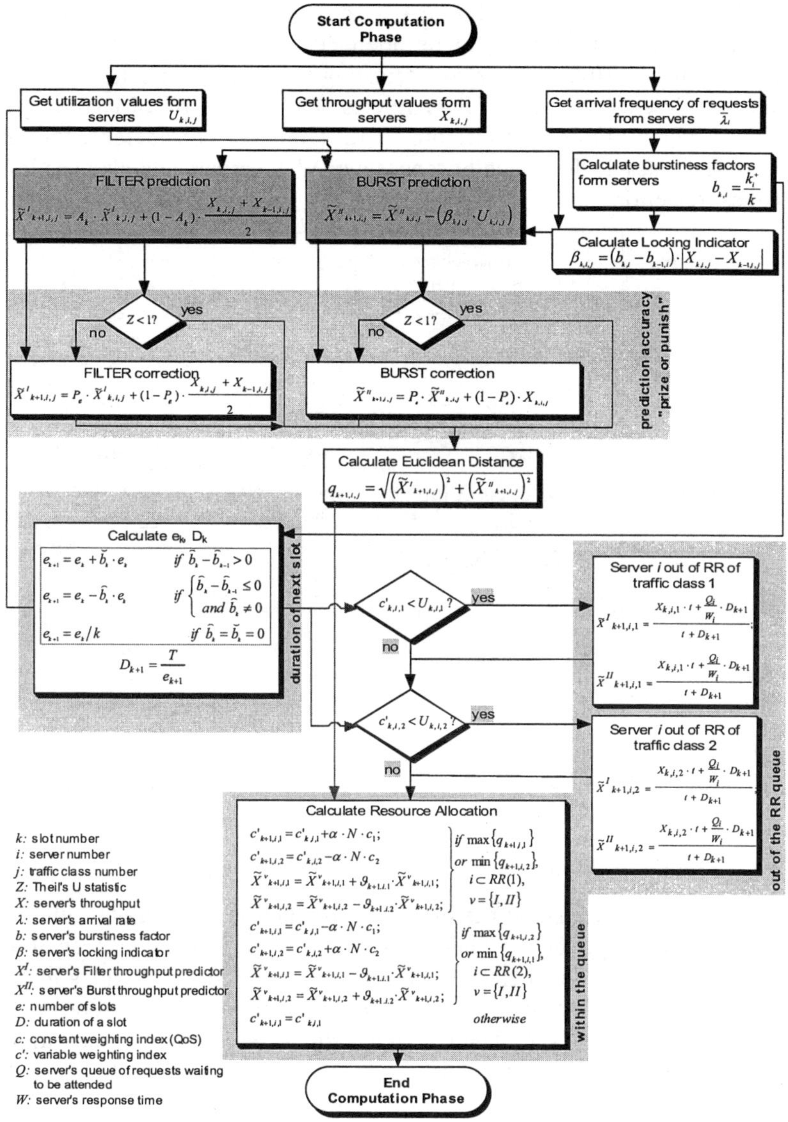

Figure 2. Computation Phase of APRA2

Let's compare the response time of our system form/to the Web switch obtained by both algorithms that is shown in figure 3. Class-1 traffic latency time in APRA2 is significantly lower than in APRA1 when the system begins to be congested

(70%...125% in X axis). In figure 4 we can observe that APRA2 has a lower queue of class-1 requests waiting to be attended while serves little bit less number of requests than APRA1. It is also interesting to compare rejections that are produced only for class-2 requests. APRA1 rejects near to 20% of all incoming requests and APRA2 rejects 11.86%. Therefore APRA1 reduces considerably the response time for traffic class-1, the queue of requests in Web servers and also has less number of request rejections.

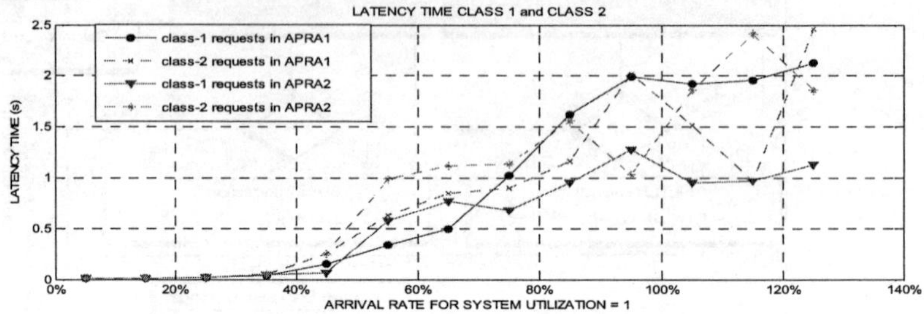

Fig. 3. Class-1 and class-2 latency times in APRA1 and APRA2

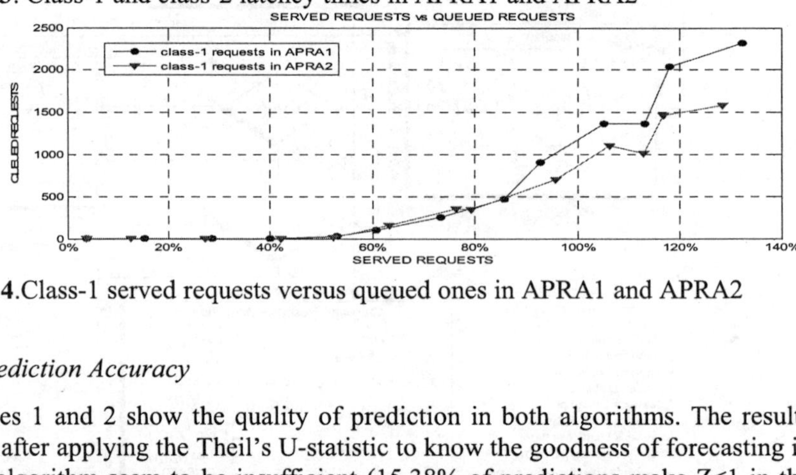

Fig. 4.Class-1 served requests versus queued ones in APRA1 and APRA2

5.1 Prediction Accuracy

Tables 1 and 2 show the quality of prediction in both algorithms. The results obtained after applying the Theil's U-statistic to know the goodness of forecasting in APRA1 algorithm seem to be insufficient (15.38% of predictions make Z<1 in the case of *Filter prediction* and in the case of *Burst Prediction* it does not reach 8%.). In the case of APRA2, Theil's U-statistic shows an important improvement in contrast to the previous one. These results are shown in table 1.

APRA2 performs better forecast when the utilization level of the system is greater than 75% that means the system is servicing a high demand of http requests. The percentage of times where predictions are revised as explained in section 5.2 and "punished" is shown in table 2.

It is also necessary to know the number of times the APRA2 algorithm has chosen a wrong "best" or "worst" server. Table 3 shows that in a total number of 148 slots (that is 296 selections), 26.35% of "best" or "worst" server choices where wrong for priority traffic class due to a failure in prediction that was corrected in the following computation phase and less than 22% for non-priority traffic class during the complete experiment. In contrast, focusing on the simulations where the servers were more stressed (second column of table 3, the percentages of mistakes decrease to 16.6% and 14.4% for each traffic class. So, if we reduce the interval of the experiment from an arrival frequency that makes the system reach 75% of its utilization level, until 125% (obviously the system rejects requests) then we can observe that the number of mistakes decrease. Therefore it is evident that algorithm APRA2 works better when the Web system begins to be congested.

Table 1. Theil's U-statistic for APRA1 and APRA2

Z<1	APRA1 (UT ≥ 75%)	APRA2 (UT ≥ 75%)
Filter Prediction	34.72 %	76.38 %
Burst Prediction	25 %	79.16 %

Table 2. Forecast Control in APRA2

Corrections in prediction	5% ≤ UT ≤ 125%	UT ≥ 75%
Filter Prediction	47.97 %	39.52 %
Burst Prediction	36.82 %	29.29 %

Table 3. Number of mistakes in the election of "best" or "worst" server

Number of mistakes	5% ≤ UT ≤ 125%	UT ≥ 75%
Traffic Class 1	78	22
Traffic Class 2	65	19
Number of slots	148	66

6 Conclusions

The main contribution of this paper is the evidence that a good prediction provides a better response in a Web system. Therefore it is necessary to control the accuracy of this prediction. The comparison among two dispatching algorithms for a Web switch, one just predicting and the other with self-correcting prediction, reveal that a *reward* scheme to control the accuracy of the predictions on real time is quite useful in an adaptive system. We have developed an algorithm that rectifies its behaviour on the basis of the error of previous predictions. Furthermore our algorithm reacts to bursty arrivals of incoming traffic by using a variable slotted checking time and also guarantees QoS requirements by adaptive resource allocation for each type of users based on the combination of two throughput estimators that forecast the system behaviour for the near future. Results obtained show that the accuracy on the prediction is absolutely necessary to ensure good performance of the system.

References

1. Aron, M., Differentiated and Predictable Quality of Service in Web Server Systems. PhD thesis, Rice University (2000).
2. Balasubramanian, J., Schmidt, D.C., Dowdy, L., Othman, O. Evaluating the Performance of Middleware Load Balancing Strategies, Enterprise Distributed Object Computing Conference, Eighth IEEE International (2004) pp. 135-146
3. Cao, J., Andersson, M., Nyberg, C., Kihl, M. Web Server Performance Modeling Using an M/G/1/K*PS Queue, 10th International Conference on Telecommunications, Papeete, vol 2 (2003) pp. 1501- 1506.
4. Gilly, K., Alcaraz, S., Juiz, C., Puigjaner, R. Comparison of Predictive Techniques in Cluster-Based Network Servers with Resource Allocation, The IEEE Computer Society's 12th Annual International Symposium on Modeling, Analysis, and Simulation of Computer and Telecommunications Systems (2004) pp. 545-552
5. Gilly, K., Juiz, C., Alcaraz, S., Puigjaner, R. Performance Analysis of a Predictive and Adaptive Algorithm in Cluster-Based Network Servers with Resource Allocation, 19th International Symposium on Computer and Information Sciences (2004) pp. 615-626.
6. Li, C., Peng, G., Golapan, K. and Chiueh, T.-C. Performance guarantees for cluster-based internet services, 9th International Conference on Parallel and Distributed Systems (2002) pp. 276-283.
7. Lu, Y., Abdelzaher, T., Lu, Ch., Sha, L. and Liu, X. Feedback Control with Queueing-Theoretic Prediction for Relative Delay, Real-Time and Embedded Technology and Applications Symposium (2003) pp. 208–217.
8. Makridakis, S., Wheelwright, S.C., Hyndman, R.J. Forecasting Methods and Applications. (John Wiley and Sons, Inc., 1998).
9. Menascé, D.A. & Almeida, V.A.F. Scaling for E-Business. (Prentice Hall, 2000).
10. Simulog Corp. The QNAP Reference Manual. V.4.
11. Vilalta, R., Apte, C. V., Hellerstein, J. L., Ma, S., Weiss, S. M. Predictive algorithms in the management of computer systems. IBM System Journal, **41**, no.3 (2002). Pp. 461-474.
12. Zhang, A., Santos, P., Beyer, D., Tang, H.K. Optimal Server Resource Allocation Using an Open Queueing Network Model of Response Time. HP Laboratories Palo Alto. HPL-2002-301 (2002).

A FUZZY-BASED VERTICAL HANDOFF SCHEME FOR INTERWORKING BETWEEN WLAN AND GSM

FATMA TANSU, MUHAMMED SALAMAH

Computer Engineering Department, Eastern Mediterranean University, Magusa, T.R.N.C, Mersin 10, Turkey

E-mail : fatma.tansu,muhammed.salamah@emu.edu.tr

The next generation wireless network environments are expected to support anywhere, anytime connectivity for high-performance applications like multimedia, full-motion video and high data rates with appropriate quality of service (QoS). To provide a solution to these demanding needs, service providers intend to combine different technologies in heterogeneous networks. In this study, we propose a fuzzy-based vertical handoff scheme for interworking between WLAN and GSM. We concentrated on crucial features like user preference, network conditions, speed, RSS and support of different service types. After extensive simulation, the results show that the proposed handoff scheme maintains a stable utilization against mobility under a specific load. Moreover, the proposed scheme provides good results for the call blocking and dropping probabilities, Grade of Service (GoS), and throughput.

1. Introduction

The next generation wireless network environments will support anywhere, anytime connectivity for high-performance applications like multimedia, full-motion video and high data rates with appropriate quality of service (QoS). At the turn of 21st century, second and third generation (2G and 3G) cellular wireless networks were successfully employed by the wireless access providers. Today, wireless data services are becoming popular, but no one technology or service can provide ubiquitous coverage with all of the desired metrics like delay, latency and cost being satisfied. To provide a solution to these demanding needs, service providers intend to combine different technologies, such as Bluetooth, IEEE 802.11 WLAN, GPRS and 3G services in heterogeneous(overlay) networks. To extend the capabilities of the 3G networks and to efficiently interoperate different wireless technologies in heterogeneous networks, research activities toward the next generation wireless networks have already started.[1,2]

Heterogeneous wireless networks have overlapping coverage areas including pico-cell, micro-cell, macro-cell and global cell in a hierarchical manner, where higher levels in the hierarchy provide lower bandwidths and higher delays over larger coverage areas. Handoff is a process of transferring a mobile station's (MS) point of attachment between cells of the same or different networks while maintaining its active connection. In cellular networks, such point of attachments is referred to as base station (BS), and in WLANs it is called access point (AP).[3]The movement of a user among different types of networks is referred to as inter-system or vertical mobility. In homogeneous networks, a handoff decision is mainly based on received signal strength (RSS) at the MS. However, in heterogeneous networks, to make an efficient vertical handoff decision other factors like service type, monetary cost, user preferences, mobile node and network conditions should be taken into account.[4]

In this paper we address the vertical handoff for interworking between WLAN and GSM. We propose a vertical handoff scheme in which the decision mechanism is based on fuzzy-logic. Related work on vertical handoff has been presented in recent research literature. In Ref. 3 RSS, speed and number of users were taken into account in the vertical handoff decision. However, in our scheme, the effect of service type, and network conditions are taken into account in addition to RSS, speed and number of users.

The rest of this paper is organized as follows: In section 2, we present our system model with possible vertical handoff scenarios. The proposed fuzzy-based vertical handoff scheme is described in section 3. The simulation model together with system parameters and performance metrics are given in section 4. In section 5, we present and explain our results. Finally, section 6 summarizes the paper and identifies areas for future research.

2. System Model

Several interworking approaches between WLAN and cellular networks have been proposed in the literature.[1–3,5] In our interworking architecture, we considered the two popular wireless networks, namely WLAN and GSM networks. Figure 1 shows the considered interworking architecture which consists of three WLAN cells and a GSM cell.

It is assumed that BS and APs are inter-connected through a heterogeneous cross over switch in which the proposed handoff scheme operates. The cross over switch decides to handoff a user from one network to another and it is also responsible for directing packets to the new point of

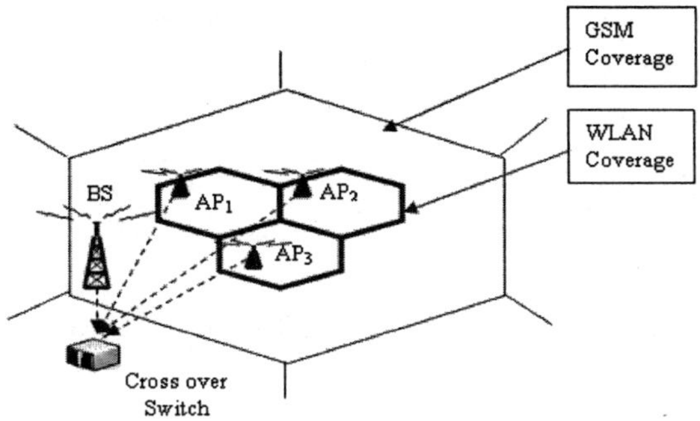

Figure 1. System Architecture.

attachment accordingly.[6] The interworking between WLAN and GSM network is based on the features of mobile IP which affects the maintenance of the mobile users' active connectivity.[1] In the rest of our paper, the term WLAN refers to IEEE 802.11b standard. A typical WLAN provides 2 Mbps bandwidth per non-overlapping channel with a small coverage area and the GSM network which covers WLAN provides variable bandwidth (e.g.384 kbps) with a larger coverage area.[7]

We assumed that the arrival traffic at the BS or an AP is either voice or data type. Taking into account that WLAN is mostly data-oriented and GSM is mostly voice-oriented, in our scheme, vertical handoff from WLAN to GSM occurs under the following conditions:(1) The MS physically moves out of the coverage of the WLAN, (2) The number of active calls in a WLAN cell reaches a level defined as Max_u at which a handoff call from other WLAN cells cannot be accommodated. On the other hand, vertical handoff from GSM to WLAN occurs when a data call enters the coverage area of a WLAN cell in which the number of active calls is less than Max_u.

3. The Proposed Fuzzy-Based Vertical Handoff Scheme

In this section, the proposed fuzzy-based vertical handoff scheme for heterogeneous network is presented. The proposed scheme for the interworking architecture given in Section 2, is based on different service types(i.e. voice, data), user preferences, speed of the user, network conditions(number of active users) and RSS. For example, fast users should remain connected to GSM and be prevented from connecting to WLAN since WLAN is designed for low velocity users and has small coverage area. Moreover, a user may prefer to connect to WLAN to send large data files or may choose GSM network to carry on a voice call. The block diagram of the proposed scheme is shown in Figure 2.

Figure 2. Block Diagram of The Proposed Scheme

When a user changes its location, *Handoff Initiation Mechanism* is started to check if handoff is needed or not by measuring the RSS of the MS. Then, the *Fuzzy Logic System* is initiated with the input metrics: speed, number of users, and RSS_{hyst},where RSS_{hyst} is a threshold to avoid unnecessary handoffs.[3] When the *Fuzzy Logic System* finishes its evaluation, it outputs **cell selection** value ranging from 1 to 10 which is used to encourage or discourage handoffs to the GSM network or a WLAN cell. Then, *Handoff Decision Mechanism* is initiated with the selected cell from *fuzzy logic system* and **service type** of the call.

There are three types of calls that can be served in WLAN: new data calls, new voice calls and handoff data calls. Taking into account WLAN's data-oriented nature and its high data rate, we allowed only data calls to make handoff from the GSM cell to a WLAN cell. The steps of the proposed algorithm for newly generated calls in a WLAN cell are as follows:

Step 1. If the newly generated call is data and the number of active calls in the current WLAN cell is above Max_u, then the call is blocked.

Step 2. If the newly generated call is voice and the number of active calls in the current WLAN cell is above Max_u, then the call is directed to the GSM cell and treated as a new voice call. We directed such voice calls to the GSM cell since GSM is a voice-oriented network.

In GSM, there are four types of calls that can be served: new data calls, new voice calls, handoff data calls and handoff voice calls. All traffic types can handoff to the GSM cell as the WLAN cells are always under the coverage area of the GSM cell. In the proposed scheme the newly (voice/data) will be blocked, if the GSM cell has no free channels.

The handoff algorithm for the calls that are currently residing in WLAN initiates handoff decision process when the user moves in the WLAN. At the beginning, the strength of the received signal at the current location (RSS_c) is measured. Then, RSS_c is compared with thresholds RSS_{tho} and RSS_{th_edge}, accordingly. As shown in Figure 3, RSS_{tho} is the threshold value of the received signal strength where a user can handoff to one of its neighbor cells because of RSS_c degradation, whereas RSS_{th_edge} is the threshold value of received signal strength at the edge of the cell.

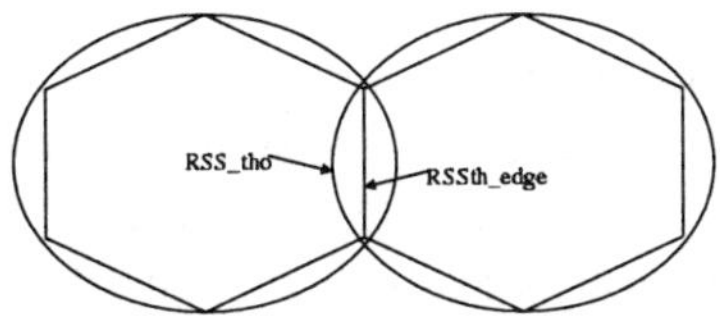

Figure 3. RSS Thresholds

The steps of the handoff algorithm from a WLAN cell to another WLAN cell or to the GSM cell are as follows:

Step 1. If call type is voice and if $RSS_c \leq RSS_{tho}$ and $RSS_c \leq RSS_{th\_edge}$, then the call may handoff to another WLAN/GSM cell or it may be dropped according to the output of WLAN-to-WLAN fuzzifier.

Step 2. If call type is data and if $RSS_c \leq RSS_{tho}$ and $RSS_c \leq RSS_{th\_edge}$, then the call may handoff to another WLAN cell or it may be dropped according to the output of WLAN-to-WLAN fuzzifier.

Note that, if the decision is **drop** the call, then the fuzzifier output is *High* with a value 6–10 according to the input parameters of *fuzzy logic system*. This value indicates that the algorithm discourages the call to make handoff. However, if the decision is **handoff** to another WLAN cell, then the fuzzifier output is *Low* with a value 1–5. These values indicate that the algorithm encourages the call to make handoff.

Step 3. If $RSS_c \leq RSS_{tho}$ and $RSS_c > RSS_{th\_edge}$, then the call may **handoff** to another WLAN cell or stay in its current cell according to the output of WLAN-to-WLAN fuzzifier.

Note that, if the decision is **handoff** to another WLAN cell, then the fuzzifier output is *Low* with a value 1–5. These values indicate that the algorithm encourages the call to make handoff.

However, if the decision is to **stay** in its current cell, then the fuzzifier output is *Low* with a value 5–6. These values indicate that the algorithm encourages the call to do nothing by staying in its current cell.

The handoff algorithm for the data calls that are currently residing in GSM initiates the handoff decision process when a user moves in GSM. Recall that we are allowing only the data calls to make handoff from GSM to WLAN cells. The steps of the handoff algorithm from the GSM cell to a WLAN cell are as follows:

Step 1. The location of the user is checked to examine if it is under the coverage area of one of the WLAN cells.

Step 2. If the user enters the coverage of a WLAN cell, the RSS of the AP of the entered WLAN cell is compared with RSS_{th_edge}. If $RSS_{AP} \leq RSS_{th\_edge}$ then a handoff occurs according to the output of GSM-to - WLAN fuzzifier. Note that, if the decision is **handoff** to a WLAN cell, then the fuzzifier output is *Low* with a value 1–5. These values indicate that the algorithm encourages the call to make handoff to a WLAN cell. Otherwise, no handoff occurs and the algorithm encourages the call to do nothing by staying in the GSM cell.

The membership functions (MFs) of WLAN-to-WLAN and GSM-to-WLAN fuzzifiers are shown in Figure 4. The rules of WLAN-to-WLAN and GSM-to-WLAN fuzzifiers are shown in Table 1.

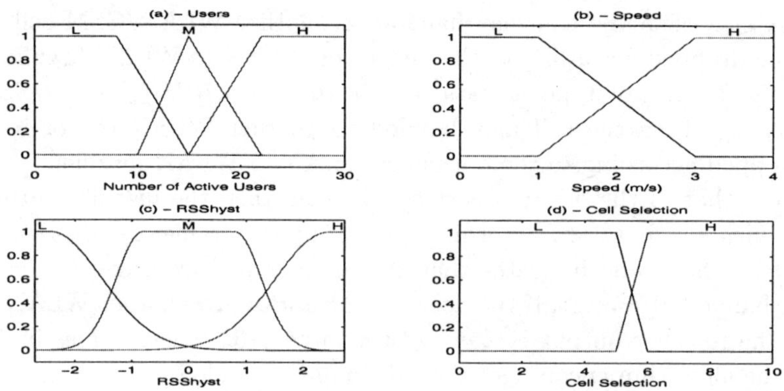

Figure 4. Membership Functions for Fuzzy Variables

4. Performance Evaluation

We evaluated the performance of the vertical handoff strategy for the interworking architecture through extensive simulation using Matlab. The simulated heterogeneous network consists of three WLAN cells and a GSM cell as in Figure 1. The channel propagation model used for received signal strength (RSS) at distance **d** is given by:[8]

$$RSS(d)[dBm] = Pt[dBm] - (PL(d0) + 10nlog(d/d0) + X_{\sigma})[dB] \quad (1)$$

Table 1. The Fuzzy Rules of WLAN-to-WLAN and GSM-to-WLAN Handoff Algorithm

Rule	Active Users	Speed	RSS_{hys}	Cell Selection Data Stay	Cell Selection Data Drop	Cell Selection Voice Stay	Cell Selection Voice Drop
1	Low	Low	Low	Low	Low	Low	Low
2	Low	High	Low	Low	Low	High	High
3	Medium	Low	Low	High	High	Low	Low
4	Medium	High	Low	High	High	High	High
5	High	Low	Low	High	High	High	High
6	High	High	Low	High	High	High	High
7	Low	Low	Medium	Low	Low	Low	Low
8	Low	High	Medium	Low	Low	Low	Low
9	Medium	Low	Medium	Low	Low	Low	Low
10	Medium	High	Medium	Low	Low	High	Low
11	High	Low	Medium	High	Low	High	Low
12	High	High	Medium	High	Low	High	High
13	Low	Low	High	Low	Low	Low	Low
14	Low	High	High	Low	Low	Low	Low
15	Medium	Low	High	Low	Low	Low	Low
16	Medium	High	High	Low	Low	Low	Low
17	High	Low	High	Low	Low	High	High
18	High	High	High	Low	Low	High	High

Rule	Active Users	Speed	Cell Selection
1	Low	Low	Low
2	Low	High	Low
3	Medium	Low	Low
4	Medium	High	High
5	High	Low	High
6	High	High	High

where Pt is the transmitted power and PL(d0) is the path loss at a distance **d0** and distributed log-normally (in dB),n is the path loss exponent, *d0* is the close-inference distance, d is the transmitter–receiver separation distance and Xσ is zero-mean Gaussian distributed random variable (in dB) with standard deviation σ (also in dB) modeling shadow fading, where σ depends on the environment and has values between 6–12.[3] Call generations in WLAN follows Poisson processes with average arrival rates λ_{W_nv} and λ_{W_nd}, for new voice and new data calls, respectively. Similarly, call generations in GSM also follows Poisson processes with average arrival rates λ_{G_nv} and λ_{G_nd} for new voice and new data respectively. The call duration follow an exponential distribution with mean T=180 sec. The system load can be defined as

$$\rho = (\lambda_{W\_nv} + \lambda_{W\_nd} + \lambda_{G\_nv} + \lambda_{G\_nd}) \times T \tag{2}$$

Note that the mean inter-movement time (M) of a user, which defines the time difference between two consecutive movements of a user, is exponentially distributed, so that, the handoff from one network to another occurs at random intervals. Therefore, the mobility mobility can be defined as:

$$\alpha = (T - M)/M \tag{3}$$

The simulation parameters are listed in Table 2. The most important performance evaluation parameters of wireless networks are new call blocking probability (P_n), handoff dropping probability (P_h), utilization and throughput. The design goals of handoff schemes should also include minimizing the Grade of Service (GoS) cost function. Although sophisticated

Table 2. Simulation Parameters

Radius of each WLAN and GSM cell	100m and 1km
Transmitted power of APs and BS	100mWatt and 1Watt
Path loss exponent n	2
σ	6.5
Number of non-overlapping channel (i.e. no. of WLAN cells)	3
Data rate of WLAN per non-overlapping channel	2 Mbps
Total WLAN capacity	6 Mbps
Data rate of GSM	384 kbps
Probability of data/voice call generations	0.3λ/0.7λ
Load	10/20/30/40/50/60 (Erlang)
Mobility	0.5/1.5/2.5
Mean call duration (T) for data and voice	180 (exp. distribution)
Mean inter-movement time (M)	50 – 120 (exp. distribution)
Speed	1-6 (m/s)
Max. number of active users in WLAN (Max_u)	25

cost functions have been proposed, in practice, a simple weighted average is useful for most design purposes. The penalty k is used to reflect the effect of the handoff dropping over the new call blocking in the GoS cost function. A penalty of 5 to 20 times is commonly recommended.[9] The GoS cost function can be defined as

$$GoS = P_n + k \times P_h \tag{4}$$

5. Results

The performance of the proposed algorithm is measured through simulation and the following results were obtained.

Fig 5.a shows the new call blocking probability P_n, against load for different mobility values. As expected P_n increases with load. The small effect of mobility increase on degrading P_n appears only at high loads. This is due to the increase in the number of allocated handoff calls at high mobility.

Fig 5.b shows the handoff dropping probability P_h versus different mobility values. Since we are not applying any priority between new and handoff calls, it can be seen that the trends of blocking and dropping probabilities are almost the same. However, we can observe that the dropping probability is more vulnerable to changes in mobility. this is because more number of handoff calls compete for resources at high mobility.

Fig 5.c shows the GoS against mobility under different load conditions. Except at high loads (50 - 60 Erlang), the proposed algorithm shows almost stable GoS under different mobility values. This is because of the increase in the P_n and P_h values at these high loads.

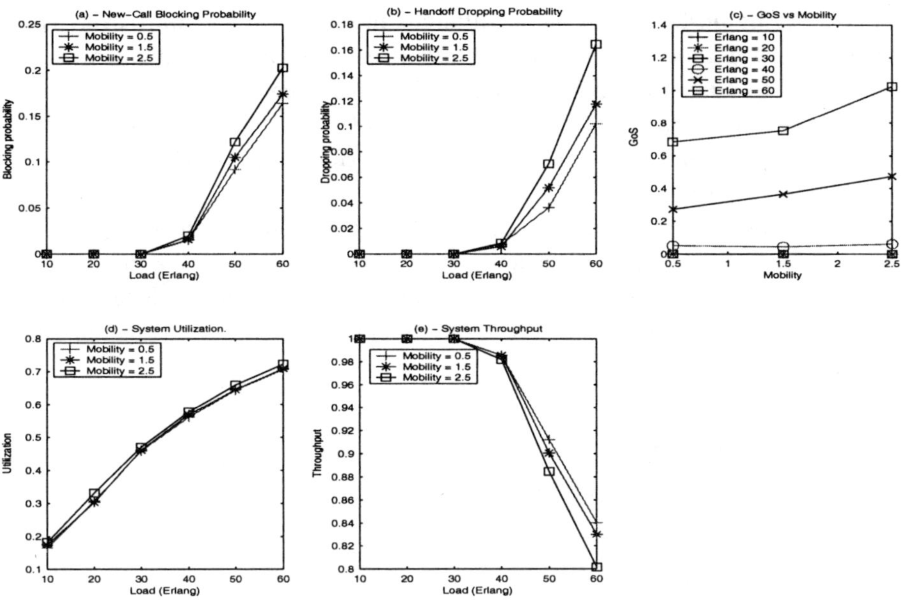

Figure 5. Simulation Results

Fig 5.d shows the system utilization versus load for different mobility values. As expected, utilization increases as load increases. It is clear that changing the mobility also does not affect the utilization. This shows the stability of the proposed vertical handoff scheme against mobility.

Finally, Fig 5.e shows the overall system throughput for different mobility values. Throughput refers to the actual data rate over the requested rate. It is clear that, for load values less than 40 Erlang, the system throughput is high and stable. However, for high loads the throughput degrades down to 0.8, which is due to the corresponding increase in P_n and P_h.

6. Conclusion

In this paper, we proposed an efficient vertical handoff scheme to improve the performance of an integrated WLAN-GSM network. The proposed scheme is based on fuzzy-logic that adapts handoff decisions dynamically taking into consideration crucial features like user preference, network conditions, speed, RSS and different service types. Generally, the performance of the proposed schemes in the literature degrades as mobility increases.[10] Our proposed scheme shows an interesting result through maintaining an almost stable performance under different mobility values. Moreover, the results show a good performance behavior of the proposed scheme and its capability to adapt to different mobility and load scenarios.

In this study, we treated new and handoff calls equally. As a future work, we are planning to investigate the performance of the system by applying a priority mechanism that favors handoff calls. Different priority levels may be applied for different service types as well. Moreover, applying such a fuzzy-based handoff scheme for interworking between more than two overlay networks is noteworthy. Finally, studying the performance of the proposed scheme can be investigated using other distributions for call generations, arrival rates and mobility rates.

Acknowledgments

The authors would like to thank Tamer Tulgar for his valuable support.

References

1. McNair, J., Zhu, F.: Vertical handoff in fourth-generation multinetwork environments. Wireless Comm. **11** (2004) 8–15
2. Salkintzis, A.: Interworking between wlans and third-generation cellular data networks. In: The 57th IEEE Semiannual Vehicular Technology Conf. (2003) 1802–1806
3. Majlesi, A., Khalaj, B.: An adaptive fuzzy logic based handoff algorithm for interworking between wlans and mobile networks. In: The 13th IEEE Int. Symp. on Personal, Indoor and Mobile Radio Comm. (2002) 2446–2451
4. Zhu, F., McNair, J.: Optimizations for vertical handoff decision algorithms. In: IEEE Wireless Comm. and Networking Conf. (2004) 867–872
5. Salamah, M., F.Tansu: On the vertical handoff performance for interworking between wlan and gsm. In: The 9th CDMA Inter. Conf. (2004) 414–418
6. Wang, S.H., Kong, P.Y.: A novel vertical handover schemefor integrated wlan and cellular wireless networks. In: The 9th Int. Conf. on Comm. Systems. (2004) 526–530
7. et al., M.Y.: Optimization scheme for mobile users performing vertical handoffs between ieee 802.11 and gprs/edge networks. In: IEEE Global Telecomm. Conf. (2001) 3439–3443
8. Rappaport, T.S.: Wireless Communications: Principles and Practice. Prentice Hall Inc. (2002)
9. Barcel, F.: Performance analysis of handoff resource allocation strategies through the state-dependent rejection scheme. IEEE Trans. on Wireless Comm. **3** (2004) 900–909
10. et.al, Y.C.K.: Dynamic channel reservation based on mobility in wireless atm networks. IEEE Comm. Magazine **37** (1999) 47–51

PERFORMANCE ANALYSIS OF RELIABLE MULTICAST PROTOCOLS

COŞKUN ÇELİK
Gazi University, 06570, Ankara, TURKEY, ccelik@gazi.edu.tr

CÜNEYT F. BAZLAMAÇCI
Middle East Technical University, 06531, Ankara, TURKEY, cuneytb@metu.edu.tr

Reliability issue of multicasting contains the challenges for detection and recovery of packet losses and ordered delivery of the entire data. In this work, existing reliable multicast protocols are classified into three main groups, namely tree based, NACK-only and router assisted, and a representative protocol for each group is selected to demonstrate the advantages and disadvantages of the corresponding approaches. The selected protocols are SRM, PGM and RMTP. Performance characteristics of these protocols are empirically evaluated by using simulation results. A public Network Simulator-2 (NS-2) implementation of RMTP was also performed as part of this study and the protocols were evaluated by investigating performance metrics of distribution delay, recovery latency and request overhead with respect to varying multicast group size and link loss rate.

1 Introduction

IP multicasting is a method for transmitting the same data packets to multiple receivers. It minimizes the bandwidth consumption since only a single copy of a multicast packet flows over each link and intermediate routers. Responsibility of group management is on the receiver side, instead of the sender, since it is difficult for a sender to maintain the size and membership state of a growing and frequently changing group. Since feedbacking of all control information from receivers to a single sender causes a burst of traffic towards the sender, a TCP-based end-to-end control mechanism is not applicable for IP multicasting. Therefore a specialized transport layer protocol should be implemented to deal with the challenges of the end-to-end reliability, congestion, flow control and scalability problems. These specialized transport layer protocols are called as Reliable Multicast Protocols.

In the literature, there exist some proposals for reliable multicast protocols. In this study we investigate these different classifications and select one of them for our comparative study. One representative protocol for each group of the selected classification is chosen and simulations for different test cases are carried out using these protocols, namely SRM, PGM and RMTP. Previous implementations for SRM and PGM exist in NS-2 but not for RMTP. In the first stage of the work, RMTP is implemented for NS-2.

In our simulation study, three performance metrics are defined for comparing the representative protocols. These performance metrics are distribution delay, recovery latency and request overhead on routers or links. Test cases are generated by varying the number of multicast group members in the network and the average loss rate of the links.

The remainder of this paper is organized as follows; the next section introduces Reliable Multicast concepts and presents a classification for reliable multicast protocols. Chapter 3 presents the details of our simulation study, including network and application model, experiment design and results of simulations. Finally, Chapter 4 concludes the paper.

2 Reliable Multicast Protocols

2.1 Introduction to Reliable Multicast

The basic definition of Multicast Reliability is stated as delivering all data units to all receivers in a multicast group. But this concept can further be classified into three subgroups, namely total reliability, semi-reliability and time-bounded reliability. Total reliability guarantees error-free delivery of all data to all receivers. File transfer applications are examples for applications requiring total reliability [1]. Semi-reliability supports retransmission of lost packet or some error correction codings but does not guarantee totally error-free delivery of data. It is used by loss-tolerant real-time applications [2]. Time-bounded reliability is also used by real-time applications but with strict jitter requirements. It states that the retransmission of a lost packet is only performed for up to a certain time [3]. The present work focuses on total reliability only.

2.2 Classification of Reliable Multicast Protocols

There are various reliable multicast protocol classifications in the literature. Some of them group the protocols according to the application requirement, while some others use the way that the protocol recovers packet losses or whether it uses router assistance [4 - 7].

In this study, we used a newer classification which adds router-assistance and forward error correction methods to the taxonomy [3, 8]. According to this, reliable multicast protocols are divided into four groups; NACK-only protocols, Tree-based ACK (TRACK) protocols, Router assisted protocols and Open Loop protocols, as shown in Figure 1. NACK-only protocols attempt to limit the traffic by only using NACKs for requesting packet retransmission. They do not require any help from the network infrastructure. TRACK protocols use ACKs. In order to avoid ACK implosion, ACKs are suppressed in a tree shaped infrastructure. Router assisted protocols also use negative acknowledgments for packet recovery. These protocols take advantage of using routers in order to constrain negative acknowledgments and retransmissions. Open loop protocols use sender-based Forward Error Correction (FEC) methods with no feedback from receivers or the network to ensure good throughput.

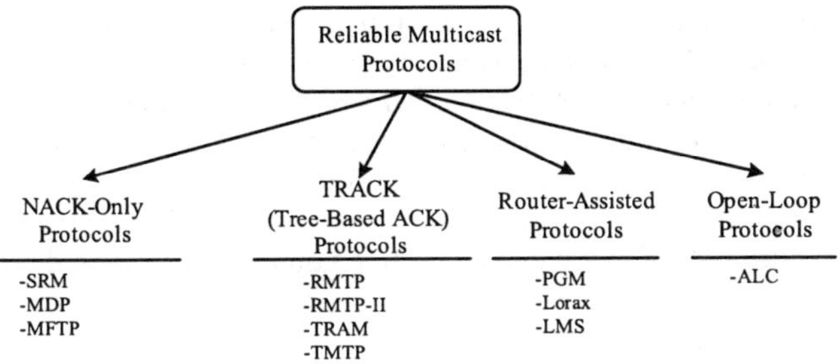

Fig. 1. Classification of Reliable Multicast Protocols

2.3 Related Work

In this section, the protocols that are selected for our simulation study, namely RMTP, SRM and PGM are explained briefly.

Reliable Multicast Transport Protocol (RMTP): The Reliable Multicast Transport Protocol (RMTP) [9] is a one-to-many, tree based positive acknowledgement protocol. It uses IP multicast to forward the multicast packets down on a delivery tree to all group members and provides reliability by using selective retransmission of lost packets. To avoid ACK implosion problem, the protocol divides the whole multicast into local regions. Each local region has a Designated Receiver (DR), which is a special receiver that assists the sender in processing ACKs and retransmitting data packets. Periodic ACK packets are unicasted to the local DR and a DR sends its ACKs to a higher level DR.

Scalable Reliable Multicast (SRM): Scalable Reliable Multicast [10] is a NACK-based reliable multicast protocol designed for many-to-many applications. SRM employs a "decentralized error recovery"; which means that, a node that detects packet loss multicasts a NACK for that packet to the whole group, and any node that has the data packet can multicast a repair packet for that loss.

All packet types of SRM (original data packets, request packets and repair packets) are multicast to the whole group. Since a repair request is multicast to the whole group, more than one receiver who have the desired packet can reply simultaneously. In order to prevent such duplicate retransmissions, SRM (1) uses a delay of some random interval before transmitting a request/repair packet (back-off), (2) suppresses transmission of a request/repair packet if someone else has already sent the same packet (suppression).

Pragmatic General Multicast (PGM): Pragmatic General Multicast (PGM) [11] is a reliable multicast transport protocol that uses router-assistance in order to obtain scalability. The protocol uses PGM-capable network elements (NE), which are routers enhanced to support PGM. In PGM, the sender multicasts sequenced data packets (ODATA) along the distribution tree to the receivers by using IP multicast. When a receiver detects a packet loss, it unicasts periodic negative acknowledgments (NACKs) containing the sequence number of the lost packet to the nearest NE. Network elements forward NACKs hop-by-hop to the sender using the reverse path of the ODATA packet, and confirm the reception at each hop by multicasting a NACK confirmation (NCF) packet. Receivers and network elements stop sending NACK at the reception of a corresponding NCF or repair data packet (RDATA). Finally, the sender receives the NACK and confirms by multicasting an NCF to the group, and then generates repair packets (RDATA). To avoid NACK implosion, PGM employs NACK elimination within network elements in order to propagate just one copy of a given NACK along the reverse path. The protocol also has a NACK suppression mechanism; receivers wait for a random time before delivering NACKs. If an RDATA or another NACK which has the same content is received during this period, the receiver cancels its own NACK.

3 Simulation Study

In the comparative part of this study, three selected protocols have been simulated in Network Simulator-2 under different test cases, for comparing some characteristics of these protocols. For this purpose, a single large network topology was created and the experiments designed for measuring different characteristics were performed on the same topology for each protocol.

RMTP, one of our selected protocols, did not exist in the Network Simulator version 2.27 [12], which was used as the simulation tool during this work. Therefore, at the first step of the simulation study, NS-2 simulation code for RMTP had been developed and appended to NS version 2.27. [13]

3.1 Network and application model

In this study, an underlying network topology was created and than the group members were selected randomly within the end nodes of this network. The network was created by using a topology generator tool, Tiers [14]. The network contains a WAN consisting of 3 WAN nodes; 4 MANs, each having 2 MAN nodes; and 5 LANs per MAN, each having 5 LAN nodes (end nodes).

The whole topology contains 131 nodes but only 100 of these are end nodes, so the members were selected within these 100 end nodes randomly. The network topology used throughout the experiments is presented in Figure 2. Bandwidths of the links were specified as E3 carrier for WAN-WAN links (34368 kbps); E2 carrier for WAN-MAN links and MAN-MAN links (8448 kbps); El carrier for MAN-LAN links; (2048 kbps) and 100 Mbps Ethernet for LAN-LAN links.

In real networks, most of the packet losses are due to the buffer overflows in routers. In order to simulate these events in NS-2, a user-defined loss rate is assigned to each link. In our simulations, all test cases are repeated under small and large loss rates, representing light and heavy background traffic, respectively.

Simulations were performed on one-to-many basis, i.e. a randomly selected sender sent a file of a predetermined size to a multicast group, which was also selected randomly. In SRM and PGM experiments, a CBR (Constant Bit Rate) traffic source was connected to the sender and it produced a packet traffic at 100 kbps. Since RMTP is window-based and its transmission rate is directly related to its protocol parameters, the RMTP sender agent was implemented in a way that it generates its own data traffic, without an external traffic source. But in each experiment, 100 packets, each containing 1000 bytes, were generated at the sender node and were transmitted to each group member, successfully.

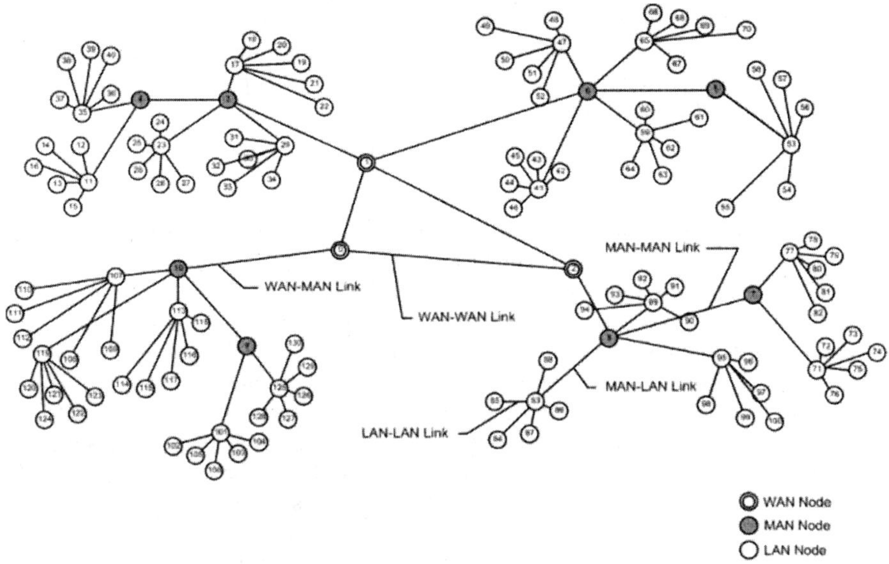

Fig. 2. Underlying network topology

3.2 Evaluation metrics

The evaluation metrics used in this study can be defined as follows:

Distribution Delay is the average time elapsed since a packet is sent from the sender until it has been correctly received by the whole group. >From the sender's point of view, distribution delay implies the minimum time for which the sender must keep the packet at memory before securely discarding it.

Recovery Latency is the average time between a packet drop being detected by a receiver and its repair packet reaching the receiver. In other words, it is the time for which a receiver should wait in order to receive retransmission for a lost packet.

Request Overhead is the additional load on intermediate nodes (routers) generated by the protocol. In order to measure this parameter, the number of request packets processed by each router is counted and the average value is calculated over all routers who participate in the multicast distribution tree. The results are presented as the ratio of the average number of request packets to the number of original packets sent by the sender. Thus, it expresses the number of request packets required for sending a definite number of packets to a multicast group.

3.3 Experiment Design

In our simulation study, different test cases were generated by changing the network parameters. In the first set of experiments, group size was increased from 10% to 90%. Each case was repeated for a small and large loss rate, i.e. 1% and 5%

respectively. The second set of experiments was performed by altering the link loss rates for simulating different network conditions.

In order to obtain reliable simulation results, each experiment was repeated many times and the average of all was calculated at the end. The number of repetitions for each experiment was determined according to a confidence interval rule. All experiments were repeated until a simulation result, whose probability of being at ± 10% closeness of the real value is 95%, is obtained.

3.4 *Simulation Results*

Distribution Delay: In Figure 3 - 4, the results obtained for distribution delay are presented. As can be seen from Figure 3.a, in case of small loss rate, increasing group size causes a smooth increase on distribution delay. This is an expected result, because as the number of members increases, the number of packet drops will increase since these packets spread more on the links. In this case, results are very similar to each other. But in case of large loss rate, (Figure 3.b) some important changes on the operation of protocols are observed. First of all, characteristic of RMTP is very similar to small loss case except a rise which is due to the increase in the number of packet losses and retransmissions. But when the SRM graph is examined, it is seen that, in spite of rising group size, distribution delay is decreasing, in other words the protocol operates faster. Since in SRM, each receiver could reply a retransmission request, it is reasonable that increasing the group size will decrease the retransmission time which will consequently decrease the distribution delay. So SRM performs better at dense multicast groups. >From Figure 3, it is seen that the variation of SRM distribution delay is opposite, i.e. it is increasing in small loss case while decreasing in large loss rate. So it is possible to conclude that, SRM operates better when the loss rate is higher. This is the result of using back-off timers before sending NACKs and repair packets. In case of high loss rate, the probability of receiving the same request or repair packet for which a receiver is running a back-off timer is higher, therefore recovering a loss packet would be faster.

Distribution delay for PGM is raising in both small and large loss rates, but the rate of increase is considerably large at large loss. In this scheme, a retransmission packet travels a longer path between the sender and the requester, so the probability of dropping this packet somewhere on the path is much higher. This situation does not effect the operation at small losses but it is an important drawback when loss rate is high.

Variation of a protocol against loss rate gives an opinion about the dependency of that protocol to the changes at network conditions. Figure 4 gives the operation at varying loss rates, or network conditions. For small loss rates, i.e. under 1%, results are very close to each other, which is supported by Figure 3.a. But as the loss rate increases, SRM shows better performance than the other two protocols. Furthermore, if the parts of the graphics between 2% and 4% of loss rates are considered in Figure 4, SRM distribution delay is almost horizontal, RMTP is very close to a horizontal line but PGM distribution delay increases from 2.5 seconds to 3.1 seconds, which means that PGM strictly depends on the network condition.

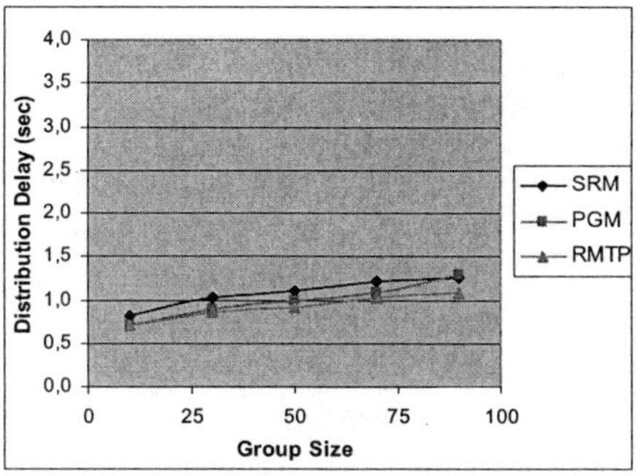

(a) small loss rates

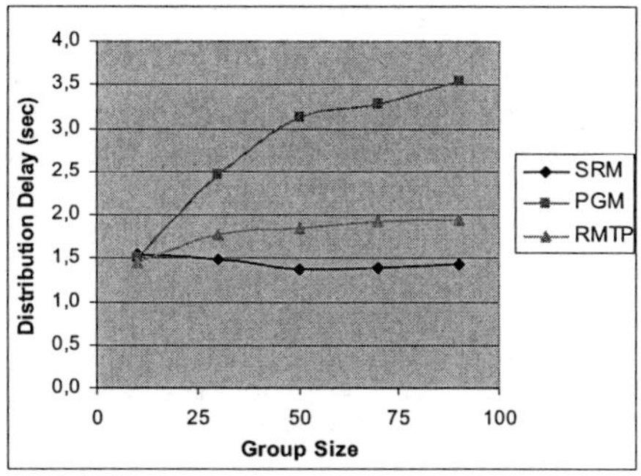

(b) large loss rates

Fig. 3. Distribution delay vs. Group size

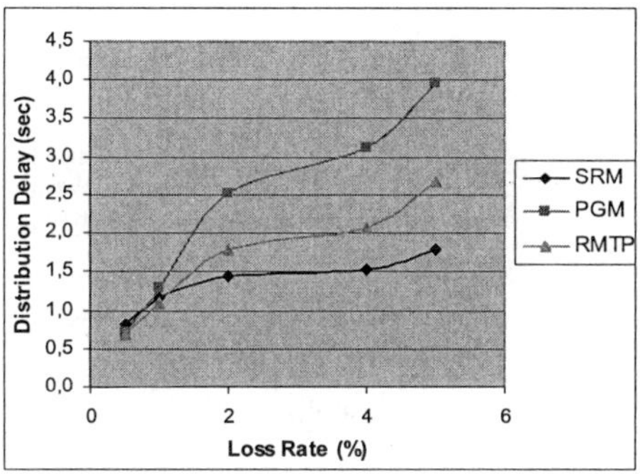

Fig. 4. Distribution delay vs. Loss rate (Group size=30)

Recovery Latency: Graphics given in Figure 5 – 6 illustrate the variation of recovery latencies against different network parameters. As can be seen in Figure 5, recovery latency for SRM and RMTP decreases as the group size increases. Since these protocols use local retransmission, not being effected by growing group size is an expected result. Since RMTP uses multicast retransmission when the demands for a lost packet exceeds a threshold value, increasing group size causes more multicast retransmission, which consequently decreases the recovery time. But in both small and large loss rate cases, the characteristics of RMTP graphics are similar, that is recovery mechanism of the protocol is not affected from the network condition. As seen in Figure 5.b, SRM is the fastest protocol to recover a packet loss, when the group density is greater than 20%, which means SRM mechanism requires dense multicast groups in order to obtain fast error recovery. PGM recovery latency against group size is almost doubled when the network goes from small loss case to large loss case. Figure 6 shows the affect of loss rate on recovery latency. Recovery mechanism of SRM and RMTP operate very stable in high loss rates, namely over 2%. But increasing loss rate raises the recovery time of PGM.

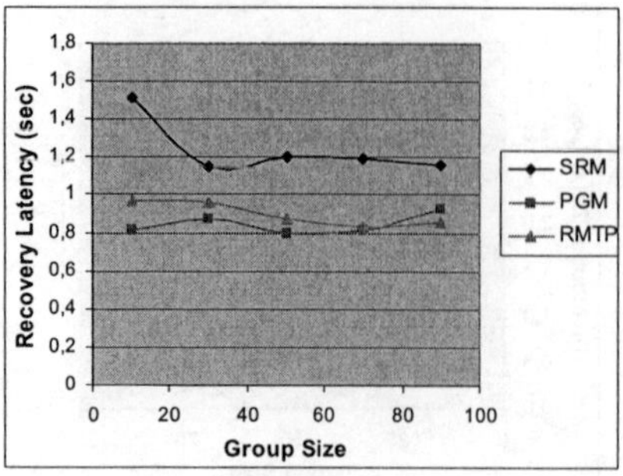

(a) for small loss rates

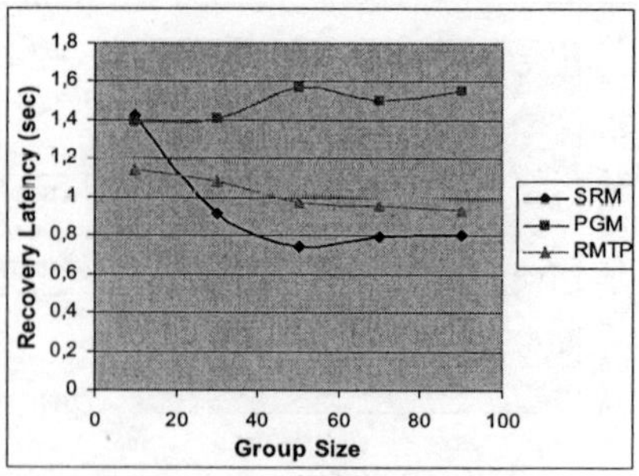

(b) for large loss rates

Fig. 5. Recovery latency vs. Group size

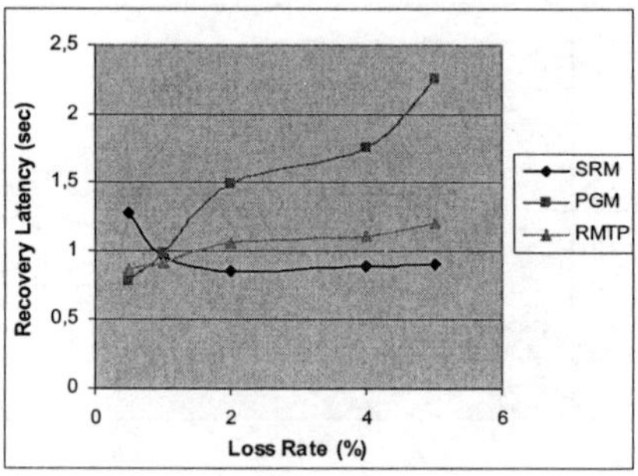

Fig. 6. Recovery latency vs. Loss rate

Request Overhead: Figure 7 – 8 shows the variation of request overhead generated by each protocol against group size and loss rate. From figures, RMTP seems to generate more request overhead as the group size increases. The first reason for that is sending periodic ACKs for requesting lost packets, instead of sending NACKs only in case of a packet drop. Therefore request overhead of RMTP is higher than others in small loss rate case, and the difference gets higher as the group size increases (Figure 7.a). Another reason is not using a suppression mechanism for request packets like the other protocols. As a result, increasing group size increases RMTP request overhead faster than the other protocols, especially in the high loss case (Figure 7.b). Since in a dense multicast group, it is likely to get a repair or request packet for a SRM receiver before its back-off timer expires and consequently its retransmission request would be discarded, SRM has a small request overhead at high group sizes, with respect to other protocols (Figure 7.b).

In case of PGM, since a request packet travels the whole network between the receiver and the sender, error probability for that request gets higher, as the link loss rates increase. Therefore especially in case of large loss rate (Figure 7.b), PGM generates more request overhead. For instance, request overhead for a group size of 10 is greater than 1, which means a router processes more request packets than the original data packets, even for a multicast group with 10 members. On the other hand, as it is seen in Figure 8, two protocols which use local retransmission do not suffer from increasing loss rate, as much as PGM.

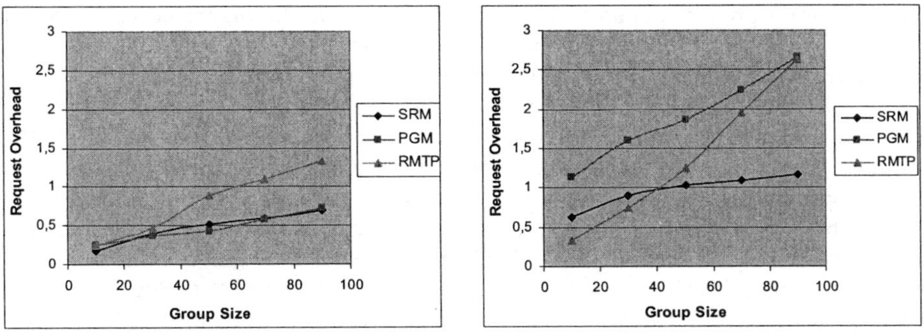

(a) for small loss rates (b) for large loss rates

Fig. 7. Request overhead vs. Group size

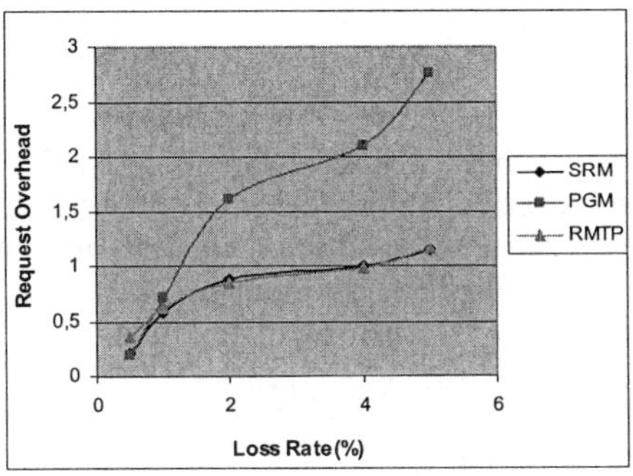

Fig. 8. Request overhead vs. Loss rate

4 Conclusion

This paper presented a performance evaluation of different class of reliable multicast protocols. Results obtained from the simulation study can be summarized as below.

Sending repair packets by multicast transmission decreases the recovery time. SRM uses multicasting for all retransmissions and from simulation results it is seen to have a good recovery latency performance especially at high loss rates. Similarly, RMTP recovery latency also decreases with increasing group size. (RMTP is likely to send multicast retransmission in large groups.)

The term of local retransmission can be used for the protocols in which not only the original sender but also a specialized receiver or any receivers who has the required data is able to reply a retransmission request. The most important advantage of using local retransmission is to keep the recovery times at a low level, as it is seen in SRM and RMTP simulations. But using a replier apart from the sender requires some additional protocol implementation efforts. For example, in SRM, each receiver should have the ability of sending a previously received packet when it is necessary. The same requirement is valid for a RMTP designated receiver, and furthermore selecting the locations of these DRs and running some extra features on them are necessary for a proper operation. These properties should be organized by a session manager. As a result, decreasing the recovery time by using local retransmission creates extra loads on protocol implementation and session management.

In this study, packet drops due to the network congestion are simulated by loss rates assigned to each link. With simulations, it is seen that recovery time of the protocols using local retransmission, namely SRM and RMTP, is not effected from the changes in loss rate, in other words, changes in network conditions. >From the results obtained, a protocol that specifies the border of its local retransmission area while establishing the session, e.g. RMTP, is independent of group density. On the other hand, since SRM does not define the local areas and obtains the locality by trying to answer a retransmission request by the nearest receiver, in sparse multicast groups the recovery latency was measured at the highest level and increasing the group size, i.e. the group density, caused a drop at the latency.

References

1. Handley M., Floyd S., Whetten B., Kermode R.: The Reliable Multicast Design Space for Bulk Data Transfer. *Network Working Group RFC 2887*, (2000)
2. Li, V.O.K., Zhang, Z.: Internet Multicast Routing and Transport Control Protocols. *Proceedings of the IEEE* , Volume: 90 , Issue: 3, (2002) 360 - 391
3. Whetten, B., Taskale, G.: An Overview of Reliable Multicast Transport Protocol II. *Network, IEEE,* Volume: 14, Issue: 1, Jan.-Feb, (2000) 37 – 47
4. Obraczka, K.: Multicast Transport Protocols: A Survey and Taxonomy. *Communications Magazine, IEEE*, Volume: 36, Issue: 1, Jan., (1998)
5. Levine, B.N., Garcia-Luna-Aceves, J.J.: A Comparison of Known Classes of Reliable Multicast Protocols. *Int. Conf. on Network Protocols*, (1996) 112 – 121
6. Maihofer, C., Rothermel, K., Mantei, N.: A Throughput Analysis of Reliable Multicast Transport Protocols. *Ninth International Conference on Computer Communications and Networks,* (2000) 250 – 257
7. Appala, S.V.,Austen, J.R.: An Evaluation of Reliable Multicast Protocols. *Southeastcon '99. Proceedings*. IEEE, March, (1999) 165-168
8. Whetten, B., Vicisano L.: Reliable Multicast Transport Building Blocks for One-to-Many Bulk-Data Transfer. *Network Working Group RFC 3048*, (2001)
9. Paul, S., Lin, J., Sabnani, K., Bhattacharyya, S.: A Reliable Multicast Transport Protocol (RMTP). *IEEE Journal on Selected Areas in Comm.*, (1997) 407 – 421
10. Floyd, S., Jacobson, V., Liu, C.G., McCanne, S.: A reliable multicast framework for light-weight sessions and application level framing. *IEEE/ACM Trans. Networking*, vol. 5, (1997) 784–803
11. Gemmell, J., Montgomery, T., Speakman, T., Crowcroft, J.: The PGM Reliable Multicast Protocols. *Network, IEEE*, Vol: 17, Issue: 1, (2003) 16 – 22
12. University of Southern California Information Sciences Institute: The Network Simulator - ns-2. http://www.isi.edu/nsnam/ns/, January 2004
13. Çelik, C.: Performance Analysis of Reliable Multicast Protocols. *Master Thesis,* Middle East Technical University, Ankara, (2004)
14. Calvert, K.I., Doar, M.B., Zegura, E.W.: Modeling Internet Topology. *Communications Magazine, IEEE,* Volume: 35, Issue: 6, (1997) 160 - 163

EMULATING AD HOC NETWORKS: DIFFERENCES FROM SIMULATIONS AND EMULATION SPECIFIC PROBLEMS

EREK GÖKTÜRK

Department of Informatics,
University of Oslo,
Postboks 1080 Blindern, 0316 Oslo, Norway.
E-mail: erek@ifi.uio.no
WWW home page: http://folk.uio.no/erek/

Simulations, emulations, and test deployments play a central role in design and development of ad hoc network protocols and software. Among these three methods, emulations have gained considerable popularity. This is partly because emulations address efficiency-accuracy trade-off of simulations by incorporating real hardware or software into the synthetic environment in a controlled manner. Although generally treated as a special case of simulations, emulation experimentation have its own problems and pitfalls. These problems do not typically show up in simulation studies, since they stem from presence of real hardware or software in the experiment. In this paper, the sketch of an emulation integrated development lifecycle is presented for establishing the boundaries of emulation experiments, and the problems specific to emulations are identified and discussed.

1. Introduction

Mobile ad-hoc networks (MANETs) are wireless networks in which participating nodes have a high degree of mobility, and where the network lacks infrastructural elements. The characteristics of ad hoc networks are different enough from wired networks, that techniques used for analyzing them appear inadequate[8].

Simulation experiments have been the main tool for testing network protocols and software. A simulation experiment is essentially the use of a set of scenarios, a model which is usually composite, and a simulation system in order to create data to be analyzed for gaining insight into the target phenomenon. Simulation experiments can be conducted long before any implementation is available. At the other end of the spectrum of available methods lie the controlled deployments of finished or partly finished implementations. For ad hoc networks, these test deployments are costly,

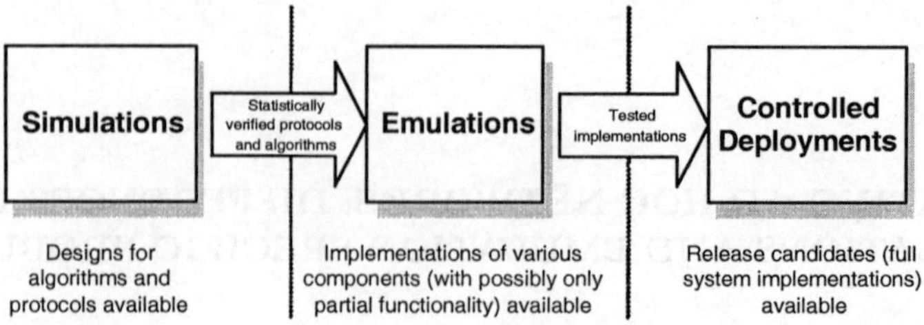

Figure 1. The emulation integrated development lifecycle.

very difficult to manage, and the results obtained hard to replicate. Such downsides are generally taken to be arguments in favor of simulations.

The gap between simulation experiments and test deployments is covered by emulation experiments. An emulation experiment is the use of a set of scenarios, a composite model of the target phenomenon parts of which are either replaced or augmented with finished or partly finished implementations (*emulated entities*), and an emulation system in order to create data to be analyzed for gaining insight into the target phenomenon. The presence of emulated entities and their interaction with the models simulated in the experiment provide new sources of problems not found in simulation experiments. While the emulation studies for ad hoc networks have recently gained considerable popularity, very few papers on the subject observe emulation related problems and explicitly discuss them.

In this position paper, we first present the boundaries of emulation experiments through sketching an emulation integrated lifecycle for development of ad hoc networking protocols and software. In the third section emulation specific problems are presented, by drawing upon various emulation studies reported in literature. The goal here is strictly the identification of problems, and solutions will not be provided. Furhermore, the problems presented might apply for other domains than ad-hoc networks, but such generalizations are beyond the conclusions of this paper. Of the problems presented, we acknowledge that not all would appear at all modeling granularities, and that the accuracy wanted and type of analysis to be performed determine how much these problems would be of concern for a specific study. The last section contains a discussion and conclusion.

2. Ad Hoc Network Emulation

The role of emulation studies is one of bridging the analytical or model level development stage with the actual real-life deployment of the system in a

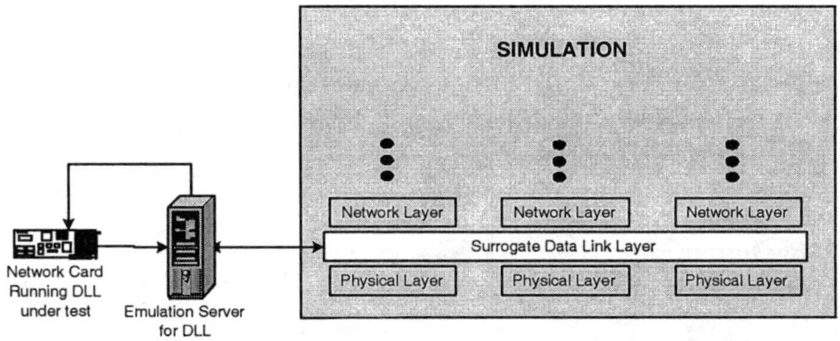

Figure 2. Horizontal emulation architecture.

smoother way. Although a very useful tool for conceptual analysis, pure simulation studies might not always provide consistent and relevant prediction or verification[2], or might miss important effects[10]. Therefore the whole spectrum from pure simulation experiments up to real system test deployments seems necessary for developing robust systems and systematically managing cross-layer concerns.

Emulation studies are not a replacement for simulations or controlled test system deployments[4]. The emulation integrated development lifecycle (see Fig. 1) may start with the simulation stage when the algorithms are available, but the actual implementations or the target platforms are not. Enrichment of the simulation environment is advised to start as soon as implementations of various components, of possibly limited functionality, become available[6]. The introduction of first implementations into the simulations is the point where the emulation experiments can be said to start. Emulation studies incorporate the whole spectrum from this point up to controlled test deployments of the system.

In simulation experiments, a simulation system is used to create the experiment scenarios, manage the models, run episodes, collect data, and even to conduct analysis. The role played by the simulation system in a simulation experiment is assumed by an emulation system in an emulation experiment. The emulation system manages the simulated parts, and in addition it provides mechanisms for integrating and managing the emulated entities.

Emulated entities can be integrated into an emulation system various ways. Two main integration methods can be identified: horizontal emulation, and vertical emulation. In horizontal emulation, a model for a specific layer functionality is replaced by the actual implementation for that layer in a simulated protocol stack (see Fig. 2). This architecture is more suit-

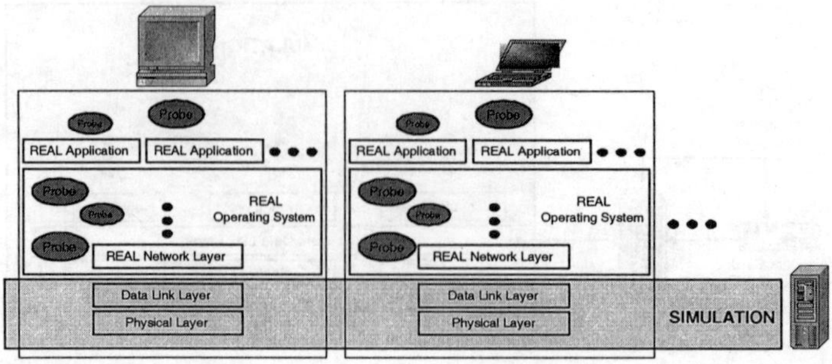

Figure 3. Vertical emulation architecture. This architecture can be said to be most typically associated with network emulation experiments.

able when the emulated entities can't be duplicated in an efficient way, or when there is a shared resource, like a scarce target platform, employed in a time-sharing manner[13]. On the other hand, in vertical emulation, the emulated software covers groups of consecutive layers of the protocol stack, and organized in per node basis (see Fig. 3). Typically, data-link layer or IP layer and upwards is emulated, whereas the lower layers are realized by a simulation system. This approach leads to an intuitive decomposition and distribution.

Distribution of execution is another important property related to the architecture of emulation systems. The distribution of execution concerns the number of available computational platforms (*physical hosts*), the way these hosts are connected, and how the emulated entities, simulation models, and the emulation system components are distributed to these hosts. There are both monolithic and distributed emulation systems reported in literature. The monolithic emulation systems are designed to conduct the whole emulation experiment on one physical host, generally in the form of a usual workstation or desktop computer. In such systems, the amount of resources available, resource contentions, and resource conflicts present the main obstacle against scalability. In distributed emulation systems, execution is done on more than one physical host in various different distributions of components.

3. Problems of Emulation

3.1. *Problems Inherited from Simulations*

Simulated models are part of emulation experiments. This implies that some or all of data generated in the emulation experiment is causally dependent on the simulated models. Therefore, the emulations inherit the problems of simulations through the models used in the experiments.

Many concerns about ad hoc network simulators and simulation experiments are expressed in the literature. The trade-off between accuracy of models used in ad hoc network simulations and efficiency of simulating them is particularly acute[13]. Since efficiency plays a major role in scalability, the scalability problem is most usually addressed by simplifying the models, thereby decreasing the accuracy considerably[9]. Such reduced accuracy is again usually justified by pointing at the requirements to argue that the level of accuracy provided by the model set is sufficient for the needs of the experiment. Although such justifications are abundant, the arguments are rarely backed up by analysis or convincing statistical results. More studies are needed to understand the effects of modeling granularity and accuracy on the results, and techniques and a generic framework for such analysis is yet to be developed.

3.2. *Simulation-Emulation Boundary Problems*

Running simulations along with emulated entities also create potential for problems stemming from the simulation-emulation boundary. The simulation-emulation boundary can be defined as the total of all data transactions between the simulated models and the emulated entities in an emulation experiment. For example, Ethernet frames in a vertical ad hoc network emulation where the physical layer is simulated are among the data transactions that crosses the emulation-simulation boundary.

One problem related to data transactions is the compatibility of granularity of the models employed at the simulation side and the emulated entities. The modeling at the emulated entities' side is complete, up to the implemented functionality in which case the data collected should be independent of the incomplete functionality. However, at the simulated side the models are generally under heavy accuracy-efficiency trade-off considerations. This may lead to the simulation side leaving out handling of some data which in a real deployment would be exchanged between two components modeled at different sides of the boundary in the emulation. Such omitted data would have to be filled in as stub values, which results in decreased accuracy transferred over the boundary to the emulated components and indirectly to the results obtained. Attention should be paid to this problem especially in ad hoc network related studies where cross-layer effects are of particular concern. Therefore, the amount of data available at the simulation-emulation boundary should be considered carefully when designing emulation experiments, and the effects of lack of data should be assessed.

3.3. *Problem of Physical Hosts in Synthetic Environment*

In simulations, the models running in the simulation system are designed to trace the states of an entity in a virtual (or synthetic) environment described in a scenario. The virtual environment itself is composed out of models. Therefore the whole system is one that traces the steps of a totally virtual world, in which space and time are not bound by physical world nor its laws. This in effect means that the physical world, in which the state tracing is done, has no effect whatsoever on the behavior of the conceptual entities in the virtual world whose states are traced by models.

However, that is not the case for emulations. The emulated entities are implementations of software or hardware, which generally work dependent on various physical entities. For the case of software, which is our main focus in this paper, the emulated entities are dependent on the computational, storage, and other resources on the physical host, and their behavior is affected considerably by it. Therefore in emulations, the system under test (SUT), which is totally virtualizable in the case of simulations, includes the physical hosts and the resources available on them as non-virtualized parts of the environment. For this reason, without proper management and virtualization of the physical hosts on which the emulated entities are executed, the emulation experiments cannot be said to provide fully synthetic environments in which to test SUT.

The main problem that comes with inclusion of physical hosts in the synthetic environment has already shown itself in the literature as the imposition of real-time constraints over the simulated models in emulation experiments[3,6,8,11]. This eventually has the effect of debalancing the accuracy-efficiency trade-off of models used in ad hoc network simulations. The remedy is sought in simplifying the models, thereby giving up on accuracy in order to decrease the computational load of the model to make it conform to real-time constraints. The justification for such simplifications is reused from the discussion on scalability of simulations, which was presented in Section 3.1. Again these justifications generally lack analytical or statistical analyses backing them. Very few papers even mention the problem[6,11]. An alternative solution to preventing imposition of real-time constraints on the simulated models is virtualization of the physical hosts themselves. The virtual machine[1], user mode kernel[5], and micro-kernel[3] based approaches can be interpreted as the first hints towards this solution.

Another problem is related to management of the experiment. In simulation experiment episodes (or runs: execution of one scenario), it is easy to provide managemental functionality such as pausing, accounting for lag in one or more of the models, saving state, restoring, etc., due to simulation system's complete control over the virtual environment. As current emulation systems lack complete control on the physical hosts as parts of the episode environment, either they provide no managemental functionality, or the functionality they provide is very limited when compared to simulation systems. This makes the emulation experiment process brittle, and causes stress on the experimenter, since the emulation systems provide little help if anything happens during the experiment that was not accounted for from the outset.

3.4. *Transparency*

The main idea behind conducting emulation studies is to incorporate real implementations into synthetic environments to investigate the behavior of the implemented system. The amount of changes necessary to run the real implementation along with the emulation system is defined as the transparency of the emulation system.

The transparency of an emulation system should preferably be as high as possible, which is the same as saying that changes in the real implementations should be kept to a minimum, preferably none. Meanwhile, an application or a protocol should run on the emulation system as if it were running on its target platform. To accomplish transparency while keeping the results accurate, an emulation system should account for many differences between the target platform and the physical hosts on which the emulated entities are executed. These differences stem from the amount of resources available, resource contention and conflict characteristics, and different implementations of abstractions at different levels, in particular operating system level abstractions. Providing high transparency presents a considerable challenge in the design of emulation systems.

3.5. *Emulation Overhead and Emulated Entity Multiplexing*

Emulation experiments are actually performance analysis studies. In performance analysis, data collection causes a well known problem called monitoring overhead problem[7]. The monitoring overhead problem is the result of using hardware and software probes which themselves eventually have effects on the system performance.

In simulation experiments, the monitoring overhead is not considered an issue, since the environment in which the models are simulated is assumed to be fully synthetic, as discussed in Section 3.3. In a properly designed simulation system, the monitoring probes are outside of the synthetic environment and the conceptual model, therefore cannot cause any unwanted effects in the events happening in the synthetic environment. However, in emulation systems, the inclusion of emulated entities brings the computational platforms they run on into the experiment environment. This was again pointed out in Section 3.3. Therefore the physical hosts become the gateway to monitoring the status and behavior of the emulated entities, in effect bringing monitoring overhead effects into the conceptual model.

It is not only monitoring overhead that the emulated entities being situated on real physical hosts cause. When observed from the point of view of one emulated entity, the rest of the emulation, which consists of the other emulated entities, the simulated components, along with the emulation system that acts as the mediator, is also a source of overhead. This kind of overhead is referred to as *emulation overhead.* The effects of emulation overhead depend on how many physical hosts are participating in the experiment, and the distribution of execution (see Section 2) over these physical hosts.

In the case of monolithic systems, the emulation overhead is one of the main factors preventing the system to scale. Even for non-monolithic, distributed systems, it is very desirable to keep the number of physical hosts in the experiment much lower than the number of emulated entities, or the nodes in the networks described in the scenarios. This is established by multiplexing the emulated entities on physical hosts, for example by running more than one node of the network on one physical host. Such multiplexing should be done with the effects well accounted for, since usually the emulated entities create resource contentions and sometimes even conflicts. The most immediately noticeable resource contention that limits the scalability happens over the CPU: Vahdat *et.al.*[12] reports decrease in the instructions per communicated byte with increasing number of emulated entities per physical host.

An initial estimation about the extent of the emulation overhead problem can be deduced from results reported in literature on the performance of the emulation systems themselves. Herrscher and Rotermel provide data[6] from which it can be observed that their system induces around 8% difference between the specified bandwidth available to nodes in the emulation and their actual throughput, without pushing the system for scalability. Jain discusses in his book on performance analysis[7] that having around 10% effect on an observed variable affects the performance analysis results considerably. Therefore Herrscher and Rotermel's data can be interpreted as showing that further studies are needed for systematic analysis of these effects, assessment of their significance, and development of a methodology and a tool set for researchers conducting emulation experiments in order to actively manage these effects.

4. Conclusion

Emulation systems fill the gap between the simulations and the deployment of the system in the development of networking software, including the software and protocols for ad hoc networks. A network emulation system's architecture can be classified by the way the emulated entities are integrated with the rest of the system as being horizontal or vertical. The two architectures are driven by different needs, and lead to different designs.

Emulations have been presented as an outgrowth of the simulation studies in the emulation integrated lifecycle, in section 2. In addition, they are generally perceived as no different than simulations. However, emulation studies pose a number of problems not typical for simulations, some of which we have identified from the literature on ad hoc network emulation experiments and discussed in this paper.

Today's network emulation systems do not seem to be built for providing support for self-monitoring, which seems to be needed for avoiding various problems discussed. As a result, we suggest that control and management systems for emulation related effects should be integrated into ad hoc network emulation systems, along with proper monitors. This is especially true considering also that analysts and emulation system designers have quite different views of the system: for one it is only a tool, whereas for the other it is the final product. Therefore, as a tool, emulation systems should provide enough support for guiding the analyst around the inaccuracies that are created by the tool itself, without calling for in-depth knowledge of the tool's implementation.

The main contribution of this paper is the identification of the problems specific to emulation studies, and establishment of their context by discussing the boundaries of emulation experimentation in ad hoc networks research and development. Based on this paper, we suggest and are now undertaking direct experiments on various emulation systems themselves, in order to assess their sensitivity for the problems discussed.

Acknowledgments

The author wishes to thank Dr. Ellen Munthe-Kaas, Dr. M. Naci Akkøk, Matija Pužar, and Katrine Stemland Skjelsvik for their valuable feedback.

References

1. Rimon Barr. *An efficient, unifying approach to simulation using virtual machines.* PhD thesis, Cornell University, May 2004.
2. David Cavin, Yoav Sasson, and André Schiper. On the accuracy of MANET simulators. In *Proc. of POMC '02*, pages 38–43. ACM Press, 2002.
3. Michael Engel, Matthew Smith, Sven Hanemann, and Bernd Freisleben. Wireless ad-hoc network emulation using microkernel-based virtual linux systems. In *Proc. of EUROSIM'04*, pages 198–203, 2004.
4. Hannes Frey, Daniel Görgen, Johannes K. Lehnert, and Peter Sturm. A java-based uniform workbench for simulating and executing distributed mobile applications. In *Proc. of FIDJI 2003*, 2003.
5. V. Guffens and G. Bastin. Running virtualized native drivers in user mode linux. In *Proceedings of USENIX 2005 Annual Technical Conference*, 2005.
6. Daniel Herrscher and Kurt Rothermel. A dynamic network scenario emulation tool. In *Proc. of ICCCN'02*, pages 262–267, 2002.
7. Raj Jain. *The Art of Computer Systems Performance Analysis: Techniques for Experimental Design, Measurement, Simulation, and Modeling.* Wiley-Interscience, New York, U.S.A., April 1999.
8. Glenn Judd and Peter Steenkiste. Repeatable and realistic wireless experimentation through physical emulation. *SIGCOMM Comput. Commun. Rev.*, 34(1):63–68, 2004.
9. Valeri Naoumov and Thomas Gross. Simulation of large ad hoc networks. In *Proc. of MSWIM'03*, pages 50–57. ACM Press, 2003.
10. Erik Nordström, Per Gunningberg, and Henrik Lundgren. A testbed and methodology for experimental evaluation of wireless mobile ad hoc networks. In *Proceedings of the Tridentcom 2005*, 2005.
11. Tanguy Pérennou, Emmanuel Couchon, Laurent Dairaine, and Michel Diaz. Two-stage wireless network emulation. In Fernando Boavida, Edmundo Monteiro, and Joao Orvalho, editors, *Proceedings of the Workshop on Challenges of Mobility held in conjunction with 18th IFIP World Computer Congress (WCC)*, pages 57–66, 2004.
12. Amin Vahdat, Ken Yocum, Kevin Walsh, Priya Mahadevan, Dejan Kostić, Jeff Chase, and David Becker. Scalability and accuracy in a large-scale network emulator. *SIGOPS Oper. Syst. Rev.*, 36(SI):271–284, 2002.
13. Brian White, Jay Lepreau, and Shashi Guruprasad. Lowering the barrier to wireless and mobile experimentation. In *Proc. of Hotnets'02*, 2002.

ENERGY EFFICIENT AND RELIABLE ROUTING WITH COOPERATIVE DIVERSITY IN WIRELESS AD-HOC NETWORKS

A. AKSU, O. ERCETIN, T. UNLUYURT, K. BULBUL, K. KILIC

Sabanci University,
34956 Istanbul, Turkey
E-mail: (aylinaksu@su., oercetin@, tonguc@, bulbul@, kkilic@) sabanciuniv.edu

The problem of maximizing network lifetime in wireless ad-hoc networks is addressed with a cooperative routing approach. The network lifetime optimization problem is defined as a linear programming problem and it is shown with simulations that networks utilizing cooperative transmission have larger lifetime than the networks not utilizing.

1. Introduction

It is well known that wireless ad hoc networks is a key to the future wireless communication because of its cheap infrastructureless property. However, its decentralized property causes the individual nodes to have a strong effect on network performance because of the fact that they have limited battery energy. All these reasons motivate the research on maximizing the network lifetime in wireless networks.

In this work we aim to prolong the lifetime of a network by routing the flow traffic such that the energy consumption is balanced among the nodes, since energy is the most important resource in wireless networks. In this study, we define the lifetime of a network as the time when the first node in the network drains out its battery which leads to a partition in the network. Our main contribution is the usage of cooperative diversity and energy efficient routing algorithms jointly which yields a cross-layer approach to the network lifetime optimization problem. We inspired from the work held by Chang and Tassiulas, [1], in which they defined a linear programming problem in order to solve the lifetime optimization problem and proposed algorithms to route traffic in order to maximize the network lifetime. Brown *et al.* in [3], proposed algorithms for sequentially maximizing the lifetime of each commodity in the network.

2. Cooperative Diversity

Improving the wireless link quality is the major problem in wireless networks, since there are several properties of wireless medium such as pathloss, fading, and lossy medium that cause problems and complexity. Therefore, to reliably transmit information over long distances, the system requires increasing power, bandwidth, and receiver complexity. Fading can be mitigated by the use of diversity without increasing power. We refer the reader to Ref. [4] for the diversity schemes used in wireless networks.

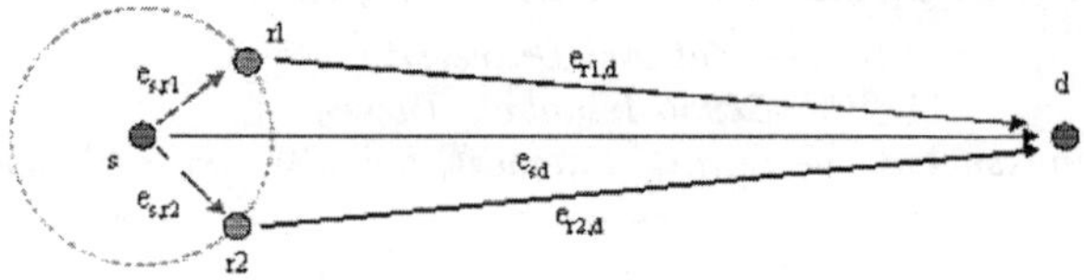

Figure 1. Cooperative transmission.

In cooperative transmission, multiple nodes transmit the same information to a common receiver, and this improves the signal quality and reliability at the receiver. Fig. 1 is an example how cooperation is working. At first, source node s sends its data to relay nodes r_1 and r_2, and then, s, r_1 and r_2 cooperates to send the information to the destination node d by less transmission energy. The transmittters send symbols using a coding scheme. Alamouti coding is a complex space-time block coding scheme in which the symbols are replicated in space and time in a specific manner and full diversity is achieved [5]. This symbol replication enables receiver to combine the signals and decode the symbol. Because there is a little chance that all fading coefficients in all transmission links will mitigate the signal quality, cooperation allows nodes to transmit their information with less power while providing a signal that can be decoded at the destination.

In cooperative routing, users share their antennas to create a virtual antenna array through a distributed transmission and signal processing as Laneman stated in [6]. Thus, in cooperative routing, each node participates and gains benefit by relaying messages for another. Khandani *et al.* proposed in their paper [7] a new way of achieving space diversity by allowing cooperation among nodes for routing purposes by creating a virtual antenna array. A study by Scaglione *et al.* is based on the continuum approximation in networks with high density [8]. Goldsmith *et al.* [9] aimed to minimize the total energy consumption required to send a given number of bits over a fading channel.

Next, we consider the power consumption of Single-Input Single-Output (SISO) and Multiple-Input Single-Output (MISO) systems.

2.1. *SISO*

In a SISO system, there are one transmitting and one receiving antenna. Let $\hat{s_0}$ and n_0 be the symbol to be transmitted and the additive noise term, respectively. Let $h = \alpha e^{j\phi}$ be the channel between the transmitter and the receiver where α is the magnitude of the channel due to fading and has Rayleigh distribution. Then, the received symbol is $r_0 = h\hat{s_0} + n_0$. Given Rayleigh fading coefficient α, SNR of this received signal, γ_{nc}, is:

$$\gamma_{nc} = \frac{|\alpha^2||\hat{s_0}|^2}{N_0}, \tag{1}$$

where $|n_0|^2 = N_0$, and N_0 is the power of the noise term.

2.2. *MISO*

MISO systems consist of multiple transmitters and a single receiver. Consider a simple example where 2×2 Alamouti code is used to achieve space and time diversity, we need two transmitters in the system. Let $h_i = \alpha_i e^{j\phi_i}$, $i = 0, 1$, be the channel between the transmitters and the receiver where α_i is the magnitude of the channel and has Rayleigh distribution. We assume that the channel is a flat fading channel. Let s_0 and s_1 be the symbols to be transmitted from transmitter 0 and transmitter 1 respectively, and n_0 and n_1 are the noise terms. The transmission matrix $\mathbf{S}$ correspoding to 2x2 Alamouti Coding is [5],

$$\mathbf{S} = \begin{vmatrix} s_0 & s_1 \\ -s_1^* & s_0^* \end{vmatrix}. \tag{2}$$

Using the transmission matrix $\mathbf{S}$ and assuming the receiver has perfect knowledge of the channel coefficients, the received symbols are linearly combined to achieve diversity gain and estimated symbols are:

$$\widetilde{s_0} = |\alpha_1^2 + \alpha_0^2|s_0 + h_0^* n_0 + h_1 n_1, \tag{3}$$

$$\widetilde{s_1} = |\alpha_1^2 + \alpha_0^2|s_1 + h_1^* n_0 - h_0 n_1. \tag{4}$$

Given fading coefficients, α_0 and α_1, SNR at the receiver will be:

$$\gamma_c = \frac{|\alpha_1^2 + \alpha_0^2||s_0|^2}{N_0}, \tag{5}$$

where $|n_0|^2 = N_0$.

Comparison of MISO and SISO cases for the same transmission powers reveals that Alamouti codes provide twice better SNR on average, i.e. diversity gain is 2.

3. Energy-Efficient Reliable Transmissions

Given Rayleigh fading coefficients and assuming modulation is BPSK and SNR is a deterministic variable, the bit error probability P_b is,

$$Prob(Bit\ error|fading\ coefficients) = Q\left(\sqrt{2\gamma}\right) = P_b\,. \tag{6}$$

Using the inverse of Q-function[a], we obtain a threshold value for SNR which is a function of bit error rate as $erfinv^2(1-2P_b)$.

However, note that since SNR of the received signals depends on Rayleigh fading coefficients which has Rayleigh distribution, γ is a random variable. Usually, there is an end-to-end average quality of service (QoS) requirement that needs to be satisfied. In our case, the QoS requirement is the outage probability, P_{out} which is defined as the probability that instantaneous combined SNR falls below a certain specified threshold.

$$P_{out} = P(\gamma < erfinv^2(1-2P_b))\,. \tag{7}$$

Next, let us determine the energy consumption of SISO and MISO systems under such QoS requirement.

For MISO case, using Eqs. (5-8) we obtain bit power, $|s_0|^2$ for given BER, P_{out}, N_0 and σ as,

$$|s_0|^2 = \frac{N_0 erfinv^2(1-2P_b)}{\gamma_u 2\sigma^2}\,, \tag{8}$$

where $|\alpha_1|^2 + |\alpha_0|^2$ in (5) has Gamma Distribution with parameters $(2, 2\sigma^2)$ and γ_u is a constant found using the properties of Gamma distribution and outage probability P_{out}.

For SISO case, using Eqs. (1) and (6-8), we obtain bit power, $|\hat{s_0}|^2$ for given BER, P_{out}, N_0 and σ as,

$$|\hat{s_0}|^2 = \frac{N_0 erfinv^2(1-2P_b)}{\gamma_y 2\sigma^2}\,, \tag{9}$$

where α^2, Y is exponentially distributed with mean $2\sigma^2$ and γ_y is a constant found using the properties of exponential distribution and outage probability P_{out}.

---

[a] $Q^{-1}(x) = \sqrt{2}\, erfinv(1-2x)$

Using Eqs. (14) and (16), for bit error probability less than 0.1, we can find the ratio of required transmission powers for SISO and MISO, i.e. $R = |\hat{s_0}|^2/|s_0|^2$ as 5.0457. Hence, the power we need for SISO case is approximately 5 times of the power needed in MISO case for an outage probability of 0.1. In Fig. 2, we can see the ratio of symbol powers for varying outage probabilities. Note that while outage probability is decreasing, energy consumed for transmision of one bit of information in SISO systems is increasing exponentially unlike MISO case.

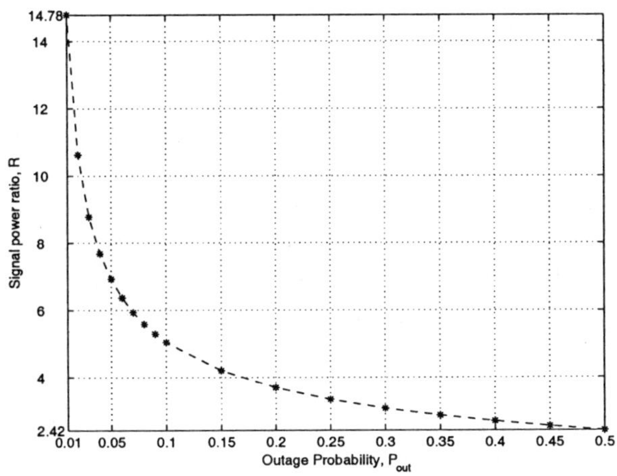

Figure 2. R for varying outage probabilities

4. Network Model

The network is modeled by a directed graph $G(N, A)$ where N is the set of nodes, A is the set of directed edges (i, j) where i, j is in N. E_i is the initial energy of node i. is the distances between ith and jth nodes. e^t_{ij} is the transmission energy required for node i to transmit an information unit to node j and proportional to the 4th power of d_{ij}, i.e., $e^t_{ij} = e^T + \epsilon_{amp} d^4_{ij}$, where e^T and ϵ_{amp} are the energy consumed at the transmitter circuitry and the energy consumed for transmitting one bit of information one meter away. e^r_{ij} is the reception energy due to receiver circuitry consumed by node j. This energy consumption model is adopted from [2].

We assume there are multiple commodities in the network. A commodity $c \in C$ is defined by a set of source nodes $O^{(c)}$ and destination nodes

$D^{(c)}$, where C is the set of all commodities. If any node in $D^{(c)}$ is reached, the information transfer of commodity c is considered to be done. Q_i is the flow generated by node i in all commodities, where $Q_i^{(c)}$ is the flow generation of commodity c by node i, and $q_{ij}^{(c)}$ is the flow rate from node i to node j of commodity c.

C_{ij} is the set of nodes that i cooperates with in order to send data to node j. Node i itself is also included in the cooperation set, since it also sends information with the other assisting nodes. Since selection of assisting nodes is an integer programming problem, we propose a method to select assisting nodes: In this method, closest n nodes are selected as assisting. In this paper, we consider only the case when $n = 1$ and Alamouti coding is used.

If node i is a source node, it consumes E_{cs} amount of energy consisting of energy required to *send* information to relay node and the sink. In particular, first term in (10) calculates the energy consumption when node i transmits data to the nodes in its cooperation set C_{ij} to send data to node j. Second term is the energy consumption, when node i transmits data to node j with transmission energy divided by R_{ij}, the ratio of energy consumption of node i in SISO case to energy consumption in MISO case when the nodes in the cooperation set of node i are used as assiting nodes.

If node i is a next hop node or a destination node for another source node j, it consumes E_{cd} (11) amount of energy because of the reception energy e_{ji}^r.

If node i is an assisting node or a relay node for another source node, it consumes E_{cr} (12) amount of energy consisting of energy required to *receive* information from the source and *send* to the sink. For this case, node i is a relay for another node k and sends data to node j with transmission energy divided by R_{kj}, the ratio of energy consumption of node k in SISO case to energy consumption in MISO case when the nodes in the cooperation set of C_{kj} are used as assiting nodes.

$$E_{cs} = \sum_{j \in N} \sum_{c \in C} q_{ij}^{(c)} \Big(\sum_{k \in C_{ij}} e_{ik}^t + \frac{e_{ij}^t}{R_{ij}} \Big) \tag{10}$$

$$E_{cd} = \sum_{j \in N} \sum_{c \in C} q_{ji}^{(c)} e_{ji}^r \tag{11}$$

$$E_{cr} = \sum_{j \in N} \sum_{k \in N : i \in C_{kj}} \sum_{c \in C} q_{kj}^{(c)} \Big(e_{ki}^r + \frac{e_{ij}^t}{R_{kj}} \Big) . \tag{12}$$

5. System Lifetime Optimization Problem and Constraints

The lifetime of node i under a given flow vector $\mathbf{q}=\{q_{ij}\}$ is given by,

$$T_i(\mathbf{q}) = \frac{E_i}{E_{cs} + E_{cd} + E_{cr}} \,. \tag{13}$$

We define system lifetime as the length of time until the first node drains out its battery. Hence, the minimum lifetime over all nodes gives the system lifetime, i.e.,

$$T_{sys}(\mathbf{q}) = \min_{i \in N} T_i(\mathbf{q}) \,. \tag{14}$$

We aim to find the flow that maximizes system lifetime under flow conservation condition, i.e.,

$$\sum_{k \in N, k \neq i} q_{ki}^{(c)} + Q_i^{(c)} = \sum_{j \in N, j \neq i} q_{ij}^{(c)} \,, \tag{15}$$

where $i \in N - D^{(c)}$ is a source node in commodity c, j is the destination node, and k is the node that sends information to node i. $Q_i^{(c)}$ is the flow generated by node i, where $c \in C$.

Given the source and destination nodes and the information generation rate at the source node, the problem of maximizing system lifetime T is equivalent to the following linear programming problem:

Maximize T, s.t.,

$$E_{cs} + E_{cd} + E_{cr} \leq E_i, \forall i \in N \tag{16}$$

$$\sum_{k \in N, k \neq i} \hat{q}_{ki}^{(c)} + TQ_i^{(c)} = \sum_{j \in N, j \neq i} \hat{q}_{ij}^{(c)}, \forall c \in C \,, \tag{17}$$

where $i \in N - D^{(c)}$ and $\hat{q}_{ij}^{(c)} = Tq_{ij}^{(c)}$ is the amount of flow transmitted from node i to node j.

6. Network Examples and Numerical Results

In this section, the optimal system lifetime for both MISO and SISO cases for a number of network examples will be given. Results are obtained by implementing the linear problem in optimization tool OPL [10]. All nodes are assumed to have equal energies, and parameter values are quoted from [2] as 10 J for initial energies, 150 nJ/bit for the energy consumption in receiver circuitry, 50 nJ/bit for transmitter circuitry and 100 pJ/bit for transmission energy of one bit of information to 1 unit far away. In the following network examples, we distributed N nodes uniformly randomly in a $d \times d\ m^2$ region, and obtained optimal flows and lifetimes through the simulations for varying N and d. In all simulations, we assume the average bit error probability of the channels is 0.1, and there are two nodes in the cooperation set of a node in MISO case. For a better understanding of the efficiency of the cooperation, we choose to compare the systems in terms of the ratio of the lifetimes obtained in MISO and SISO cases.

In Table 1, the ratio of the lifetimes are shown, where initial energies of nodes are equal, and there are one source and one destination node in the network. When nodes are closer to each other as in $10 \times 10\ m^2$ area, optimal lifetimes in both cases are the same, since the efficiency of cooperative transmission in Rayleigh fading channels appears in long distance transmissions. When the area is wider, MISO system lifetime obtained is more than the lifetime in SISO case.

Table 1. $T_{coop}/T_{noncoop}$, equal initial energies.

	$N = 5$	$N = 10$	$N = 25$	$N = 50$
10×10	1	1	1	1
50×50	1.841	1.5478	1.0487	1.0378
75×75	1.3733	1.252	1	1.1344

A network example is shown in Fig. 4, where 10 nodes are distributed in a $50 \times 50\ m^2$ area, 4th and 7th nodes are selected as source and destination nodes respectively. Direct transmissions are shown by solid lines and cooperative transmissions are shown by dotted lines. In a sample route following the path 4-3-5-7, node 4 cooperates with node 6 to send information to node 3, node 3 cooperates with node 2 to send information to node 5, and node 5 cooperates with node 1 to send information to node 7. When we obtain the lifetime ratio for the case where initial node energies are uniformly randomly distributed between 5 Joules and 10 Joules, the results in Table 2 shows that MISO systems performs better in most of the network examples than the SISO systems. However, when 25 nodes are distributed in $50 \times 50\ m^2$ area, SISO gave a better solution than the cooperation. The reason is that when the node energies are too low, by forcing to cooperate, we consume more energy.

Table 3 shows the lifetime ratio where initial energies are equal, and there is only one commodity, but source and destination nodes are randomly selected. Results show that, in the worst case, performances of MISO and SISO case are equal; and in the best case, the MISO system can perform

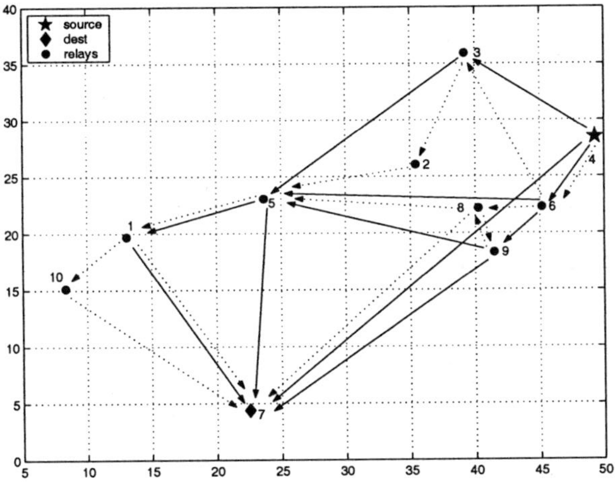

Figure 3. 50×50, $N = 10$, $T_{coop}/T_{noncoop} = 1.5478$

Table 2. $T_{coop}/T_{noncoop}$, random initial energies, single commodity, single source-sink pair.

	$N = 5$	$N = 10$	$N = 25$	$N = 50$
10×10	1	1	1	1
50×50	1.8612	1.639	0.95145	1.0265
75×75	1.0989	1.1921	1	1.4634

Table 3. $T_{coop}/T_{noncoop}$, equal initial energies, single commodity, multiple sources and sinks.

	$N = 5$	$N = 10$	$N = 25$	$N = 50$
50×50	1	1	1.0496	2.0113
75×75	1.3713	1.096	1.7415	1.8742

twice better than the SISO system as in the example with 50 nodes in 50×50 m^2 area.

Table 4 shows the ratio of the lifetimes where there are two commodities in the networks, and the source-sink sets in commodities are randomly selected. Note that if any node in destination set is reached, the information transfer of that commodity is considered to be done. For such a network, SISO systems can have higher lifetime if the number of source nodes is large, because enforced cooperation in MISO systems causes the nodes to consume more energy.

Table 4. $T_{coop}/T_{noncoop}$, equal initial energies, two commodities.

	$N = 5$	$N = 10$	$N = 25$	$N = 50$
50×50	0.9275	1.0000	1.0272	0.9700
75×75	1.0000	1.0000	0.6075	1.9481

7. Conclusions and Future Work

In this paper, the goal is to find the flow traffic among nodes so that the system lifetime is maximized when cooperation is utilized. Our results indicate that optimized network lifetime can be increased even by using a single relay node.

In this work, since we assume always two nodes cooperate without solving the optimum cooperation set for each transmission, in some network examples, SISO system had higher lifetime. A future direction is to jointly optimize the selection of the cooperating set and routing.

References

1. Chang J.-H. and Tassiulas L., Energy conserving routing in wireless ad hoc networks, *Proc. IEEE INFOCOM* (Tel Aviv, Israel, 2000) pp. 22–31.
2. Chang J.-H. and Tassiulas L., Maximum lifetime routing in wireless sensor networks, *IEEE/ACM Transactions on Networking* , Vol. 12, No. 4 (2004).
3. Brown T., Zhang Q. and Gabow H., Maximum flow life curve for a wireless ad hoc network, *ACM Symp. Mobile Ad Hoc Networking and Computing, (MobiHoc 2001)* (Long Beach, CA, 2001).
4. Rappaport T. S., Wireless Communications, Principles and Practice (Prentice Hall, 2002).
5. Alamouti S. M., A simple transmit diversity technique for wireless communications, *IEEE Journal on Select Areas in Communications*, Vol. 16 (1998) pp. 1451–1458.
6. Laneman J. N., Wornell G. W. and Tse D. N. C., An efficient protocol for realizing cooperative diversity in wireless networks, *Proc. IEEE ISIT* (Washington, D. C., 2001) p. 294.
7. Khandani A., Abounadi J., Modiano E. and Zhang L., Cooperative routing in wireless networks, *Allerton Conference on Communications, Control and Computing* (2003).
8. Sirkeci-Mergen B. and Scaglione A., A continuum approach to dense wireless networks with cooperation, *IEEE Infocom* (2005).
9. Cui S., Goldsmith A. J. and Bahai A., Energy-efficiency of MIMO and cooperative MIMO techniques in sensor networks, *IEEE Journal on Selected Areas of Communications*, Vol. 22, No. 6 (2004).
10. http://www.ilog.com, 2004.

VISUAL DEVICE IDENTIFICATION FOR SECURITY SERVICES IN AD-HOC WIRELESS NETWORKS*

DONGWAN SHIN

Computer Science Department,
New Mexico Tech,
Socorro, NM 87801, USA
E-mail: doshin@nmt.edu

SEUNGHYUN IM

Computer Science Department,
University of North Carolina at Charlotte,
Charlotte, NC 28223, USA
E-mail: sim@uncc.edu

This paper discusses a novel approach to identifying entities involved in ad-hoc wireless communications through using an efficient visual code system called UbiCode. UbiCode, used in an out-of-band channel in order to bootstrap trust between entities unknown to each other, facilitates a mechanism for demonstrative identification of entities involved in ad-hoc wireless communications. We present the design of UbiCode as well as identification protocols leveraging the system. We also demonstrate our approach through a proof-of-concept implementation.

1. Introduction

The lack of both trusted third party and physical restraint in ad-hoc wireless networks makes it hard to provide security services for mobile nodes. One of the key problems in those environments, especially where those nodes need to communicate in a secure and spontaneous manner, is the identification of the other entity (typically device) in a communication preceding authenticated key establishment. Demonstrative identification is a must in order to bootstrap other security services; it is often referred to as one based on physical context (for example, audio with limited transmission range is used to demonstratively identify each other in a communication) [4].

*This work is partially supported by a startup grant from the research and economic development office of the New Mexico Tech.

1.1. *Motivating Examples*

Suppose people in ad-hoc wireless networks want to exchange information with nearby people or devices. Establishing secure communications are required in many cases in these environments where information to be exchanged must not be eavesdropped or tampered. For instance, Alice wants to send sensitive business information from her PDA to a mobile device of her business partner; Bob needs to send a document from his mobile device to a public printer in a conference room and pay for the print job using his electronic wallet in his mobile device; and a team of project members has to share electronic versions of paper documents during a project meeting.

In each of those scenarios, before some sensitive information being exchanged, two preparatory steps are generally required for establishing secure communications: obtaining the correct network address belonging to the device and sharing a secret key for cryptographic operations. However, often in ad-hoc wireless network environments, those two tasks become non-trivial both because communication channels tend to be established dynamically (or *spontaneously*) [9,14] without any prior electronic information about the entities involved and because online connectivity tends to be very limited such that any well-established trust relationships are little anticipated. For example, before sending his print job to the printer in the conference room, Bob is likely to create a dynamic association between his device and the printer without any pre-existing information about the printer in his device. An interesting but challenging problem we want to address in this paper is related to how to authenticate the other entity in an association and how to secure the association. In other words, how can Bob be assured that his device is actually talking to the printer in the conference room, *not* in the lobby, and his communication is secure?

1.2. *Our Objective*

According to [4], which discusses the problem of secure communication and authentication in ad-hoc wireless networks, the demonstrative identification of devices over a location-limited channel works as a catalyst in bootstrapping secure wireless communication. Audio and infrared are named as a good candidate for communication technologies for demonstratively identifying entities in a communication. In this paper, we propose a novel approach to using a visual code system called UbiCode in order to provide a means for identifying mobile devices as well as establishing a secure communication in ad-hoc wireless networks. UbiCode works as a basis of network address acquisition as well as public key verification for devices to be spontaneously associated, and it can be captured with built-in digital cameras in mobile devices which, once considered to be a special hardware, are becoming a standard equipment due to their growing popularity. Our approach is to embed the minimal amount of cryptographic key information as well as the network address of an entity involved in an association into the visual code. Capturing the visual code using cameras can be thought of as using a direct optical channel which is generally believed to be as secure as connecting two devices using non-shared wires. We also demonstrate our approach through a proof-of-concept implementation.

The rest of this paper is organized as follows. Section 2 shows background technologies and previous research related to our work. Section 3 presents how to design UbiCode, followed by Section 4 which describes identification protocols leveraging UbiCode. Implementation details are described in Section 5. Section 6 discusses lessons learned from our experiment and concludes the paper.

2. Background and Related Works

The main focus in current practices with various visual code systems is on providing an inexpensive and reliable solution to bridge the gap between the real world and the virtual world. CyberCode [13] is included in this category. When users want to download the electronic copy of a paper document, they capture the visual code printed on the paper with a camera integrated in mobile devices; the visual code works as a link to the corresponding electronic data stored in the database. Similar visual codes proposed in [11,12] also function as a pointer to the actual electronic data or service related to the physical object. Even though these previous approaches address how to obtain the network address of the object of interest, none of them deals with how to use visual codes as a basis of secure communication channels.

2.1. *Secure Spontaneous Association*

There have been several previous approaches to tackling the problem of validating and securing spontaneous associations by using different out-of-band channels in addition to the radio frequency communication channel as a means of main data communication [3,8,9,16]. Some of them require extra hardware, such as a laser pointer to get the network address and set up a session key, and others require extensive user involvement, such as waving hands to confirm the secure association.

Stajano and Anderson suggested a solution to the problem of secure spontaneous associations in the form of the *resurrecting duckling protocol* in [14]. In their protocol, a shared secret key is exchanged over an authenticating 'physical' channel; they suggested direct electrical contact between the devices, as well as displaying hashes of keys for users to compare. Various authors expanded on that idea of authenticating key exchange using physical properties. In [10] Kindberg and Zhang employed a variety of longer-range *physically constrained* channels to achieve the transfer of data in such a way that the user can tell with which physical device the data originated, without having to physically touch that device. Those channels include infrared beacons, lasers, and combinations of radio frequency and ultrasound signals [9], all of which are attenuated by walls and can be directed with some degree of accuracy. Balfanz et al pursued a similar idea, using what they termed *location-limited* channels, including infrared and audio signals in [4]. They observed that it can be preferable to send authenticating materials, which does not have to be secret, on the constrained or limited channel, and use that to verify messages sent over the wireless network.

The requirement to achieve secure associations spontaneously eliminates several other solutions. Virtual Private Network connections (often used over 802.11) require pre-registration and login. Bluetooth, putting other concerns aside, requires response to a challenge that can only be communicated verbally from one human to another.

3. Our Approach

UbiCode is a visual code system which enables a demonstrative identification of devices and thus bootstraps other security services such as authentication, confidentiality, and integrity in ad-hoc wireless environments.

3.1. *Design Principles*

Before we discuss in detail our visual code system, we first discuss the design principles of our system.

- Security Goals: Our visual code system will achieve or facilitate the following security goals: *identification*, *confidentiality*, and *integrity*. The identification of a device in a communication can be done through the verification of the public key belonging to the device. Device identification can be considered as a pre-authentication process described in [4]. Instead of using expensive

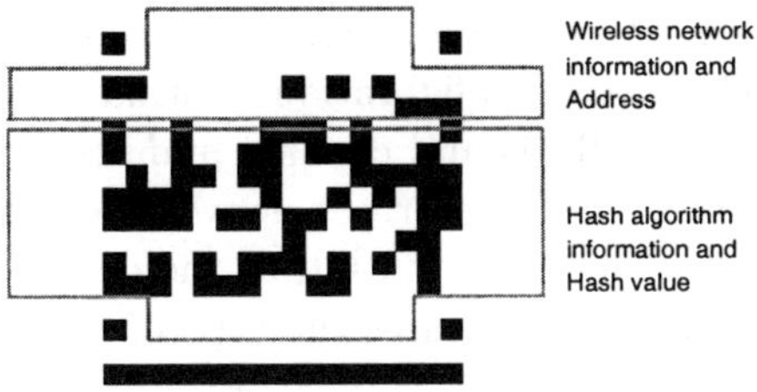

Figure 1. The UbiCode and Data Embedded

PKIs, our visual code system leverages inexpensive and memory-efficient cryptographically-secure hash functions (e.g., MD5).

- Ease-of-Use: Using our system to set up a secure association is similar to taking a picture. Users should not be disturbed by multiple steps in order to establish the association. This principle helps reduce security risks caused by the complexity of system usages.
- Minimal Data Transmission: Generally using out-of-band channels for physically validating an association is expensive. Minimal amount of data transmission is preferred.
- Line-of-Sight: Our target environment is the personal area network (PAN) where associations are usually set up within line of sight. Users with mobile devices will greatly benefit from hundreds of surrounding wireless devices in the environment.

The ideal approach to designing the visual code system is to encode minimal data necessary to represent the network address and the public key of an entity in an association in the code. Most of two dimensional barcodes currently used in automated tagging systems, such as PDF417 or data matrix [1,2], have the encoding capacity of a few thousand bits, which is bigger than the key size of popular public key algorithms such as RSA. However, the reason why we are not using those existing barcode systems is that they are not initially designed for secure device associations and do not contain the information we need for our purposes.

3.2. *Data Components*

Figure 1 shows our visual code called UbiCode. Data components embedded are as follows:

- Wireless Network Information: This indicates which wireless technology is used for communication, such as 802.11b or Bluetooth. This also includes the configuration information about the wireless network, such as BSSID and channel number if 802.11b is used.

- Network Address: This describes network address, such as IP or MAC address, and subnet mask that the device is configured.
- Hash Algorithm: This indicates the type of hash algorithm used in the visual code, such as MD5 or SHA1.
- Hash Value: This consists of actual hash value of either the public key or the secret value, depending on protocols used.

The size of the visual code can vary depending on the wireless technology and hash implementation. In general, visual code images require that they be taken from a very short distance when low cost and low resolution CCD/CMOS cameras are used. More importantly, for given dimensions, as the amount of encoded data becomes smaller, image recognition capability becomes better under the same device and an image processing algorithm used because each bit can be represented with bigger size. Obviously, we can increase reading and decoding capabilities of our visual code by increasing the size of the code image. However, there are certain limitations enforced by the size of the physical objects, e.g., a visual code in a smart cup [5] can't be bigger than a few inches.

4. Our Protocols

In this section, we show how to use our visual code system to demonstratively identify devices as well as to bootstrap other security services such as authentication and confidentiality in ad-hoc wireless networks.

4.1. *One-directional Identification Protocol*

The general steps in one-directional identification protocols including the step for authenticated key establishment are as follows:

- Step 1 (*Encoding Phase*): An entity (A) in an association prepares a visual code by encoding its network information as well as the hash value of its public key into the code. The code can be displayed on the screen or printed out and attached on the device.
- Step 2 (*Decoding Phase*): Another entity (B) in the association captures and decodes the visual code in order to extract both the network address and the public key hash value of A.

One-directional identification using UbiCode

1. A -> B : $E_{IMG}(addr_A, h(pub_A))$

Authentication and secret key exchange protocols

1. A -> B : CLIENT_HELLO

...

$E_{IMG}(X)$: Visual code encoding

Figure 2. One-directional Identification Protocol

- Step 3 (*Key Exchange Phase*): B connects to A via a radio frequency based channel and fetches its public key.
- Step 4 (*Key Verification Phase*): B hashes A's public key and compares it with the hash value retrieved in step 2. If they match, the identification of A in B succeeds. Otherwise, it fails.
- Step 5 (*Secret Key Generation Phase*): Only after the key verification phase was successful, both A and B generate a shared secret[a] key and start exchanging information in a confidential and integrity-preserving channel.

Figure 2 shows our one-directional device identification protocol. At the end, each entity should be in possession of the secret key newly generated on the basis of successful identification.

4.2. *Mutual Identification Protocols*

Assuming that both devices can perform public key operations, a simple mutual identification is possible through running the one-directional identification protocol in both directions in each of those phases (excluding the last phase) where the two devices' roles are switched. Note that after successful device identification, entities can use any public key exchange protocol such as SSL/TLS, requiring the proof of the possession of a corresponding private key. At the end of a correct run of the protocol, each entity should be able to verify the other entity in an association and be in possession of the secret key newly generated on the basis of their public key exchanged. This is shown in Figure 3(A). UbiCode can also be used in single public key protocol, where only one device can perform expensive

[a]Detailed discussion on various types of secret key generation protocols falls outside of the purview of this paper. Diffie-Hellman key agreement protocol can be, for instance, one of those protocols.

Mutual device identification using UbiCode

1. A -> B : E_{IMG} (addr$_A$, h(pub$_A$))
2. B -> A : E_{IMG} (addr$_B$, h(pub$_B$))

Authentication and secret key exchange protocols

1. A -> B : CLIENT_HELLO

...

(A) Basic Mutual Identification Protocol

Mutual device identification using UbiCode

1. A -> B : E_{IMG} (addr$_A$, h(pub$_A$))
2. B -> A : E_{IMG} (addr$_B$, h(S_B))

Authentication and secret key exchange protocols

1. A -> B : pub$_A$
2. B -> A : E_{pubA} (S_B)

...

E_{pubA} (S_B) : the encryption of S_B under pub$_A$

(B) Modified Basic Mutual Identification Protocol

Figure 3. Mutual Identification Protocols

public key operation. The protocol, shown in Figure 3(A), is based on and modified from one in [4]. The other device B has an arbitrary secret S_B instead of its public key, preparing a visual code by encoding the hash value of the secret into the code.

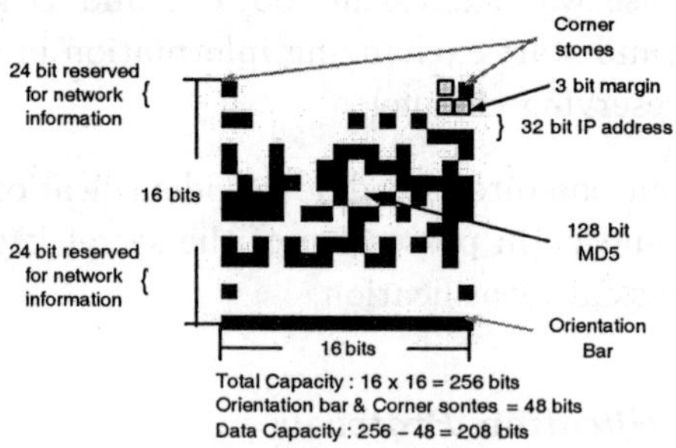

Figure 4. Our Implementation of UbiCode

5. Implementation Details

Figure 4 shows our implementation of UbiCode. The code consists of 256 squares in a 16 by 16 array. One orientation bar and four corner stones are used to identify the code from other objects. Maximum data capacity available for both network and hash information is 208 bits excluding the regions for identification. We used 128 bit MD5 for a hash function for key verification, and 802.11b wireless ad hoc mode as a main communication channel. For simplicity, the code only contains 32 bit IP address. A wide variety of image processing algorithms were employed to obtain the vidual code data from an image; Adaptive threshold [17] to correct the distortion

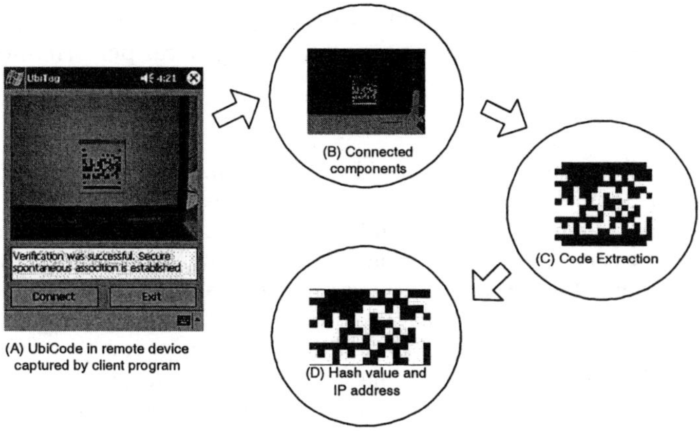

Figure 5. Overall Process of Data Extraction at Client Side

of the captured image, connected component labelling [6] to find the clusters of adjacent pixels, second order moments [15] to distinguish bars and corner stones from other shapes, and projective mapping [7] to extract a sequence of bits. We implemented one-directional identification protocol on one laptop with 1.4GHz Pentium 4 running Windows XP for the server (public display device) and one HP iPAQ 5450 PDA with 400MHz PXA CPU and built-in 802.11b card running Windows Pocket PC 2002 for the personal device. The code was written in C♯ using Visual Studio .NET 2003. On the client side, we used 640x480 pixel images taken by a Sony digital camera[b]. Figure 5 illustrates the overall process of data extraction at client side.

6. Discussion and Conclusion

Demonstrative identification of devices in ad-hoc wireless networks is required in order to bootstrap other security services such as authentication, confidentiality, and integrity. In this paper, we presented a novel approach to using a visual code system called UbiCode with a view to establish secure communications between mobile devices over ad-hoc wireless networks.

Our immediate future work will focus on the optimization of our implementation, since the overall performance of recognizing a single UbiCode

[b]Our target platform was a cell phone equipped with a digital camera running Microsoft Smartphone OS (e.g. Motorola MPx220 or Audiovox SMT 5600) However, such a device was not available at the time of implementation. Future work will include such devices.

needs to be improved at the client side. The computation time for the server, however, did not significantly affect the general performance.

References

1. International Organization for Standardization Information Technology - International Symbology Specification - Data Matrix, ISO/IEC **16022**, (2000).
2. International Organization for Standardization: Information Technology - International Symbology Specification - PDF417, ISO/IEC **15438**, (2001).
3. N. Asokan and P. Ginzboorg, Key-agreement in ad-hoc networks. *Computer Communications*, **23(17)**, (2000).
4. D. Balfanz, D. Smetters, P. Stewart, and H. Wong, Talking to strangers: Authentication in ad hoc wireless networks. In *Proceedings of the 9th Annual Network and Distributed System Security Symposium*, San Diego, CA, (2002).
5. H.-W. Gellersen, M. Beigl, and H. Krull, The mediacup: Awareness technology embedded in an everyday object. In *Proceedings of 1st International Symposium on Handheld and Ubiquitous Computing*, Karlsruhe, Germany, (1999).
6. S. L. Haralick, R.M., *Computer and Robot Vision*, **1** (Addison-Wesley, 1992).
7. P. Heckbert, Fundamentals of Texture Mapping and Image Warping. Master's thesis, Univ. of California, Berkeley, (1998).
8. T. Kindberg and A. Fox, System software for ubiquitous computing. *IEEE Pervasive Computing*, **1(1)**, (2002).
9. T. Kindberg and K. Zhang, Validating and securing spontaneous associations between wireless devices. In *Proceedings of the 6th Information Security Conference*, Bristol, UK, (2003).
10. T. Kindberg, K. Zhang, and N. Shankar, Context authentication using constrained channels. In *Proceedings of the Fourth IEEE Workshop on Mobile Computing Systems and Applications*, Callicoon, NY, (2002).
11. S. R. Klemmer, J. Li, J. Lin, and J. A. Landay, Papier-mache: Toolkit support for tangible input. In *CHI Letters, Human Factors in Computing Systems*, **6(1)**, (2004).
12. J. Rekimoto and Y. Ayatsuka, Cybercode: Designing augmented reality environments with visual tags. In *Proceedings of Designing Augmented Reality Environments*, Elsinore, Denmark, (ACM, 2000).
13. M. Rohs and B. Gfeller, Using camera-equipped mobile phones for interacting with real-world objects. In *2nd International Conference on Pervasive Computing*, Linz/Vienna, Austria, (2004).
14. F. Stajano and R. Anderson, The resurrecting duckling: Security issues for ad hoc wireless networks. In *Proceedings of the 7th International Workshop on Security Protocols*, Cambridge, UK, (1999).
15. R. C. Veltkamp and M. Hagedoorn, State of the art in shape matching. *Technical report*, **27**, Utrecht University, Netherlands, (1999).
16. M. Weiser, The computer for the 21st century. *Scientific American*, **265(3)**, (1991).
17. P. D. Wellner, Adaptive thresholding for the digitaldesk. *Technical report*, **93-110**, Rank Xerox Research Centre, Cambridge, UK, (1993).

A NEW ALGORITHM FOR HORIZONTAL HANDOVER MANAGEMENT IN WIRELESS MOBILE NETWORKS

A. TÜYSÜZ, M. YILDIRIM

Department of Computer Engineering, Bogazici University,
Bebek, Istanbul, 34342, TURKEY
e-mail: {aysegul.tuysuz,.meltem.yildirim}@ boun.edu.tr.

Mobile IP (MIP) is the current standard for supporting mobility in wireless mobile networks. However, the latency and packet losses faced during handovers may significantly degrade the quality of seamless connection in Mobile IP. Thus, minimizing handover latency and the number of lost packets during a handover is an important task in wireless mobile networks. In this paper, we propose a new mobility management scheme to handle the movements of Mobile Nodes (MNs) among different cell in the same wireless network to reduce data loss and maintain uniform connectivity. We also provide the performance results both for the proposed and basic horizontal handovers in wireless mobile networks. The simulation results show that the proposed model profoundly decreases latency at the expense of slightly increased data traffic.

1. Introduction

Wireless networking has become an increasingly important way to provide global information access for users regardless of time and location. Mobile IP (MIP) is the current standard for supporting mobility in wireless networks [1]. MIP provides a good framework for allowing users to roam outside their home networks. However, the MIP model needs to be enhanced to manage the movement across multiple subnetworks within a single network or domain. MIP may result in disruption to user traffic during handoff; it also has high control overhead due to frequent notifications to the home network resulting in high packet loss and high handover latency. Thus, minimizing handover latency is crucial for wireless applications supporting MIP. In this paper, we focus on reducing latency and disruption as the mobile user roams among the cells of the same wireless network. We present the basic handover scheme MIP for handover management, discuss their drawbacks and compare them with the proposed scheme which is determined to provide a seamless service to roaming end-users.

The rest of this paper is organized as follows. Section 2 presents horizontal handover process. Section 3 briefly explains the Mobile IPv6 (MIPv6) and its components. The solution for horizontal handover management in Mobile IPv6 and the proposed models for horizontal handover are presented in Section 4 with the basic schemes and simulation results. Finally, Section 5 concludes this work.

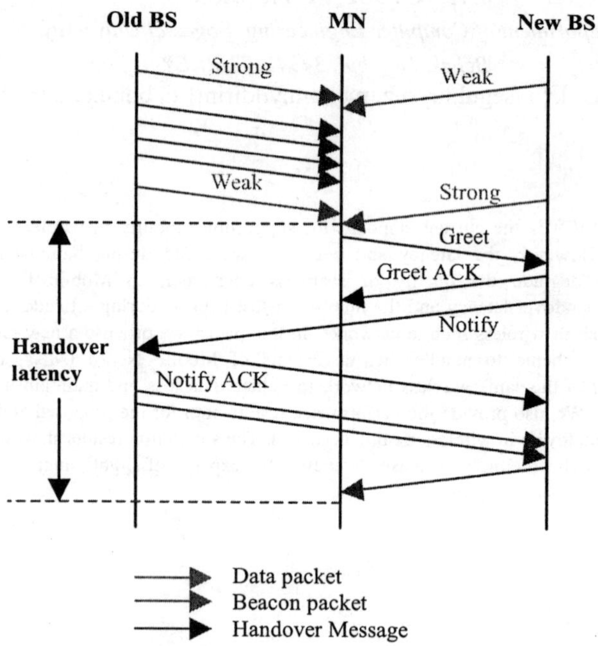

Figure 1. Horizontal Handover Steps.

2. Horizontal Handover

Horizontal handovers are the conventional handovers which take place while the MN switches between cells of the same network. Therefore, the MN does not need to change the network interface it is using. Fig. 1 shows how a horizontal handover occurs [2]. There is a handover from the old base station (BS) to the new BS; both of them having the same wireless network interface. The beacons, which are generated by the BSs, help the MN to determine if a horizontal handover is necessary or not. The MN checks the signal strengths of all beacons. If a new BS sends stronger signals than the old one, the handover mechanism is triggered by the MN. The MN sends the handover request to the new BS and receives an acknowledgement. The new BS also sends a notification to the old BS and waits for an acknowledgement from the old BS. Meanwhile, the old BS buffers the packets coming to MN until getting the notification from the new BS. These packets are sent to the new BS after the notification acknowledgement. Therefore, MN's packets, which arrive during the handover operation, are not lost. As depicted in Fig. 1, handover latency is the time between the moment when the MN instructs the new BS for a handover start and the moment when the new BS sends the first data packet to the MN.

3. Mobile IPv6

A MIPv6 node can continuously change its location on an IPv6 network and still be connected. The connectivity of the node is maintained by various messages going back and forth between the MIPv6 components [3]. This section discusses the MIPv6 components and how they communicate [4].

3.1. Nodes

The mobile node (MN) is the node that travels between IPv6 subnets. It acquires new temporary addresses as it roams into new subnets and maintains its connectivity by using its unchanging home address. The Correspondent Node (CN) is the node that wants to exchange data with the MN. The Home Agent (HA) is the router on the MN's home subnet and provides communication between MN and CN. If the MN is away from its home, it registers its current temporary address with the HA and the HA forwards data, which come to the MN's home address, to the MN's temporary address. The Foreign Agent (FA) is the Home Agent of the foreign subnet the MN roams. HA and FA are either Access Routers (AR) or Access Points (AP).

3.2. *Links*

Home Link is established between MN and HA. The MN obtains its home address from this link. Foreign Link is between the MN and the FA. The MN obtains its temporary address from this link.

3.3. *Addresses*

Home Address always identifies the MN even if it is outside the home subnet. It is used on Home Link. Care-of address is the temporary address assigned to the MN when it is attached to a foreign link and provides information about the MN's current location. It is used on Foreign Link.

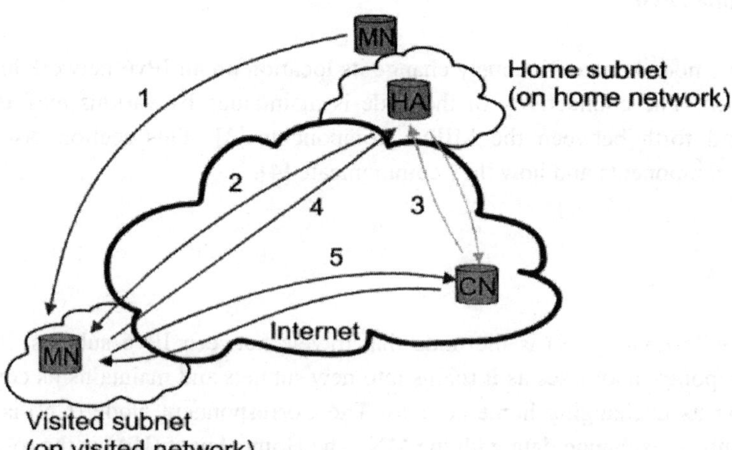

Figure 2. Communication of MIPv6 components [5].

3.4. *Communication Between Mobile IPv6 Components*

Fig. 2 illustrates the communication lines between the components of MIPv6 [5]. In this figure, the MN travels from its home subnet to the foreign subnet, registers with the foreign subnet and gets a new address called the care-of address (1). Then, the MN transmits this address to the HA (4) and sometimes to the CN (5) if the CN is MIPv6 capable. This message, which enables a mapping between the MN's home address and care-of-address, is called a "binding update". Then, HA sends a "binding acknowledgment" (2) to the MN. If the CN is not MIPv6 capable, it sends data to the MN's home-address and HA collects the data to deliver it to the MN's care-of address (3). The MN sends its response to the CN over HA but this type of communication increases the burden of routing at HA. On the other hand, if the CN is MIPv6 capable, it may directly send data to and receive data from the MN's care-of address (5). As a result of binding, it can be said that there is a dynamic tunnel between home address and care-of address at any time.

Moreover, it is worthy to note that the FA periodically sends a message called the "Router Advertisement". This contains the globally unique routing prefix that is used to formulate a care-of address by the MN. As soon as the MN switches its network, it can send a "Router Solicitation" message to the FA before receiving the periodic Router Advertisement message.

4. Horizontal Handover Models

4.1. Present Solution in Mobile IPv6

Previously, it has been explained that MN registers with the foreign subnet and gets a new care-of address as soon as it enters a new foreign subnet. Fig. 3 depicts this registration process. As explained in [4], first, MN creates its own care-of address by making use of "Router Advertisement" messages sent from FA. Then, MN sends a request to FA to check the uniqueness of the care-of address it has just created (1). FA performs Duplicate Address Detection (DAD), which takes considerable amount of time, and sends the result back to MN (2). Finally, if the newly created care-of address is unique, the MN registers with the foreign subnet (3 and 4). Otherwise, MN has to create another care-of address and the same procedure starts all over again.

One of the major drawbacks of this model is certainly starting the handover process *after* the MN enters the new subnet. No matter how fast the signals are transmitted or how fast the DAD operation is done, it is impossible to get rid of the handover latency. If the handover process could start *before* the MN actually enters the new subnet, then the handover latency can be decreased to some extent. Secondly, DAD takes a very long time. If the AR could keep track of all the care-of addresses in its coverage area and could generate a new care-of address for the MN, then time would not be wasted for the DAD operation.

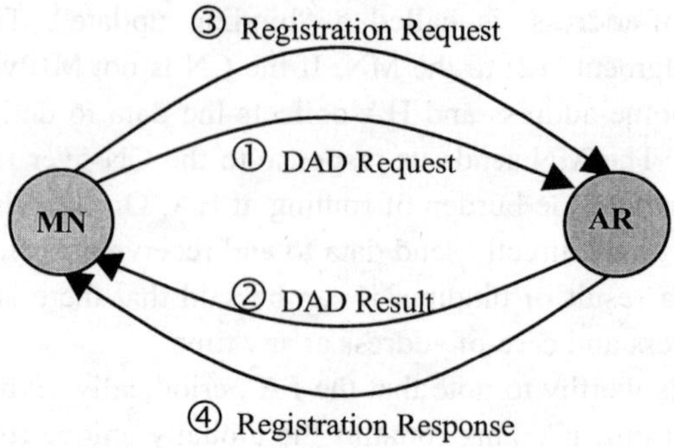

Figure 3. Present solution for horizontal handover IN Mobile IPv6.

4.2. A New Algorithm for Horizontal Handover Management

The horizontal handover model proposed in this paper focuses on the two major drawbacks of the present system described above. First, it reduces the handover latency significantly since the MN's handover process starts before the MN physically enters a new subnet. Moreover, since the care-of addresses are generated by the ARs instead of the MNs, the amount of time wasted for DAD is also eliminated.

According to our model depicted in Fig.4, all the ARs know each other in advance. As the MN moves away from its current AR (approximately 90% of the subnet's coverage radius), it sends a handover signal to its current AR noting that it is about to perform a handover (1). The handover signal also contains the MAC address of the MN and necessary information that identifies the target AR. Then, the current AR requests a care-of address for the MN from the target AR (2) by sending the MAC address of the MN. The target AR generates a new care-of address and sends it to the current AR (3). The target AR also reserves the generated address for a certain amount of time so that the address is not generated for other new comer MNs. The current AR informs the MN of its new care-of address (4). Having obtained its new care-of address, the MN registers to the new subnet (5, 6).

Although this model decreases the horizontal handover latency considerably, it has some hidden costs. First, all the ARs have to be aware of each other in advance. Second, the messaging traffic is considerably increased since there is more signalling done in this model.

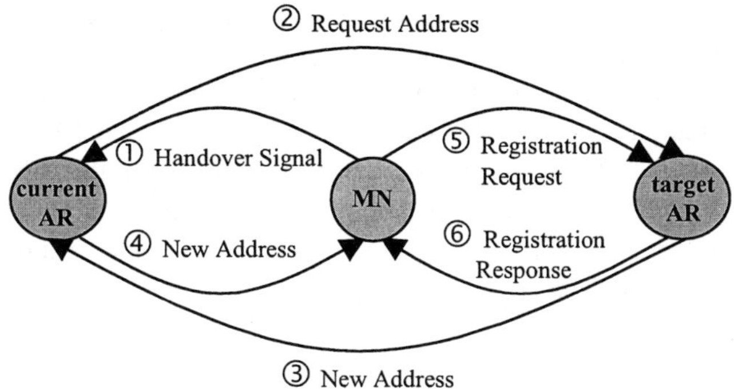

Figure 4. Proposed solution for horizontal handover.

4.3. Simulation Results

In order to compare the performances of the two horizontal handover schemes explained above, we perform a set of simulations. In the simulations, the ARs are assumed to be base stations whose radius of coverage is approximately 500 meters. The base stations are assumed to support 50 MNs at most. The handover latencies are measured separately for each model as the MN moves from one base station to another. The simulation of the proposed model is performed for two different MN velocities: 80 km/hour which is assumed as the approximate velocity of an automobile, and 8 km/hour which is assumed as the approximate velocity of a pedestrian.

Fig. 5 presents the performances of present and proposed models. Note that no value for MN's velocity is given for the present model. The handover latency of the present model is independent of the MN's velocity since the handover starts after the MN enters the subnet. However, the MN's velocity plays an important role in the proposed model because the handover process starts as the MN's distance from the old AR approaches 90% of the AR's total coverage radius. Therefore, if the MN is not highly mobile, a pedestrian, it can be registered to the new subnet before even stepping into it and in such a case there is no handover latency.

As depicted in Fig. 5, the handover latency of the present solution increases as the number of nodes in the subnet increase. As the subnet approaches its limit (30-50 MNs), the probability of the MN's generating a unique care-of address decreases significantly. As a result, the MN tries to generate another care-of address and the

DAD procedure starts all over again for that newly generated address. However, in our model, the time for generating a care-of address is independent of the number of MN in a subnet. Therefore, the handover latency of our model is almost constant. Finally, if the number of MNs in a subnet is between 0 and 10, the present model's performance is better than that of the proposed model for MN's velocity = 80 km/hour. Therefore, one can conclude that the present model is more appropriate if the subnet does not contain many MNs whereas our model is more appropriate for highly crowded subnets.

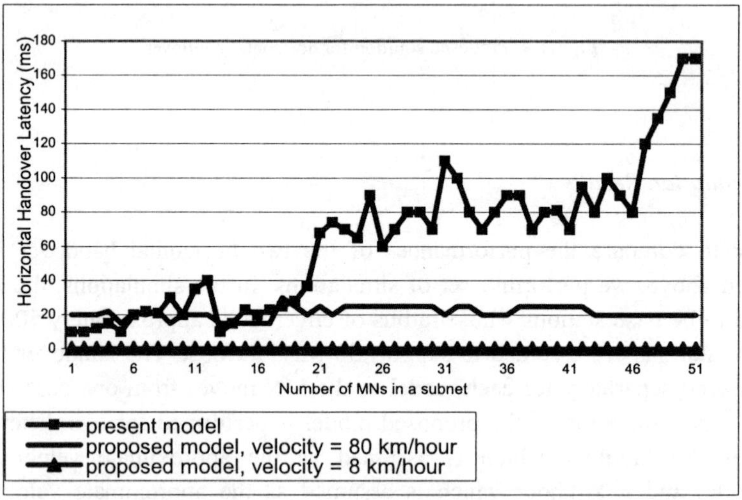

Figure 5. Horizontal handover latency vs. number of MN.

5. Conclusion

In this paper, we presented the design, implementation, and simulation of a new horizontal handover management model for wireless mobile networks. The main design goals of our model were low packet loss, and low handover latency during handover to provide seamless handover between cells of a wireless network. We showed through simulation how the proposed scheme performs better than the Mobile IP in terms of reduced handover latency and packet loss rate. Our handover management model decreases latency significantly at the expense of slightly increased traffic while decreasing packet loss rate by eliminating the amount of time wasted for DAD in MIP. Generating care-of address for MN is done by communication of old and new ARs before the MN hands over the new subnet. In other words, in the target AR, the new care-of-address is reserved for MN; thus the handover latency is decreased.

References

1. Perkins C., *IP Mobility Support*, IETF RFC 2002, Oct. 1996.
2. Badis H. and Agha K.A., *An Efficient Mobility Management in Wireless Overlay Networks*, The 14th IEEE 2003 International Symposium on Personal, Indoor and Mobile Radio Communication Proceedings (2003), 2500-2504.
3. Saha D., Mukherjee A., Misra I.S. and Chakraborty M., *Mobility Support in IP: A Survey of Related Protocols,* IEEE Network (2004), 34-40.
4. Montavont N. and Noël T., *Handover Management for Mobile Nodes in IPv6*, IEEE Communications Magazine (2002), 38-43.
5. Strand L., *Linux Mobile IPv6 HOWTO,* http://www.tldp.org/HOWTO/Mobile-IPv6-HOWTO/ (June 2005), 1-2.
6. Ramjee R., *HAWAII: A Domain-Based Approach for Supporting Mobility in Wide-Area Wireless Networks,* IEEE/ACM Transaction Network, Vol. 10 (2002), 396-410.

AN AAA BASED SOLUTION FOR THE SECURE INTEROPERABILITY OF 3G AND 802.11 NETWORKS

B. TURGUT

Fintek Inc., Eskisehir Yolu 4.km
Ankara, Turkey

M. U. ÇAGLAYAN

Department of Computer Engineering,
Bogazici University, Bebek, Istanbul, Turkey

Third Generation mobile telecommunications systems enable multimedia services combining the growth in mobile communications with the growth of the Internet. On the other hand, WLAN's are easy to implement, cheaper to construct and provides high speed services compared with other wireless technologies. In order to achieve access independence and to maintain a smooth interoperation with wireline and wireless terminals across the Internet, security is an important issue that must be handled. One step to achieve interoperability may be providing secure interoperability between the 802.11 WLAN and 3G networks. Although both systems have authentication mechanisms in their own domain, there is not a single mechanism that provides seamless authentication between two domains. In this paper, an AAA based authentication mechanism is presented between 3G networks and 802.11 networks. The authenticaton mechanism provides seamless authentication between two domains using the existing authentication mechanisms in each domain and provides a way for distributing session key and encryption algorithm between 3G core network and 802.11 core network.

1 Introduction

After the explosion of Internet growth, we are now witnessing the merging of wireless and mobile technologies with the Internet. WLAN technology and 3G cellular networks are some of the wireless technologies that provide Internet access. It is important to provide seamless interconnection between different wireless technologies.

The problem we are trying to solve here is secure interoperability of two different wireless technologies. Each security domain has its own structure and security mechanism. Certainly, one of the most challenging problem of such merged structure is providing security between two domains, which have different security architectures. The case is: One end point in one domain tries to communicate with another end point in the other domain. The proposed solution should not affect the security mechanism in each domain. Moreover, no hardware or software modifications in clients of different domains are allowed.

Third Generation mobile telecommunications systems enable multimedia services combining the growth in mobile communications with the growth of the Internet. On the other hand, WLANs are easy to implement, cheaper to construct and provides high speed compared with the other wireless technologies. In this paper, problem of authentication between IEEE 802.11 WLAN (Wireless LAN) and Third Generation cellular network is attempted to be solved. Third Generation cellular networks are treated in the context of 3GPP (Third Generation Partnership Project) specifications. In this paper, we propose an authentication mechanism that uses the existing structures and protocols that meet the requirements given above. The proposed authentication mechanism is based on the

- AAA (Authentication Authorization Accounting) protocols and infrastructure; for authentication between two domains
- 3G AKA (Authentication and Key Agreement) authentication algorithm; for authentication in 3G network
- 802.1x and PPP (Point to Point) EAP (Extensible Authentication Protocol) protocols; for authentication in 802.11 network

IEEE 802.11 and 3G Cellular Networks are two different wireless technologies that have their own system and security architecture. So to provide a secure interconnection between them, it is important to understand their own structure and what capabilities they provide firstly. Overview of the security mechanisms in the 802.11 and 3G networks will be given in the beginning. Next, the problems about the authentication between 802.11 and 3G networks are described. Finally, the proposed scenario for the authentication of 802.11 and 3G networks is discussed and conclusions are given.

2 The Time Threshold Based Scheme (TTS)

To understand the security mechanisms in 3G and 802.11 domains, understanding of the 802.11 and 3G structures is needed. The structures of the 802.11 and 3G networks may be found in the given references [6, 7, 8, 10, 14, 24]. IEEE 802.11 security will be discussed briefly in the first part of this section. The security of 3G systems will be given in the second part.

2.1. Overview of IEEE 802.11 Security

IEEE 802.11 has a Medium Access Control (MAC) layer security mechanism and uses Wired Equivalent Privacy (WEP) protocol for encryption. Authentication is not an explicit goal of WEP but considered to be a feature of WEP. Security will be examined in two parts, encryption and authentication.

Encryption aims to provide a level of security that wired systems have. WEP (Wired Equivalent Privacy) uses 40-bit RC4 algorithm for encryption. The same key is used to encrypt and decrypt the data.

There are a lot of problems with WEP. And mostly it is not thought to be safe. Walker [1] has shown that WEP is unsafe at any key size independent from the key size. RC4 is not suitable for the WEP environment. Also Fluhrer, Mantin, and Shamir offered an attack to break WEP [2].

Walker has offered AES block cipher in Offset CodeBook Mode (OCP) to use in WEP. Some offer not to rely on the link layer security offered by 802.11 and use higher level security mechanisms such as IPSec and SSH and treating all 802.11 systems as external [2].

In terms of computational complexity WEP is efficient. WEP can be implemented in hardware and software and allows low-MIPS devices to implement in software. Since RC4 is a stream cipher, it performs encryption and decryption much faster than block ciphers. RC4 encryption and decryption are fast, about 10 times faster than DES [3]. When we look at the AES block cipher it is thought to be as good as any symmetric cipher and allows very efficient implementations over a very wide range of environments, it has very low RAM and ROM requirements so it is suitable to restricted space environments [5].

There are two types of authentication, Open System Authentication and Shared Key Authentication. Open System Authentication is the default authentication service. Any terminal may request authentication. The terminal receiving the request may grant it doing nothing or looking for a special list to control. In Shared Key Authentication, shared secret key is involved to authenticate the station to AP. It is based on the challenge response mechanism. Mutual authentication requires two cycles of messaging [4].

Key management is not specified in 802.11. This is a quite inefficient and unacceptable situation, especially in wireless infrastructure network mode with a large number of mobile terminals (MT). Also, there are no authentication and encryption services in wireless adhoc network mode.

The shared key authentication is easily broken by a passive attack by eavesdropping [3]. It is recommended to use a higher-level security mechanism like IPSec. Since 802.11 protocols do not provide sufficient security in authentication, work is still being done on new authentication mechanisms [16].

The use of IEEE 802.1x [15] and RADIUS (Remote Authentication Dial In User Service) server [19] addresses the security limitations of 802.11. 802.1x can be used to derive authentication and encryption keys for use with any cipher and can also be used to periodically refresh keys and re-authenticate. IEEE 802.1X is not a single authentication method; rather it utilizes Extensible Authentication Protocol (EAP)[20,21]. EAP is a general protocol for authentication that supports multiple authentication mechanisms. Using IEEE 802.1x and a RADIUS server, authentication is handled in layer 2 rather than in layer 1 as specified in 802.11. The authentication procedure using 802.1x and RADIUS may be found in [15].

In the draft specification for enhanced Security in 802.11 networks [16], Enhanced Security Network(ESN) is defined as follows: 802.11 ESS relying on

IEEE 802.1x for its authentication and key management services. ESN offers a new WEP2 algorithm and AES in Offset Codebook mode for eacryption. WEP2 is similar to the WEP. It relies on the RC4 but provides a larger encryption key and larger IV. ESN capable 802.11 MT and AP agreed on to use which authentication mechanism and encrytion method during the association.

2.2. Overview of 3G Security

In this section, we will be the summarizing the 3G security aspects according to the specifications of the 3GPP [17,25].

3GPP security is based on the GSM security [9,13] but it aims to cure some weaknesses of the GSM and adds several newer security features. GSM and GPRS security is based on one-way authentication using a long-term shared key between SIM card and home network. 3GPP supports mutual authentication. GSM and GPRS provide link level protection over the air and no protection in the core network [9,11,12,13]. 3GPP supports security in the core network.

In 3GPP, five security feature groups are defined [25]. To send an IP packet securely through the 3G domain, we will only emphasize the network access security and the network domain security among the five security feature groups.

2.2.1. Network Access Security

It provides network authentication to the user and user authentication to the network. Authentication vector delivered by the Home Network of the user is used. In addition to mutual authentication, it provides session key for encryption cipher key (CK) and session key for integrity check (IK) between the user and the network.

The mechanism is based on the secret K shared between the user and AuC (Authentication Centre) in the user's Home Environment (HE) and the challenge/response mechanism very similar to the GSM authentication and key agreement mechanism with the difference that it uses sequence number.

After the authentication and key agreement HE decides which algorithms to use for encryption and integration and sends this to the MT. If they agree on which algorithms to be used then they start ciphering and deciphering according to the selected algorithms.

Integrity algorithm f9 is implemented in the MT and RNC (Radio Network Controller). Confidentiality function f8 is used on dedicated channels between the MT and RNC. Kasumi may be used for f8. There may be other options in the future.

2.2.2. Network Domain Security

The term Network Domain Security is used for the security of networks that are managed by a single administrative authority. For native IP-based protocols, security is provided by IETF defined IPSEC security protocols specified in RFC-2401.

3 Interoperability in 802.11 and 3G Authentication

The problem to be solved is the secure interoperability of the IEEE 802.11 WLAN and Third Generation Cellular protocols. IEEE 802.11 wireless protocol coverage area and the entities in this area constitute the 802.11 domain. Similarly 3G cellular protocol coverage area and the entities in this area constitute the 3G domain. For any kind of data communication between two domains, the first step is to mutually identify the peers in 802.11 domain and 3G domain. 802.11 WLAN terminals can be authenticated in 802.11 domain [3] and 3G terminals can be authenticated according to the proposed methods given in 3GPP specifications [25] in 3G domain.

There are several problems that must be handled to achieve authentication between 3G domain and 802.11 domain. The problems are described below.

i. Authentication consists of two parts; the claim of identity and the proof of identity. Each system uses its own identification scheme. 3GPP uses User Services Identity Module (USIM) contained in a smart card and IEEE 802.11 MT uses terminal id, MAC address or something else depending on the implementation. There should be a common way of identifying the peers.

ii. The authentication mechanism should verify the identity of 802.11 WLAN MT to the 3G MT and verify the 3G MT to the 802.11 WLAN MT. In other words mutual authentication should be provided.

iii. Authentication mechanism must provide key agreement. For the confidentiality and integrity of the communication, there should be secret keys shared between the 802.11 WLAN MT and 3G MT. For this reason authentication mechanism should provide key agreement. Agreed keys will be used for encryption mechanism later.

iv. 802.11 WLAN uses link layer authentication in its own domain. Also authentication is done in layer2 in 3G domain. 3G cellular networks and IEEE 802.11 networks use different protocols and technologies for the physical and link layers. They should use upper layer authentication.

v. Secure exchange of authentication messages between intermediate nodes is required. Intermediate nodes are the nodes between the core networks of two domains.

vi. Interdomain security of authentication messages is required. This corresponds to the security in each domain. Each domain has an authentication scheme as briefly described in section two.

vii. Computational and communication efficiency: This is the number of messages to execute the protocol and the bandwidth required. This is important because of the low processing power and battery resources of wireless equipments.

4 Proposed Scenario for Interoperability in Authentication

4.1 General Approach

The proposed solution handles each domain independently from each other. It does not modify the security mechanisms in each domain at all. It is based on the communication of two AAA servers in each domain. Both 802.11 MT and 3G MT authenticate themselves in their own system successfully and indicate the communication request to the Authentication clients in their domain. Authentication clients do the necessary operations and send the authentication request to the authentication server with the appropriate identity that allows the authentication request to be routed its home destination. The following scenario solves the problems for the authentication of 3G MT and 802.11 MT as follows:

i. NAI (Network Access Identifier) [23] format name is used for each terminal.
ii. Mutual authentication is provided with the use of a shared secret between two AAA servers in AAA protocol.
iii. AAA protocol provides a way of establishing a secure tunnel between two domains with the given properties and session key [22].
iv. Since authentication between two domains will be provided using the AAA protocol, Network or upper layer authentication would be used according to the AAA protocol.
v. AAA protocols provide different kind of mechanisms for confidentiality and integrity besides the authentication of the message. One of them may be using the MAC of entire message.
vi. The security mechanism of each domain has been briefly described above. The messages will be protected using the security mechanism of the each domain.
vii. Messaging for the authentication of the terminals between the 802.11 and 3G domain is not handled by the mobile terminals, so it does not effect the battery or processing power of the mobile terminals. AAA clients in the core network in the each domain sends message to the AAA servers for authentication.

The basic structure and operation are shown in the Figure 1.

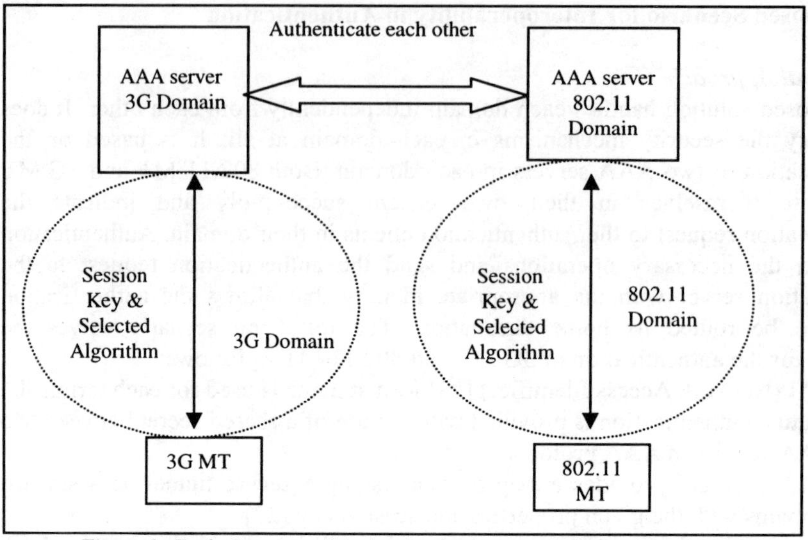

Figure 1. Basic Structure of Authentication between 3G Domain and 802.11 Domain

4.2 Details of Proposed Scenario

The scenario below demonstrates message transfer from 3G MT to 802.11 MT in detail.

i. When a 3G terminal is powered on, connection set up procedure is called. Connection set up procedure includes AKA, which provides mutual authentication between the 3G MT and 3G network. The 3G-SGSN (Serving GPRS Support Node) performs the authentication procedure. At the end of the Connection Set Up Procedure [25], IK(i) and CK(i) are established between the SGSN and 3G MT. Encryption algorithm f_8 is used for the messages between the 3G MT and SGSN. RNC performs the ciphering procedure based on the algorithm.

ii. 3G MT should access the PS (Packet Switched) Domain to send a message to a Packet Data Network (PDN) outside the 3G network. PDP (Packet Data Protocol) context should be activated for the 3G MT. Before the PDP context activation, 3G MT should perform a GPRS attach to the SGSN. In the attach procedure, SGSN obtains the subscriber data of the 3G MT from the HLR (Home Location Register) which will be used in the PDP context activation. Attach procedure is explained in [18]. At the end of this procedure, SGSN obtains the APN list of the subscriber, which will be used in the PDP context activation.

iii. PDP Context Activation procedure is initiated by the 3G MT. SGSN finds out information about the GGSN (Gateway GPRS Support Node) from the

APN (Access Point Name) setting of the 3G MT. SGSN uses the APN list of the subscriber that it received in GPRS attach process to control if the 3G MT has access to the selected APN. Messaging between SGSN and GGSN occurs during PDP context activation through the G_n interface and G_n interface uses User Datagram Protocol UDP/IP protocol. Activation of PDP context is GTP (GPRS Tunneling Protocol) control plane function. According to the specifications GTP-C (GTP Control Plane Signaling) is protected with IPsec security protocol [17]. IPsec security protocol will always be in ESP (Encapsulating Security Payload) mode. SA (Security Association) mode will always be in tunnel mode. PDP context activation procedure is explained in detail in [18]. At the end of this step, a session is established between the 3G MT and 3G GGSN. GGSN will give an IP address to the 3G MT using a DHCP (Dynamic Host Configuration Protocol) server or it supplies an IP address from its own address space.

iv. After the successful context activation procedure, 3G MT may send a packet data to the 802.11 using the PDP context established in the previous step. The message is encrypted with the f_8 algorithm and the established CK(i) in the first step from the MT to SGSN. In summary:

3G MT -> SGSN :f_8[CK(i), COUNT-,BEARER,DIRECTION,LENGTH]⊕ Plaintext
COUNT-C : a time dependent input
BEARER: The bearer identity
DIRECTION: The direction of transmission
LENGTH: the length of the key stream required (1)

v. The message is sent from the SGSN to GGSN using the GTP User Plane (GTP-U). All PDP PDU's (Packet Data Unit) are encapsulated with GTP. Specifications force the use of IPSec for GTP-C messages but don't say anything for the GTP-U messages. In this scenario, since SGSN and GGSN are in the same security domain, there is no need to use IPSec between SGSN and GGSN. For implications that are critical about security, IPSec may be used in this interface. GTP is specified in 3G TS 29.060.

vi. GGSN finds out the domain of the receiver of the message from the destination address of the message using DNS. GGSN constructs the identity of the 3G MT and 802.11 MT in NAI format (3G MT_{id}, 802.11 MT_{id}). GGSN functions as an AAA Client and carries out the necessary security functions when a message arrives through a PDP context that is established using special APNs. GGSN asks the AAA server in 3G domain if there is an identity with the 802.11 MT_{id} in the 802.11 domain and indicating that it has a user with 3G MT_{id} using a AAA Request Message. AAA Request message also has the related attributes that offer how a secure tunnel will be established between the domain of the receiver and the 3G domain. Attributes about the secure channel may change according to the security mechanism that the GGSN will offer. The whole message is signed with the shared key between GGSN and 3G AAA Server (K_{GGSN3G}). GGSN will get the properties of the tunnel from the APN configuration. An example APN configuration is given in Table 1.

Table 1. Example APN Configuration

APN Label	SecureCommunication
GGSN access mode	Transparent
IP address allocator	GGSN
IP address type	Ipv6
DHCP server IP address	-
Maximum number of active PDP contexts	100.000
Maximum number of simultaneous active users	50.000
Security Enabled	True
SA mode	Tunnel
Security protocol	ESP
Address of the SGW	IP address of the SGW in 802.11 domain

Note that Security Enabled, SA mode, Security protocol and address of the SGW information are new and are not currently stored for APN but we propose that the security configurations for APN will exist in the APN configuration to enable the IP level security between 3G domain and 802.11 domain.

vii. AAA server in 3G domain decrypts the message using K_{GGSN3G}. If the validation of the AAA Request is successful, AAA server in 3G domain searches for the user in the AAA request. If user is determined to be a member of 802.11 domain, which has mutually authenticated with a 3G AAA Server, 3G AAA Server forwards the Access Request message to the 802.11 AAA server, signing the message with the shared secret between the 3G AAA server and 802.11 AAA server ($SK_{3G80211}$).

viii. AAA server in the 802.11 domain verifies the incoming Access Request. If the verification is successful, 802.11 AAA Server validates the user and the tunnel properties offered by the 3G AAA Server.

ix. If the validation of user is unsuccessful, AAA server in the 802.11 domain rejects the request message of the AAA server in the 3G domain. AAA server in 3G domain passes this information to the GGSN. GGSN may initiate the PDP context deactivation procedure for the PDP context that the 3G MT uses to talk with 802.11 MT.

x. If the user validation process is successful, AAA server in the 802.11 domain examines the properties of the secure tunnel and decrypts the session key offered. At this point, AAA server in 802.11 domain checks if the user has rights to use given security mechanism. If no security mechanism is defined for the user, Reject Message is sent to the 3G AAA server. If more than one security mechanism is defined for the user and one of them has the same properties with the offered security mechanism by the 3G domain, AAA Server in 802.11 domain honors that mechanism. Also, it may be the case that a security mechanism is defined for the user, but it does not match with the offered one. In both cases, AAA server in the 802.11 domain prepares a response message indicating that it accepts the user and sends the message to the 3G AAA server signing with the key $SK_{3G80211}$.

xi. If the packet is verified, 3G AAA server signs the response message with the key SK_{GGSN3G} and sends the response message to GGSN.

xii. If the message is verified, GGSN examines the properties of the tunnel. The result may be one of the following cases: The peer accepts all the properties and the session key it has offered or the peer does not accept one or more properties or session key it has offered. The first case is covered in the following item. In the second case, if the GGSN has support the properties offered by the 3G domain, it may prepare a new request packet with these properties and restarts the messaging again. If it does not support the properties, it may start the deactivation of PDP Context process, since a secure connection cannot be established.

xiii. In the first case, a secure tunnel is established with the properties decided in the authentication step. Encryption algorithm and encryption keys (or key distribution mechanisms in some applications) were also decided in the upper steps, so GGSN sends PDUs that come from the 3G MT to the 802.11 domain by using the encryption algorithm through the established secure tunnel, as follows:

GGSN <-> 802.11 AP secure tunnel is established
GGSN -> 802.11 AP : Alg_{GGSNAP}_$Encrypt_{KGGSNAP}$[PDU]
Alg_{GGSNAP}: Agreed IPSEC protocol, it may be AH (Authentication Header) or ESP
K_{GGSNAP}: Agreed key to be used in encryption (2)

xiv. It is assumed that Enhanced Security Network (ESN) is used to provide security features to the 802.11 domain [16]. 802.11 AP sends the message to the 802.11 MT with the selected encryption method using the configured key.

802.11 AP -> 802.11 MT : $Alg_{APMT}\_Encrypt_{KAPMT}$ [3GMTid || $802.11MT_{id}$ || Msg]

K_{APMT}: Key between the 802.11 AP and 802.11 MT, distributed manually or by some automated key management technique.

Alg_{APMT}: Negotiated cipher suite between the 802.11 AP and 802.11 mobile terminal, it may be WEP, WEP2, AES (3)

The exchange of messages corresponding to the proposed scenario is given in Figure 2.

5 Conclusions

There has been too much study about the security problems in wireless networks. Some of them specialize on the 3G networks [28]. In [28] VPN is used for end-to-end security. IKE protocol proxy schema is proposed for VPN initialization giving the complex computational work to the network. Mostly TLS is told to be used but it is a resource consuming protocol for mobile devices. Solutions are proposed based on TLS introducing an intermediate node and giving some computational operations from wireless client to the intermediate node.[29] TLS handshake phase is extended to provide this messaging.

An AAA based solution for the secure interoperability of 3G and 802.11 networks is proposed. In the proposed solution, all message transfers from 3G MT to 802.11 MT are presented. AAA protocol and the existing authentication mechanisms in each domain are used for the authentication of 3G MT and 802.11 MT. In the near future, it seams like both 3G domain and 802.11 domain will have AAA technology in their structure. In 3G domain, IP Multimedia subsytem uses AAA protocols for the authentication of a user [26]. ESN capable 802.11 networks also use AAA infrastructure for the authentication [18]. Therefore, it is expected that there will be no need to define a new mechanism for authentication within these two domains and AAA infrastructure could be used for interoperability.

In the proposed solution, no new software need be installed on the 3G MT's and 802.11 MT's. Since 802.11 MT and the 3G MT are authenticated in their own security domains, the authentication interoperability is mostly handled by a number of messages between the GGSN of 3G domain, AP of 802.11 domain and AAA servers of each domain. This approach will provide seamless authentication between 3G MT and 802.11 MT. GGSN of the 3G domain, AP of the 802.11 domain and the AAA servers of each domain should have the proposed functionality for such seamless authentication between 3G MT's and 802.11 MT's.

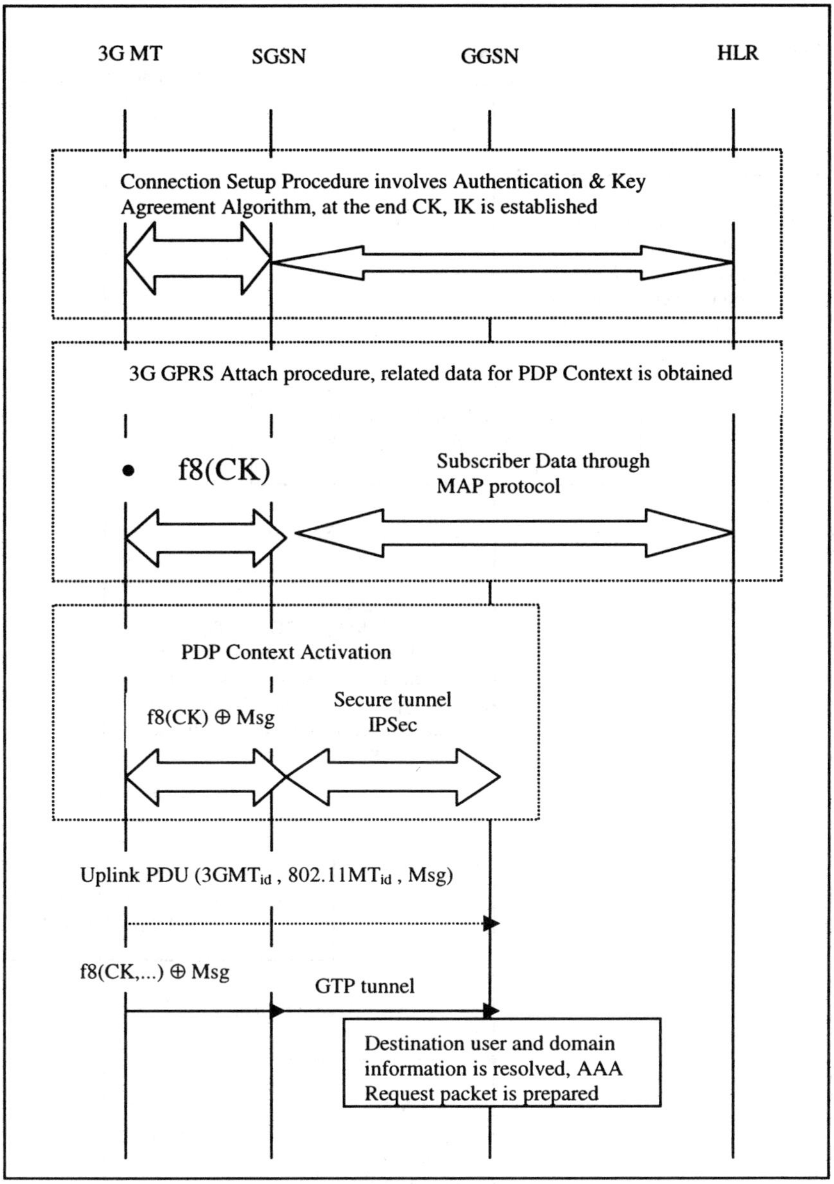

Figure 2-a. Message Exchange In Proposed Solution (Part A)

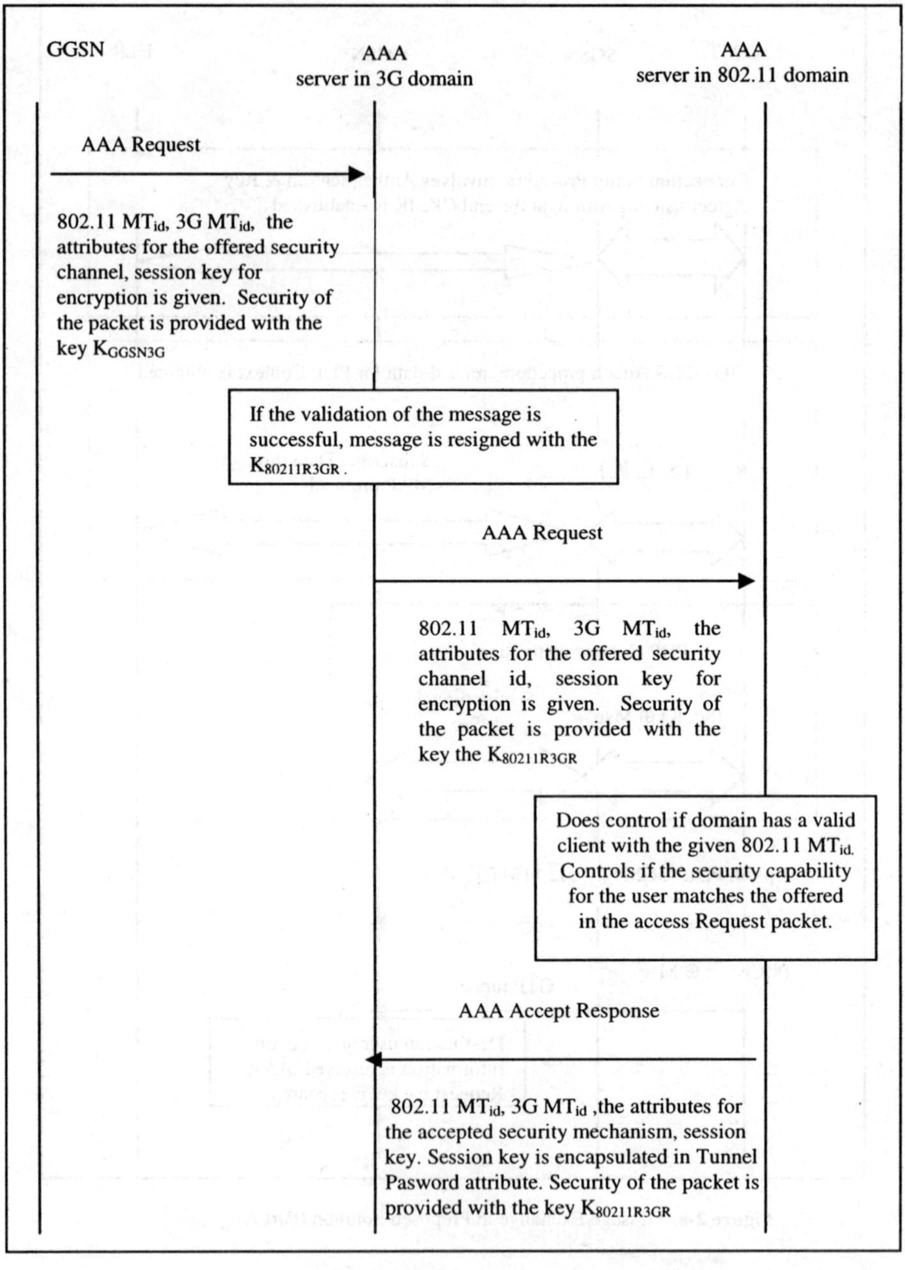

Figure 2-b. Message Exchange In Proposed Solution (Part B)

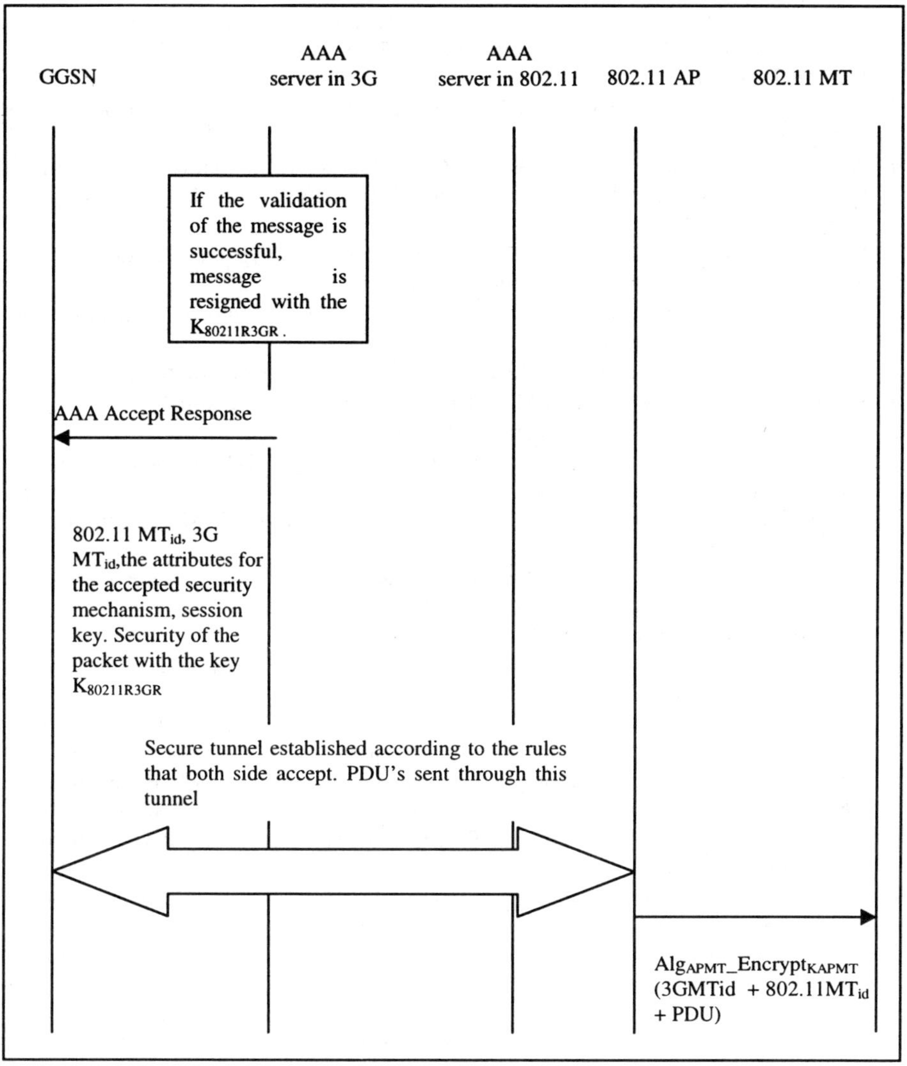

Figure 2-c. Message Exchange In Proposed Solution (Part

References

1. Walker J.R., Unsafe at any key size; An analysis of WEP encapsulation (Intel Corporation, 2000).
2. Stubblefield A., Ioannidis J, and Rubin A.D., Using the Fluhrer, Mantin and Shamir Attack to Break Web (Computer Science Dept. Rice University, AT&T Labs-Research, Florham Park, NJ).
3. Weatherspoon S., Overview of IEEE 802.11b Security (Network Communications Group, Intel Corporation).
4. Arbaugh W. A., Shankar N., and Wan Y. C. J., Your 802.11 Wireless Network has No Clothes (Department of Computer Science University of Maryland College Park, Maryland , 2001).
5. Report on the Development of the Advanced Encryption Standart (AES); http://csrc.nist.gov/encryption/aes/round2/r2report.pdf.
6. Brenner P., A Technical Tutorial on the IEEE 802.11 Protocol (http://www.sss-mag.com/pdf/802_11tut.pdf).
7. Scourias J., Overview of the GSM Cellular System(University of Waterloo).
8. Rahnema M., Overview of the GSM System and Protocol Architecture.
9. Brookson C., GSM(and PCN) Security and Encryption.
10. ANSI IEEE Std 802.11 1999, Information technology- Telecommunications and Information Exchange between Systems - LAN/MAN Networks – Specific Requirements - Part 11: Wireless LAN Medium Access Control (MAC) and physical layer (PHY) specifications.
11. Rautpalo J., GPRS Security – Secure Remote Connections over GPRS (Helsinki University of Technology, Department of Computer Science).
12. Brookson C., GPRS Security(2001).
13. Peng C., GSM and GPRS Security (Telecommunication Software and Multimedia Laboratory, Helsinki University of Technology).
14. Lin Y., Herman C.,H.Rao, and Chlamtac I, General Packet Radio Service (GPRS): architecture, interfaces, and deployment (Department of Computer Science and Information Engineering, National Chiao Tung University, AT&T Research Labs, Center for Advanced Telecommunication, Systems and Services University of Texas).
15. Ayyagari A., and Fout T., Making IEEE 802.11 Networks Enterprise-Ready (Microsoft Corporation, 2001).
16. IEEE Draft 802.11eS/D1, Draft Supplement to STANDARD FOR Telecommunications and Information Exchange between Systems - LAN/MAN Specific Requirements - Part 11: Wireless Medium Access Control (MAC) and physical layer (PHY) specifications: Specification for Enhanced Security"(2001).
17. 3GPP Technical Specification 3GPP TS 33.210, Technical Specification Group Services and System Aspects; 3G Security; Network Domain Security; IP network layer security (Release 5)(3rd Generation Partnership Project, 2002-01).

18. 3GPP Technical Specification 3GPP TS 23.060, Technical Specification Group Services and System Aspects; General Packet Radio Service (GPRS); Service Description (3rd Generation Partnership Project, Stage 2 Release99).
19. RFC 2865, Remote Authentication Dial In User Service (RADIUS).
20. RFC 2869, RADIUS Extensions.
21. RFC 2284, PPP Extensible Authentication Protocol.
22. RFC 2989, Criteria for Evaluating AAA Protocols for Network Access.
23. RFC 2486, The Network Access Identifier.
24. 3GPP Technical Specification 3GPP TS 23.002, Technical Specification Group Services and System Aspects; Network Architecture (Release 5)(3rd Generation Partnership Project, 2002-01).
25. 3GPP Technical Specification 3GPP TS 33.102, Technical Specification Group Services and System Aspects; 3G Security; Security Architecture (Release 1999), (3rd Generation Partnership Project, September 2001).
26. Salvela J., Access Security in Third Generation Mobile Networks (Technology Research Center of Finland).
27. 3GPP Technical Specification 3GPP TS 23.228, Technical Specification Group Services and System Aspects; IP Multimedia (IM) Subsystem –Stage 2 (V2.0.0) (3rd Generation Partnership Project, 2001-03).
28. Xenakis C. and Merakos L., Computer Communications , 27 (2004), 638-650
29. Badra M., Serhrouchni A. And Urien P., Computer Communications , 27 (2004), 1738-1745

